Bourne on Company Law

SEVENTH EDITION

An ideal introductory textbook, *Bourne on Company Law* offers a succinct overview of the fundamental areas covered in LLB and GDL courses. The text is clear and easy to follow, being presented in short, sub-headed sections for ease of navigation, and is thoroughly cross-referenced to highlight connections across topics.

Written for both law and non-law students, this text offers straightforward explanations of all key cases, as well as chapter summaries and end of chapter questions to aid understanding. The book is also supported by a companion website offering self-test questions, a useful glossary and annotated web links.

Nicholas Bourne worked as a Company Secretary after qualifying as a Barrister. He taught widely in Company Law in the United Kingdom and the Far East. He became a Professor of Law and later a Member of the National Assembly for Wales. He was appointed to the House of Lords in 2013 and in May 2015 was appointed Under-Secretary of State at the Department of Energy and Climate Change and the Wales Office.

Bourne on Company Law

SEVENTH EDITION

Nicholas Bourne

 Routledge
Taylor & Francis Group

LONDON AND NEW YORK

First published 2016
by Routledge
2 Park Square, Milton Park, Abingdon, Oxon OX14 4RN

and by Routledge
711 Third Avenue, New York, NY 10017

Routledge is an imprint of the Taylor & Francis Group, an informa business

British Library Cataloguing in Publication Data
A catalogue record for this book is available from the British Library

Library of Congress Cataloging-in-Publication Data
Names: Bourne, Nicholas, author.
Title: Bourne on company law / Nicholas Bourne.
Other titles: Company law
Description: Seventh edition. | Abingdon, Oxon ; New York, NY : Routledge, 2016. | Includes bibliographical references and index.
Identifiers: LCCN 2015047383| ISBN 9781138897748 (hbk) | ISBN 9781138911895 (pbk) | ISBN 9781315692296 (ebk)
Subjects: LCSH: Corporation law–Great Britain. | LCGFT: Textbooks
Classification: LCC KD2079 .B685 2016 | DDC 346.41/066–dc23
LC record available at http://lccn.loc.gov/2015047383

ISBN: 978-1-138-89774-8 (hbk)
ISBN: 978-1-138-91189-5 (pbk)
ISBN: 978-1-315-69229-6 (ebk)

Typeset in Times New Roman
by Wearset Ltd, Boldon, Tyne and Wear

Printed and bound in Great Britain by
TJnternational Ltd, Padstow, Cornwall

To the memory of my dear parents, Joan Bourne and John Morgan Bourne.

Outline contents

Contents

Preface

The Companies Act 2006 is the longest statute on any subject ever to pass through the Westminster Parliament. That is the measure of the challenge, both for an author and for students of company law particularly when added to the formidable panorama of decided cases.

The pace of change in company law is sometimes bewildering but the subject matter is always fascinating.

This book is written primarily for students. It is hoped, however, that some of the ideas will be of interest to the researcher and some of the analyses relevant for the practitioner.

Although for simplicity 'he' is used throughout, the pronoun should of course be read as equally applicable to men and women.

As always, I am grateful to colleagues and to students past and present for their help. I am very grateful to my editorial team for their patience and assistance, and I am also extremely grateful to Lee Chong who provided invaluable editorial assistance and to Sandra Morgan for her inexhaustible patience in decoding manuscripts and dictated disks.

The law may be complex and increasing in volume and complexity, but since Jonathan Swift commented as long ago as 1711 that, 'If books and laws continue to increase as they have done for 50 years past; I am in some concern for future ages, how any man will be learned or any man a lawyer', perhaps we have, in reality, no reason to fear that volume and complexity!

Nicholas Bourne, Cardiff, February 2016

Table of cases

Table of statutes

Statutory Instruments

International Legislation

European Legislation

Directives

Regulations

Chapter 1

Introduction

Chapter Contents

1.1 A company or a partnership

When a group of people get together and decide to start a business, one decision that they will need to make early on is whether to operate as a company or as a partnership (or 'firm'). There are certain advantages, and indeed certain disadvantages, that attach to incorporation, which is the process of creating a company. A partnership is unincorporated and is defined in the Partnership Act 1890 as the carrying on of a trade or profession with a view of profit (s 1). The following are, therefore, matters which those setting up a business will need to consider. The essence of the company is that it is a separate person in law, see *Salomon v A Salomon & Co Ltd* [1897] AC 22 (see section 2.1). The partnership does not have legal personality. The partners are agents of the partnership (s 5 of the Partnership Act 1890). From this very basic difference between the company and the partnership flow many of the advantages and disadvantages of incorporation.

Unlike the company where there is, at least in theory, a clear division between shareholders who invest in the business and the directors who manage the business, in partnership law there is no such division. In partnership law a person who invests in the firm's business will inevitably find that he is a partner in the firm and fully liable for the firm's debts (unless he is a limited partner within the Limited Partnerships Act 1907 or the Limited Liability Partnerships Act 2000).

It is possible for the partnership to employ people but the partners themselves are not employed by the firm. The two relationships are mutually exclusive. The position of a director, even a sole director, is quite different. He may be employed by the company, see *Lee v Lee's Air Farming* [1961] AC 12.

Sometimes the position of the salaried partner causes particular difficulty. The position is used most prevalently in professional firms as a 'first step on the ladder'. If a person is represented to the outside world as a partner, then, of course, he may bind the firm by his actions, see *United Bank of Kuwait Ltd v Hammond* [1988] 1 WLR 1051. However, within the partnership itself, the position will be affected by the question of whether a salaried partner is, in reality, an employee or a partner, see *Stekel v Ellice* [1973] 1 WLR 191.

The most obvious advantage in incorporation is the access to limited liability. Not all companies are limited companies. Unlimited companies do not need to file accounts so sometimes this is an attraction for those setting up a business. However, the possibility of limiting the liability of the participators to the amount of the issued shares is an attractive one. Sometimes this advantage is, of course, more apparent than real. If a small private company goes to a bank and asks to borrow a large sum of money, the bank is unlikely to be satisfied with the possibility of recourse against the company's assets. In practice, the bank manager will require some collateral security from the company's directors. In a partnership, however, all the partners will have unlimited liability for the business's debts and liabilities. This is the case except in a limited partnership governed by the Limited Partnerships Act 1907. In a limited partnership under this Act, however, only sleeping partners may have limited liability and it is not possible to form a partnership made up entirely of limited partners. There must always be somebody who is 'picking up the tab' with no limitation of liability.

Under the Limited Liability Partnerships Act 2000, it is possible to opt for a new form of business association, namely a limited liability partnership (LLP). The relationship between the members is like that of a general partnership but the institution has to be registered with the Registrar of Companies. Members of a limited liability partnership are not responsible for its debts. Limited liability partnerships are regarded as legal persons with their own rights and obligations. Accounts have to be prepared and audited although there is no requirement to prepare the equivalent of a directors' report.

A further advantage of the company is the possibility of separating ownership from control. In a partnership, all of the partners are agents for the firm. In a company, and this is particularly the case in public companies, the ownership and the control are separated. Those people owning the share capital will not generally be the people who are running the business (however, in private companies, the owners and the managers may well be the same).

An attraction of incorporation is what is sometimes termed perpetual succession. This means that the company need never die. Companies do go into liquidation but they need not do so. There is no theoretical reason why a company cannot go on for ever. The Hudson's Bay Company has been running for well over 300 years, for example. In the case of partnerships, however, wherever there is a change of partners, there has to be a drawing up of partnership accounts and a re-formation of the partnership.

Incorporation is an attractive business medium where the participators wish to be able to transfer their shares at some later stage. In a company, shares are freely transferable, subject to the terms of the company's constitution (section 7.4). In a partnership, by contrast, a partner's share is not so transferable unless the agreement so provides. The advantage of transferability is seen at its clearest where a company is quoted on the Stock Exchange or the Alternative Investment Market (AIM). At this stage, there will be a market mechanism for disposing of and purchasing shares.

It is said to be easier to raise finance where a company is formed as opposed to a partnership. Clearly, if a company is quoted, it has access to the Stock Exchange to raise finance by issuing its shares and debentures (collectively called securities) to the public (Chapter 20). In the case of debentures, these may be secured by a floating charge over all of the company's assets and undertaking (section 20.6), although this does not in general provide advantages for companies on or after 15 September 2003 (section 20.6). The device of the floating charge is open to the company and a general partnership cannot take advantage of this means of raising finance, although it is open to limited liability partnerships to create floating charges.

It is probably the case that there is more prestige attached to the company than to the partnership. There is no reason that this should be the case but probably the trading and investing public sees a company in a more favourable light than a partnership.

A further consideration, although it might not be an advantage for companies, is taxation. Companies will pay corporation tax on their profits. In the case of partnerships, the profits of the partnership business are attributable to the partners of the firm, who will pay schedular income tax on those profits. It is not possible to say in isolation from factors concerning the circumstances of the participators and their other sources of income whether this is an advantage or not. It will depend on the circumstances.

The disadvantages that attach to incorporation are not numerous. There are clearly formalities to be complied with. A partnership agreement need not even be written (provided it is not a limited or a limited liability partnership). Clearly, it is desirable to have a written agreement for evidential purposes but there is no legal reason why the agreement should be in writing. Companies are subject to a comprehensive code of rules contained in the Companies Act 2006 and elsewhere; the general partnership is not subject to a detailed statutory regime although the Partnership Act 1890 does set out some rules.

The Limited Liability Partnership Regulations 2001 (S1 2001/1090) do apply detailed rules to limited liability partnerships which are similar to the regime that applies to companies.

In the case of a company, there are various formalities to be complied with. A constitution has to be drafted. Articles of association (the constitution) have to be delivered to the Registrar at Companies House in Cardiff in the case of English and Welsh companies, together with a statement of capital and a statement of compliance. A certificate of incorporation will then be issued to the company. There are various ongoing formalities for a company, including the filing of an annual return, the filing of annual accounts (unless the company is unlimited) and the filing of various forms connected with changes of directors, issue of shares, issue of debentures, change of company secretary, etc. Companies also have to comply with formalities regarding the holding of meetings, which is not the case in a partnership. Private companies are not required to hold AGMs but may do so if they wish.

Together with these formalities, there is the disadvantage of publicity in the case of the company. This is generally seen as a disadvantage as a company has no option but to make certain of its affairs public. These would include the names of the company's directors and company secretary, the accounts of the company (unless unlimited), the annual return of the company, the company's constitution and various registers that have to be kept at the company's registered office.

Together with formalities and publicity, one may add expense as a disadvantage. However, the expense of setting up a company is not great. There is a charge for the issue of a certificate of incorporation and an annual fee for filing the company's annual return, but few other charges are made by the company's registry. The cost of the annual audit may well be a deterrent, however, in the case of a limited company, although small companies are exempted from the statutory audit.

Two other disadvantages of incorporation may be mentioned here. These are the rules on the maintenance of capital that apply to companies – and which are much stricter than in relation to partnerships – and the remaining vestigial rules on ultra vires that limit a company's freedom of manoeuvre. Partnerships by contrast are free to do what is legal within the law of the land.

Sometimes an individual may elect to run a business as a sole trader. This is, in essence, the firm without partners. There will be no limit on liability but no formalities either. It is almost invariably a small business.

Comparison of partnerships and limited companies

Partnership	Limited company
No separate legal personality	Separate legal personality
Governed by Partnership Act 1890	Governed by Companies Act 2006 and Insolvency Act 1986
No comprehensive statutory rules	Complex rules which need interpreting by a lawyer

Partnership	Limited company
Partnership profits allocated to partners and taxed under normal income tax rules	Company profits liable for corporation tax
Partners have generally unlimited liability	Shareholders' liability limited to paying for the number of shares they have taken up
Partnership may be ended on death or bankruptcy of partner, or by notice	Company perpetual – can go on for ever
Difficult to realise investment	Investment readily available through trading shares in the Stock Exchange (if quoted)
Debts secured against assets of individual partners	Debts secured against company assets
All partners are agents of the firm	Possible to separate ownership and control (members own; directors control)
Difficult to raise money	Easier to raise money by debentures and shares
No requirement to make any information public in general	Required to make information public, and file information with Registrar of Companies including filing of annual accounts

1.2 Types of companies

There are various classifications of companies that may be made.

1.2.1 Chartered company

A company may be chartered, that is, set up by a charter from the Crown, and may then derive its powers from the charter. The very first companies were of this variety, for example the East India Company, the Massachusetts Bay Company and the Hudson's Bay Company. Today, chartered companies are not of economic significance but they still exist. Generally, they are not trading concerns. They may be professional organisations – the Institute of Chartered Accountants of England and Wales is an example. They may be local government corporations, for example, the Corporation of Chesterfield. Perhaps the most famous chartered company of them all is the British Broadcasting Corporation.

1.2.2 Statutory company

A further type of company is the statutory company. In Victorian England, there was a great plethora of incorporations. Each company had to be set up by a separate Act of Parliament. During this period of industrial revolution, the great mass of companies involved public utilities such as gas and water, or transportation such as canal companies and railway companies. Today, there are few statutory companies. The process is too cumbersome for periods of massive economic activity, as each company is incorporated by a separate Act of Parliament.

1.2.3 Registered company

The third type of company in this classification is the most common of all. This is the registered company. There were problems with incorporation by charter or by statute in that these forms of incorporation were cumbersome and inconvenient. This ultimately led Parliament to act to make it simpler to incorporate. Registered companies originated with the Joint Stock Companies Act 1844 when Gladstone was President of the Board of Trade. Limited liability was not introduced until the Limited Liability Act 1855. The current Companies Act under which registration may be sought by companies is the Companies Act of 2006. Provided a company complies with the formalities set out in the Act, it will be registered – that is, its name will be added to the list of registered companies and a file will be opened in its name at Companies House in Cardiff. In fact, today, clearly a manual register is not opened, but the company's registered details are kept and are available for inspection at Cardiff and in London (and in Edinburgh for Scottish companies).

The Registrar of Companies for England and Wales is situated at Crown Way, Cardiff, CF14 3UZ. The Registrar is head of a government agency called Companies House.

The Registrar of Companies for Scotland is based at Companies House, 4th Floor, Edinburgh Quay 2, 139 Fountainbridge, Edinburgh, EH3 9FF.

The Registrar of Companies for Northern Ireland is at Companies House, 2nd Floor, The Linenhall, 32–38 Linenhall Street, Belfast, BT2 8BG.

Further information about the operation of Companies House may be obtained from the website at www.gov.uk/government/organisations/companies-house.

As noted, in order to register a company, the company's constitution, the articles of association, must be delivered to the Registrar. This is submitted together with an application for registration providing information such as the company's name, the part of the United Kingdom where the registered office is to be situated and whether members have limited liability, and, if so, whether it is limited by shares or by guarantee. It will also state whether the company is public or private. If the company is to have a share capital then a statement of capital and initial shareholdings must also be filed together with the application for registration. If the company is a company limited by guarantee, then a statement of the guarantee must be filed.

There needs to be a statement of who the directors are and if the company is a public company then there must be a statement of who is to be the secretary.

These documents must be accompanied by a statement of compliance to the effect that the requirements of the Act have been complied with.

Companies can be incorporated by electronic filing. This is likely to become more significant.

1.2.4 Limited and unlimited company

Another form of classification of companies is the distinction between a company limited by shares, a company limited by guarantee, a company limited by guarantee with share capital and an unlimited company.

Most companies are limited by shares. Trading companies will need to raise share capital with which to purchase assets which they need for running their businesses. Companies limited by guarantee are the media usually utilised by charities, including educational institutions such as the London School of Economics. Such companies do not need capital with which to trade but may wish to have some of the other advantages of incorporation such as the ability to hold property in their own name. Since the Companies Act 1980, it has not been possible to create new companies limited by guarantee with a share capital, but there are some companies falling into this category which existed in 1980 and remain registered companies. Public companies must be limited by shares or limited by guarantee with share capital. If the company is an unlimited one, as has already been mentioned, there will be no obligation to file annual accounts. However, this advantage must be balanced against the disadvantage that the members of the unlimited company will have unlimited liability and may be called upon to contribute to the company's assets if the company goes into liquidation.

1.2.5 Public and private company

Long in gestation, the Companies Act (CA) 2006 ultimately reached the statute book. One of the declared aims of the statute is to cater for private companies as a priority. Thus, for example, there is a provision for model articles for private companies limited by shares and by guarantee, quite distinct from model articles for public companies.

A fundamental distinction pervading the whole of company law is the distinction between public and private companies and this, of course, is retained. Most companies are private but the more important larger companies are public companies. The basic distinction is that a public company may offer its shares and debentures to the public whilst a private company may not do so (see s 755 CA 2006).

Section 757 CA 2006 provides for a prohibition order restraining a proposed contravention of the section. If a company acts in contravention of s 755 then it may be required to re-register as a public company under s 758 CA 2006. Whilst, if the court does not make an order for re-registration, it may either make a remedial order under s 759 CA 2006 requiring any person knowingly concerned in the contravention of the section to offer to purchase any of the securities on appropriate terms where a person is affected by the contravention, or may make an order for the compulsory winding up of the company.

A further distinction is the capital requirement first introduced in the Companies Act 1980 which requires that a public company must have a minimum subscribed share capital of £50,000 (s 763 CA 2006). This must be paid up to at least 25 per cent so at least £12,500 must already have been raised by the issue of shares. A public company must furthermore have a trading certificate before it begins trading, in addition to its certificate of incorporation (s 761 CA 2006). This trading certificate will only be issued once the Registrar of Companies is satisfied that the company has fulfilled the formalities of the Act and raised the required minimum capital.

A private company need have only one director and no secretary; a public company must have a minimum of two directors and a secretary (s 273 CA 2006).

The name of the company will indicate whether the company is public or private. The description 'public limited company' or, as abbreviated, 'plc' (or Welsh equivalent 'ccc' and 'cwmni cyhoeddus cyfyngedig') will indicate that the company is a public one. By contrast, if the company is expressed to be 'limited' or, as abbreviated, 'ltd', or 'cyfyngedig' or, as abbreviated, 'cyf', the company is a private company (see ss 58 and 59 CA 2006).

Private companies may qualify as small (ss 381–384 CA 2006) or medium sized (ss 465–467 CA 2006) in which case they enjoy certain accounting exemptions (see sections 17.1.2 and 17.1.3).

Public companies have to abide by stricter regimes in relation to distributions (see section 8.1.3), payment for shares (see section 4.7) and the making of loans and quasi-loans, and the entering of credit transactions in favour of directors (see section 10.9).

1.2.6 Community interest company

A new form of company was created by the Companies (Audit, Investigations and Community Enterprise) Act 2004 (see s 6 of the Companies Act 2006). The Companies (Audit, Investigations and Community Enterprise) Act 2004 provides in s 26 that this is a new type of company for those wanting to establish social enterprises. The community interest company must set out an object in its memorandum such that a reasonable person might consider that the carrying on of the object would be for the benefit of the community (s 35(3) of the 2004 Act). Furthermore, surpluses should normally be reinvested for the purposes of the community interest company rather than being distributed to shareholders (s 30 of the 2004 Act).

Such companies will not have charitable status, even if their objects are wholly charitable. A community interest company should register with Companies House as a company limited by guarantee or a company limited by shares, and then will apply for community interest company status to the community interest company regulator (ss 27 and 36 of the 2004 Act). They must adopt a suitable constitution providing for the pursuit of the community interest object and provisions consistent with community interest companies such as restrictions on the transfer and distribution of the company's assets, and if the regulator is satisfied that the company will pursue purposes beneficial to the community, then the company will be registered as a community interest company.

Community interest companies must produce an annual community interest report. This report will set out what the company has done during the year to benefit the community.

Community interest companies are regulated by an independent officer appointed by the Secretary of State for Business, Innovation and Skills. Among the officer's duties are the promotion of community interest companies and the provision of guidance.

Some companies such as party political institutions may not gain community interest company status, by virtue of regulation.

Community interest companies will be more lightly regulated than charities but do not enjoy charitable status. It may be the appropriate vehicle for social enterprise if it is felt appropriate to incorporate with limited liability, and if flexibility is desired along with an organisational structure, membership and governance.

The name of the community interest company, if it is private, must end with 'Community Interest Company' or 'CIC', or 'Cwmni Buddiant Cymunedol' or 'CBC' for companies registering documents in Welsh, whereas if it is a public limited community interest company, then the appropriate company names will end with 'Community Interest Public Limited Company' or 'Community Interest PLC', or 'Cwmni Buddiant Cymunedol Cyhoeddus Cyfyngedig' or 'Cwmni Buddiant CCC', if it is desired to register documents in Welsh.

1.3 Legislation

Over the years company law has become increasingly complex and there is a very large and detailed set of rules governing company law in addition to the great welter of cases that affects this area.

The Companies Act 2006 is the current consolidation measure of company law. It is the longest piece of legislation on any subject to have passed through the British Parliament.

Additionally, there are other pieces of legislation, for example, the Insolvency Act 1986, as well as the Financial Services and Markets Act 2000, which are also important.

1.3.1 Bribery Act 2010

One piece of legislation that impacts upon company law is the Bribery Act 2010. The Bribery Act deals with the criminal law relating to bribery. The Act repeals previous statutory and common law provisions in relation to bribery and corruption and replaces these provisions with the crimes of bribery, being bribed, the bribery of foreign public officials, and also the failure of commercial organisations to prevent bribery conducted on their behalf. Facilitation or grease payments (small bribes paid to 'get things done or done faster') is also an offence within the Act.

The maximum penalty for committing a crime under the Act is ten years' imprisonment plus an unlimited fine, as well as the potential for the disqualification of directors, and the confiscation of property.

In relation to commercial organisations, s 7 creates a new offence of the failure of such organisations to prevent bribery conducted on their behalf. It applies to all commercial organisations that are conducting business in the United Kingdom. It is not exclusive to the organisation itself, so individuals may also be guilty of the offence. It is an offence of strict liability with no need to prove any *mens rea*.

Section 7(2) provides a defence if the organisation can demonstrate that it has in place 'adequate procedures designed to prevent persons associated with the organisation from undertaking such conduct'. The burden of proof for proving such a defence is placed upon the organisation concerned. The burden of proof is on the balance of probabilities.

Guidance has been published in relation to the liability of businesses. The guidance demonstrates the need for a clear code of conduct for corporations, which should ensure that their employees are aware of the scope of the Act. Appropriate training should also be provided in relation to the impact of the Act for a company's employees. Such measures on the part of corporations would help establish that adequate procedures had been put in place.

In relation to prosecution, the prosecution must be sanctioned by the director of the appropriate prosecution agency (s 10). Section 11 provides that the penalty to be placed on the commercial organisation is an unlimited fine. In addition, of course, individuals or the company itself may be subject to a confiscation order under the Proceeds of Crime Act 2002. Directors may also be disqualified for their conduct.

In 2011 it was announced that the Attorney General's office was consulting on the possibility of bringing in plea bargaining to help in the pursuit of white-collar crime. This would potentially strengthen the UK's position in enforcing the Bribery Act 2010.

A plea-bargaining agreement would permit prosecuting authorities to grant an amnesty to corporations in return for assistance with an investigation.

The Director of the Serious Fraud Office and the Director of Public Prosecutions published a consultation in June 2013 on rules which came into force in 2014 on a draft Code of Practice explaining how they intend to use Deferred Prosecution Agreements. The first one was agreed with Standard Bank plc in November 2015. Deferred Prosecution Agreements were introduced in Sch 17 of the Crime and Courts Act 2013.

1.4 European law

The United Kingdom joined the Common Market, as it then was, in 1972. Membership became operative from 1 January 1973. Increasingly Directives and Regulations have a considerable effect on United Kingdom company law. The European Union (EU), as it now is, has a commanding hold on many aspects of British law.

Lord Denning described the Treaty of Rome as being 'like an incoming tide which flows into the estuaries and up the rivers of English law' (*HP Bulmer v J Bollinger SA* [1974] Ch 401).

Although this tide has not flowed into all of the channels of company law, it has gushed into its streams and affected English company law.

There is provision in the European Union's treaties for the harmonisation of the laws of member states in certain areas. The Council and the Commission are authorised to coordinate 'to the necessary extent the safeguards which, for the protection of the interests of members and others, are required of companies or firms "...with a view to making such safeguards equivalent throughout the Community"' (Art 44(2) (g) Treaty of Rome).

This process of harmonisation is carried out by means of Directives. These are measures addressed to member states of the European Union to enact their provisions as law, leaving it to the member state to determine exactly how this is to be achieved.

In fact, the First Directive on company law was already in force when the United Kingdom joined the Common Market.

The First Council Directive (68/151/EEC) provides for the coordination of regulations concerning disclosure and the validity of obligations entered into by companies with limited liability and the power of representation of the company's organs. In everyday terms, the First Council Directive required mitigation of the ultra vires doctrine in favour of outsiders and provisions to the effect that those dealing on behalf of unformed companies could enforce transactions and, in turn, be made liable on transactions on behalf of unformed companies.

The Second Council Directive (77/91/EEC) concerns the coordination of provisions on the formation of public limited liability companies, minimum share capital requirements, dividends to shareholders and increases and reductions in capital. The Directive is particularly important in relation to provisions relating to the maintenance of capital and the consequent protection of creditors.

The Third Council Directive (78/855/EEC) concerns mergers between public limited liability companies within the same Member State.

The Fourth Council Directive (78/660/EEC) coordinates provisions within Member States concerning the presentation and content of companies' annual accounts and annual reports, the methods of valuation and the publication of accounts in respect of companies with limited liability.

The Sixth Council Directive (82/891/EEC) concerns the division of public limited liability companies. This Directive sets out rules concerning divisions of public limited liability companies within the same Member State.

The Seventh Council Directive (83/349/EEC) coordinates national laws on consolidated accounts (group accounts).

The Eighth Council Directive (84/253/EEC) sets out those persons who are appropriate to carry out the statutory audits of accounting documents for companies subject to audit.

The Tenth Council Directive was passed in 2005 (2005/56/EC). It relates to cross-border mergers of limited liability companies. The Directive is intended to facilitate cross-border mergers and provides for the reduction of costs of such mergers.

The Eleventh Council Directive (89/666/EEC) concerns disclosure requirements in respect of companies with branches in another Member State which are governed by the laws of another state to ensure an equivalent level of protection for shareholders and third parties.

The Twelfth Council Directive (89/667/EEC) provides for single-member private limited liability companies. In addition, where Member States allow single-member companies in the case of public limited companies, the Directive is also applicable.

The Thirteenth Council Directive (2004/25/EC) relates to takeover bids and the protection of shareholders (especially minority shareholders), employees and others. The Directive provides for notification of employees or their representatives in the offeree and offeror companies.

Work on a draft Fourteenth Directive on the transfer of a company's registered office from one Member State to another has ceased.

In 2007 a Directive was passed on the exercise of shareholders' voting rights (2007/36/EC). This Directive provides for the rights of shareholders to information relevant to general meetings and the facilitation of cross-border exercise of voting rights, by correspondence and by proxy. Furthermore, it provides for the abolition of share blocking and related practices, and provides for the right to ask questions at general meetings.

In addition there are amending directives.

Directive 2003/58/EC amends the First Council Directive on company law in relation to disclosure requirements.

Directive 2006/68/EC amends the Second Council Directive on company law regarding the formation of public limited liability companies and the maintenance and alteration of their capital.

Directive 2007/63/EC amends the Third Council Directive and the Sixth Council Directive regarding mergers and divisions of public limited liability companies relating to the requirement of an independent expert report (see also section 5.9 in relation to prospectuses).

1.4.1 Controversial Directives

There has been considerable controversy over the proposed Fifth Directive dealing with two-tier boards and employee representation at board level. This has lapsed.

The Draft Ninth Directive on Corporate Groups was also controversial. The approach on matters of protection of shareholders and creditors within groups is dealt with differently in Germany from other Member States and consequently no progress was made on this Directive, which was subsequently withdrawn.

1.4.2 High Level Group of Experts

In 2001, the Commission appointed a High Level Group of Experts to make 'recommendations for a modern regulatory European company law framework'. Their final report was published in 2002 (*Final Report of the High Level Group of Company Law Experts on A Modern Regulatory Framework of Company Law in Europe –* Brussels, 4 November 2002).

The High Level Group of Experts placed emphasis on providing legal structures for doing business rather than protection for shareholders and others. This approach was largely accepted by the Commission in 2003.

At the same time that there was a shift of emphasis, the Commission moved to simplify legislation adopting the Simpler Legislation for the Single Market Initiative (SLIM) in 1996. This was, in fact, a general initiative and was not limited to company law. It led to amendments of the First, Second, Third and Sixth Directives (referred to above).

In 2006, the Commission adopted an updated simplification programme with a view to measuring administrative costs and reducing burdens that unnecessarily hamper the economic activity of European business. The aim of this is to enhance the competitiveness of EU companies by reducing burdens imposed under the European Company Law Directives where this can be achieved without major negative impact on other stakeholders. The action programme and the aim of it to reduce administrative burdens by 25 per cent by the year 2012 were both endorsed by the Spring European Council in March 2007.

In July 2007, the Commission adopted a communication setting out proposals for simplifying the areas of company law, accounting and auditing.

The UK government is strongly in favour of simplification and has welcomed the benefits that simplification of reporting requirements will bring to Member States.

1.4.3 Securities regulation

The European Union has adopted a number of directives on securities regulation (see section 5.8).

In 2002, Regulation 1606/2002/EC in the securities market context required companies with securities issued on recognised stock exchanges to produce accounts in accordance with International Accounting Standards (see section 17.1.1).

1.4.4 Supremacy of European law

The primacy of European law was an issue that arose in *Centros Ltd v Erhvervs-og Selskabsstyrelsen* [2000] Ch 446. This case concerned two businesspeople in Denmark, a husband and wife, shopping around for the best place to incorporate their business. Mrs Bryde was the sole director of Centros Ltd, which was registered as a private company in England and Wales in May 1992. There were, and are, no minimum capital requirements for private companies in England and Wales. She then approached the Danish Companies Board wishing to register a branch. The company's object covered a range of economic activity but it was only intended to operate as a wine importer and exporter. The only other member of the company was Mrs Bryde's husband, Mr Bryde.

It should be noted that in Denmark 200,000 Danish kroner were needed at the time to register a private company.

The Companies Board in Denmark rejected the application to register the Danish branch and this was upheld on appeal.

The matter was then referred to the Court of Justice in the European Union. The Court of Justice held that a refusal to register a branch of a company having its registered office and formed in accordance with the laws of another Member State constituted an obstacle to the right of freedom of establishment under the EU Treaty and was so precluded. The branch should therefore be registered in Denmark.

1.4.5 Societas Europaea

From October 2004, it has been possible under Regulation (EC) No. 2157/2001 to set up a European public limited liability company or 'Societas Europaea'. Such companies can be set up where there is cooperation between at least two European companies from different Member States.

A Societas Europaea can be set up by merger, as a holding company or as a subsidiary. Once registered, a Societas Europaea has legal personality. It must have a registered office and the head office must be in the same Member State. Companies

House produces an introductory guide on the Societas Europaea. It is available on the Companies House website: www.companieshouse.gov.uk.

Regulations are set out in the European Public Limited-Liability Company Regulations 2004(SI 2004/2326). These came into force in October 2004.

There are few in the UK and few throughout the EU.

1.4.6 The European Private Company

The Societas Privata Europaea was a Commission proposal for a Council Regulation on the statute of a European private company (COM (2008) 396/3). There have been various compromise proposals but the issue remained unresolved as at December 2015. The United Kingdom has broadly welcomed the proposal although it has made some reservations, most significantly to require that the vehicle could only operate where companies had a presence in more than one Member State.

It should be noted that there are some 23 million small and medium-sized enterprises in the EU, and 99 per cent of all companies are within this category. More than 40 per cent would like to develop cross-border activity but within the EU only 5 per cent do so (in the UK this is 7.5 per cent).

1.4.7 European Economic Interest Grouping

Another business institution at European level is the European Economic Interest Grouping (EEIG). This institution has separate personality and is made up of two or more legal persons from two or more Member States. The association allows its members to retain their individual identity whilst setting up an additional activity such as joint research.

The structure is similar to that of a company and in the UK the EEIG must register at Companies House.

1.5 The Department for Business, Innovation and Skills

Companies are administered within the Department for Business, Innovation and Skills. Overall responsibility for the Department lies with the Secretary of State for Business, Innovation and Skills.

The Department's main office is 1 Victoria Street, London, SW1H 0ET. The department's website is www.gov.uk/government/organisations/department-for-business-innovation-skills.

The Department is committed to fostering competitive markets in the UK, the EU and worldwide. By fighting anticompetitive practices and promoting open markets, it enables companies to compete freely and fairly, giving UK consumers more choice and better value.

The Companies Investigation Branch is also situated within the Department. The branch investigates existing companies where there is suspicion of corporate abuse or other grounds to investigate. In April 2006 it merged with the Insolvency Service, an Executive Agency of the Department of Business, Innovation and Skills.

Summary

A company or a partnership

A company is a separate entity in law and certain advantages flow from this:

(a)   access to limited liability;
(b)   separation of ownership from control;
(c)   perpetual succession;
(d)   transferability of shares;
(e)   raising finance.

A partnership may be set up without formalities, without publicity and without expense.

The profits of a company are subject to corporation tax; the profits of a partnership are subject to schedular income tax in the hands of the partners.

Types of company

There are various classifications of companies:

(a)   Companies may be chartered, statutory or registered. The vast majority are registered.
(b)   Companies may be limited by shares, limited by guarantee or unlimited. A few are limited by guarantee with a share capital. Unlimited companies do not need to file annual accounts.
(c)   An important distinction is between private companies and public companies. Most companies are private, but only public companies can offer their shares or debentures to the public. All companies quoted on the Stock Exchange are public.
(d)   Companies engaged in social enterprise may engage in activity via incorporation by becoming community interest companies.

European law

European law has had an impact on the development of company law.

Self-test questions

1.1   How does a company differ from a partnership?

1.2   What are the different types of company?

1.3   Set out the names of the major pieces of legislation relevant to company law today.

1.4   How important is European Law in company law as it applies in the United Kingdom today?

1.5   Which government department is responsible for the area of company law today?

Further reading

IGF Cath, 'Freedom of Establishment of Companies: A New Step Towards Completion of the Internal Market' 6YB of European Law 1986 247.

J Freedman, 'Small Business and the Corporate Form: Burden or Privilege?' (1994) 57 MLR 555.

A Hicks, 'Corporate Form: Questioning the Unsung Hero' (1997) JBL 306.

C Howell, 'The Company White Paper: A Descriptive Overview' (2005) 26 Co Law 203.

FG Jacobs, 'The Basic Freedoms of the EEC Treaty and Company Law' (1992) 13 Co Law 4.

O Kahn-Freund, 'Some Reflections on Company Law Reform' (1944) 7 MLR 44.

AF Konard, 'The European Alternative to Uniformity in Corporation Laws' (1991) 89 Mich L Rev 2150.

E Micheler, 'The Impact of the Centros Case on Europe's Company Laws' [2000] Comp Law 179.

F Saifee and B Makowicz, 'Societas Privata Europaea: The European Private Company' (2009) 30 Co Law 227.

S Sheikh, 'UK Company Law Reform: Towards a 21st Century Corporate Revolution' (1996) 7 ICCLR 119.

Chapter 2

The *Salomon* principle and the corporate veil

2.1 Introduction

As has been noted, a key feature of the company is that it is a legal person with a separate existence from the company's members (i.e. shareholders where the company has shares) or its directors. From this separate personality flow many consequences.

The House of Lords' decision in *Salomon v A Salomon & Co Ltd* established the separate identity of the company.

Aron Salomon and his boot and shoe business have done for company law what Mrs Carlill and her smoke ball did for the law of contract and what Mrs Donoghue and her adulterated ginger beer did for the law of tort.

Mr Salomon transferred his business to a limited company and he and six other members of his family subscribed the company's memorandum; the purchase price was £38,782. Salomon took 20,001 shares and the six other family members took one share each. Debentures (loan stock) of £10,000 and £8,782 cash were paid to Salomon as the balance of the purchase price. The business foundered and was wound up with liabilities in excess of its assets by £7,733. The company's liquidator claimed that the company's business was still Salomon's, in that the company was merely a sham to limit Salomon's liability for debts incurred in carrying it on, and the repayment of Salomon's debenture should be postponed until the company's other creditors were satisfied. At first instance, Vaughan Williams J agreed with the liquidator. He held that Salomon's sole purpose in forming the company was to use it as an agent to run his business for him.

The Court of Appeal reached the same conclusion but for different reasons. It took the view that the principle of limited liability was a privilege conferred by the Companies Acts only on genuinely independent shareholders and not on 'one substantial person and six mere dummies'.

The House of Lords unanimously reversed the Court of Appeal decision. Lord Halsbury LC in *Salomon v A Salomon & Co Ltd* said:

> I must pause here, to point out that the statute enacts nothing as to the extent or degree of interest which may be held by each of the seven [subscribers] or as to the proportion of influence possessed by one or the majority of the shareholders over the others. One share is enough. Still less is it possible to contend that the motive of becoming shareholders or of making them shareholders is a field of enquiry which the statute itself recognises as legitimate. If there are shareholders, they are shareholders for all purposes; and even if the statute was silent as to the recognition of trust, I should be prepared to hold that if six of them were the cestuis que trust of the seventh, whatever might be their rights *inter se*, the statute would have made them shareholders to all intents and purposes with their respective rights and liabilities, and dealing with them in their relation to the company, the only relations which I believe the law would sanction would be that they were corporators of the body corporate.

This case thus established one of the basic articles of faith of British company law, indeed of company law of all common law systems, that a company is a legal person independent and distinct from its shareholders and its managers.

This, at least, was the theory. However, the principle in Salomon's case has not been without its detractors. Otto Kahn-Freund in 'Some Reflections on Company Law Reform' in (1944) MLR 54, was critical of the principle in the case. He says:

However, owing to the ease with which companies can be formed in this country, and owing to the rigidity with which the courts applied the corporate entity concept ever since the calamitous decision in *Salomon v Salomon & Co Ltd*, a single trader or a group of traders are almost tempted by the law to conduct their business in the form of a limited company, even where no particular business risk is involved, and where no outside capital is required.

This state of affairs would not necessarily call for reform, if it were not for the fact that the courts had failed to give that protection to the business creditors, which should be the corollary of the privilege of limited liability.

Kahn-Freund continues (p. 57):

What can be done? How is it possible to check the one-man company and other abuses of company law for purposes which it was never meant to serve? Is it conceivable that Salomon's case can be abrogated by legislation? Could the interests of outside creditors be protected by a general clause under which persons owning a controlling interest in a company would be liable for its debts? Or could there be a provision according to which a company would be deemed to act as agent for the owners of controlling interests?

Nor is Kahn-Freund alone. Clive Schmitthoff in 'The Wholly Owned and the Controlled Subsidiary' [1978] JBL 218, considers problems that present themselves in connection with wholly owned and controlled subsidiaries (see section 2.2.2.2).

Schmitthoff looks at the decision in Salomon in the narrower context of subsidiary companies, although he analyses the decision and points out some difficulties that it presents.

He looks specifically at two separate problems; one concerns the problem of jurisdiction where the courts of the host country (of a subsidiary) may wish to exercise jurisdiction over the parent company in the home country. He also considers the separate problem of the liability of the parent for the debts of subsidiaries.

As regards jurisdiction, the courts and authorities of the host country should assume jurisdiction over the parent company if it carries on substantial business in the host country by means of wholly owned or controlled subsidiaries, or by means of branch offices.

As regards liability, the parent company should be liable for the debts of wholly owned and controlled subsidiaries if it employed these dependent companies as agents, and it should be rebuttably presumed that it used these subsidiaries in that manner.

Schmitthoff continues:

If the subsidiary is wholly owned, there should be a conclusive presumption that it is controlled by the parent, and if the parent holds more than 50% of the voting power of the subsidiary, but does not own the subsidiary wholly, there should be a rebuttable presumption to the effect that the subsidiary is controlled.

(p. 229)

Notwithstanding such statements and occasional exceptional judicial instances apart, the principle of separate identity has been consistently applied.

In the New Zealand case of *Lee v Lee's Air Farming Ltd* [1961] AC 12, which went to the Privy Council, Lee owned all the shares but one in the company that he founded. His wife held the other share. Lee was governing director of the company, whose business was spraying crops from the air. When he was killed in a flying accident while on company business, his widow was held to be entitled to recover compensation from the company for his estate as the company was quite separate and distinct from her husband, its employee.

It has sometimes been said that the American Realist school in jurisprudence explains far more about how judicial decisions are made than the system of precedent. Thus decisions may be put down to whether the judge has a fondness for, or aversion to, redheads, and what the judge has had for breakfast. This may explain some of the cases in this area of law, which are notoriously difficult to reconcile one with another.

It is proposed to contrast some cases here. The case of *Lee v Lee's Air Farming Ltd* can be contrasted with *Malyon v Plummer* [1964] 1 QB 330. Here the claimant's husband had been killed in an accident. This had been caused by the admitted negligence of the defendant. The husband owned all but one of the shares in a company. He worked a six-day week for the company and was the only breadwinner. The claimant owned the other share and received a substantial salary for a limited amount of part-time work, which she performed on a casual basis. The wife sought to claim for the loss of her livelihood, asserting that when the husband was killed, the company was also effectively killed.

In the Court of Appeal, Sellers LJ said,

> In my opinion, the inter-position of FP Malyon Ltd, if that is how it should be regarded, does not prevent the court assessing truly the loss which the wife has suffered. The husband's business, FP Malyon Ltd, has been destroyed by the loss of the husband, and it is clear that the revenue was, in substance, derived from him. The decision in *Salomon v Salomon Co* need not blind one to the essential facts of dependency and require a finding of fact that is contrary to the true financial position as distinct from an artificial or fictitious one.

The common feature in *Lee v Lee's Air Farming Ltd* and *Malyon v Plummer* is that, in a loose sense, justice can be seen to have been done in both cases. In *Lee*, by asserting the separate identity of the company, the widow was able to benefit from the New Zealand Workman's Compensation Act and obtain compensation. In a similar way, by destroying the corporate façade in *Malyon v Plummer*, the widow was able to assert that when the husband died the company also died, and that they were one and the same thing, and thus she was able to recover compensation for the loss of livelihood. Two widows recovering compensation by opposite legal arguments. Judges of a certain age may well have an instinctive sympathy for widows!

It is often difficult to reconcile the cases and to find a coherent body of doctrine in this area.

Two further cases may be contrasted: *Buchan v Secretary of State for Employment* and *Ivey v Secretary of State for Employment* [1997] 1RLR 80, on one hand and *Secretary of State for Trade and Industry v Bottrill* [2000] 1 All ER 915 on the other hand.

In *Buchan v Secretary of State for Employment* and *Ivey v Secretary of State for Employment*, the Employment Appeal Tribunal distinguished the Privy Council decision in *Lee* in two joined appeals. The two directors involved held a half and a controlling interest respectively in their companies. It was held that they were not employees for the purpose of making a claim against the National Insurance Fund.

The tribunal considered that such directors could block decisions at board level, including decisions relating to their dismissal, and that this was not consistent with being an employee. No doubt, the context of the dispute influenced the decision as the directors were seeking compensation as employees for dismissal. The Employment Appeal Tribunal took the view that it is not the purpose of the legislation to fund compensation for those whose businesses have failed.

However, in *Secretary of State for Trade and Industry v Bottrill*, the veil was not lifted. Bottrill was managing director of Magnatac UK Ltd. He held the only share. There was one other director. Bottrill had a contract of employment which set out all his duties, his hours, sick pay, etc. He paid tax and national insurance. The company became insolvent and he applied for a redundancy payment. It was held by the Court of Appeal, with Lord Woolff MR presiding, that it was a question of fact whether Bottrill was an employee or not. The fact that he was a controlling shareholder was not decisive. The question was whether there was a genuine contract. In the instant case the tribunal had been entitled to conclude that there was a genuine contract.

Two further cases may be contrasted.

In *Macaura v Northern Assurance Company Ltd* [1925] AC 619, where the owner of a timber business incorporated the business but continued to insure the property in his own name, it was held when the property was destroyed that he had no insurable interest and so could not claim on the policy. The property was no longer his; it now belonged to the company. It may well have been relevant in this case that the fire occurred soon after the insurance policy had been renewed. There was at least a hint in the case that this may have been a relevant factor in the decision. Is this a hint of arson?

Nevertheless, the case may be contrasted with the Supreme Court of Canada decision in *Constitution Insurance Co of Canada v Kosmopoulos* (1987) 34 DLR (4th) 208. Kosmopoulos was the sole shareholder and director of a company, Kosmopoulos Ltd, which carried on a retail business. He conducted the business as a sole proprietorship (as it had formerly been), and was himself the lessee of the business premises. He took out insurance in his own name. Damage was caused by fire to the assets of the company, and the insurers denied liability. Kosmopoulos's action succeeded at trial and in the Ontario Court of Appeal. On further appeal by the insurers to the Supreme Court of Canada, the appeal was dismissed. It was held that it was not necessary that the insured should have a legally enforceable interest in the property. It was sufficient if he had a relation to, or concern in, the subject matter of the insurance, whereby he would suffer a loss upon the occurrence of the insured risks. Wilson J in the Supreme Court said that:

> Mr Kosmopoulos, as a sole shareholder of the company, was so placed with respect to the assets of the business as to have benefit from their existence and prejudice from the destruction. He had a moral certainty of advantage or benefit from those assets but for the fire. He had, therefore, an insurable interest in them, capable of supporting the insurance policy and is entitled to recover under it.

There is no suggestion that the law in Canada is materially different from the law in the United Kingdom. Common law countries all seem to suffer from the same confusion of clinging to the *Salomon* principles of the basic separation of the company from its controllers, while at the same time undermining it with a variety of exceptions and qualifications which are considered in this chapter. Those hoping for a clear and consistent message in this area will hope in vain, as the above cases demonstrate.

Demonstrating the separate nature of the company in *R v Buxton* [2010] All ER 215, the Court of Appeal held that a restraining order could be issued to safeguard a company from harassment.

While the decision in Salomon's case has certainly been open to criticism, and the cases are far from consistent, in *Adams v Cape Industries plc* [1990] Ch 433, the Court of Appeal held that an English company, whose business was mining asbestos in South Africa, was not present in the United States through another member of the corporate group. Slade LJ had said: 'save in cases which turn on the wording of particular statutes or contracts, the court is not free to disregard the principle of *Salomon v A Salomon & Co Ltd* merely because it considers that justice so requires'.

In fact, Adams identified two further areas where the veil may be lifted, namely where the company is a 'façade' such as a fraudulent construct, and also where there is an agency express or implied.

However, the Court of Appeal's view in *Adams v Cape Industries plc* has not always been followed faithfully. In *Creasey v Breachwood Motors Ltd* [1993] BCLC 480, Richard Southwell QC, sitting as a deputy High Court judge, allowed the substitution of one company for another as defendant holding the second company liable for the debts of the first. This decision, however, was itself disapproved in *Ord & Another v Belhaven Pubs Ltd* [1998] 2 BCLC 447 by the Court of Appeal. The defendant, Belhaven Pubs Ltd, appealed against a decision of Judge Alton whereby the deputy judge ordered that the claimants be granted leave to substitute Ascot Holdings plc as the defendant in an action brought by the claimants against Belhaven Pubs Ltd, claiming damages for misrepresentation and breach of warranty. The Court of Appeal held that, in the absence of any impropriety, sham or concealment in the restructuring of the Group, it would be wrong to lift the corporate veil in order to make the shareholders of the defendant company liable instead of the company itself.

The principle of separate identity was also restated by Lightman J in *Acatos and Hutcheson plc v Watson* [1995] 1 BCLC 218. He considered that the principle of separate identity should be upheld unless there was a specific statutory provision or some other contractual term or established common law principle to the contrary. He said that 'outside these exceptions [the company] is entitled to organise and conduct its affairs in the expectation that the court will apply the principle of *Salomon v A Salomon & Co Ltd* in the ordinary way'. The case concerned the company acquiring all the issued share capital of a company called Acatos Ltd and Acatos and Hutcheson plc sought a declaration that the proposal did not fall foul of the provision prohibiting a company from purchasing its own shares, where Acatos Ltd's sole asset was a 29 per cent holding in Acatos and Hutcheson plc. It was held that there was no breach of the provision.

2.2 Lifting the veil – exceptions to the *Salomon* principle

However, the principle in Salomon's case does give way to exceptions where the veil of incorporation is lifted. These are of two types: statutory and judicial.

2.2.1 Statutory exceptions

It was formerly the case that if an officer of the company did not use the company name in full on any letter, order for goods or money etc. then that company officer was liable to the other party and also liable to a fine (s 349(4) Companies Act 1985). However, the Companies Act (CA) 2006 alters this provision. Section 82 CA 2006 provides that the Secretary of State may make regulations requiring companies to display specified information at specified locations, on documents, and on request to those with whom they deal. This information would include the name of the company. If the company then sought to enforce contractual rights against the other party, then these proceedings would be dismissed if the other party had a claim against the company which he was unable to pursue by reason of the company's breach of regulations, or if he had suffered some financial loss by reason of the company's breach of the regulations unless the court considered it just and equitable to permit the proceedings to continue (s 83 CA 2006). Breach of the regulations under s 82 would also amount to a criminal offence on the part of the company and on the part of every officer in default (s 84 CA 2006) (see in general section 6.2).

If the company's business has been carried on with intent to defraud creditors or for any fraudulent purposes, the court, on the application of the liquidator, may declare that the persons who were knowingly parties to the fraud are liable to make such contributions (if any) to the company's assets as the court thinks proper (s 213 of the Insolvency Act 1986). Whatever contributions the court orders will be distributed among the company's creditors and should therefore compensate for the loss caused to creditors by the fraudulent carrying on of the business (*Morphitis v Bernasconi* [2003] Ch 552). This section has a criminal counterpart in s 993 of the Companies Act 2006. The section is applicable not merely to directors but to other persons who are trading through the medium of the company. By contrast, s 214 of the Insolvency Act 1986, which deals with wrongful trading, empowers the court to make a declaration in the situation of insolvent liquidation against a person who was a director or shadow director who knew, or ought to have known, that there was no reasonable prospect of the company avoiding insolvent liquidation (see section 25.3).

In *Re Produce Marketing Consortium (No 2)* [1989] BCLC 520, Knox J drew attention to two material differences from s 213:

> First, the requirement for an intent to defraud and fraudulent purpose was not retained as an essential, and with it goes what Maugham J called 'the need for actual dishonesty involving real moral blame'.

He continued:

> The second enlargement is that the test to be applied by the court has become one under which the director in question is to be judged by the standards of what can reasonably be expected of a person fulfilling his functions, and showing reasonable diligence in doing so.

On the facts of the case, two directors of a fruit-importing business were held liable. The directors of the company had been warned by the company's auditors of the company's serious financial plight.

In this case, the judge ordered that the directors should contribute to the company's assets the amount by which they had been depleted by the directors' conduct, i.e. once again the aim is compensatory.

In *Re Purpoint Ltd* [1991] BCLC 491, the judge decided that the right measure of liability for wrongful trading was the increase in the net liabilities of the company which had been occasioned by the continuance of trading after the director should have known that the company was destined for liquidation (see wrongful trading in section 25.3).

There are some other situations in respect of insolvency where the veil is lifted. Section 216 of the Insolvency Act 1986 makes it an offence for a person who is a director, or shadow director, of a company that has gone into insolvent liquidation to be in any way concerned in the next five years in the formation or management of a company with a name similar to that of the original company. Section 217 makes such persons personally liable in such a situation.

A further provision applicable in situations of insolvency is s 15 of the Company Directors Disqualification Act 1986, which provides that a person who has been disqualified from acting in the management of a company is personally liable for the company debts if he acts in contravention of this order.

In the case of a public limited company, if it acts before it has obtained its trading certificate, then the company and its officers are liable to fines. Furthermore, if the company fails to comply with its obligations within 21 days, the directors of the company are jointly and severally liable to indemnify any other party to the transaction in respect of any loss or damage suffered by reason of the company's failure to comply with its obligations (s 767(3) CA 2006).

Group accounts have to be filed where companies are in a group. This is in addition to the separate sets of accounts that have to be filed for each of the constituent companies. In order to determine if a company is part of a group, clearly the veil is being lifted. To determine if a holding/subsidiary relationship exists, it is necessary to examine ownership of the shares, membership of the board of directors, or control of the board or company in general meeting (s 399 CA 2006) (see section 17.2.2).

There are many other statutory examples. For example, under s 6 of the Law of Property Act 1969, it is provided that an individual landlord is able to resist the renewal of a tenancy if he can show that he needs the premises for his own commercial purposes. This is extended to cover the situation where he needs the premises for the purposes of a company which he controls. See *Tunstall v Steigmann* [1962] 2 QB 593.

Under EU competition law, a parent company and its subsidiaries can be treated as an economic unit or an undertaking i.e. economic units which consist of an unitary organisation of personal tangible or intangible elements which pursue a specific economic aim on a long-term basis (see *Shell International Chemical Co Ltd v Commission* (case T-11/89)) for the purposes of establishing whether the whole undertaking has breached competition rules pursuant to the rules of competition outlined in Arts 101 to 106 of the Treaty on the Functioning of the European Union (2012/C 326/01).

2.2.2 Judicial lifting of the veil

It is difficult to identify a consistent thread running through the decided cases indicating when the veil will be lifted. It seems to be, as the American Realists (commenting on the nature of legal decisions) indicate, and as previously noted in section 2.1, dependent on the particular judge and what the judge has had for breakfast! However, it is possible to identify certain consistent themes in the cases.

As Murray Pickering in 'The Company as a Separate Legal Entity' (1968) 31 MLR 481 has demonstrated, there is a remarkable range of judicial descriptions used where difficulties are experienced by the courts in separating the company as a legal entity from its members. These include, as Pickering notes, for example, 'a mere nominee', 'a mere fraud', 'an agent', 'a trustee', 'a mere device', 'a myth and a fiction' (*Broderib v Salomon* [1895] 2 Ch 323), 'a pretended association' (*Salomon v A Salomon & Co Ltd* [1897] AC 22), 'a bubble' (*Re Carl Hirth* [1899] 1 QB 612), 'an unreal' procedure (*Attorney General for Dominion of Canada v Standard Trust Co of New York* [1911] AC 498), 'an alias', 'a name' (*Re Darby* [1911] 1 KB 95), 'an artificial legal thing', 'a legal abstraction' (*Continental Tyre & Rubber Co (GB) Ltd v Daimler Co Ltd* [1915] 1 KB 95), 'mere machinery' (*Daimler Co v Continental Tyre & Rubber Co* [1916] 2 AC 307), 'a metaphysical conception' (*Lennards Carrying Co Ltd v Asiatic Petroleum Co Ltd* [1915] AC 705), 'a sham or bogus' (*R v Grubb* [1915] 2 KB 683), 'an abstract conception' (*Houghton & Co v Nothard Lowe & Wills Ltd* [1928] AC 1), 'a simulacrum' (*EBM Co Ltd v Dominion Bank* [1937] 3 All ER 555), 'a cloak' (*Gilford Motor Co Ltd v Horne* [1933] Ch 935), 'a mere alter ego' (*Pegler v Craven* [1952] 2 QB 69), 'an abstract being' (*Austin Reed Ltd v Royal Assurance Co Ltd* [18 July 1956 CA] unreported), 'a creature' (*IRC v Lithgows Ltd* (1960) 39 TC 270), 'a screen' (*Barclays Bank v IRC* [1960] 3 WLR 280) and even 'a blacksheep' (*IRC v Sansome* [1921] 2 KB 492).

2.2.2.1 Fraud situations

The court will lift the veil to prevent fraud or sharp practice. In *Jones v Lipman* [1962] 1 All ER 442, a vendor of land sought to evade a decree of specific performance of a contract for the sale of a piece of land by conveying the land to a company which he had purchased for the purpose of sidestepping the obligation.

The court held that the acquisition of the company and the conveyance of the land to it was a mere 'cloak or sham' to evade the contract of sale. The veil was lifted.

By contrast, in the Australian case of *Electric Light and Power Supply Co Ltd v Cormack* [1911] HSR 352, the veil was not lifted. Here the New South Wales Supreme Court neglected to lift the veil. The defendant contracted to use the claimant's power in his business for two years exclusively. During this time he sold his business to a company he managed which used another source of power. Rich AJ refused to lift the veil, saying there was no intention to create injustice. It seems that the intention aspect was the determining factor in the case. This, of course, was not held to be significant in *Jones v Lipman*. In the opinion of the author, the *Jones v Lipman* decision is preferable. It should not be necessary to show an intention to create injustice in such cases, merely that injustice has been the result of the defendant's actions.

In *Gilford Motor Co v Horne* [1933] Ch 935, an employee who was subject to a restraint of trade clause set up a company to circumvent the restriction. He claimed that the company was not bound by the restrictive covenant as it was a separate legal person distinct from himself and was not a party to the contract between him and his former employer. He proceeded to operate a garage in Highgate, London through the company in competition with his former employer. The company's shares were allotted to his wife and an employee of the company who were appointed directors. The court held that, since the defendant in reality controlled the company, its formation was a sham. An injunction was therefore issued against him restraining him from competing through the medium of the company.

A similar desire to prevent abuse is evident in *Re Bugle Press Ltd* [1961] Ch 270. The issued capital of Bugle Press Ltd was £10,000; £4,500 each was held by two directors, Jackson and Shaw. The applicant Treby held the other £1,000 of shares. Jackson and Shaw formed another company of which they were the only two members and this company offered to acquire all the shares of Bugle Press Ltd.

The intention of Jackson and Shaw was to compulsorily acquire the shares of Treby under what are now the 'squeeze-out' and 'sell-out' provisions contained in Part 28 Chapter 3 of the Companies Act 2006. In short, they were using the takeover provisions to rid themselves of a difficult dissentient member. The court held that Treby was entitled to a declaration that Jackson and Shaw could not acquire his shares as the offeror and the holders of 90 per cent of the acquired company were the same and the section was being used to expropriate the shares of a minority shareholder (see also section 24.8).

Fraud was also at issue in *Wallersteiner v Moir* [1974] 1 WLR 991. In this case, the defendant Moir had accused the claimant of a number of fraudulent acts. The court had to consider whether a loan made by a company to another company which was under the control of its director was illegal under s 197 of the Companies Act 1948, which prohibits the giving of a loan to a director. Lord Denning MR considered that the company was the puppet of Dr Wallersteiner as the company was his creature and therefore that the loan should be treated as a loan made to him.

In *Trustor AB v Smallbone (No 2)* [2001] 2 BCLC 436, the veil was lifted where the company transferred money to a company owned and controlled by Smallbone's managing director. The money was transferred in breach of fiduciary duty.

The cases of *Gilford v Horne* and *Jones v Lipman* and indeed the fraud situations and other judicial exceptions to the piercing of the corporate veil now need to be read in the light of the Supreme Court case decisions of *VTB Capital plc v Nutritek International Corporation* [2013] UKSC 5 and of *Prest v Petrodel Resources Limited* [2013] UKSC 34. *VTB Capital* is considered here. The case of *Prest* is considered in more detail under 2.2.2.3 below.

In *VTB Capital plc v Nutritek International Corporation* [2013] UKSC 5, VTB, a bank argued that it had entered into a loan in reliance on fraudulent misrepresentations by Mr Konstantin Malofeev. He was alleged to be the owner of both the borrower and the vendor (Nutritek).

The borrower defaulted and VTB sought leave to sue Malofeev and Nutritek. This involved piercing the corporate veil.

This was the first time that the piercing of the corporate veil principle had been considered by the Supreme Court (or the House of Lords).

The Supreme Court overruled the case of *Antonio Gramsci Shipping Corporation v Stephanovs* [2011] EWHC 333 (Comm) which allowed the corporate veil to be pierced so that controllers of a company could themselves be sued where the contract had been concluded by the company.

The effect of the decision is clearly to limit lifting the veil in cases of fraud.

2.2.2.2 Group situations

Another situation where the veil is often lifted is in group situations where the parent company and a subsidiary are treated as one entity if they carry on the same business. The principle does not seem to be consistently applied, however. In *Smith, Stone and Knight Ltd v Birmingham Corporation* [1939] 4 All ER 116, the court treated a subsidiary company as the agent of its holding company (an approach that is at odds with the decision in the *Salomon* case itself).

Similarly, in *Firestone Tyre & Rubber Co Ltd v Llewelyn* [1957] 1 WLR 464, an American company which operated through a wholly owned subsidiary in England was held liable to pay United Kingdom tax as the American company was carrying on business in the United Kingdom through the subsidiary.

In contrast, in *Harold Holdsworth & Co (Wakefield) Ltd v Caddies* [1955] 1 All ER 725, the question arose as to whether the director of a holding company could be assigned duties in relation to subsidiary companies. The House of Lords held that this was indeed possible on the basis that the companies were part of the same group enterprise.

In *DHN Food Distributors Ltd v Tower Hamlets London Borough Council* [1976] 1 WLR 852, the Court of Appeal had to consider a case involving the expropriation of property. A company, DHN Food Products, was formed to carry on the business of importing and distributing groceries. The premises the company traded from were in fact owned by Bronze, a wholly owned subsidiary of DHN. Bronze and DHN had the same directors. The London Borough of Tower Hamlets acquired the property to build houses on the site. Compensation was payable under the relevant legislation for loss of title. Compensation was also payable for disturbance of the business. However, compensation for disturbance of the business was only payable if the business disturbed belonged to the title holder. The operator of the business here was the holding company; the title holder was the subsidiary company.

The Court of Appeal treated the companies as one entity. Lord Denning MR said:

> We all know that, in many respects, a group of companies are treated together for the purpose of general accounts, balance sheets, profit and loss account. They are treated as one concern.... This is especially the case when a parent company owns all the share of the subsidiaries, so much so that it can control every movement of the subsidiaries.

Lord Denning MR relied heavily on the House of Lords decision in *Harold Holds-worth & Co (Wakefield) Ltd v Caddies* in *DHN* (1976) at p. 860. He claimed it was a striking instance of 'the tendency to ignore the separate legal entities of various companies within a group'. In fact, Viscount Kilmuir LC, Lord Morton of Henryton and Lord Reid all arrived at their decisions because the appellant company owned all the shares in the subsidiary and could therefore procure the appointment of the respondent as managing director of the subsidiary company. There is nothing in their judgment to suggest that the separate identities of parent and subsidiary companies in a group should be disregarded.

The approach is not consistent. In *Lonrho Ltd v Shell Petroleum Company Ltd* [1980] 1 WLR 627, the House of Lords considered a claim by the claimant for discovery of documents in the possession of companies that were wholly owned subsidiaries of the defendant companies. The wholly owned subsidiaries were incorporated and resident in South Africa and Zimbabwe (or Southern Rhodesia as it then was). The House of Lords took the view that even though these companies were wholly owned subsidiaries, there was a degree of autonomy consequent upon these companies operating overseas. It felt that it was inappropriate to lift the veil in such a situation distinguishing *DHN Food Distributors Ltd v Tower Hamlets London Borough Council*. Interestingly, the Court of Appeal had taken the same view as the House of Lords and Lord Denning MR had stated that the parent companies had no 'power' over the subsidiaries. He considered the case to be quite different from the *DHN Food Distributors* case.

Similar issues were raised in *Woolfson v Strathclyde Regional Council* [1979] 38 P&CR 521. The House of Lords in this case considered the situation where a compulsory purchase order had been made over certain shops in Glasgow. The shops were owned by Solomon Woolfson and by Solfred Holdings Ltd, the shares of which were held two-thirds by Woolfson and one-third by Woolfson's wife. The shop premises were occupied by a company called M and L Campbell (Glasgow) Ltd, which operated the business of costumiers of wedding garments. The share capital of Campbell was 1,000 shares of which 999 of these shares were held by Woolfson, the remaining share by his wife. Woolfson was the sole director of Campbell and he managed the business. His wife also worked for Campbell and provided valuable expertise in relation to the selling of the garments. Woolfson and Solfred Holdings Ltd claimed compensation for disturbance of the business. They argued that the business carried on on the premises was truly their business, conducted by Campbell as their agent so that, since they were the true occupiers of the premises, they were also entitled to compensation for disturbance. They placed reliance upon the decisions in *Smith, Stone and Knight Ltd v Birmingham Corporation* and *DHN Food Distributors Ltd v Tower Hamlets London Borough Council*.

Lord Keith, in the course of his judgment in the House of Lords, considered that the case was distinct from the decision in *DHN Food Distributors*. The position in that case, his Lordship said, was that compensation for disturbance was claimed by a group of three limited companies. In the case before him, the company that carried on the business, Campbell, had no control whatever over the owners of the land, Solfred and Woolfson. It may be seen that it is sometimes difficult to reconcile the decisions in this area.

Generally the decision in *DHN* has been seen as an 'aberration' (Rixon, 'Lifting the Veil Between Holding and Subsidiary Companies' (1986) 102 LQR 415). It has been said that the separate entity principle is 'unchallengeable by judicial decision' (in *Re The Albazero* [1977] AC 774). Nevertheless, the veil may well be lifted in group situations as it was in *Kensington International Ltd v Congo* [2007] EWCA Civ 1128 where there were dishonest intercompany transfers.

Although *Salomon* is generally applied in group situations, problems do arise where there has been undercapitalisation within a group situation. Lynn Gallagher and Peter Ziegler in 'Lifting the Corporate Veil in the Pursuit of Justice' [1990] JBL 292 analysed some American cases where undercapitalisation has been the ground for lifting the veil.

In *Chatterley v Omnico* (1971) 485 P 2d 667, the Supreme Court of Utah held a parent company liable for the unpaid wages owed to the employees of a subsidiary company. Similarly, *Herman v Mobile Homes Corporation* (1947) 26 NW 2d 757 provides an example of the undercapitalisation factor being applied. The Supreme Court of Michigan held that the subsidiaries were merely the alter ego of the parent company as they were undercapitalised. The action had been brought by the claimant against Mobile Homes for defective workmanship. Even here, however, the decisions are not uniform. In *Bartle v Home Owners Co-operative* (1955) 127 NE 2d 832, the veil was not lifted although there was undercapitalisation. Froessel J held there was no fraud, no misrepresentation and no illegality.

One United States Supreme Court decision where the veil was lifted, where there was undercapitalisation, is *Taylor v Standard Gas and Electric Company* (1939) 306 US 307. Deep Rock Oil Corporation was involved in the production of oil and gas, and was a subsidiary of Standard Gas and Electric Company, the defendant. The defendant held virtually all the shares in Deep Rock and controlled its board of directors. The subsidiary was placed in liquidation and the holding company claimed as a creditor. This claim was challenged by the preference shareholders of Deep Rock, who argued that Deep Rock was merely the alter ego of Standard. The United States Supreme Court agreed.

In the United States, it is possible therefore to discern a separate doctrine, where the veil of incorporation is often lifted where there is undercapitalisation within a group. This does not appear to have been a factor in the cases in the United Kingdom, where much seems to depend upon the particular judge or court involved, and there cannot be said to be a coherent thread through the cases. Such is the impact of Lord Denning that the *DHN Food Distributors* case is often cited as the leading case in this area, although the House of Lords has, as has been noted above, on occasion taken a completely different line, refusing to lift the veil where the Court of Appeal, particularly when Lord Denning was active, showed a very different approach and was much more willing to lift the veil in group situations.

It seems pretty clear to the author that the *DHN* decision is the aberration rather than the decision setting out the general rule in relation to disregarding the separate identity of companies within a group. An interesting analysis of decided cases from before 1960 up to 1999 is provided in Charles Mitchell's analysis in 'Lifting the Corporate Veil in the English Courts, An Empirical Study' (1999) 3 CFILR 15. Mitchell's analysis demonstrates that in decided cases around half of the cases involved situations where the veil is lifted. The rate of lifting the veil in decided cases was highest in the 1970s. This could well be the influence of Lord Denning in the Court of Appeal, but interestingly the number of decided cases where the veil is lifted goes up again in the 1990s despite the *dicta* in the Court of Appeal decision in *Adams v Cape Industries plc*.

Other countries may arrive at different results from the UK. This appears to be the case in continental Europe. For example, in Italy, Article 2362 of the Civil Code of 1942 provides that in cases of insolvency of companies limited by shares, the single person who holds the shares of the company will be liable for the debts of the company. This would seem to apply to both natural and legal persons.

Section 322 of the German Code provides that the parent shall be liable jointly and severally for the debts of the wholly owned subsidiary. Similarly, as noted by Schmitthoff in 'The Wholly Owned and the Controlled Subsidiary' [1978] JBL 218, the final draft of the statute for European companies (Bulletin of the European Companies 4/75) provides for the debts and liabilities of dependent companies within the group to be owed of the parent company.

In *Chandler v Cape plc* [2012] EWCA (Civ) 525 the Court of Appeal found that a parent company owed a duty of care to an employee of a subsidiary company.

See also *Barings plc v Coopers & Lybrand* [1997] 1 BCLC 427 (see section 18.1.6.4).

2.2.2.3 Miscellaneous situations

There are numerous other decisions where the veil has been lifted. It is difficult to classify these cases. It is therefore appropriate to examine this potpourri of cases.

A decision of all the members of a company may be binding as a company decision notwithstanding that the decision has not been taken at a company meeting. To determine if the decision is one of all the members the veil has clearly to be lifted; see, for example, *Re Express Engineering Works Ltd* [1920] 1 Ch 466.

The veil may also be lifted to determine a company's nationality by reference to the nationality of its members. This occurred in *Re FG Films Ltd* [1953] 1 All ER 615, where the court held that the film *Monsoon* (never an international blockbuster!) was not a British film. Although the company producing it was incorporated in England, it was controlled by an American corporation.

In *Daimler Co Ltd v Continental Tyre & Rubber Co (GB) Ltd* [1916] 2 AC 307, the House of Lords decided that the company, although it was incorporated in England, was an enemy alien as all of its shareholders were German. In *Trebanog Working Men's Club & Institute Ltd v Macdonald* [1940] 1 KB 576, the device of the trust was used to circumvent the principle of separate personality. A club incorporated to provide leisure facilities for its members purchased alcohol. The alcohol was sold to the members. The club was prosecuted for selling alcohol without a licence. The court acquitted the club of the charge since it was held that there was no sale as the members in reality owned the alcohol, which was purchased on their behalf by the committee of the club. It was held that the club held the alcohol as trustee for its members and that therefore the beneficial ownership in the alcohol was vested in the members collectively with the result that there was not a sale at all and therefore no criminal offence had been committed.

In *Prest v Petrodel Resources Limited* [2013] UKSC 34, the Supreme Court took the opportunity to rationalise some of the exceptions to the piercing of the corporate veil. The Court stated that it would only pierce the corporate veil when it is necessary to do so, that is when 'other more conventional remedies have proved to be of no assistance'. Lord Sumption drew a difference between the concealment principle which was not, in his view, a true instance of piercing the corporate veil but merely looking behind the façade as opposed to the evasion principle where the corporate veil may be pierced.

He said of the concealment principle:

> the interposition of the company (or several companies) so as to conceal the identity of the real actors will not deter the courts from identifying them, assuming their identity is legally relevant. In these cases the court is not disregarding the 'façade' but only looking behind it to discover the facts which the corporate structure is concealing.

In *Prest v Petrodel Resources Limited*, following a divorce and the claim of ancillary financial relief, it fell to be determined whether the husband, Mr Prest, was entitled to residential properties held by several companies owned and controlled by him, for the purposes of the Matrimonial Causes Act 1973. One of the properties was the matrimonial home for which no rent was paid and three others had been bought by the company for only £1 each. Others were seemingly bought by the company using the money of Mr Prest. Mr Prest was found entitled to the properties under principles of trust law. In making an order under the Matrimonial Causes Act, the Court held unanimously that piercing the corporate veil could not be used to treat the company's assets as belonging to Mr Prest, not simply because he was the owner and controller of the companies but the evidence showed that the companies held the assets in trust for Mr Prest because of the circumstances in which the properties were acquired.

In essence, application of the concealment principle may reveal a company to have received assets wrongfully or illegally transferred to it by the controller of the company and therefore an order for repayment by the company could be made as agent or nominee of the wrongdoer to the rightful owner, just as it would if the money had been passed to another person.

The evasion principle occurs when an individual uses the vehicle of a company so as to evade or frustrate the enforcement of obligations, liabilities or restrictions. Most of these are the fraud situations covered in 2.2.2.1 above although it was pointed out in *Prest v Petrodel Resources Limited* that piercing the corporate veil was not necessary in *Gilford v Horne* and *Jones v Lipman,* as other traditional remedies were applicable e.g. liability may be imposed in other ways on the controller such as a joint tortfeasor or fraudulent trading, where applicable.

More recently, the principles in *Prest v Petrodel Resources Limited* were followed and applied in *Pennyfeathers Ltd v Pennyfeathers Property Co Ltd* [2013] EWHC 3530 (Ch).

There is therefore a distinction to be made between piercing of the veil as opposed to merely looking behind it to discover the actual facts. The case of *Prest v Petrodel Resources Limited* reaffirmed the sanctity of separate legal personality. Where other remedies or tools are available and applicable, these should be used instead and piercing the veil should only be the last resort. It would be interesting to see whether there are any novel situations where the tools currently available for the courts to use are inadequate but it would seem that these situations would be very rare.

2.3 Companies – torts and crimes

Companies can commit torts. Thus in *Campbell v Mayor, Aldermen and Councillors of the Metropolitan Borough of Paddington* [1911] 1 KB 869, the claimant was in possession of a house in London from which there were uninterrupted views of the thoroughfare of Edgware Road where the funeral procession of King Edward VII was to have taken place. Albert Ginger agreed to rent a room on the first floor to view the procession. Meanwhile the council corporation erected a stand for the councillors to view the procession in front of the premises, obstructing the view. This was illegal.

The claimant released Ginger from the contract as it was felt unfair to hold him to the contract. The claimant also lost other potential customers. She claimed for loss because of the public nuisance and the unlawful interference with her use and enjoyment of her house.

The court upheld her claim. Avory J said at p. 875,

> To say that because the Borough Council had no legal right to erect it, therefore the corporation cannot be sued, is to say that no corporation can ever be sued for any tort or wrong ... that would be absurd.

In other words, the claim of ultra vires in relation to a tort by a company is of no effect.

It used to be the case that companies were only liable for torts vicariously committed by employees if they were committing an authorised act in an unauthorised way. They were not liable for unauthorised acts. This is no longer the case and the context of the tort must be examined.

In *Lister & Others v Hesley Hall Ltd* [2002] 1 AC 215, the claimants had been residents in a school for boys with behavioural difficulties. The defendants employed Grain to take care of the boys as warden. Unknown to the defendants, Grain was sexually abusing the children. The claimants brought this action against the defendants alleging that they were vicariously liable for the torts of their employee.

The Court of Appeal said there was no liability as they were not doing an authorised act in an unauthorised way. This was, of course, the test at the time.

The House of Lords, however, on appeal held that the question of vicarious liability was on the basis that the defendants had undertaken care of the boys through the services of Grain and that there was a very close connection between his employment and his torts. The acts were so closely connected that the defendants were liable. Furthermore, the crimes had been committed in the company's time and on the company's premises.

In *Dubai Aluminium Co Ltd v Salaam & Others (Livingston & Others Third Party)* [2003] 1 BCLC 32, the defendant company was the victim of a fraud by which they were induced to pay a large consultancy fee to the participants in the fraud who were partners in a firm. The question arose as to whether the firm was vicariously liable for their acts.

It was held that liability depended on the closeness of the connection between the duties which, in broad terms, the partners or employees were authorised to perform, and the firm, and that there was such a close connection in this case.

Note that although a partnership authority, there is a clear analogy between partnership law and company law.

Companies may be found liable for offences of strict liability, so no *mens rea* is needed in such cases.

This approach requires the precise interpretation of statutes to determine whether a strict liability offence is in issue. This is of importance in areas of licensing, pollution, food safety, etc. In *Alphacell Ltd v Woodward* [1972] AC 824, the case involved strict liability of a company.

The claimant manufactured paper from Manila fibres on the banks of the River Irwell in Lancashire. The company was charged with causing polluting matter to enter the river. It was held that no knowledge was necessary for the commission of this offence as knowingly was not implied in the offence, and accordingly the company was held liable.

However, often, there is a due diligence defence and if the company can demonstrate that it practised due diligence and that the lack of diligence was on the part of a person who was not the true embodiment of the company, it will escape liability. In *Tesco Supermarkets Ltd v Nattrass* [1972] AC 153, the company was charged with an offence under the Trade Descriptions Act 1968 in that certain goods stated to be available were not. The company demonstrated that it had introduced a system to try to ensure that this did not happen. The failure was held to be that of the store manager and not of the company, and the company was held not liable.

In *R v Gateway Foodmarkets Ltd* [1997] 3 All ER 78, a company was held liable under s 2(1) of the Health and Safety at Work etc. Act 1974. This provides for liability where there is a failure to ensure the health, safety and welfare at work of any employee unless all reasonable precautions have been taken by the company or on its behalf.

The company had failed to provide for the safety of a duty manager at one of its Sheffield branches. He fell to his death into a lift shaft where a trap door had been left open in the control room floor.

In *R v British Steel* [1995] 1 WLR 1356, the court held that it was no defence for the company that the senior management had taken all reasonable care to avoid a breach of the statutory duty, even though the strict liability was qualified by a defence if all reasonably practical steps had been taken. The court took the view that this reasonably practical defence applied not just to senior management but also to those in charge of the dangerous activity, i.e. both must take reasonably practical steps to avoid harm.

In *Tesco Supermarkets Ltd v Nattrass*, the principle of identification had been established. This means that the state of mind and will of the director can be attributed to the company.

Shortcomings in the identification approach were recognised in the Privy Council case of *Meridian Global Funds Management Asia Ltd v Securities Commission* [1995] 2 AC 500. The Privy Council held that in certain cases the court has to determine whose act or knowledge was the company's. Generally, this would be the directing mind and will of the company, but not necessarily so.

Meridian was unusual in that a company was convicted of a crime where the individual, whose knowledge was attributed to the company, was not part of the company's directing mind and will. As Lord Hoffman said:

Whose act (or knowledge or state of mind) was for this purpose intended to count as the act, etc. of the company? One finds the answer to this question by applying the usual canons of interpretation, taking into account the language of the rule (if it is a statute) and its content and policy.

The policy of the New Zealand Securities Amendment Act 1988 which was at issue in *Meridian* was to require the immediate disclosure of a substantial security holder. The person here whose knowledge was attributed to the company was the person who acquired the relevant interest with the company's authority. In *Stone and Rolls Ltd v Moore Stephens* [2009] 1 AC 1391, in a case involving auditors' civil liability the House of Lords confirmed that the attribution rules identified by Lord Hoffmann in *Meridian* were part of English law.

Sometimes decisions may be surprising, as in *Richmond on Thames Borough Council v Pinn and Wheeler* [1989] RTR 354, where a company was charged with driving a goods vehicle exceeding 16.5 tonnes in a restricted street in Greater London. The regulations were made under the Road Traffic Regulations Act 1984. There was a conviction by Justices of the Peace but the Crown Court allowed the appeal on the basis that the company was not able to commit the offence of 'driving' contrary to the regulations. A further appeal was dismissed by the court. Pill J said: 'The act of driving a lorry is a physical act which can be performed only by natural persons.'

However, the principles are reasonably straightforward. Difficulties do arise, however, where the crime requires *mens rea* on the part of the company. Here the courts have traditionally required that the guilty mind should be that of the company's directing mind and will, or, as was said by Lord Denning MR in *Bolton Engineering v TJ Graham & Sons* [1957] 1 QB 159, 'The brain and nerve centre of the company'.

In *John Henshall (Quarries) Ltd v Harvey* [1965] 2 QB 233, the issue of the knowledge of the company was central to the case. John Burrell was employed by the defendants as a weighbridge operator. He weighed an eight-wheel lorry driven by Hobson on the defendant's weighbridge near Holywell in Flintshire, North Wales. He issued a conveyance note which actually showed that the vehicle was overweight but allowed the driver to drive away due to an oversight.

The defendant company was convicted of aiding, abetting, counselling and procuring Hobson to use a vehicle in contravention of the Road Traffic Act 1960. On appeal it was held:

(i)   the master must have actual knowledge where aiding and abetting etc. is the charge that is being made; and

(ii) the master could only be fixed with the knowledge of Burrell if he was the 'brains of the company'. This was not the case here.

The defendant company was therefore not guilty of the offence and the appeal was allowed.

Thus in *Lennard's Carrying Co Ltd v Asiatic Petroleum Co Ltd* [1915] AC 705, the House of Lords based identification on a person 'who is really the directing mind and will of the corporation, the very ego and centre of the corporation'.

These decisions should now be interpreted in the light of the *Meridian* decision.

Three cases in the 1940s established that companies could commit crimes involving dishonesty: *DPP v Kent and Sussex Contractors Ltd* [1944] KB 146; *R v ICR Haulage Ltd* [1944] KB 551; and *Moore v Bresler* [1944] 2 All ER 515.

There must be no double counting in the punishment of companies.

In *R v Rollco Screw & Rivet Co Ltd & Others* [1999] IRLR 439, the prosecution arose due to a serious incident of asbestos contamination in a factory in the Birmingham area. The company employed some 12 or more employees in the manufacture of screws and rivets.

The company's roof was in a very poor condition. The father and son directors of the company became aware that it was asbestos. In fact it was brown asbestos, the most dangerous type of asbestos.

It was established that the stripping of the asbestos was done with inadequate equipment and none of the workers used had the appropriate asbestos licence. Furthermore, 200 to 300 bags of the asbestos were dumped on sites around Birmingham.

In giving the judgment of the court, Bingham LCJ said,

> One must avoid a risk of overlap. In a small company the directors are likely to be the shareholders, and therefore the main losers if a severe sanction is imposed on the company. We accept that the courts must be alert to make sure that it is not, in effect, imposing a double punishment.

The points made in the case therefore in holding the company liable is that if fines are also being imposed against the directors, to fine the company as well where the directors are the only shareholders is to impose a double punishment.

Debate rages on the potential extent of a company's criminality. Some offences cannot be committed by a company. It seems clear that companies are incapable of committing offences of a sexual nature, or the offence of bigamy. Companies cannot commit murder. This is not because of a technical problem but because the offence carries a statutory sentence of life imprisonment, and companies cannot be imprisoned. There is no conceptual problem with holding a company liable for manslaughter. There have been very real practical difficulties in securing convictions, however, and this has been the subject of fierce debate in recent years.

2.3.1 Corporate manslaughter

In passing it is worth noting that in some common law jurisdictions a company may not be convicted of manslaughter. In *R v Murray Wright Ltd* [1970] NZLR 476, in the New Zealand Court of Appeal, the appellants were chemists and supplied the wrong medicine to Miss Keepa. She died as a result of taking the medicine. The appellants tried to quash an indictment issued in relation to this.

Henry J refused, saying the company could be convicted of manslaughter. However, in the New Zealand Court of Appeal this was reversed, as s 58 of the Crimes Act 1961 says that homicide is the killing of a human being by another, and on that basis a company could not be found guilty of homicide.

There is no such problem in the UK. However, in *Re Attorney-General's Reference (No 2 of 1999)* [2000] QB 796, the Court of Appeal refused to apply the

Meridian approach to identification in relation to manslaughter by negligence. This means a company can only be convicted if an identifiable human being, who is the directing mind and will of the company, can be shown to have committed the crime. It is therefore difficult to obtain convictions in relation to larger companies. Where there have been convictions, the companies have been small, as in *R v Kite* [1996] Cr App Rep (S) 295, where the managing director of the company that had organised a leisure trip for teenagers was found guilty of manslaughter, as was the company, where four teenagers died in a canoeing disaster in Lyme Bay.

In *R v Jackson Transport (Ossett) Ltd* (1996) (unreported), the company concerned was somewhat larger, employing about 40 people. James Hodgson was killed in May 1994 while he was cleaning behind a tanker vehicle containing chemicals. He died when he used steam equipment to clean a valve in the tanker blocked with toxic chemicals. The company had not provided proper equipment, training or supervision. The company was convicted of manslaughter.

In August 2001, English Bros Ltd, a Wisbech construction company, pleaded guilty to the manslaughter of Bill Larkman, an employee who died in June 1999 (unreported), when he fell through a fragile roof to his death. The company had been warned previously about failing to provide correct safety equipment. The company was fined £25,000.

In October 2002, Dennis Clothier & Sons and one of its directors were found guilty of the manslaughter of Steven Hayfield (unreported). He had died when he was hit by a 20-tonne trailer which became detached from a tractor because it was dangerously loaded.

In April 2000, Teglgaard Hardwood (UK) Ltd (unreported) and one of its directors pleaded guilty to the manslaughter of a labourer, Christopher Longrigg, who died when a stack of timber fell on him while he was working for the company in a shipyard.

In Scotland, there has only ever been one company charged with homicide. This was Transco plc, the gas supply company. It was charged with the homicide of four people who died in December 1999 when a massive explosion destroyed a family house in Larkhall. Scotland's Court of Criminal Appeal dismissed culpable homicide charges against the company.

It seems that the argument for enacting a new offence of corporate killing applies equally in England, Wales and Scotland.

It has so far proved impossible to convict larger companies of manslaughter. There has been, and remains, considerable pressure for reform. The background to this pressure has been some horrific disasters like the Southall rail crash (1997) and the *Herald of Free Enterprise* disaster off Zeebrugge (1987).

In the *Herald of Free Enterprise* case (*R v P & O European Ferries (Dover) Ltd* (1991) 93 Cr App Rep 72), perhaps one of the most famous corporate manslaughter cases, an inquest jury had returned verdicts of unlawful killing in 187 cases. However, the prosecution case for corporate manslaughter failed as the facts of negligence could not be attributed to any individual who was a controlling mind of the company. This case demonstrated problems with the old law of corporate manslaughter.

In the Clapham rail disaster of 1988, where 35 people were killed, there was an admission of liability by the British Rail Board for the accident. A considerable sum of compensation was paid, reaching £1 million in some cases. There was no prosecution for corporate manslaughter, however.

In *Transco*, the Scottish case in 2003 referred to above, an appeal court in Edinburgh rejected a charge of 'culpable homicide' (this is the equivalent in Scotland of corporate manslaughter in England). However, prosecutions under s 3 and s 33 of the Health and Safety at Work etc. Act 1974 were successful and the company was fined £15 million.

See also the Fennell Report into the King's Cross Underground Fire (1988) and the Cullen Report into the *Piper Alpha* Disaster (1990).

The Law Commission consulted on the law of corporate manslaughter in Consultation Paper No 135 (1994). The Law Commission recommended a new offence based on whether the company's conduct fell significantly below what could reasonably be expected of it in the context of the significant risk of death or injury of which it should have been aware.

In a later report, *Legislating the Criminal Code: Involuntary Manslaughter* (1996) (Law Commission Report No. 237), the Law Commission in its final report calls for a new offence of corporate killing comparable to killing by gross negligence. The focus of this offence would be on the quality of the company's operating systems rather than on the guilt of individuals. In 2000, a Private Member's Bill was introduced on corporate killing. It was introduced by Andrew Dismore MP. The Corporate Homicide Bill proposed to create a new criminal offence of corporate killing where the conduct of the company falls well below what could reasonably be expected. This was not pursued when the government announced its intention to bring forward legislation.

Legislation was announced in May 2003 by the Home Secretary, David Blunkett. The new offence was to be of death caused by management failure if the way in which the company's activities were managed or organised failed to ensure the health and safety of persons employed in it, or they were affected by its activities. The maximum penalty was to be an unlimited fine.

The Queen's Speech in November 2003 made no mention of the reform of the law of corporate manslaughter. In March 2005, the government published a White Paper on the matter (see *Corporate Manslaughter: The Government's Draft Bill for Reform* (CM6497)).

Attitudes have changed, as noted by Celia Wells in 'Corporate Manslaughter: A Cultural and Legal Form', 6 CLF 45. In *R v Cory Brothers* (1927), Cory Brothers put up an electrified fence, fearing pilfering in the coal strike of 1926, and an unemployed miner who was out ratting was electrocuted and killed. There was a prosecution for manslaughter but the trial judge directed that the company could not be indicted.

Deaths in major construction projects were once regarded as routine. In Radnorshire, in the area once represented by the author in the National Assembly for Wales, over 100 people were killed in the construction of the reservoirs of the Elan Valley at the start of the twentieth century.

In the opinion of the author, it was high time for the law to be reformed in this area and put on a statutory basis. There had been far too much talk about this area of law by successive governments and little or no action. The proposals contained in the Law Commission Reports were ultimately acted upon before the reports gathered dust on the ministerial bookshelves in the Home Office. At last reform was forthcoming.

Companies may also commit torts. Not only will a company be liable for the torts of employees committed in the course of their employment on the basis of vicarious liability, but they may also be liable in their own right. Thus a company may be liable for nuisance, etc.

In March 2005, the government issued a White Paper, *Corporate Manslaughter: The Government's Draft Bill for Reform* (CM6497). The Home Secretary, in the foreword to the White Paper, states:

> This government is committed to delivering safe and secure communities, at home and in the work place, and to a criminal justice system that commands the confidence of the public. A fundamental part of this is providing offences that are clear and effective. The current laws on corporate manslaughter are neither, as a number of unsuccessful prosecutions over the years stand testament.

The proposals were designed to strike a balance. Companies and other organisations must be held properly to account for gross failings by their senior management which have fatal consequences. However, as an offence of homicide, corporate manslaughter charges must be reserved for the very worst cases of management failure. It is intended that the offence will complement rather than replace other forms of redress such as prosecutions under health and safety legislation.

A draft Bill set out proposals for a new specific offence of corporate manslaughter. An organisation would be prosecuted if a gross failing by its senior managers to take reasonable care for the safety of their workers and members of the public caused a person's death. The new offence would apply as now to all companies, and also to other types of incorporated body including many bodies in the public sector, such as local authorities. Government departments and other Crown bodies would also be liable to prosecution.

It was considered by the White Paper that the current problem with the law is the need to find a very senior individual personally guilty of gross negligence, occasioning manslaughter, before the company itself can be convicted. At the heart of the new offence, therefore, was a more effective means of attributing failures in the way its activities are organised or managed at a senior level in an organisation. It remains the case that an organisation must owe a duty of care to the victim and the high threshold that conduct must have been grossly negligent.

Clear and explicit links were also built into the offence to duties that organisations must already comply with under health and safety legislation, providing clarity about the standards against which conduct will be judged. Consultation on the proposals ended on 17 June 2005. The Bill became law on 26 July 2007 as the Corporate Manslaughter and Corporate Homicide Act.

The proposals in the draft Bill had their starting point in the Law Commission's 1996 report *Legislating the Criminal Code: Involuntary Manslaughter* (Law Com No. 237). The government subsequently issued a consultation paper in 2000 titled *Reforming the Law on Involuntary Manslaughter: The Government's Proposals*.

2.3.1.1 The offence

The Corporate Manslaughter and Corporate Homicide Act 2007 came into force on 6 April 2008 across the United Kingdom.

The Act presents a new approach in relation to corporate manslaughter. Previously a company could only be convicted of corporate manslaughter where an individual's gross negligence caused the manslaughter and that individual was considered to be 'the directing mind' of the organisation. In practice this meant that successful prosecutions of small companies were possible as the directors were likely to be much more closely involved with day-to-day management. In contrast those companies other than small companies would generally escape successful prosecution as no blame could be directly attributed to the company's directors.

The 2007 Act sets out a new offence for convicting an organisation where there has been a gross failure in the way that activities were managed or organised, and those activities result in a person's death. The offence is called corporate manslaughter in England and Wales and Northern Ireland, and corporate homicide in Scotland.

Under the new approach, courts will look at management systems and practices adopted by the organisation in considering whether prosecution is appropriate for the worst corporate failures of health and safety provision resulting in death. The Ministry of Justice has stated that

> This is an oppotunity for employers to think again about how risks are managed. The offence does not require organisations to comply with new regulatory standards. But organisations should ensure that they are taking proper steps to meet current legal duties.
>
> (Ministry of Justice, 'Understanding the Corporate Manslaughter and Corporate Homicide Act 2007')

The offence set out in the Corporate Manslaughter and Corporate Homicide Act 2007 is designed to tackle the difficulties created by the identification principle. The problem is addressed through a new test focusing on management failure.

An organisation to which the Act applies is guilty of an offence if the way in which its activities are managed or organised:

(a) causes a person's death; and
(b) amounts to a gross breach of a relevant duty of care owed by the organisation to the deceased.

The Act further provides that an organisation is guilty of an offence under the Act only if the way in which its activities are managed or organised by its senior management is a substantial element in the breach (s 1(3)).

The heart of the new offence lies in the requirement for a management failure, a substantial element of which must be a gross failure at a senior management level. It focuses on the way in which a particular activity is being managed or organised. Organisations are not to be liable on the basis of any intermediate operational negligence causing death, or indeed for the unpredictable, maverick acts of its employees. Instead, the Act focuses responsibility on the working practices of the organisation. It also allows senior management conduct to be considered collectively as well as individually.

The definition of senior management is drawn to capture only those who play a role in making management decisions about or actually managing the activities of the organisation as a whole or a substantial part of it. In addition, the definition requires that the person play a 'significant' role (s 1(4)).

The new offence is targeted at the most serious management failings that warrant the application of a serious criminal offence. It is not the intention of the legislation to catch companies or others making proper efforts to operate in a safe or responsible fashion, or where efforts have been made to comply with health and safety legislation but appropriate standards are not quite met.

The sanction to be applied is a financial penalty – an unlimited fine. The Act makes provision for this and organisations found guilty of manslaughter would face an unlimited fine (s 1(6)).

In addition, a remedial order may be made against a company requiring steps to be made by the company (s 9). The steps required may include action to remedy:

(a) the breach;
(b) any matter that appears to the court to have resulted from the breach and to have been a cause of the death; and
(c) any deficiency as regards health and safety matters in the organisation's policies, systems or practices of which the relevant breach appears to have been an indication.

The court will provide for a period within which a company must comply with the remedial order (s 9(4)(a)).

In addition, under s 10 of the Corporate Manslaughter and Corporate Homicide Act 2007, the court may make an order (a Publicity Order) requiring the organisation to publicise in a specified manner:

(a) the fact of conviction;
(b) specified particulars of the offence;
(c) the amount of any fine; and
(d) any terms of any remedial order that has been made.

By s 10(3) the court will designate a period within which the organisation must comply with the order.

As employers have a legal responsibility to report incidents at work, including work-related deaths, this would lead to a police investigation to ascertain if a criminal offence (other than under health and safety law) is suspected. The police will work in partnership with the Health and Safety Executive, local authority or other regulatory authority.

The government indicated via the Ministry of Justice that it expects cases of corporate manslaughter and homicide to be rare as it is only intended to cover the most serious incidents of failure across an organisation to manage health and safety appropriately.

In England and Wales cases are managed and prosecuted by the Crown Prosecution Service (CPS). In Northern Ireland they are undertaken by the Public Prosecution Service. In Scotland they are prosecuted by the Procurator Fiscal.

It is entirely possible, of course, for health and safety charges to be brought at the same time.

2.3.1.2 Case law

The CPS authorised a charge of corporate manslaughter on 23 April 2009 against Cotswold Geotechnical Holdings Ltd in relation to the death of a geologist, Alexander Wright, who worked for the company and was killed on 5 September 2008. Mr Wright was working in a pit when it collapsed on him as he was taking soil samples and he was crushed to death.

In the first conviction of corporate manslaughter under the 2007 Act the company was found guilty of corporate manslaughter and fined £385,000 at Winchester Crown Court (15 February 2011) and the conviction was upheld by the Court of Appeal (*R v Cotswold Geotechnical Holdings Ltd* [2011] EWCA Crim1337).

Summary

Introduction

The company is a separate entity in law. It is capable of owning property, concluding contracts and committing torts and crimes.

On occasion, the so-called corporate veil is lifted or pierced and the deeds of the company are identified as those of its directors or shareholders.

Exceptions to the *Salomon* principle

The situations where the veil is lifted may be classified as statutory or judicial.

Statutory exceptions

Statutory exceptions include:

(a) Sections 82 and 83 of the Companies Act 2006 – criminal liability for misdescription of the company.
(b) Section 213 of the Insolvency Act 1986 and s 993 of the Companies Act 2006 – fraudulent trading.
(c) Section 214 of the Insolvency Act 1986 – wrongful trading by a company director.
(d) Sections 216 and 217 of the Insolvency Act 1986 – prohibition on directors of insolvent companies being associated with a company with a similar name.
(e) Section 15 of the Company Directors Disqualification Act 1986 – personal liability of a disqualified person who acts in the management of a company.
(f) Section 767(3) of the Companies Act 2006 – liability of officers where a public company trades without a trading certificate.
(g) Section 399 of the Companies Act 2006 – the obligation to file group accounts.
(h) There are many situations under the companies' legislation where obligations are placed on groups, or where rules apply to directors of companies within the same group. Wherever there is a group situation the veil may be lifted depending on particular circumstances.
(i) Section 6 of the Law of Property Act 1969 – landlord refusing to renew a tenancy where he needs the premises for the purposes of a company which he controls.

(j) Under the Finance Act 2014, HMRC is able at its discretion trigger a reallocation of profits in a hybrid partnership where there is no commercial justification for the profit sharing ratios. Specifically, HMRC can re-allocate an 'excessive' profit share to the individual partner(s) under the new s 805C of the Income Tax (Trading and Other Income) Act 2005.

(k) Arts 101 to 106 of the Treaty on the Functioning of the European Union pertaining to EU competition law.

Judicial exceptions

It is difficult to categorise the judicial exceptions to the *Salomon* principle. Certain themes can be identified, however:

(a) The veil is generally lifted to prevent fraud. However, fraud situations should be seen in conjunction with the evasion principle enunciated in *Prest v Petrodel Resources Limited*.

(b) Sometimes, the veil is lifted in a group situation, treating companies within the same group as part of the same enterprise. This is particularly true where a company is a wholly owned subsidiary of a holding company. Even here, there is no universal rule.

(c) Sometimes the device used to lift the veil is agency, sometimes trust, sometimes in a group situation the group enterprise, but this should now be read in line with the concealment principle – *Prest v Petrodel Resources Limited*.

(d) Some cases turn on their special facts, e.g. the consent of all members is the consent of the company – *Re Express Engineering Works Ltd*, all the shareholders of a company were German, therefore the company was an enemy alien – *Daimler Co Ltd v Continental Tyre & Rubber Co (GB) Ltd* was decided during the First World War.

(e) The courts will pierce the veil only if necessary to do so when other more conventional remedies have failed.

Companies and crimes and tort

Companies may commit crimes, although some crimes by their nature, such as bigamy, cannot be committed by companies. In relation to strict liability offences, if there is a defence of due diligence in the statute, the company may escape liability by demonstrating that the lack of care was that of an employee who was not part of the directing mind or will of the company. Companies may also commit torts.

Legislation is now providing for a clearer approach to corporate manslaughter.

Self-test questions

2.1 What is the significance of the *Salomon* decision?

2.2 Is there scope to extend the *Salomon* principle in light of recent case law?

2.3 Where has the legislature intervened to lift the corporate veil? Do you think legislative intervention has been sensible?

Further reading

D Bromilow, '*Creasey v Breachwood Motors*: Mistaken Identity Leads to Untimely Death' (1998) 19 Co Law 198.

D Burles, 'The Criminal Liability of Corporations' (1991) 141 NLJ 609.

CMV Clarkson, 'Kicking Corporate Bodies and Damning Their Souls' (1996) 59 MLR 557.

DW Elliott, 'Directors' Thefts and Dishonesty' [1991] Crim LR 732.

E Ferran, 'Corporate Attribution and the Directing Mind and Will' (2011) 127 LQR 239.

L Gallagher and P Ziegler, 'Lifting the Corporate Veil in the Pursuit of Justice' [1990] JBL 292.

R George, 'The Veil of Incorporation and Post-Divorce Financial Remedies' (2014) 130 LQR 373.

J Gobert, 'Corporate Criminality: Four Models of Fault' (1994) 14 LS 393.

J Gobert, 'Corporate Killing at Home and Abroad – Reflections on the Government's Proposals' (2002) 118 LQR 72.

J Gobert, 'The Corporate Manslaughter and Homicide Act 2007 – 13 years in the Making But Was It Worth the Wait?' (2008) 71 MLR 413.

S Griffin, 'Section 349(4) of the Companies Act 1985 – An Outdated Victorian Legacy' [1997] JBL 438.

C Hare, 'From Solomon to Spiliada: Orthodoxy and Uncertainty in the Supreme Court' (2013) CLJ 280.

C Hare, 'Family Division 0, Chancery Division 1: Piercing the Corporate Veil in the Supreme Court (Again)' (2013) CLJ 511.

O Kahn-Freund, 'Some Reflections on Company Law Reform' (1944) 7 MLR 54.

Law Commission, 'The Law of Corporate Manslaughter', Consultation Paper No 135, 1994, London: HMSO.

Law Commission, 'Legislating the Criminal Code: Involuntary Manslaughter', Consultation Paper No 237, 1996, London: HMSO.

W McArdley and G Jones, 'Prest v Petrodel Resources and VTB Capital v Nutritek: A Robust Corporate Veil' (2013) 14 BLI 295.

C Mitchell, 'Lifting the Corporate Veil in English Courts, an Empirical Study' [1999] 3 CF1LR 15.

S Ottolenghi, 'From Peeping Behind the Corporate Veil to Ignoring It Completely' (1990) 53 MLR 338.

M Petrin, 'Assumption of Responsibility in Corporate Groups: Chandler v Cape plc' (2013) 76 MLR 603.

MA Pickering, 'The Company as a Separate Legal Entity' (1968) 31 MLR 481.

FG Rixon, 'Lifting the Veil Between Holding and Subsidiary Companies' (1986) 102 LQR 415.

A Samuels, 'Lifting the Veil' [1964] JBL 107.

CM Schmitthoff, 'Salomon in the Shadow' [1976] JBL 305.

CM Schmitthoff, 'The Wholly Owned and the Controlled Subsidiary' [1978] JBL 218.

G Slapper, 'Corporate Punishment' (1994) 144 NLJ 29.

GR Sullivan, 'The Attribution of Culpability to Limited Companies' (1996) 55 CLJ 515.

A Talwar and A Dawson, 'Corporate Killing' (2003) 153 NLJ 908.

CH Tan, 'Veil Piercing: A Fresh Start' (2015) JBL 20.

G Virgo, 'Stealing From the Small Family Business' [1991] CLJ 464.

V von Wachter, 'The Corporate Veil' (2007) 157 NLJ 990.

KW Wedderburn, 'Corporate Personality and Social Policy: The Problem of the Quasi-corporation' (1965) 28 MLR 62.

C Wells, 'Corporate Liability and Consumer Protection: Tesco v Nattrass Revisited' (1994) 57 MLR 817.

C Wells, 'The Corporate Manslaughter Proposals: Pragmatism, Paradox and Peninsularity' [1996] Crim LR 545.

M Whincup, 'Inequitable Incorporation – The Abuse of a Privilege' (1981) 2 Co Law 158.

RJ Wickins and CA Ong, 'Confusion Worse Confounded: The End of the Directing Mind Theory?' [1997] JBL 524.

Chapter 3

Promoters and pre-incorporation contracts

Chapter Contents

3.1 Promoters

Somebody has to set up the company and, in order to set up a company, there have to be promoters. The promoters will purchase property from which the company is going to operate and undertake the preliminary steps to set the company up. They will thus be acting before the company has been formed.

In Victorian Britain, there used to be professional company promoters. These promoters were often dishonest and acted fraudulently. The Anglo-Bengalee Disinterested Loan and Life Assurance Company, mercilessly lampooned by Dickens in *Martin Chuzzlewit*, is typical of the sort of situation that arose. Indeed Albert Grant, who features in some of the prominent late Victorian cases concerning company promotion, is assumed to be the inspiration for the villain Augustus Melmotte in Trollope's *The Way We Live Now*.

A code of rules therefore developed to ensure that promoters acted with integrity in setting up the company.

There are few statutory rules in this area and indeed no satisfactory statutory definition of a promoter. Section 67 of the Companies Act 1985 formerly defined a promoter in s 67(3) as a person who is 'a party to the preparation of the prospectus or a portion of it'.

In the absence of any precise definition in statute, resort must be had to judicial statements relating to promotion. As Gross notes in 'Who Is a Company Promoter?' [1970] 86 LQR 493, the term 'promoter' is ill-defined by companies legislation. The usual dictum referred to in defining a promoter is that of Cockburn CJ in *Twycross v Grant* (1877) 2 CPD 469, where he said that a promoter is 'one who undertakes to form a company with reference to a given project and to set it going and who takes the necessary steps to accomplish that purpose'. This definition is clearly somewhat general. In *Whaley Bridge Calico Printing Co v Green* (1880) 5 QBD 109, Bowen J said: 'The term promoter is a term not of law, but of business, usefully summing up in a single word a number of business operations familiar to the commercial world by which a company is generally brought into existence.' The old, Victorian rogue promoters responsible for finding directors to manage a company and for drafting prospectuses to raise capital from the public are largely a thing of the past. Most companies are promoted as private companies by those who will subsequently be managing the business. Rules are still necessary to protect those investing in the business and to protect creditors.

3.2 Promoters' duties

A company promoter owes fiduciary duties to the company that he is setting up. Fiduciary duties are basically duties of good faith and integrity. Most obviously, where a promoter is selling property to a company, he must ensure that he discloses any profit that he is making on the deal. The disclosure may be made to all of the shareholders, actual and potential, as was the case for example in *Salomon v A Salomon & Co Ltd* (1897). Disclosure to the shareholders was also the method employed successfully in *Lagunas Nitrate Company v Lagunas Syndicate* [1899] 2 Ch 392. Alternatively, the disclosure may be made to the company's directors.

However, in such an instance the disclosure can only be effective if it is to an independent board of directors. In *Erlanger v New Sombrero Phosphate Co* (1878) 3 App Cas 1218, a syndicate had purchased a lease of a Caribbean island called Sombrero. The syndicate was selling the island to a company that had been formed for the purpose.

The syndicate owed promotional duties in relation to the sale. They disclosed the profit that was being made in selling the island to the company to the board of directors. There were five directors; two were abroad at the material time, two were associated with the syndicate and the fifth was the Lord Mayor of London who was too busy to give proper attention to the affairs of the company. It was held in the circumstances that this was not a full disclosure to an independent board of directors. The company was able to rescind the contract.

When a promoter discloses a profit that he is making upon a deal, he must take care to ensure that he is disclosing the entire profit that he is making from the arrangement. In certain cases, there may well be some collateral profit as well as the direct profit from the sale. It was thus in *Gluckstein v Barnes* [1900] AC 240, where a syndicate had purchased the exhibition hall, Olympia. The syndicate disclosed the profit that it was making in re-selling the hall to the company but failed to disclose a profit that it was making in relation to certain mortgages over the hall which it had purchased at a discount. This meant that, when the syndicate purchased the hall, there was a further reduction of £20,000 since the price of the purchase also included an amount to be set off against debts which were now owed to the syndicate. Lord MacNaghten said:

> They issued a prospectus representing that they had agreed to purchase the property for a sum largely in excess of the amount which they had, in fact, to pay. On the faith of this prospectus, they collected subscriptions from a confiding and credulous public. And then comes the last act. Secretly, and therefore dishonestly, they put into their own pockets the difference between the real and the pretended price.

The case clearly represents a breach of promoters' duties and the promoter in question, Gluckstein, was ordered to repay his share of the secret profit.

Particular problems may arise where a promoter has acquired property before the promotion began. In such a situation, where the promoter then sells the property to the company without fully disclosing the profit that is being made upon the transaction, there is a difficulty in awarding an appropriate remedy. If the company were to seek an account of profits in such a case, the question would arise as to what portion of profits properly belongs to the pre-promotion period and so would be rightfully the property of the promoter, and what part of the profit could be said to belong to the post-promotion period and so belong to the company. In such cases, therefore, the view of the courts is that it is not possible to sue for an account of profits but merely for rescission of the contract, always assuming that the right to rescission has not been lost. See *Re Cape Breton Co, Cavendish-Bentinck v Fenn* (1887) 12 App Cas 652 and *Ladywell Mining Co v Brookes* (1887) 35 ChD 400. These decisions have been criticised notably by Xuereb in 'Secret Profit – Re Cape Breton Company Revisited' (1987) 5 CLD 9 on the basis that some apportionment of the profit could be made by the court.

3.3 Remedies for breach of promoters' duties

Promoters owe fiduciary duties to the company which they are promoting. The duty is akin to the duty owed to the unborn child as no company is yet in existence. However, there is a range of remedies that will be available against a promoter who has breached his duty and failed to disclose the extent of the profit that he is making where he has sold property to the company. A possible remedy is for rescission of the contract of the sale between the promoter and the company. The usual bars to rescission will apply. Thus, rescission is not available where there has been affirmation, where it is impossible to restore the parties to their pre-contractual positions or where third party rights have intervened.

An alternative remedy is for the company to sue for a return of the profit. If the company wishes to keep the property in question and merely recover the profit, this is clearly the appropriate remedy to seek. This was the remedy awarded, for example, in *Gluckstein v Barnes* (1900).

These are the two usual alternative remedies. However, in one case, the remedy of damages was awarded against a promoter. This occurred in *Re Leeds and Hanley Theatres of Varieties Ltd* [1902] 2 Ch 809. In this case, the claim was for breach of duty of care in the promoter selling property to the company at an overvaluation. Damages were awarded against the promoter. This is a rare instance of damages being awarded against a promoter, but it is interesting to note that the measure of damages was the same as the profit made by the promoter.

It may be on occasion that a single shareholder can bring a claim as a derivative action on behalf of the company. The shareholder must fit within one of the exceptions to the rule in *Foss v Harbottle* (1843) 2 Hare 461 or s 260 Companies Act (CA) 2006 (see Chapter 15). This could occur where the promoters are in control of the company and are using their management and/or voting powers in general meeting to prevent an action being brought in respect of an undisclosed profit that has been made by promoters.

A further remedy may be available in the particular instance of the company's liquidation. Section 212 of the Insolvency Act 1986 permits the court to order in a liquidation that a promoter restore to the company any property or money obtained in breach of duty. This may be done on the petition of the liquidator or on the petition of a creditor or member (see also section 25.3).

3.4 Payment for the promoters' services

A promoter cannot have a contract with the company which he is going to form. The company is not yet in existence and, therefore, is unable to contract. In *Re National Motor Mail Coach Company Limited, Clinton's Claim* [1908] 2 Ch 515, it was accepted that there could be no contract between a promoter and his unformed company such that a promoter could claim reimbursement of expenses incurred in setting up the company. Furthermore, the court held that there could be no quasi-contractual remedy in this case, based on the company having received a benefit.

Generally, in such cases, no problem will arise. The promoters who have been setting up the company will also be the first directors and will take care to ensure that they are reimbursed for their expenses and receive payment for the services that they have performed. However, where problems do arise, a fresh contract after incorporation may be the answer. It is important that this new contract should be supported by some element of fresh consideration or be concluded under seal, as otherwise the contract will be invalid for want of consideration since the consideration is past.

In Scottish law, past consideration for the payment of promoters' expenses is permissible as past consideration is good consideration in Scottish law. See *Park Business Interiors v Park* [1992] BCLC 1034.

3.5 Pre-incorporation contracts

Where a person enters into a contract on behalf of an unformed company, a conceptual problem arises. It is clear in such instances that the company itself cannot be bound since the company does not exist.

3.5.1 Common law

In *Kelner v Baxter* (1866) LR 2 CP 174, the claimant had delivered goods to the defendants. The goods had been ordered on behalf of the proposed Gravesend Royal Alexandra Hotel Co. Ltd. The question arose as to whether the company was liable upon this contract. The Court of Common Pleas held that the company could not be liable since it did not exist at the time of the contract. In fact, the defendant, who had acted on behalf of the unformed company, was held liable on this contract.

Gross states in 'Pre-Incorporation Contracts' (1971) 87 LQR 367 that it is rare to hear such widespread and common opposition against any aspect of company law as that against the rule in *Kelner v Baxter*.

This is the position at common law before statute intervened. The position was not uniform, however, and in some cases it was held that there was no contract. In *Newborne v Sensolid (Great Britain) Ltd* [1954] 1 QB 45, Leopold Newborne (London) Ltd purported to sell a quantity of ham to the defendant. The defendant refused to take delivery of the ham. The company sued for breach of contract. It transpired that the company had not been registered until the day after the contract was concluded.

The claimant continued the action in his own name. The claimant was a promoter and director of the company. It was held in the Court of Appeal that there was no contract in this case. The fact that the agreement had been signed 'Yours faithfully, Leopold Newborne (London) Ltd' and the signature of the director added beneath indicated that there was no intention that personal liability should attach to the director. It was therefore held that there was no contract. Similarly, in the Australian case of *Black v Smallwood* [1966] ALR 744 (High Court of Australia), it was held that where a contract was concluded where the purchaser was described as Western Suburbs Holdings Pty Ltd with the signatures of Robert Smallwood and J Cooper added subsequently as directors, there could be no contract between the claimant Black and the defendant Smallwood. In this case, all the parties believed that the company did exist, whereas in fact at the time of the contract it did not. The court held that in the circumstances there could be no contract. Although a contract may take effect between the person purporting to act for the unformed company and the other contracting party, it is clear from the cases that there can be no adoption or ratification of that agreement by the company once it comes into existence. This is clear from the opinion of the Privy Council in *Natal Land and Colonisation Co Ltd v Pauline Colliery and Development Syndicate Ltd* [1904] AC 120 (an appeal from the Supreme Court of Natal). In this case, the contract had been entered into between the Natal Land Company and one Mrs de Carrey for coalmining rights on Natal Land's property. Mrs de Carrey then assigned the contract to Louch, who was to become a director of the Pauline Colliery Company which was about to be registered. Natal Land agreed to this substitution of the contracting party under the agreement. Later Natal Land contended that there was no contract as the respondent did not exist at the time of the purported assignment. The court accepted this view.

The appropriate course of action in such a situation where a person acting for the company is bound is that, once the company comes into existence, it should enter into a new contract on the same terms.

3.5.2 Statutory provision

When the United Kingdom joined the European Communities by the European Communities Act 1972, s 9(2) of the European Communities Act implemented part of the first EC Company Law Directive. Section 9(2) is now contained in s 51(1) of the Companies Act 2006.

> A contract which purports to be made by or on behalf of a company at a time when the company has not been formed has effect, subject to any agreement to the contrary, as one made with the person purporting to act for the company or as an agent for it, and he is personally liable on the contract accordingly.

This statutory provision will mean that, in both *Kelner v Baxter* and *Newborne v Sensolid*, the person purporting to act for the company will be liable upon the contract as well as being able to hold the other party to the contractual agreement. In *Phonogram Ltd v Lane* [1982] QB 938, the court had to consider the effect of what is now s 51(1) where a company called Fragile Management Ltd was in the process of being incorporated. The company was to manage a pop group called Cheap, Mean and Nasty.

The defendant was the manager of the pop group. He agreed with the claimants that the claimants would supply finance. He signed an agreement undertaking to repay the monies that had been advanced on behalf of Fragile Management Ltd if the contract was not completed before a certain time. Subsequently, the claimants sued the defendant for the money that had been advanced. The defendant argued he was not personally liable. It was suggested on his behalf that the contract was not 'purported' to be made by the company as it was known that the company was not in existence. Indeed, it was known by both parties that the company had not yet been formed. However, Lord Denning MR took the view (a view shared by Shaw and Oliver LJJ) that a contract can purport to be made on behalf of a company even though the company is known by both parties not to have been formed. He took the view that, although what is now s 51(1) can be excluded by contrary agreement, this contrary agreement should be express. This view was shared by the other members of the Court of Appeal.

It seems that the Contracts (Rights of Third Parties) Act 1999, which permits enforcement of a contract by a third party, does not apply to pre-incorporation contracts. The contract in question is one on behalf of a third party, not one for the benefit of a third party.

It is possible in certain situations that a promoter may act on behalf of a company to be bought 'off the shelf'. In such a situation, the company does exist where the promoter is acting so that it is open to the company subsequently to ratify what the promoter has done provided that the promoter made it clear that he was acting on behalf of the company. It may be that the company subsequently alters its name; this will not change the legal situation.

In *OshKosh B'Gosh Inc v Dan Marbel Inc Ltd* [1989] BCLC 507, an off-the-shelf company was acquired. The company resolved to change its name to Dan Marbel Inc Ltd but no certificate of incorporation recording the change of name was obtained. The Court of Appeal took the view that the company had been formed although trading under a different name. What is now s 51(1) was therefore inapplicable.

Similarly, in *Badgerhill Properties Ltd v Cottrell* [1991] BCLC 805, the company was already in existence although its name had been wrongly stated. The Court of Appeal took the view that the section did not apply.

Cotronic (UK) Ltd v Dezonie [1991] BCLC 721 is a rather different situation. The claimant company sued for monies owed in relation to work done as subcontractors for a company, Wendaland Builders Ltd, controlled by the defendant. The defendant joined the owner of the property as third party.

The owner of the land argued that, when it entered into the agreement, Wendaland Builders Ltd had been struck off the register and so did not exist, so there was no contractual liability. The defendant argued that what is now s 51(1) applied. The Court of Appeal took the view that this was not a pre-incorporation situation. The defendant did not purport to be concluding a contract on behalf of a new company. (Note that the defendant did succeed on the basis of a *quantum meruit*.)

In *Rover International Ltd v Cannon Film Sales Ltd* [1987] BCLC 540, it was held that what is now s 51(1) did not apply to companies not registered in the UK. *Rover* was reversed on a different point.

The person purporting to act for the company will be able to hold the other party to the contractual agreement. The matter was put beyond doubt in *Braymist Ltd v Wise Finance Co Ltd* [2002] Ch 273. Here a contract had been made on 28 January 1993 by the vendor, Braymist Ltd, which had not yet been incorporated. It was purporting to sell land. The title was held by another company, Plumtree Ltd. Braymist was to become a 100 per cent subsidiary of Plumtree.

Mr Poole, who had management control of Plumtree, instructed solicitors, William Sturgess, to act. The solicitors signed for Braymist Ltd. A notice to complete the contract was subsequently given, and it was attempted to enforce the contract against Wise by or on behalf of the unformed company.

Etherton J held that what is now s 51(1) operated with mutuality so that it could be enforced against Wise. The proper person to enforce was the person who was acting for the unformed company, Braymist, namely William Sturgess, solicitors. This was upheld by the Court of Appeal.

Savirimuthu analyses this decision in 'Pre-Incorporation Contracts and the Problem of Corporate Fundamentalism – Are Promoters Proverbially Profuse' [2003] Co Law 196. Further reform of the law to allow ratification of pre-incorporation contracts by statute would be a sensible move. Prentice in 'Section 9 of the European Communities Act' [1973] 89 LQR 518 believes that the opportunity should be taken to deal with this problem by permitting ratification of pre-incorporation contracts. This view is echoed by Green in 'Security of Transaction after Phonogram' [1984] 47 MLR 671, and Griffiths' 'Agents without Principals: Pre-Incorporation Contracts in Section 36 C(1) of the Companies Act 1985' (1993) 13 LS 241.

Another case involving what is now s 51(1) is the decision in *Hellmuth, Obata and Kassabaum Incorporated t/a HOK Sport v Geoffrey King* [2000] All ER (D) 1394. HOK had carried out planning work for a proposed sports arena in Hannover. They claimed fees against King, who had acted for Arena Hannover AG (a company in formation). The action was allowed in respect of the work being undertaken. The judge, Colin Reese QC, held *obiter* that the section applied to quasi-contractual claims for a *quantum meruit* as well as to contractual claims.

In *Royal Mail Estates Limited v Maple Teesdale Borzou Chaharsough Shirazi* [2015] EWHC 1890 (Ch) the court considered whether an assignment clause 'the benefit of this contract is personal to the buyer' amounted to a contrary agreement allowed by s 51 CA 2006. In this case, Maples Teesdale, a firm of solicitors signed a contract for acquisition of a property for £20 million for their client. Unknown to them or the seller, the buyer had not been incorporated. Maple Teesdale signed the contract 'for and on behalf of the buyer' and 'Maples Teesdale pp buyer' which apparently is not an uncommon practice in conveyancing.

Maples Teesdale argued that they were not liable on the basis of certain wording in the contract which stated that the contract was personal to the company named as a party. The Court found no evidence of an agreement to the contrary and consequently, Maples Teesdale was liable under the contract.

There needs to be a clear agreement to exclude the operation of s 51 and a contractual provision which was merely inconsistent with the consequences of the application of s 51 (i.e. that the agent would be personally liable for the contract) was not sufficient to amount to an agreement to the contrary. The Court noted that one of the purposes was to protect third parties in dealing with a non-existent company. The court also stated that an agreement to the contrary did not need to be contained in the contract itself but could be in a separate agreement.

Summary

Promoters

There is no statutory definition of promoters. One must therefore turn to the cases. A promoter is a person 'who undertakes to form a company with reference to a given project and to set it going and who takes the necessary steps to accomplish that purpose', per Cockburn CJ in *Twycross v Grant* (1877).

Promoters owe fiduciary duties to the companies they are forming. They must disclose any profit they are making from the promotion – either to the members of the company or to an independent board.

The company may sue for disgorgement of the profit or for rescission (if this is not barred) where there is a breach of this duty.

Pre-incorporation contracts

A conceptual problem arises where a person concludes a contract for the as yet unformed company. At common law, the position was confused. Sometimes, the person acting for the unformed company was held to be contractually bound but much depended on the form of words used. Since the European Communities Act 1972 the position has been standardised. Section 51(1) of the Companies Act 2006 now provides that where a person acts for an unformed company, that person is contractually bound unless there is an agreement to the contrary.

Self-test questions

3.1   What is a promoter?

3.2   What duties are owed by promoters?

3.3   What are the remedies available to an injured party where there has been a breach of promoters' duties?

3.4   How may promoters be reimbursed for their services to a company?

3.5   What is the essence of the conceptual problem in relation to pre-incorporation contracts?

Further reading

J Gold, 'The Liability of Promoters for Secret Profits in English Law' (1943) 5 UTLJ 21.

NN Green, 'Security of Transaction After Phonogram' (1984) 47 MLR 671.

A Griffiths, 'Agents Without Principals: Pre-incorporation Contracts and Section 36C of the Companies Act 1985', (1993) 13 LS 241.

JH Gross, 'Who Is a Company Promoter?' (1970) 86 LQR 493.

JH Gross, 'Pre-incorporation Contracts' (1971) 87 LQR 367.

B McCrea, 'Disclosure of Promoters' Secret Profits' (1969) Univ of BCLR 183.

J McMullen, 'A Case Note on Phonogram v Lane' [1982] CLJ 47.

DD Prentice, 'Section 9 of the European Communities Act' (1973) 89 LQR 518.

A Roberts, 'Three Ring Circus' (on S36C(l) CA85) (2003) 147 SJ 458.

J Savirimuthu, 'Pre-Incorporation Contracts and the Problem of Corporate Fundamentalism – Are Promoters Proverbially Profuse?' (2003) Co Law 196.

PG Xuereb, 'Secret Profit – Re Cape Breton Revisited' (1987) 5 CLD 9.

Chapter 4

Shares and payment of capital

Chapter Contents

4.1 The nature of a share

Where a company is limited by shares, the capital of the company is divided into shares. These are units of a given amount defining a shareholder's proportionate interest in the company. The nature of a share was discussed in *Borland's Trustee v Steel Bros & Co Ltd* [1901] 1 Ch 279. The relevant facts of this case were that the company's constitution provided that on any manager or assistant ceasing to hold such office, or on his death or bankruptcy, he must, on receiving notice, transfer his shares.

The significance here is in the judgment of Farwell J in his definition of a share. Farwell J defined a share as follows:

> The share is the interest of the shareholder in the company measured by a sum of money, for the purpose of liability in the first place, and of interest in the second, but also consisting of a series of mutual covenants entered into by all the shareholders *inter se* [in accordance with what is now s 33 of the Companies Act (CA) 2006].

4.1.1 Main features

The main features of a typical share are as follows:

(a)   a right to dividends declared on the shares;
(b)   generally (unless it is a non-voting share) a right to vote at general meetings;
(c)   on the liquidation of the company or on a reduction of capital, the right to receive assets distributed to shareholders of that class;
(d)   an obligation to subscribe capital of a given amount which will sometimes be the nominal value of the share if the share is issued at par and sometimes will be in excess of this if the share is issued at a premium (the issue of shares at par and at a premium is discussed below in section 4.8);
(e)   rights of membership attached to the shares as defined in the company's memorandum and articles (discussed above in relation to the s 33 membership contract in section 7.7); and
(f)   a right to transfer the share in accordance with the articles of association (discussed below in section 4.4).

4.2 Different classes of shares

Often, a company will only have one class of share. These will be ordinary shares or the equity of the company. On occasion, the company may have more than one class of share. The classes will be differentiated by reference to rights to dividend, rights to repayment of capital, rights to vote, etc. Where this is the case, matters of the variation of class rights may arise where it is proposed to alter the company's articles and that alteration varies the rights attaching to a particular class of share (these matters are considered under variation of class rights in section 7.6).

4.2.1 Preference shares

It is perhaps appropriate here to say something about the nature of a preference share, which is probably the most common type of share other than ordinary shares.

The most common feature of a preference share is that it confers a right to a preferential dividend up to a specified amount, for example, 8 per cent of its paid-up value. This dividend is paid before any dividend is paid on the ordinary or equity share capital of the company. Preference shares may also have other preferential rights such as preferential voting rights or a right to repayment of capital in priority to other shares on a winding up.

The rights of the preference shares will depend upon what is set out in the terms of issue or in the articles of association of the company.

In relation to dividends, the preference shareholder is only entitled to a preferential dividend when this dividend is actually declared. Even if there are available profits there is no obligation upon the directors to declare a dividend (the question of dividends is considered separately, see Chapter 8). If, however, a dividend is not declared in any given year in relation to preference shares, the right to that dividend is carried forward. This presumption of the preference dividend being cumulative can be rebutted by a provision in the articles or in the terms of issue but, in the absence of any express statement, it is assumed that the right to a preference dividend is cumulative. Therefore, if a preference dividend of 8 per cent is not paid in year one, the right to that dividend carries forward into year two and so on.

If the preference dividend is paid in full, there is no further right to any additional dividend unless the terms of issue or articles say so. If there is such a right to an additional dividend, the preference shares are termed participating preference shares.

In relation to capital, there is no automatic priority for preference shares in a winding up or in a reduction of capital. The right only exists if the terms of issue or the articles set out such a right. If preference shares are given a priority in a winding up, then once their capital has been returned, this is exhaustive of their rights unless the terms of issue or the provisions of the articles provide otherwise; that is, preference shares do not participate in any surplus assets on a winding up.

4.3 Other classes of shares

The possible types of class of shares are many. It is not uncommon for a company to have redeemable preference shares. These shares are shares that mirror preference shares except they are redeemable at a set date or at the option of the company.

A company may issue deferred or founders' shares. These shares rank after ordinary shares in respect of dividends and sometimes in relation to a return of capital. They will usually, however, have additional voting rights. Typically, they would be taken up by a company's promoters.

Many large public companies have separate management shares, for example, the Savoy Hotel Group. These shares carry additional voting rights and they are thus able to outvote the ordinary shares of the company. In other respects, their rights will often be the same as the ordinary shares, for example, in relation to dividends and return of capital.

4.4 Transfer of shares

Shares are freely transferable unless the company's articles impose restrictions on transfers. It was formerly the case before the Companies Act 1980 that private companies had to restrict the transferability of their shares in some way as a condition of their private status. This requirement was swept away by the Companies Act 1980.

If the articles contain no restriction at all, then the motive of the transferor in disposing of his shares is immaterial. In *Re European Bank (Masters' Case)* (1872) 7 Ch App 292, 12 days before a banking company stopped business, a shareholder transferred shares to his son-in-law. The shares were partly paid shares. The court held that the transfer could not be set aside. The court would not inquire into the bona fides of the transferor. In *Re Smith, Knight & Co* (1868) LR 4 Ch App 20, the court held that the directors of the company have no discretionary powers except those that are given to them by the company's constitution to refuse to register a transfer which has been made bona fide.

Restrictions on share transfer can only apply to non-quoted companies. Transfers of uncertificated shares, i.e. those quoted on an exchange, cannot be subject to restrictions. They are carried out anonymously and not face to face and, if the company is a UK one, they must permit transfer in uncertificated form.

4.4.1 Restrictions on transferability

What happens where there is some restriction on transferability? The restriction may take one of many forms. Articles of association may give the directors an absolute discretion to refuse to register a transfer of shares. This was the position in *Re Smith and Fawcett Ltd* [1942] Ch 304 (see section 12.5.2). In this case, the court held that the directors had a total discretion as to registering transfers. The only limitation on their discretion was that it should be exercised bona fide in the interest of the company. The Court of Appeal refused to draw an inference that it was being exercised mala fide. It is clear that, where the directors have an absolute discretion to refuse to register a transfer, the courts are reluctant to interfere. It should be noted, however, that a refusal to register a transfer of shares may justify a petition under ss 994–996 (considered under minority protection, Chapter 15).

Sometimes the refusal to register may only be exercised on certain grounds. A familiar power is one that the directors can exercise if, in their opinion, it is contrary to the interests of the company that the proposed transferee should become a member.

In *Re Bede Steam Shipping Co Ltd* [1917] 1 Ch 123, which concerned a Newcastle-based steamship company, the court held that such a power only justifies a refusal to register on grounds that are personal to the proposed transferee. It does not, for example, justify a refusal to register transfer of single shares or shares in small numbers because the directors do not think it is desirable to increase the number of shareholders. The refusal to register was exercised on the ground that the directors did not want the shares to be held by many people. Lord Cozens-Hardy MR cited Chitty J in *Re Bell Bros* (1891) 65 LT 245 with approval:

> If the reasons assigned are legitimate, the court will not overrule the directors' decision merely because the court itself could not have come to the same conclusion, but if they are not legitimate, as, for instance, if the directors state that they

rejected the transfer because the transferor's object was to increase the voting power in respect of his shares by splitting them among his nominees, the court would hold the power had not been duly exercised.

Articles too, cannot be altered with retrospective effect to enable directors to refuse to register a transfer that has already happened: see *W and A M'Arthur Ltd v Gulf Line Ltd* [1909] SC 732.

4.4.2 The issue of pre-emption

Often, the restriction on transfer may be one of pre-emption, giving other shareholders the right to purchase the shares of the transferor at a fair value before they are offered elsewhere. This situation arose in *Curtis v JJ Curtis & Co Ltd* [1986] BCLC 86 in the New Zealand Court of Appeal. Here, the company's articles of association provided that a shareholder who wished to transfer his shares to an outsider had first of all to offer them to existing shareholders. This was not done. Cooke J held that a perpetual injunction would be granted against the transferor preventing him from transferring them other than in accordance with the articles.

A pre-emption clause was the restriction which was utilised in *Rayfield v Hands* [1958] 2 All ER 194, to preserve control in a few people in a small company. Similarly in *Greenhalgh v Mallard* [1943] 2 All ER 234, an article provided that, if a member wished to transfer his shares to a non-member, they must first be offered to existing members. Another article provided that, if a member wished to sell his shares, he must notify the fact to the directors. A member transferred his shares to other members. Greenhalgh, another member, sought to have the transfers declared invalid on the ground that the restriction on transfer of shares applied to sales to existing members as well as to non-members and, in this case, the shares had not been first offered to members as a whole.

This argument was rejected by the Court of Appeal because the articles were not sufficiently clear to restrict a transfer to existing members. The restriction was held to apply only to the case of sales of shares to non-members.

Lord Greene MR stated:

> Questions of constructions of this kind are always difficult but, in the case of the restriction of transfer of shares, I think it is right for the court to remember that a share, being personal property, is prima facie transferable, although the conditions of the transfer are to be found in the terms laid down in the articles. If the right of transfer, which is inherent in property of this kind, is to be taken away or cut down, it seems to me that it should be done by language of sufficient clarity to make it apparent that this was the intention.

The issue of pre-emption also came up in *Tett v Phoenix Property and Investment Co Ltd* [1986] BCLC 149, where the articles of association of the company restricted the right of the shareholder to transfer his shares. On the facts of the case, it was held that the directors had offered the shares to existing shareholders and the offer had not been taken up so that sale elsewhere was effective. Registration of the transfer was appropriate.

The courts will lean against an interpretation of any power in the directors which hampers the right to transfer shares.

On the other hand, the courts will not carry out a literal construction so far that it defeats the obvious purpose of the provision. Thus, in *Lyle & Scott Ltd v Scott's Trustees* [1959] AC 763, where the articles provided for a right of pre-emption in the other shareholders where a shareholder was desirous of transferring his ordinary shares, and some shareholders sold their shares to a takeover bidder and received the purchase price and gave him irrevocable proxies to vote on his behalf, the House of Lords held that in the context 'transferring' meant assigning the beneficial interest and not the process of having a transfer registered. The shareholders had indicated their intention to sell their shares and could not continue with the sale without giving the other shareholders their right to exercise their pre-emption rights.

It is most important, if the company wishes to protect some shareholders from the effect of shares being held by others, to ensure that the power of refusal to register a transfer of share also applies on transmission (cases where shares pass on death or bankruptcy).

In *Safeguard Industrial Developments Ltd v National Westminster Bank Ltd* [1982] 1 WLR 589, a shareholder held the balance of control between two rival brothers. He died leaving the shares to one of the brothers' children. The question arose as to whether pre-emption applied on transmission or simply where a shareholder wished to transfer his shares during his lifetime.

The court held that the provision could only apply in respect of transfer, not transmission. Likewise, a renunciation of an allotment in favour of another person is not considered a transfer in the context of articles providing for directors' approval to register a transfer: *Systems Control plc v Munro Corporation plc* [1990] BCLC 659.

Careful wording is therefore needed to protect companies and their shareholders in such situations.

4.4.3 Directors' rights to reject on prescribed grounds

If, on the true construction of the company's articles, the directors are only entitled to reject on certain prescribed grounds, and if it is proved that they have rejected on others, the court will interfere as in *Re Bede Steam Shipping Co Ltd*. This still holds true but the CA 2006 has made changes to the law. It used to be the case that interrogatories may be administered to determine on which of certain prescribed grounds the directors have acted but not as to their reasons for rejecting on those particular grounds: see *Sutherland (Duke) v British Dominions Land Settlement Corporation Ltd* [1926] Ch 746.

However, if the directors do state their reasons, the court will investigate them to determine whether they have acted on those grounds. They will overrule their decision if they have acted on considerations that should not have influenced them.

Even where the right to refuse is a qualified one, in certain situations the directors may not be obliged to give their reasons. In a case concerning Tottenham Hotspur Football Club, it was established that, even if the directors can only refuse to register a transfer on certain grounds, they cannot be obliged to give the reason if the articles provide they need not do so (*Berry and Stewart v Tottenham Hotspur Football & Athletic Co Ltd* [1935] Ch 718).

Section 771(1) of CA 2006 has somewhat changed the position. The reason for refusal to register must now be given. The section stipulates that in the event of a transfer being lodged with the company, it must either register the transfer or give the transferee notice of refusal to register, together with reasons for its refusal. This must be done as soon as practicable and in any event, within two months of the date of lodgement. Section 776 also provides that unless the company has refused registration, it must complete and issue the certificates within the two months, otherwise this is a criminal offence.

Should the transfer be refused, the company must provide the transferee with such further information as the transferee may reasonably request, about the reasons for the refusal.

4.4.4 Positive act of board

In relation to transfer generally, it should be noted that a refusal to register a transfer must be a positive act of the board. In *Re Hackney Pavilion Ltd* [1924] 1 Ch 276, the two directors of the company were divided on the question of whether the proposed transfer should proceed. The company secretary was asked to write to the executrix's solicitors and return the transfer documents indicating that the transfer could not go ahead. The High Court ordered that the transfer must go ahead. Astbury J said:

> Now, the right to decline must be actively exercised by the vote of the board ad hoc. At the actual board meeting, there was a proper quorum but, as the board was equally divided, it did not and could not exercise its rights to decline.

In such situations, the transfer must, therefore, go ahead.

4.4.5 Refusal must be exercised within a reasonable time

As discussed above, another restriction on refusal of registration of a transfer is that the refusal must be exercised within a reasonable time. This rule has statutory force from s 771 CA 2006, which provides that when a transfer of shares in or debentures of a company has been lodged with the company, the company must either register the transfer or give the transferee notice of refusal, together with the reasons for the refusal, as soon as is practicable, and in any event not later than two months after the date on which the transfer is lodged. Failure to comply with this section constitutes an offence. During the two-month period, however, the transferee cannot claim to be registered as a member, even though there are no directors, so that the company cannot exercise the right to refuse to register: see *Re Zinotty Properties Ltd* [1984] 1 WLR 1249.

Section 994 CA 2006 probably enables members to apply for a remedy in cases where directors fail to register a transfer of shares and this failure constitutes unfair prejudice to the members concerned. This may now enable a member to obtain a remedy in cases such as *Re Smith & Fawcett Ltd* (1942) (see section 12.5.2). Other transfer situations may involve this section. Section 994 was involved in *Re a Company (No 007623 of 1984)* [1986] BCLC 362, where a rights issue was made which the petitioning shareholder was unwilling to accept.

Hoffmann J held that the remedy was to offer to sell his shares to the other members under pre-emption provisions. The pre-emption provisions of this company contained a mechanism for determining a fair value of the shares by means of a valuation conducted by auditors. This procedure should have been employed without recourse to the courts. The inference of the decision is that a remedy would have been available under s 994 had there been no pre-emption provisions.

The area of law relating to share transfer, and particularly restrictions on transferability, is increasingly important as more and more people buy shares and as more and more set up their own businesses where they may wish to keep control and ownership within a tightly knit group.

4.5 Share warrants

Section 122 of the Companies Act 2006 provides that on the issue of a share warrant, the company must enter in the register of members the fact of the issue of the warrant, a statement of the shares included in the warrant and the date of issue of the warrant, and amend the register if necessary so that no person is named on the register as the holder of the shares specified in the warrant. A share warrant is a title document confirming the bearer of the document as the owner of the shares specified.

Subject to the company's articles on surrendering the share warrant for cancellation, the bearer is entitled to have his name entered as a member in the register of members.

4.6 Pre-emption rights

Section 561 of the Companies Act 2006 provides that a company must not allot equity securities to a person on any terms, unless it has made an offer to each person who holds ordinary shares in the company to allot to him on the same or more favourable terms a proportion of those securities that is, as nearly as practicable, equal to the proportion in nominal value held by him of the ordinary share capital of the company, and the period during which any such offer may be accepted has expired or the company has received notice of the acceptance or refusal of every offer so made.

Section 562 provides for the need of communication of the pre-emption offer to shareholders and s 563 provides that failure to comply with s 561 and s 562 constitutes an offence for which the company and every officer in default is liable to compensate any person to whom an offer should have been made in accordance with the provisions of the sections.

Section 564 provides an exception to the pre-emption right in relation to the allotment of bonus shares. Section 565 provides for an exception where shares are issued for non-cash consideration, wholly or in part, and s 566 provides for an exception where securities are held under an employees' share scheme.

In the case of private companies with only one class of share, the right to pre-emption may be excluded generally in relation to the allotment by the company of equity securities generally, or in relation to allotments of a particular description (s 569 CA 2006).

In addition to this, s 570 provides for the disapplication of pre-emption rights where directors of a company (i.e. public and private) are generally authorised for the purposes of s 551 (power of directors to allot shares, etc.; authorisation by company): they may be given power by the articles or by a special resolution to allot equity securities as if s 561 (right of pre-emption) did not apply to the allotment or as if it did apply subject to modification.

Section 571 provides for disapplication of pre-emption rights by special resolution in relation to a specified allotment of equity securities. Where the directors of a company are authorised, whether generally or otherwise, to allot shares, the company may, by special resolution, resolve that s 561 (right of pre-emption) does not apply to a specified allotment or applies to such an allotment with modifications.

Finally, s 573 CA 2006 disapplies pre-emption rights in relation to the sale of treasury shares (see section 9.6).

4.7 Payment for shares

Section 580 provides that shares may not be allotted at a discount. Section 581 provides for different amounts to be paid on shares. Section 582 provides that shares allotted by a company and any premium on them may be paid up in money or money's worth (including goodwill and know-how). Section 583 provides for the meaning of 'payment in cash'. Section 585 provides that public companies must not accept an undertaking to do work or perform services in return for shares. Section 586 provides that public companies' shares must be paid up to at least one-quarter, and the whole of any premium.

Section 587 provides that public companies must not allot shares as fully or partly paid otherwise than in cash if the consideration for the allotment is or includes an undertaking which is to be, or may be performed, more than five years after the date of the allotment.

Section 593 provides that a public company must not allot shares as fully or partly paid up otherwise than in cash unless:

(a)   the consideration has been independently valued;
(b)   the valuer's report has been made to the company during the six months immediately preceding the allotment; and
(c)   a copy of the report has been sent to the proposed allottee.

This section does not apply to the allotment of shares in a company arrangement where Company A, in return for the transfer to that company of shares of Company B, or the cancellation of all or some of the shares of Company B, allots shares (s 594).

Section 595 provides that s 593 does not apply to the allotment of shares by a company in connection with a proposed merger with another company. This is where one of the companies proposes to acquire all the assets and liabilities of the other in exchange for the issue of shares or other securities of that one to shareholders of the other, with or without any cash payment to shareholders.

Although the statutory provision (s 593) applies only to public companies, there is a common law rule that all companies must only issue shares for non-cash assets if the value of those assets is at least equal to the value of the shares. In general, however, in a private company situation the courts will not interfere with the valuation placed upon those assets.

It may do so, however, if there is fraud; see *Re Wragg* [1897] 1 Ch 796. In this case a summons was taken out by the Official Receiver as the liquidator of Wragg Ltd. The company had carried on the business of omnibus and coach proprietors, livery stable keepers and job masters in Whitechapel, London. Originally the business was unincorporated but they incorporated it in 1894. It was contended by the liquidator that shares had been sold without any cash or kind being offered for those shares.

The Court of Appeal considered that the Official Receiver had failed to make out that the consideration was a sham and therefore the shareholders who were being impeached were held not liable to pay any additional sums on their shares.

This rule that shares cannot be issued at a discount is already clearly stated in common law. In *Ooregum Gold Mining Co of India Ltd v Roper* [1892] AC 125, the House of Lords held that shares could not be issued at a discount. That is to say, that the company must always obtain at least the nominal value (or par value) of the shares in payment for them.

In this case, the operations of the mining company had not been successful and a winding-up order was obtained against the company. Subsequently the order was stayed and the company sought to introduce fresh capital by means of an issue of shares at a discount.

The respondent, George Roper, challenged this issue saying that the defendant company had no power to issue shares at a discount. The House of Lords upheld this argument.

There are some exceptions to the rule that shares cannot be issued at a discount. It is possible to issue shares to underwriters under ss 552 and 553 of the Act at a commission of up to 10 per cent on the par value of the shares. Another exception is that a company may issue debentures at a discount (debentures are considered in Chapter 20). The debentures may be convertible into shares. Provided that the right to convert is not immediate, there will be no contravention of s 580; see *Koffyfontein Mines Ltd v Mosely* [1911] AC 409.

4.8 Issue of shares at a premium

Shares may sometimes be issued at a premium. Shares are issued at a premium if they are issued at more than par or nominal value. The amount of any premium must be fully paid on allotment if the issue is in a public company.

The amount of the premium is paid into a share premium account. Section 610 CA 2006 provides that if a company issues shares at a premium, whether for cash or otherwise, a sum equal to the aggregate amount or value of the premiums on those shares must be transferred to an account called 'the share premium account'.

For most purposes, the share premium account is treated just as if it were ordinary share capital. There are certain exceptions to this principle. They are that the money in a share premium account may be used to pay up fully paid bonus shares or to pay off the company's preliminary expenses or to pay up any commitment or discount allowable on the issue of shares or debentures of the company or in providing for the premium payable on redemption of debentures of the company.

There is no statutory rule requiring a company to obtain the best possible premium on an issue of shares in the way that there is a similar rule to obtain at least the par value and, therefore, not to issue shares at a discount. Yet if shares are issued at well below the market price, this may constitute a breach of directors' duties.

4.9 Return of allotments

Section 555 of the Companies Act 2006 provides that a company limited by shares and a company limited by guarantee and having a share capital must, within one month of making an allotment of shares, deliver to the Registrar a return of the particular allotment.

The return must set out the total number of shares of the company, the aggregate nominal value of the shares, and for each class of shares prescribe particulars of the rights attaching to the shares, the total number of shares of the class and the aggregate nominal value of that class, and also the amount paid up and the amount (if any) unpaid on each share.

Section 556 requires a return of allotment by an unlimited company where it is allotting new classes of shares. Here the company must, within one month of making such an allotment, deliver to the Registrar a return setting out the prescribed particulars of the rights attached to the shares.

Section 557 provides that it is an offence to fail to comply with the requirement to make a return under s 555 and s 556.

Summary

Introduction

A share is the interest of the shareholder in a particular company. There are various different types of shares such as ordinary, preference, deferred and management shares.

Transfer of shares

Shares are said to be freely transferable but, in the case of private companies, it is often the case that there are various restrictions on transferability.

Sometimes, the restriction on transferability will give the company's directors the power to refuse to register a transfer. The power may be a general power of refusal or it may be exercisable on specified grounds. It is a power to refuse – so, if the directors are evenly split, the transfer must go ahead. If the directors have a general power to refuse, they cannot be obliged to give reasons for their refusal to agree to the transfer.

Sometimes, the restriction provides that shares must first be offered for sale to existing members. If this is so, the provision will be construed strictly (as it will in all cases of restriction on transfer) so that, if it is desired to restrict shares being transmitted in cases of death and bankruptcy, this would have to be set out clearly.

Issue of shares

When shares are issued, the directors must take care to ensure that the statutory pre-emption provisions are honoured. These pre-emption provisions may be excluded or modified in various ways.

When shares are issued, the directors must also take care to ensure that the company receives full payment for the shares. Here, again, there are statutory provisions to ensure that the company pays in full. In particular, shares must not be issued at a discount, i.e. at less than par value.

Once shares have been issued, a return of allotment of shares has to be made to the Registrar of Companies setting out the shares that have been issued and the consideration that has been received.

Self-test questions

4.1   What are the essential features of a share?

4.2   Set out some different types of shares.

4.3   What is the nature of management shares?

4.4   What restrictions may apply on the transfer of shares?

4.5   What is the nature of a share warrant?

4.6   How does pre-emption apply in relation to a company's issue of shares?

4.7   What are the restrictions that apply in relation to payment for shares?

4.8   What does an issue of a share at a premium mean?

4.9   What is a return of allotments?

Further reading

C Napier and C Noke, 'Premiums and Pre-acquisition Profits – The Legal and Accountancy Professions and Business Combinations' (1991) 54 MLR 810.
RR Pennington, 'Can Shares in Companies Be Defined?' (1989) 10 Co Law 140.
MA Pickering, 'The Problem of the Preference Share' (1963) 26 MLR 499.
Pre-emption Rights: Final Report (URN05/679) (London DTI, 2005).
DG Rice, 'The Legal Nature of a Share' (1957) 21 Conv (NS) 433.

Chapter 5

Financial Conduct Authority – issue of shares to the public

Chapter Contents

5.1 Background

As has been noted in section 1.2.4, most companies are limited by shares. Public companies may issue shares to the public (section 1.2.5).

The Financial Services and Markets Act (FSMA) 2000 has replaced the Financial Services Act 1986 and related legislation in regulating the financial services industry. The 2000 Act brought the financial services industry under the supervision of the single regulator, the Financial Services Authority. This included the regulation of the banks, a job it took over from the Bank of England.

Later during the financial crisis of 2007–8, the Financial Services Authority came in for much criticism in relation to its handling of the banks. As a result of this, and in the wake of the crisis, the 2000 Act was significantly amended by the Financial Services Act 2012. This set out a new system of regulation with the aims of protecting and improving the United Kingdom economy. The Act created the Financial Conduct Authority and the Prudential Regulation Authority.

The purposes of the Financial Conduct Authority are to ensure markets work effectively to protect consumers, to maintain and ensure the integrity of the market, and to regulate financial services and ensure that the financial services market is competitive.

The Prudential Regulation Authority is responsible for the prudential supervision and regulation of banks, building societies, credit unions, insurers and investment firms. It works alongside the Financial Conduct Authority.

5.2 Financial Conduct Authority

The Financial Conduct Authority is an independent organisation. It is funded by the firms that it regulates. Whilst it is not a government organisation it is accountable to the Treasury and through the Treasury to Parliament. It is a company limited by guarantee. The members of the Financial Conduct Authority are appointed by the Treasury and the Secretary of State, whilst the Bank of England's Deputy Governor for Prudential Regulation is automatically a member of the governing body.

The Financial Conduct Authority's stated approach to regulation is that it has a proportionate approach, prioritising work on the areas and firms that pose a higher risk to the Authority's objectives.

The Financial Conduct Authority authorises firms or individuals in relation to regulated activity. It supervises firms and individuals and has enforcement powers to ensure that firms and individuals follow the rules and do not damage consumer interests or the integrity of and confidence in the financial markets.

The Financial Conduct Authority has a mandate to ban financial products that pose unacceptable risks to consumers. It has powers to ban misleading financial promotions and remove them immediately from the market.

Many of the processes of the Financial Services Authority are carried over to the Financial Conduct Authority. Thus, for example, the new Authority will take account of the applicant's integrity, financial soundness, honesty and record in relation to approving individuals.

The Financial Conduct Authority has stated it is committed to bringing more enforcement cases and tough penalties to bear and getting consumers compensation.

The Financial Conduct Authority is held accountable for its actions in various ways. These include:

(i) **The Board**: The Board is made up of executive and non-executive members
(ii) **Panels**: There are four independent panels – the Financial Services Practitioner Panel, the Smaller Businesses Practitioner Panel, the Financial Services Consumer Panel and the Markets Practitioner Panel which represent the interests of their constituencies to the Financial Conduct Authority.
(iii) **Complaints, Freedom of Information and Audits**: There is a formal process for dealing with complaints concerning the Financial Conduct Authority and this is subject to the Freedom of Information Act. The National Audit Office is the statutory authority for the Financial Conduct Authority.
(iv) **Investigations into regulatory failure**: The Financial Conduct Authority must investigate and report to the Treasury if there has been a significant regulatory failing.

5.3 Principles of Good Regulation

The Financial Conduct Authority has set out Principles of Good Regulation. These are:

(i) **Efficiency and Economy**: This refers to the need to use the resources in the most efficient and economical way. As part of this process the Treasury can commission 'value for money' reviews of the operation of the Financial Conduct Authority.
(ii) **Proportionality**: The Financial Conduct Authority must ensure that any burden or restriction that it imposes upon a person for any activity is proportionate to the benefits that are expected to accrue.
(iii) **Sustainable Growth**: The Financial Conduct Authority must ensure there is a desire for sustainable growth in the economy of the UK in the medium or long term.
(iv) **Consumer Responsibility**: Consumers should take responsibility for their decisions.
(v) **Senior Management Responsibility**: A firm's senior management is responsible for the firm's activities and for ensuring that its business complies with the relevant regulations. This principle helps to secure an adequate but proportionate level of regulatory intervention by holding senior management responsible for risk management and controls within firms.
(vi) **Recognising the differences in the businesses carried on by different regulated persons**: Where appropriate the Financial Conduct Authority exercises its functions in a way that recognises differences in the nature of and objectives of businesses carried on by different persons, subject to requirements imposed by or under the Financial Services and Markets Act.

(vii) **Openness and Disclosure**: The Financial Conduct Authority states that this reinforces market discipline and improves consumers' knowledge about financial matters.

(viii) **Transparency**: The Financial Conduct Authority is pledged to exercise its functions as transparently as possible, providing appropriate information on regulatory decisions and being open and accessible to the regulated community and the general public.

These, therefore, are the principles that the Financial Conduct Authority sets itself.

5.4 Principles for Business

In addition, the Financial Conduct Authority sets out principles for businesses. These are as follows:

(i) **Integrity**: A firm must conduct its business with integrity.

(ii) **Skill, Care and Diligence**: A firm must conduct its business with due skill, care and diligence.

(iii) **Management and Control**: A firm must take reasonable care to conduct its affairs responsibly and effectively with adequate risk management systems.

(iv) **Financial Prudence**: A firm must maintain adequate financial resources.

(v) **Market Conduct**: A firm must observe proper standards of conduct.

(vi) **Customer Interests**: Appropriate regard must be had to the interests of customers.

(vii) **Communications with Clients**: A firm must have proper regard to the information clients need and communicate information to them in a clear way.

(viii) **Conflicts of Interest**: Any conflicts of interest must be managed fairly.

(ix) **Customer Relationships of Trust**: A firm must ensure that customers are entitled to rely upon the firm's judgment.

(x) **Client Assets**: A firm must arrange adequate protection for clients' assets.

(xi) **Relations with Regulators**: A firm must deal with regulators in an open and cooperative way.

5.5 Regulated activities

The Financial Services and Markets Act 2000 provides that the Financial Conduct Authority controls 'regulated activities'. Regulated activities include dealing in securities, whether as principal or agent, arranging deals in securities which include shares, and advising on investments.

Regulated activities can only be carried on in the United Kingdom by authorised persons and exempt persons. Authorised persons would include firms who are given authority by the Financial Conduct Authority. Exempt persons would include, for example, solicitors and accountants providing a limited range of financial services which are incidental to the provision of professional services.

5.6 The London Stock Exchange

The Financial Conduct Authority is responsible for maintaining an official list of securities which are admitted to trading on at least one recognised investment exchange.

The United Kingdom is a global centre for issuing shares and bonds. The Financial Conduct Authority maintains this system and helps to ensure that investors can have confidence in the securities market. It does this through:

(i)   Monitoring market disclosures by issuers and others and through enforcing action in compliance with the Financial Conduct Authority Disclosure and Transparency rules.

(ii) Reviewing and approving prospectuses published by issuers and offerors of securities, and through enforcing the Financial Conduct Authority prospectus rules.

(iii) Operating the UK listing regime which requires listed issuers to comply with the Financial Conduct Authority listing rules. The Financial Conduct Authority maintains the Official List which lists recognised investment exchanges. The London Stock Exchange is the principal recognised investment exchange in the United Kingdom. It admits a listed company's securities to trade on its listed market. It also operates the Alternative Investment Market which provides a marketplace for shares of medium size or less mature companies. It also operates the Professional Securities Market. There are other UK-based recognised investment exchanges such as the London Metal Exchange, as well as recognised overseas exchanges.

5.7 The Financial Conduct Authority Handbook and Market Conduct

The Financial Conduct Authority Handbook includes several requirements about standards of market conduct which users of the UK markets are obliged to follow.

The handbook is made up of several sections:

(i)   High level standards
(ii)   Prudential standards
(iii) Business standards
(iv)   Regulatory processes
(v)   Redress
(vi)   Specialist sourcebooks
(vii) Listing, Prospectus and disclosure
(viii) Handbook guides
(ix)   Regulatory guides
(x)   Glossary

There is a designated Financial Conduct Authority Handbook website. This is www.handbook.fca.org.uk

Contact details for the Financial Conduct Authority are as follows:

The Financial Conduct Authority
25 The North Colonnade
Canary Wharf
London
E14 5HS
Company number: 01920623
Complaints line: 020 7066 9870

5.8 Regulation

There are various aspects relating to the public offer of shares which are regulated. These are the recognised investment exchanges themselves, the market for the sale and purchase of shares and the issue of securities, as well as the involvement of those buying and selling securities.

5.9 Prospectuses

In lay terms, a prospectus is a legal document that is used to describe company securities that are on offer to potential buyers. The prospectus will commonly set out for investors relevant information about the investments to include a description of the company's business, financial statements and forecasts, biographies of directors, and other material information.

The principle of the Prospectus Directive (2003/71/EC) is to provide that where there is a public offer of securities or a request for admission of securities to trading on a regulated market, then a prospectus must be published (Article 3 of the Directive). The prospectus in question must be approved by the appropriate authority in the issuer's state. As noted (sections 5.1 and 5.6), the Financial Conduct Authority is the competent authority in the United Kingdom (s 85(7) FSMA 2000).

In addition to satisfying the Prospectus Directive rules, there is an additional regulatory regime for admission to listing. The United Kingdom has always had significant, additional requirements for admission to the London Stock Exchange for example. These include:

(i)   Obligations and marketability of shares
(ii)   Provision of information
(iii)   Rules as to working capital

The Financial Conduct Authority made a full suite of changes to the listing rules in May 2014.

5.10 Content

The obligatory content of a prospectus is specified in the Directive. It must contain all information necessary to enable investors to make an informed assessment of the assets and liabilities, financial position, profits and losses, and prospects of the issuer of the securities and the rights attaching to them. This is provided for in FSMA s 87A (1)(b) and (2).

The prospectus should contain information about the issuer of the securities, about the securities themselves, and should also contain a summary.

A supplementary prospectus has to be forwarded to the Financial Conduct Authority and published where appropriate if there arises something of significance relating to the information in the prospectus before the offer of securities has closed, and after the approval of a prospectus (FSMA s 87G).

5.11 Exemptions

An offer of securities that is addressed to qualified investors may be made without the publication of a prospectus (FSMA 2000 s 86(1)(a)). Furthermore, there is no obligation to publish a prospectus if the offer is made to fewer than 100 persons who are not qualified investors (FSMA 2000 s 86(1)(b)).

Certain small issues are also exempt from the requirement for a prospectus, if the total consideration for the offer is less than 2.5 million euros, provided that this exemption can only be used once in every 12 months (FSMA ss 85(5)(a) and 87, and Sch 11A, para. 9). This is an EU limit across the whole of the EU and would not apply to each Member State separately.

Additionally, there is no obligation to publish an approved prospectus if the consideration cannot exceed 100,000 euros. Again, this exemption can only be used once in every 12 months (s 86(1)(e)).

Large issues of shares, where the minimum consideration paid by each investor is 50,000 euros, are also exempt from the requirement to publish a prospectus (s 86(1)(c) and (d)).

It is worth noting in the case of each of these exemptions, other than the one exempting the publication of a prospectus where the offer is solely to qualified investors, that although publication of a prospectus is not needed in relation to the offer, if the securities are to be admitted to trading on a regulated market then a prospectus will normally be required.

5.12 Powers of the Financial Conduct Authority

The Financial Conduct Authority has powers under ss 87K and 87L to suspend or prevent a public issue of securities, or an application for trading of securities on a regulated market, if it discovers or reasonably suspects that there has been a contravention of the relevant provisions of Part VI of the Act or of prospectus rules, or of other obligations under the Prospectus Directive.

It may also impose financial penalties (s 91(1)(A)) or issue a public statement of censure (s 91(3)) for contravention of the Act or of the prospectus rules or of any provision in the Prospectus Directive. The following persons may be penalised:

(i) an issuer of transferable securities;
(ii) a person offering transferable securities to the public or seeking their admission to trading on a regulated market;

(iii)   an applicant for the approval of a prospectus;

(iv)   a person upon whom an obligation has been imposed under s 87K or s 87L;

(v)   any other person to whom the Prospectus Directive applies; and

(vi)   a director of any of the above knowingly concerned in the contravention that is in issue (s 91(2)).

5.13   Remedies for misleading prospectuses

5.13.1   Common law and statute – misrepresentation in contract

If a claimant has been induced to purchase securities on the strength of a misrepresentation in the listing particulars, he may have a remedy for the misrepresentation.

The claimant may seek rescission of the contract against the company. He must demonstrate a material misrepresentation of fact which has induced him to enter into the contract. Non-disclosure of a relevant fact may amount to a misrepresentation if it can be demonstrated that the omission renders the listing particulars misleading. Thus, in *Coles v White City (Manchester) Greyhound Association Ltd* (1929) 45 TLR 230, a prospectus described land as eminently suitable for greyhound racing. The prospectus failed to state that the local authority would have to give planning permission for the erection of stands for viewing and for greyhound kennels.

A shareholder sought rescission on the basis of the omission. It was held that the description was misleading in that the omission distorted what was actually stated.

Rescission is not dependent upon whether the person making the statement or omission is fraudulent or not and is available for fraudulent, negligent and innocent representations. However, the court has a discretion to refuse to order rescission and to award damages in lieu of rescission if it considers this appropriate (s 2(2) of the Misrepresentation Act 1967).

The right to rescission is lost in certain circumstances. Thus, a claimant may not rescind a contract if it is not possible to restore the parties to their pre-contractual position. This is sometimes stated as *restitutio in integrum impossibile est*. This bar to rescission will apply if the company is in liquidation; see *Oakes v Turquand* (1867) LR 2 HL 325. Another bar to rescission is if the claimant affirms the contract after discovering the misrepresentation. This may occur, for example, if the claimant votes at a meeting of members after discovering the misrepresentation; see *Sharpley v Louth and East Coast Railway Company* (1876) 2 ChD 663. In a similar way, if the claimant fails to set the contract aside promptly after discovering the misrepresentation, he will not be able to rescind.

In addition to the remedy of rescission, damages may also be awarded under s 2(2) of the Misrepresentation Act 1967, unless the misrepresentor can prove he had reasonable grounds to believe and did believe up to the time the contract was made that the facts represented were true. This section only applies if the misrepresentor is a party to the contract. This, therefore, can only apply against the company itself. Additionally, in contract, it is sometimes the case that a misrepresentation is incorporated into the resulting contract. Where this occurs, it will then be open to the injured party to frame a claim for contractual damages.

5.13.2 Common law and statute – damages in the tort of deceit

Damages may be claimed against a person who has accepted responsibility for a part of the listing particulars or authorised the contents of part or all of the listing particulars for a statement of fact which that person made knowing it to be false or reckless as to its truth. In *Derry v Peek* (1889) 14 App Cas 337, a prospectus was issued by a tramway company. The company was empowered to use horse-drawn trams in Plymouth. The prospectus stated that the company was empowered to use steam-driven vehicles. In fact, this was not the case though application had been made to the Board of Trade for permission to do so. Permission was not granted and an investor who had relied on the prospectus brought an action for damages for fraud against the directors. It was held that since the directors honestly believed the statement to be true, they were not liable in fraud.

Although an action in the tort of deceit may be brought against the company itself as well as against the directors, since an action may be brought under s 2(1) of the Misrepresentation Act 1967, where the company itself has made the misrepresentation, the action in tort is not relevant in such a situation. An exception to this, however, is where a later market purchaser brings an action in tort. Generally, actions will be brought by those who have subscribed for shares or debentures directly from the company. However, if a later purchaser can show that the prospectus was directed to encouraging purchases on the open market, he may be able to sustain an action in tort where clearly no action in contract would be possible. Generally, the view used to be taken that prospectuses were intended to encourage subscription for shares rather than purchases on the stock market; see, for example, *Peek v Gurney* (1873) LR 6 HL 377. However, in *Possfund Custodian Trustees Ltd v Diamond* [1996] 1 WLR 1351, Lightman J refused to strike out a claim that the court should recognise that prospectuses are intended to encourage purchases in the aftermarket (here, on the USM (Unlisted Securities Market) – the old second market).

5.13.3 Common law and statute – damages in the tort of negligent misstatement

An action will lie in damages against a person who makes a negligent statement which causes economic loss provided there is a relationship of sufficient proximity. The range of potential defendants certainly includes the company and its directors and experts who have consented to the contents of part or all of the prospectus.

The case establishing potential liability in this area is *Hedley Byrne & Co Ltd v Heller & Partners Ltd* [1964] AC 465. As in the case of the tort of deceit, it is possible that the range of potential claimants in the tort of negligent misstatement will include not just those who have subscribed for shares or debentures direct from the company but also those who have purchased securities on the open market. In such a situation, the tortious remedy may be relevant against the company but otherwise, where a contractual relationship exists, s 2(1) of the Misrepresentation Act 1967 is the appropriate remedy. However, it seems that the scope of liability in the tort of negligent misstatement is limited. The House of Lords in *Caparo Industries plc v Dickman* [1990] 2 AC 605 held that no duty of care was owed to potential investors in relation to the auditing of the company's accounts. Lord Bridge of Harwich said:

> To hold the maker of the statement to be under a duty of care in respect of the accuracy of the statement to all and sundry for any purpose for which they may choose to rely on it is not only to subject him, in the classic words of Cardozo CJ to 'liability in an indeterminate amount for an indeterminate time to an indeterminate class' [*Ultramares Corporation v Touche* (1931) 174 NE 441], it is also to confer on the world at large a quite unwarranted entitlement to appropriate for their own purposes the benefit of the expert knowledge or professional expertise attributed to the maker of the statement.

This principle was applied in *Al-Nakib Investments (Jersey) Ltd v Longcroft* [1990] BCC 5187, where there was a claim against the directors of a company in relation to a share purchase on the stock market following an allegedly misleading prospectus. The court considered that the prospectus was intended to encourage subscriptions for shares so that there was no remedy for purchasers on the open market. There seems to be no settled rule in this area. *Caparo plc v Dickman* (1990) and *Al-Nakib Investments Ltd v Longcroft* [1990] 3 All ER 321 lean in favour of a restrictive approach while the statutory provisions in the Financial Services and Markets Act 2000 and the decision in *Possfund Custodian Trustees Ltd v Diamond* (1996) lean in favour of a more inclusive view of the purposes of a prospectus.

5.13.4 Financial Services and Markets Act 2000 – remedies

Section 90 provides that any person responsible for a prospectus (s 86) is liable to pay compensation to a person who has (a) acquired securities to which the particulars apply; and (b) suffered loss in respect of them as a result of:

(i)   any untrue or misleading statement in the particulars; or
(ii) the omission from the particulars of any matter required to be included by s 80 or s 81. (The general duty of disclosure and the duty to supplement it with details of any significant new matter or change.)

Compensation may be payable by:

(i)   the issuer of the shares;
(ii) every director of the issuer, unless published without the director's knowledge or consent, as where on becoming aware of its publication the director gives reasonable public notice that it was published without his knowledge or consent;
(iii) every person named in the document as a director or as having agreed to become a director, provided this was done with the person's authorisation; and
(iv) every person who accepted and is stated in the document as accepting responsibility for the document or part of it, and every person who has authorised the contents of the document or any part of it. Where a person is responsible for only part of a document, liability can only arise in respect of that part.

5.13.4.1 Defences

Various defences are available:

1   **Reasonable belief**: If, after making reasonable enquiries the defendant reasonably believed that the statement in question was true and not misleading, or that the matter which was omitted was properly omitted. One of the following four circumstances must also be proved:

(i)   the defendant continued in that belief until the shares were acquired; or

(ii)   they were acquired before it was reasonably practicable to bring a correction to the attention of persons likely to acquire the shares in question; or

(iii)   before the shares were acquired, the defendant took all reasonable steps to secure that a correction was brought to the attention of persons likely to acquire the shares; or

(iv)   the shares were acquired after such a lapse of time that the defendant ought, in the circumstances, to be reasonably excused, provided that the defendant continued to believe the statement or omission was proper until after dealings in the shares commenced.

(FMSA 2000, Sch 9, para 5 and Sch 10 para 1)

2   **Expert's statement**: If the defendant reasonably believed on reasonable grounds that the expert was competent to make the statement and had consented to its inclusion in the form and context in which it was included. One of the following four circumstances must also be proved:

(i)   that the defendant continued in that belief until the shares were acquired; or

(ii)   they were acquired before it was reasonably practicable to bring the fact that the expert was not competent or had not consented to the attention of persons likely to acquire the shares in question; or

(iii)   that before the shares were acquired, the defendant had taken all reasonable steps to secure that the fact of the non-competence or non-consent was brought to the attention of persons likely to acquire the shares in question; or

(iv)   the shares were acquired after such a lapse of time that the defendant ought, in the circumstances, to be reasonably excused, provided that the defendant continued to believe in the expert until after dealings in the shares commenced.

(FMSA 2000, Sch 9, para 5 and Sch 10 para 2)

3   **Reasonable steps to correct the defect**: If the defendant took reasonable steps to bring a correction or the fact of an expert's lack of competence or consent to the attention of potential investors, then this is a defence.

(FMSA 2000, Sch 10, paras 3 and 4)

4   **Official statements and documents**: It is a defence to show that the statement which caused the loss accurately and fairly reproduces a statement made by an official person or contained in an official document.

(FMSA 2000, Sch 10, para 5)

5 **Claimant's knowledge of the situation**: It is a defence to prove the person claiming compensation acquired the shares in question with knowledge that the statement was false or misleading, or that there was a material omission. (FMSA 2000, Sch 10 para 6)

5.14 Invitations to invest

Section 21 of the Financial Services and Markets Act 2000 provides that a person must not in the course of business communicate an invitation or inducement to engage in investment activity, unless that person is an authorised person under the Act or unless the content of the communication is approved by an authorised person. The section does not apply to communications originating outside the United Kingdom (s 21(3)). Where the section is contravened a criminal offence triable, either way, is committed by the person who makes the communication (s 25). On contravention, a person is guilty of an offence and liable:

(a) on summary conviction, to imprisonment for a term not exceeding six months or a fine not exceeding the statutory maximum, or both; or

(b) on conviction on indictment, to imprisonment for a term not exceeding two years or a fine, or both.

It is a defence for a person to demonstrate that:

(a) he believed on reasonable grounds that the content of the communication was prepared or approved under s 21 by an authorised person; or

(b) that he took all reasonable precautions and exercised all due diligence to avoid committing the offence.

The Financial Services and Markets Act 2000 (Financial Promotion) Order 2001 elaborates on the financial promotion restriction and exemptions from it (SI 2001/1335).

Article 19 of the Order provides that the financial promotion restriction does not apply to a communication that:

(a) is made only to recipients whom the person making the communication believes on reasonable grounds to be investment professionals; or

(b) may reasonably be regarded as directed only at such recipients.

The financial promotion restriction is not applicable to 'non-real time communications' or to 'solicited real time communications' made by a company to certain persons. A non-real time communication is a communication other than one made in the course of a personal visit, telephone conversation of other interactive dialogue (Article 7).

A real time communication is solicited where it is made in the course of a personal visit, telephone call or other interactive dialogue if the call, visit or dialogue (a) was initiated by the recipient of the communication, or (b) takes place in response to an express request from the recipient of the communication (Article 8).

In relation to non-real time communications or solicited real time communications, the restriction does not apply to communications by a company to creditors or members concerning its own investments or those of another undertaking in the same group (Article 43). Furthermore, the restriction does not apply to such communications made to a 'common interest group'. A common interest group is a group in relation to a company made up of persons who at the time the communication is made might reasonably be regarded as having an existing and common interest in each other and the company in:

(a) the affairs of the company; and
(b) what is done with the proceeds arising from any investment to which the communication relates (Article 52).

The financial promotion restriction does not apply to communications by a director or employee of a company speaking on a television or radio broadcast, or webcast (Article 20A).

The financial promotion restriction does not apply either to any non-real time communication or any solicited real time communication made by a supplier to a customer of his in relation to the sale of goods or supply of services or a related sale or supply (Article 61).

The financial promotion restriction does not apply to communications made between companies in the same group (Article 45).

The financial promotion restriction does not apply to one-off communications (Articles 28 and 28A).

The financial promotion restriction does not apply to communications to what are termed 'certified high network individuals' (Article 48). Such individuals must have a certificate signed by their accountant or employer certifying an annual income of a specified amount or the holding of net assets of a specified value.

The financial promotion restriction does not apply to the publication of a company's annual accounts and directors' report provided it does not contain any invitation or advice to underwrite, subscribe for, or otherwise acquire or dispose of the company's shares or debentures (Article 59).

The financial promotion restriction does not apply to publication in relation to listing particulars, prospectuses or supplementary versions of these (Articles 70 to 73).

The financial promotion restriction does not apply to communications in relation to participation in employee share schemes (Article 60). Furthermore, the restriction does not apply to communications for the purpose of selling a controlling interest in a company (Article 62), or in connection with the takeover of certain unlisted companies (Articles 63 to 66 and Schedule 4).

Summary

Financial Conduct Authority

The Financial Conduct Authority is an independent non-governmental organisation responsible for regulating the financial services industry in the United Kingdom under the terms of the Financial Services and Markets Act 2000 as amended by the

Financial Services Act 2012. The Prudential Regulation Authority created by the Financial Services Authority 2012 is responsible for the regulation of banks, insurers and investment firms, while the Financial Conduct Authority is responsible for promoting confidence in financial services and markets and the protection of consumers.

Issue of shares to the public

The Financial Services and Markets Act 2000 as amended by the Financial Services Act 2012 provides for the publication of a prospectus where shares are issued to the public. It enacts into the United Kingdom's law the provisions of the Prospectus Directive (Directive 2003/71/EC).

The Financial Conduct Authority is the appropriate regulator under the Act and is responsible for maintaining confidence in the financial system, promoting public awareness of the financial system, securing the appropriate degree of protection to consumers, and reducing the extent to which it is possible for financial services businesses to be used in connection with financial crime.

Recognised investment exchanges, which include the London Stock Exchange, are recognised by the Financial Conduct Authority for the purposes of transactions in securities.

Content of prospectuses

Prospectuses should contain information to enable investors to make an informed assessment of the assets and liabilities, financial position, profits and losses, and prospects of the issuer of the securities and the rights attaching to them. This information must be presented in a clear and comprehensible format.

There are certain exemptions from the requirement to publish prospectuses, such as if the only potential investors are qualified investors, broadly speaking those who are steeped in trading in securities. Certain small and large issues are also exempted from the requirements of publication, though in these cases a prospectus is still needed if the securities are to be traded on a recognised investment exchange.

Remedies

Remedies are available under statute and at common law in relation to misleading prospectuses.

Self-test questions

5.1   What legislation applies in relation to public issues of shares?

5.2   What organisation has oversight of the issue of shares to the public?

5.3   What are the functions performed by the organisation charged with oversight of the issue of shares to the public?

5.4   What are the statutory objectives of the organisation charged with oversight of the issue of shares to the public?

5.5   Set out the principles of good regulation of the organisation charged with over-sight of the issue of shares to the public.

5.6   Who is regulated by the organisation charged with the oversight of the issue of shares to the public?

5.7   Describe the approach of the regulator to oversight of financial services.

5.8   What are the standards of market conduct which are required by users of the UK markets?

5.9   Describe the market operated by the London Stock Exchange.

5.10   What activities related to the public offer of shares are regulated?

5.11   How is the content and issue of prospectuses regulated?

5.12   What is the obligatory content of a prospectus?

5.13   What exemptions are there in relation to the regulation of prospectuses?

5.14   What are the powers of the organisation charged with responsibility in this area in relation to the public issue of securities?

5.15   Set out the various remedies for misleading prospectuses.

5.16   What constitutes an invitation to invest?

Further reading

A Alcock, 'Public Offers in the UK: The New Regime' (1996) 17 Co Law 262.
AC Page, 'Self-Regulation: The Constitutional Dimension' (1986) 49 MLR 141.
LS Sealy, 'The "Disclosure" Philosophy and Company Law Reform' (1981) 2 Co Law 51.

Chapter 6

The company's constitution – some vital considerations

Chapter Contents

6.1 Introduction

The Companies Act (CA) 2006 makes a fundamental change to the company's constitution.

Henceforth the company will effectively have a single constitution. The articles of association will become the company's constitution. Formerly there were two components to the constitution; the memorandum of association (which covered matters like the company's name and its objects) and the articles of association.

The memorandum of association is now defined in s 8 of the Act. It is a much shorter document and is in prescribed form, simply stating that the subscribers wish to form a company and agree to become members of that company and take at least one share each.

The memorandum of association must be delivered to the Registrar, together with an application for registration, stating the company's proposed name, situate of the registered office, whether England and Wales, Wales, Scotland or Northern Ireland, whether the liability of the members of the company is to be limited and, if so, whether by shares or by guarantee, and whether the company is to be a private or public company (s 9 CA 2006).

If the company is to have a share capital there should also be submitted a statement of capital and initial shareholdings (s 10 CA 2006).

If the company is a company limited by guarantee there should be a statement of guarantee submitted (s 11 CA 2006).

Additionally, there should also be a statement of the company's proposed officers (s 12 CA 2006) delivered together with the application for registration.

The application must also contain a statement of the intended address of the company's registered office and a copy of any proposed articles of association (s 9(5) CA 2006).

A statement of compliance is also required to be delivered to the Registrar stating that the requirements of the Act as to registration have been complied with (s 13 CA 2006).

The articles of association now form the company's constitution and those provisions of an existing company's memorandum that do not come within the ambit of a new-style memorandum (such as the objects of the company and the name of the company) will be treated as if they were provisions of the company's articles (s 28 CA 2006).

It is intended in this chapter to set out some of the fundamental considerations that will influence a company in drawing up its constitution. These clearly include the name of the company, the company's status (particularly whether it is public or private) and the company's objects. In relation to the company's objects a brief history of the development of objects clauses is set out to explain the context of the present law.

6.2 The name of the company

In general, those setting up a company are free to choose any name they wish. They are, however, constrained by certain rules.

6.2.1 Indications of type of company

A limited company must generally indicate this at the end of its name by the words 'Public Limited Company' or 'plc', or in the case of a Welsh company 'cwmni cyhoeddus cyfyngedig', or 'ccc', although this does not apply to community interest companies; see s 33(3) and (4) of the Companies (Audit, Investigations and Community Enterprise) Act 2004 (s 58 Companies Act 2006). If the company is a community interest company which is public, then the appropriate company names will end with 'Community Interest Public Limited Company', or 'Community Interest PLC', or 'Cwmni Buddiant Cymunedol Cyhoeddus Cyfyngedig' or 'Cwmni Buddiant CCC' (see section 1.2.6).

Private limited company names should end with 'Ltd', or in the case of Welsh companies with 'cyf' (s 59 CA 2006). Certain companies are exempt from this requirement.

A private company is exempt from s 59 if:

(a) it is a charity;
(b) it is exempted from the requirement of that section by regulations made by the Secretary of State; or
(c) it meets the conditions specified in s 61 (continuation of existing exemption for companies limited by shares), or s 62 (continuation of existing exemption for companies limited by guarantee).

Sections 61 and 62 provide for exemption if the company was previously exempt and did not include the word 'Limited' or any other permitted alternatives, and the objects of the company are the promotion of commerce, art, science, education, religion, charity or any profession, and anything incidental or conducive to any of those objects, and the company's articles require its income to be applied in promoting its objectives, prohibit the payment of dividends or return of capital to its members and require all the assets otherwise available to the members to be transferred on its winding up, either to a similar body or to another body, the objects of which are the promotion of charity and anything incidental or conducive thereto.

6.2.2 Permitted characters

Section 57 of the Companies Act 2006 provides that the Secretary of State may make provision by regulation:

(a) as to the letters or other characters, signs or symbols (including accents and other diacritical marks) and punctuation that may be used in the name of a company registered under the Act; and

(b) specifying a standard style or format for the name of the company for the purposes of registration.

The regulations may prohibit the use of specified characters, signs or symbols, when appearing in a specified position (in particular at the beginning of a name).

6.2.3 Prohibited and restricted use of names

Section 53 of the Companies Act 2006 prohibits the use of certain names. A name must not, in the opinion of the Secretary of State, be offensive or such that its use by the company would constitute an offence.

In *R v Registrar of Companies ex p Attorney General* [1991] BCLC 476, Lindi St Clair, a famous prostitute, formed a company to carry out the service of prostitution. She initially attempted to call the company 'Prostitutes Ltd', 'Hookers Ltd' and 'Lindi St Clair (French Lessons) Ltd'. All of these titles were rejected by the Registrar of Companies. Subsequently the company was registered as 'Lindi St Clair (Personal Services) Ltd' and this action was then brought to challenge the registration of the company since the company's purposes were unlawful. In the upshot, the company was struck off the register.

The practice of creating 'phoenix' companies with similar names to companies that have gone into liquidation is outlawed by s 216 of the Insolvency Act 1986. Contravention of the section leads to civil and criminal sanctions (see also section 2.2.1).

There are various statutes other than the Companies Act which also prohibit the use of certain names e.g. using a name that includes the words 'credit union' or any similar words unless the company is registered as a credit union (Credit Unions Act 1979) or misleadingly representing itself by using a name to give the impression that it is a building society without being registered as one (see Building Societies Act 1986).

6.2.4 Index of names

The name must not be the same as one already appearing on the index of names kept by the Registrar of Companies (s 66 CA 2006).

The Secretary of State may make provision by regulation supplementing the section. The regulations may make provision:

(a) as to the matters that are to be disregarded; and

(b) as to words, expressions, signs or symbols that are, or are not, to be regarded as the same, for the purposes of the section.

The regulations may provide:

(a) that registration by a name that would otherwise be prohibited under this section is permitted:

(i) in specified circumstances; or

(ii) with specified consent; and

(b)   that if those circumstances obtain or that consent is given at the time a company is registered by a name, a subsequent change of circumstances or withdrawal of consent does not affect the registration.

Section 67 provides that the Secretary of State may direct a company to change its name if it has been registered in a name that is the same as, or, in the opinion of the Secretary of State, too like:

(a)   a name appearing at the time of the registration in the Registrar's index of company names; or
(b)   a name that should have appeared in that index at that time.

Any such direction must be given within 12 months of the company's registration by the name in question and must specify the period within which the company is to change its name. Failure to comply with the direction constitutes an offence by the company and every officer of the company in default (s 68 CA 2006).

6.2.5 Specific permission required

The approval of the Secretary of State is required for a company to be registered under the Act by a name that would be likely to give the impression that the company is connected with:

(a)   Her Majesty's Government, any part of the Scottish Administration the Welsh Assembly Government or Her Majesty's Government in Northern Ireland;
(b)   a local authority; or
(c)   any public authority specified for the purposes of this section by regulations made by the Secretary of State (s 54 CA 2006).

Other sensitive words or expressions are covered by s 55 CA 2006. The approval of the Secretary of State is required for a company to be registered under the Act by a name that includes a word or expression for the time being specified in regulations made by the Secretary of State.

The Secretary of State may, by regulations made under either s 54 or s 55, require that in connection with an application for approval of the Secretary of State, the applicant must seek the view of a specified government department or other body (s 56 CA 2006).

6.2.6 Tort of passing off and company names adjudicators

The choice of name may also be limited by the possibility of an action being brought against the company for the tort of passing off. If the name chosen by the company is similar or the same as the name used by an existing business, then the proprietor of that business may bring an action to injunct the company from using the name and may also seek an account of profits. Thus, in *Ewing v Buttercup Margarine Co Ltd* [1917] 2 Ch 1, the claimant, who operated as a sole trader under the name of The Buttercup Dairy Company, sought to restrain the defendants from using the name

Buttercup Margarine Co Ltd. The action was successful. To succeed in an action for passing off, the claimant would have to show evidence of confusion and that he had suffered economic loss from this confusion. In *Salon Services Hairdressing Supplies Ltd v Direct Salon Services Ltd* (1988) SLT 414, there was no evidence of economic loss and therefore no injunction was applied.

In this case, the Scottish Court recalled interdicts on the basis that confusion and economic loss were unlikely to arise from a minor similarity between the names of the two companies. This was particularly the case since they traded in different areas and used different brand names for their products.

Note that the tort of passing off can also extend to the position whereby a company's name is being applied to goods by the defendants so that consumers may be led to believe that they are goods emanating from the company.

Provisions in the Companies Act 2006 allow for the first time for objections to a company's registered name where there is similarity to a name in which a person has goodwill.

A person (the applicant) can object to a company's registered name on the grounds:

(a) that it is the same as a name associated with the applicant in which he has goodwill; or
(b) that it is sufficiently similar to mislead by suggesting a connection between the company and the applicant (s 69).

The objection must be made by application to a company names adjudicator (see s 70). The respondents must then demonstrate if the ground specified in (a) or (b) above is established by the applicant that:

(a) the name was registered before the commencement of the activities on which the applicant relies to show goodwill; or
(b) that the company

    (i) is operating under the name; or
    (ii) is proposing to do so and has incurred substantial start-up costs in preparation; or
    (iii) was formerly operating under the name and is now dormant; or

(c) that the name was registered in the ordinary course of a company formation business and the company is available for sale to the applicant on the standard terms of that business; or
(d) that the name was adopted in good faith; or
(e) that the interests of the applicant are not adversely affected to any significant extent.

If none of these is shown, the objection shall be upheld. If one of the defences (a), (b) or (c) is established, the objection will still be upheld if it is shown that the main purpose of registering the name was to obtain money or a benefit from or the applicant or prevent him from registering the same name (s 69(5) CA 2006).

The Secretary of State shall appoint persons to be company names adjudicators (s 70 CA 2006), and one of the adjudicators shall be appointed chief adjudicator (s 70(4) CA 2006).

The Secretary of State may make procedural rules in relation to proceedings before a company names adjudicator (s 71 CA 2006).

The adjudicator may make an order requiring the respondent company to change its name, and requiring all the respondents to take such steps as are within their power to facilitate the making of that change, and not to cause or permit any steps to be taken calculated to result in another company being registered with a name that is an offending name.

The order must specify a date by which the respondent company's name is to be changed, and may be enforced as a court order (s 73 CA 2006).

An appeal lies from the adjudicator's decision to the court (s 74 CA 2006).

6.3 Change of name

Section 77 of the Companies Act 2006 provides that a company may change its name by special resolution or by any other means provided for by the company's articles. This is significant as the company's articles may provide, for example, that the company's name could be changed by a board resolution. Whether the change is by a special resolution, by a board resolution or by other means, the company must give notice to the Registrar (s 78).

A change of name may be made conditional upon the happening of an event, and on the happening of the event the company must then give notice to the Registrar (s 78(2) CA 2006).

When a new certificate of incorporation with the new name is issued, the change of name is effective (s 81).

In addition, the name of a company may be changed:

(a) by resolution of the directors under s 64 (change of name to comply with a direction of the Secretary of State where a company ceases to be entitled to exemption from using the word 'Limited' or permitted alternative); or
(b) by order under s 73 (the order of an adjudicator following objection to a company name) (see above section 6.2.6).

Mention has already been made of the Secretary of State's power to require a company with a name that is similar to an existing name to change its name (s 67) (section 6.2.4). In addition, the Secretary of State has the power, within five years of the registration of a company, where it appears that misleading information has been given for the purposes of registration of a particular name, or that an undertaking or assurance has been given for that purpose and has not been fulfilled, to direct the company to change its name (s 75 CA 2006).

Furthermore, if, in the opinion of the Secretary of State, the name by which a company is registered gives so misleading an indication of the nature of its activities as to be likely to cause harm to the public, the Secretary of State may direct the company to change its name. Such a direction must be complied with within a period of six weeks from the date of the direction, or such longer period as the Secretary of State may think fit to allow. There is no time limit in relation to exercise of this power (s 76 CA 2006).

In *Re Association of Certified Public Accountants* [1998] 1 WLR 164, Jacob J refused to set aside a direction issued by the Secretary of State for Trade and Industry who had directed the company to change its name. The Association of Certified Public Accountants had been set up to provide a professional association for accountants. Membership of the Association was chiefly drawn from people who did not have formal accountancy qualifications. The Secretary of State took the view that use of the word 'certified' indicated some type of formal qualification.

Jacob J agreed that the name was misleading and that since people would be likely to pay more to qualified accountants the name was likely to cause harm.

Companies may trade under names other than their corporate ones. Consent is still required, however, if a connection is suggested with HM Government or any local authority, as it is if the word is one of the sensitive ones set out in regulations.

6.4 Business names

Part 41 of the Companies Act 2006 deals with business names, i.e. names adopted by businesses and not just companies. This part of the Act is applicable additionally to any business carried on by a sole trader or by any business carried on as a partnership (see s 1192 CA 2006).

A person may not, without the approval of the Secretary of State, carry on business in the United Kingdom under a name that would be likely to give the impression that the business is connected with:

(a) Her Majesty's Government;
(b) any part of the Scottish administration;
(c) the Welsh Assembly Government;
(d) Her Majesty's Government in Northern Ireland;
(e) any local authority or public authority specified in regulations made by the Secretary of State (s 1193 CA 2006).

Any person who contravenes the section commits an offence.

Furthermore, a person may not, without the approval of the Secretary of State, carry on a business in the United Kingdom under a name that includes a word or expression for the time being specified in regulations made by the Secretary of State (s 1194 CA 2006). Once again, a person who contravenes this section commits an offence.

Section 1195 of the Companies Act 2006 provides that the Secretary of State may, under s 1193 or s 1194, require that in connection with an application for approval to the Secretary of State, the applicant should seek the view of a specified government department or other body. If such a requirement applies, the applicant must request the specified department or other body in writing to indicate whether it has any objections to the proposed name and, if so, why. He should submit to the

Secretary of State a statement that such a request has been made and a copy of any response that is received.

The Secretary of State, after giving approval, may withdraw the approval under s 1193 or s 1194 if it appears to the Secretary of State that there are overriding considerations of public policy that require such approval to be withdrawn.

Section 1197 covers names that are misleading and considered inappropriate because they are associated with a particular type of company or form of organisation, or are similar to words, expressions or other indications associated with a particular type of company or form of organisation.

A person who uses a name in contravention of regulations under this section once again commits an offence.

Section 1198 provides that a person must not carry on business in the United Kingdom under a name that gives so misleading an indication of the nature of the activities of the business as will be likely to cause harm to the public. Once again contravention of the section involves the commission of an offence.

Section 1199 provides that in relation to ss 1192–1196 (sensitive words or expressions), and s 1197 (inappropriate indication of company, type or legal form), where a person carries on a business under an existing name immediately before the coming into force of this part of the Act and the use of the name is lawful, then it will remain lawful. Where a business is transferred to a person on or after the date on which this part of the Act comes into force, and the business is carried on under the same name, then the name for a period of 12 months continues to be lawful, and after that time the transition of lawfulness will end.

Chapter 2 of Part 41 of the Act deals with disclosure that is required in the case of individuals or partnerships. The Chapter applies to an individual or partnership carrying on business in the United Kingdom under a business name (s 1200 CA 2006). The information that is required to be disclosed in the case of an individual is his name, and in the case of a partnership is the name of each member of the partnership (s 1201 CA 2006).

Section 1202 provides that the information is required on:

(a)   all business letters;
(b)   written orders for goods or services to be supplied to the business;
(c)   invoices and receipts issued in the course of the business; and
(d)   written demands for payment of debts arising in the course of the business (s 1202 CA 2006).

Section 1203 allows for exemption for certain large partnerships if they have more than 20 persons if the following conditions are met:

(a)   that the partnership maintains at its principal place of business a list of the names of all the partners;
(b)   no partner's name appears in the document except in the text or as a signatory;
(c)   the document states in legible characters the address of the partnership's principal place of business and that the list of the partners' names is open for inspection there (s 1203 CA 2006).

Additionally s 1204 requires that a person to whom this part of the Act applies must, at the business premises, display in a prominent position so that it may easily be read by customers or suppliers a notice containing the information required, i.e. the name of the sole trader or the names of all the partners.

Section 1205 provides for the criminal consequences of failure to make the required disclosure, and s 1206 provides for the civil consequences of failure to make disclosure. Section 1206 provides that in any legal proceedings brought by a person arising out of a contract made in the course of a business in respect of which, at the time the contract was made, there was a breach in failing to disclose in business documents or disclose at business premises the required information, then the proceedings shall be dismissed if the defendant shows:

(a) that he has a claim against the claimant arising out of the contract that he has been unable to pursue by reason of the latter's breach of the requirements of disclosure; or

(b) that he has suffered some financial loss in connection with the contract by reason of the claimant's breach of those requirements.

6.5 A company's registered office

A company must, at all times, have a registered office to which all communications and notices may be addressed (s 86 CA 2006).

A company may change the address of its registered office by giving notice to the Registrar (s 87 CA 2006).

The registered office is important in relation to inspection of registers, indexes and documents, and also as to the statement of the address of the registered office on company documents (s 87(3) CA 2006). This subsection provides that when a company has given notice to the Registrar of the change in the address of its registered office, it may act on the change from that date and, in any event, no later than 14 days from notice in relation to changing the place for inspection and changing the address of the registered office on relevant documents.

Welsh companies may register as such if their registered office is situated in Wales. This allows such companies to file documents in Welsh although translations into English must be made available.

The place where the company is incorporated i.e. registered is also important in fixing the domicile of the company and in particular the legal system which applies to it as well as the courts within that legal system which would have jurisdiction over the internal affairs of the company, where applicable. A company domiciled in one jurisdiction cannot change its domicile like a natural person unless by the passing of a private Act of Parliament.

6.6 Changes of status

6.6.1 Re-registration of a private company as a public company

Sections 90 to 96 of the Companies Act 2006 provide for re-registration of private companies as public companies.

A special resolution for re-registration must be passed (s 90(1)).

The company must have a share capital and the nominal value of the allotted share capital must be not less than the authorised minimum, and each of the company's allotted shares must be paid up at least as to one-quarter of the nominal value plus the whole of any premium. If the shares have been fully or partly paid up by an undertaking given by the person to do work or perform services, then that undertaking must have been performed or otherwise discharged, and if the shares have been allotted as fully or partly paid, otherwise than in cash, and the consideration includes an undertaking other than the one referred to above, then that undertaking must have been performed or discharged, or there must be a contract between the company and the other individual that the undertaking is to be performed within five years of the date of the special resolution (s 91 CA 2006).

Additionally, there must be a balance sheet prepared for no earlier than seven months before the date on which the application is delivered to the Registrar, an unqualified report by the auditors on the balance sheet, a written statement by the auditors that, in their opinion, at the balance sheet date the amount of the company's net assets was not less than the aggregate of the called-up share capital and undistributable reserves, and between the balance sheet date and the date on which the application for re-registration is delivered there must be no change in the company's financial position, resulting in the net assets becoming less than that aggregate (s 92 CA 2006).

If shares are allotted by the company in the period between the balance sheet date and the passing of the resolution otherwise than for cash, then any valuation required on property in return for non-cash consideration must be appropriately carried out (s 93).

The application for re-registration must be accompanied by a statement of the company's proposed name on re-registration (s 94) and of the company's proposed secretary (s 95), together with a copy of the special resolution, a copy of the company's amended articles as proposed, a copy of the balance sheet and other documents required under s 92, and if s 93 applies a copy of the valuation report. A statement of compliance should accompany the documents that the relevant requirements of this part of the Act have been complied with as to re-registration as a public company (ss 94–95).

On an application for re-registration as a public company, the Registrar, if satisfied that the company is entitled to be so re-registered, shall re-register it and issue a certificate of incorporation (s 96).

6.6.2 Re-registration of a public company as a private company

A public company may re-register as a private limited company if a special resolution is passed and if the conditions below are met (s 97 CA 2006).

The conditions are that first there must be no application for cancellation of the resolution. Section 98 provides that there may be an application to cancel a resolution by the holders of not less than 5 per cent in nominal value of the company's issued share capital or any class of the company's issued share capital, or if the company is not limited by shares by not less than 5 per cent of its members or by not less than 50 of the company's members. The members must be dissenting members, i.e. they must not have consented to or voted in favour of the resolution.

The application must be made within 28 days of the passing of the resolution. The court may then make an order cancelling or confirming the resolution.

The application should contain a statement of the company's proposed name on re-registration and a copy of the company's articles as proposed to be amended, together with a statement of compliance that the requirements of the Act have been complied with (s 100 CA 2006).

On application for re-registration the Registrar, if satisfied that the company is entitled to be re-registered, shall re-register it and issue a new certificate of incorporation (s 101 CA 2006).

6.6.3 Re-registration of a private limited company as unlimited

Section 102 of the Companies Act 2006 provides that a private limited company may re-register as an unlimited company if:

(a) all the members of the company have assented to its being so re-registered;
(b) an application is delivered for re-registration in accordance with s 103 of the Act;
(c) the company has not previously been re-registered as limited.

The application must be accompanied by a statement of the company's proposed name on re-registration, the prescribed form of assent authenticated by or on behalf of all of the members, and a copy of the proposed amended articles, together with a statement of compliance which must contain a statement by the directors that the persons by whom or on whose behalf the form of assent is authenticated constitute the whole membership of the company and, if members have not authenticated the forms themselves, that the directors have taken all reasonable steps to satisfy themselves that each person who acted as agent was lawfully empowered to do so (s 103 CA 2006). Section 104 provides for a certificate of incorporation to be issued on re-registration.

6.6.4 Unlimited private company becoming limited

Section 105 of the Companies Act 2006 provides that an unlimited company may re-register as a private limited company if a special resolution is passed for re-registration, and if the application is made with the accompanying documents provided by s 106 of the Act, provided that the company has not previously been re-registered as unlimited. The section provides that the application must be accompanied by a statement of the company's proposed name on re-registration, together with a copy of the resolution, and if the company is to be limited by guarantee, a statement of the guarantee, and, in either case, a copy of the proposed new articles of the company.

A statement of guarantee must state that each member undertakes that if the company is wound up while he is a member, or within a year of his ceasing to be a member, he will contribute to the assets of the company as may be required for:

(a)   payment of the debts and liabilities contracted before he ceases to be a member;
(b)   payment of the costs, charges and expenses of winding up; and
(c)   any adjustment of the rights of the contributories among themselves, not exceeding a specified amount (s 106(3)).

A statement of compliance must accompany the documents (s 106(4)) and a new certificate of incorporation on re-registration will then be issued if the documents are in order (s 107 of the Act).

A company that, on re-registration under s 107, already has allotted share capital must, within 15 days after the re-registration, deliver a statement of capital to the Registrar setting out the number of shares of the company, the aggregate nominal value of the shares and for each class of shares:

(i)   prescribed particulars of the rights attached to the shares;
(ii)   the total number of shares of that class;
(iii)   the aggregate nominal value of shares of that class; and
(iv)   the amount paid up and the amount (if any) unpaid on each share (s 108).

Failure to comply with the section is an offence committed by the company and every officer of the company who is in default.

6.6.5 Re-registration of a public company as a private and unlimited company

Section 109 of the Act provides that a public company limited by shares may be re-registered as an unlimited private company with a share capital if:

(a)   all the members agree;
(b)   an application for re-registration is made in accordance with s 110 of the Companies Act 2006; and
(c)   the company has not previously been re-registered as limited or unlimited.

The application must contain a statement of the company's proposed name on re-registration and must be accompanied by the prescribed form of assent by or on behalf of all the members, and a copy of the company's proposed amended articles.

The statement of compliance made with the application must contain a statement by the directors that:

(a)   the persons by or on whose behalf the form of assent is authenticated constitute the whole membership of the company; and
(b)   if it is authenticated by any agents that the directors have taken reasonable steps to satisfy themselves that they are lawfully empowered to act on behalf of the people they are purporting to act for.

Section 111 provides for the issue of a certificate of incorporation on re-registration.

6.7 Objects of the company

A company henceforth will have unrestricted objects unless the company's articles specifically restrict its objects (s 31). Therefore a company will be able to do anything that is lawful except to the extent that its articles state otherwise. Many companies will, of course, wish to have restricted objects and those companies that already have restricted objects clauses may continue with them.

What was previously the memorandum of the company would have contained a statement of the company's objects. Historically, this statement of objects was envisaged as a short, crisp statement of what the company was set up to do. It will be seen that this turned out to be extremely wide of what occurred in practice.

The Registrar of Companies does not exercise any supervisory role in relation to a company's objects except to ensure that those objects are legal. Mention has already been made of *R v Registrar of Companies ex p Attorney General* (1991) (see section 6.2.3). Registration of the company is not, however, conclusive evidence of the fact that its objects are legal – indeed the legality of its objects may be questioned: see *Bowman v Secular Society Ltd* [1917] AC 406.

However, the statement of a company's objects is important for other reasons. A company may be restrained from doing something which is outside the scope of its objects clause. Thus, in *Simpson v Westminster Palace Hotel Co* (1860) 8 HL Cas 712, a shareholder sought to restrain the hotel company from letting out rooms as office space. In the event, it was held that this was not ultra vires or beyond the company's objects but it was held that had it been so an injunction could have been issued. In *Stephens v Mysore Reefs (Kangundy) Mining Co Ltd* [1902] 1 Ch 745, a gold-mining company that was set up to mine in India was restrained from mining for gold in West Africa as this was beyond its objects clause (see now s 40(4) CA 2006).

A second reason why a company's statement of objects is important is that if the substratum of the company (its *raison d'être*) is destroyed, then a petitioner may apply to wind the company up on the just and equitable ground under s 122(1)(g) of the Insolvency Act 1986 (see section 15.6.2). Thus, in *Re German Date Coffee Company* (1882) 20 ChD 169, a company was set up to work a German patent to manufacture coffee from dates. The German patent was not granted. The company did, however, obtain a Swedish patent. A petition brought by two shareholders to wind the company up on the grounds that its objects had failed was successful despite the fact that some shareholders wished to continue with the company's activities in Sweden. Such petitions are a rarity.

An important area in relation to a company's objects clause is the question of to what extent a contract beyond the capacity of the company is enforceable, either against the company or by the company. It was formerly the case that such contracts were void at common law. Thus, in *Ashbury Railway Carriage & Iron Co Ltd v Riche* (1875) LR 7 HL 653, the company's objects were stated to be making, selling and hiring railway carriages. The company entered into a contract to build a railway in Belgium. The contract was approved by the shareholders at a general meeting of the company. It was held that the contract was ultra vires the company and that it made no difference that the shareholders had affirmed the contract as it was void *ab initio*. The company was thus able to avoid the contract and was not liable for damages to the other party to the agreement. The validity of ultra vires contracts has been altered dramatically by statute, as will be demonstrated below.

6.8 Drafting the objects clause

Although not as crucial as formerly when ultra vires contracts were void, the drafting of a company's objects clause is still clearly important where companies elect to have objects clauses. The consequences of a company engaging in activities outside of its objects clause have just been examined. The history of objects clauses and their interpretation is largely a history of conflict between the judiciary on the one hand, which wished to confine objects clauses to short crisp statements of the company's activities, and entrepreneurs on the other hand, who wished to provide companies with as much latitude as possible in their activities. In *Re Crown Bank* (1890) 44 ChD 634, North J held that a company's *intra vires* activities were limited to its main economic activity and that other matters stated in the company's objects clause could only exist in relation to that main economic activity. The company had been formed to carry on the business of banking. It was a country bank with an office in London. Later it ceased to do banking and carried on the business of land speculation in London and was also engaged in setting up a foreign business and investing in shares and securities. The objects of the company were drawn in very wide terms. North J said the objects were 'so wide that it might be said to warrant the company in giving up banking business and embarking in a business with the object of establishing a line of balloons between the earth and moon'. He allowed a petition from a shareholder to wind the company up.

The effect of this decision was at issue in *Cotman v Brougham* [1918] AC 514. In this case, the House of Lords had to consider the objects clause of Essequibo Rubber & Tobacco Estates Ltd. The objects clause enabled the company to carry on virtually every type of activity. In the Court of Appeal, Lord Cozens-Hardy MR had said: 'Now we are familiar with an enumeration of objects which extends the full length of the alphabet, and sometimes beyond it, so that you get sub-clauses (aa) and (bb) after you have exhausted all the other letters.' The last subclause of the objects clause in this case provided that every subclause should be construed as a substantive object of the company and that none of the sub-clauses should be deemed to be subsidiary or auxiliary to the principal object. At issue was the matter of underwriting certain shares in an oil company. Applying the principle in *Re Crown Bank*, underwriting could only exist as an *intra vires* business in relation to rubber and tobacco. However, the statement in the company's objects clause was held to be valid, with the result that the activity was held to be *intra vires*. The House of Lords thus reluctantly held the provision in the memorandum to be valid.

Another drafting device used to extend the scope of a company's permitted activities was at issue in *Bell Houses Ltd v City Wall Properties Ltd* [1966] 2 QB 656. The company was engaged in acquiring land and building houses. A subclause of the objects clause permitted the company to carry on any other trade or business whatsoever which can, in the opinion of the board of directors be advantageously carried on by the company in connection with or as ancillary to any of the above businesses or the general business of the company.

The claimant company had introduced a financier to the defendant company for an agreed fee. In this case, the claimant company was suing for this fee. The defendants meanwhile alleged that the contract was ultra vires as the claimants were in the business of developing property, not helping others to do so. At first instance, the action of the claimants for their fee was dismissed on the ground that the contract was ultra vires. The claimants appealed to the Court of Appeal. The appeal was successful. It was held that the objects clause permitted the directors to carry on any business which they considered could be advantageously carried on with the main business. It is, however, worth stressing that this decision of itself did not permit a company to register an objects clause where the directors could simply decide that some other activity is advantageous and profitable. This is because there are limiting words in the subclause, namely 'in connection with or as ancillary to'. Therefore, there had to be some nexus between the new business and the company's principal business.

The interpretation of an objects clause was also in issue in *Re New Finance and Mortgage Company Limited (in liquidation)* [1975] Ch 420. The objects clause of this company provided that the company could act 'as financiers, capitalists, concessionaires, bankers, commercial agents, mortgage brokers, financial agents and advisers, exporters and importers of goods and merchandise of all kinds, and merchants generally'. The company in fact ran two garages and garage shops. The company went into voluntary liquidation and Total Oil (Great Britain) Ltd sought to prove in the liquidation in relation to the sale of motor oil to the company. The liquidator rejected the proof as he contended that the purchase of the oil was ultra vires. The court held that the words 'and merchants generally' were broad enough to cover all types of commercial transactions and that therefore the purchase of the motor oil was *intra vires*.

The impresario, Sir David Frost, has also indirectly contributed to the law in this area. In *Newstead (Inspector of Taxes) v Frost* [1980] 1 WLR 135, the objects clause of a company that authorised it to carry on and execute all kinds of financial, commercial, trading or other operations was held to be valid. Some doubts were expressed on this by Viscount Dilhorne in the House of Lords but the objects clause was nevertheless upheld. At issue was the validity of a tax savings scheme entered into by David Frost with the company. The case is analysed by Pettet in 'Unlimited Objects Clauses' [1981] 97 LQR 15.

The combined effect of the jurisprudence of these various cases is to indicate that by ingenious drafting it was possible to give a company an extremely wide capacity within which to act. Such decisions inevitably led to a questioning of the law in this area and prompted reform. This will be examined below.

As noted above, unless a company's articles specifically restrict the objects of the company, its objects are unrestricted (s 31(1) CA 2006).

Where a company amends its articles to add, remove or alter a statement of the company's objects, it must give notice to the Registrar, and the Registrar on notice will register the amendment, and once entered on the register the amendment is effective (s 31(2) CA 2006).

6.9 *Ultra vires* contracts and common law

It has already been noted that, at common law, contracts that were outside of a company's objects clause were ultra vires and void. Such contracts could not be enforced by the company or against the company: see *Ashbury Railway Carriage & Iron Co Ltd v Riche* (1875). It made no difference whether the person dealing with the company knew what the company's objects were or not.

The whole doctrine of ultra vires rested on the principle of constructive notice, the rule in *Ernest v Nichols* (1857) 6 HL Cas 401, whereby a person dealing with a company was deemed to know what was in its constitution. A person dealing with a company was, however, entitled to assume that where an activity could have been executed in an ultra vires or an *intra vires* way it would be executed in an *intra vires* way. Thus, in *Re David Payne & Co Ltd* [1904] 2 Ch 608, where a company borrowed money that was in fact applied to its ultra vires business, the lender of the money was entitled to sue on the contract as he was entitled to assume that the loan was to be used for *intra vires* activities.

This did not help the outsider if he actually knew the purpose of the loan, even though he might not have realised it was ultra vires. The combination of actual knowledge of the activity and constructive notice of its ultra vires nature would be fatal. Thus, in *Re Introductions Ltd* [1970] Ch 199, where the company went into the ultra vires business of pig breeding, the lender of money, knowing that the purpose of the loan was for pig breeding, was unable to enforce the loan (nor could the lender rely upon a substantive provision permitting the company to borrow contained in the objects clause, as the court held that borrowing of itself could not stand as a substantive separate object of a company). In *Re Jon Beauforte (London) Ltd* [1953] Ch 131, a supplier provided a company with coke. In fact, the coke was used for the ultra vires activity of manufacturing veneered panels. The *intra vires* business was stated in the company's objects clause inter alia as costumiers, gown, robe, dress and mantle makers. At common law, the supplier had constructive notice of the objects clause. The order for the coke was placed on notepaper that showed that the company was in the business of manufacturing veneer panels. The court held that this combination of actual notice (by virtue of the notepaper) and constructive notice was fatal to the supplier's claim.

The whole area of ultra vires contracts and unauthorised acts of directors (an area that will be examined below) came up for consideration in *Rolled Steel Products (Holdings) Ltd v British Steel Corporation* [1986] Ch 246. The state of the law could scarcely be said to be satisfactory before the decision in *Rolled Steel Products*. The decision in this case further adds to the mosaic of rules in relation to ultra vires acts of a company and unauthorised acts of directors.

Rolled Steel Products owed money to S Ltd. One of the directors of Rolled Steel Products (S) was also a director of S Ltd. S Ltd owed money to Colvilles Ltd, which was a subsidiary of British Steel Corporation. This debt was guaranteed personally by S, the director of Rolled Steel Products and S Ltd. Colvilles believed that S and S Ltd would have insufficient assets to pay back their debt. They therefore proposed that they would lend money to Rolled Steel Products, who would use this money to pay off S Ltd, who could then pay part of the debt owed to Colvilles and that Rolled Steel Products would guarantee payment of the remainder of the debt, creating a debenture to secure the debt.

Rolled Steel Products had a provision in its constitution permitting it to give guarantees and security. The board resolution passed by Rolled Steel Products to grant the guarantee was only quorate by virtue of S's presence. S should have declared an interest and should not have counted in the quorum. The meeting was therefore insufficient for these purposes.

At first instance, Vinelott J held that the guarantee and the debenture were void as they were for purposes other than those authorised by the constitution. This reasoning is consistent with the reasoning in *Re Introductions Ltd*.

On appeal, however, the Court of Appeal held that since the company had the power in its constitution to give guarantees and to provide security, the company had contractual capacity to make the guarantee and debenture and that therefore the acts were not ultra vires the company. This clearly casts doubt on the decision in *Re Introductions Ltd* although it was not overruled.

The Court of Appeal went on to say, however, that the directors were acting beyond their powers in providing a guarantee and security for purposes other than those authorised by the constitution and since the defendant knew of this lack of authority, they could acquire no rights under the guarantee or the debenture.

It is to be noted that, although the decision in *Rolled Steel Products* was made in 1985, the relevant facts arose in 1969 and, therefore, were unaffected by the first statutory intervention in this area under the European Communities Act 1972.

The whole issue of judicial control of objects clauses and ultra vires activity is considered by Rajak in 'Judicial Control: Corporations and the Decline of Ultra Vires' (1995) CLR 9, where Rajak notes that the high-water mark of the doctrine of ultra vires was in the 1870s, and that by the end of the 1980s it had largely ceased to exist in any meaningful way.

The somewhat confused and arbitrary decisions in relation to what contracts were enforceable and what contracts were not, together with the decisions on the interpretation of objects clauses, prompted the government to consider statutory reform of the ultra vires rule and led to the commissioning of the Prentice Report, which is considered below. In the meantime, however, British membership of the European Communities had necessitated reform of British company law in line with the first directive on EC company law which had been passed in 1968 (68/151).

6.10 Section 9(1) of the European Communities Act 1972

Article 9 of the first EC directive on company law provides as follows:

(i)   Acts done by the organs of the company shall be binding upon it even if those acts are not within the objects of the company, unless such acts exceed the powers that the law confers or allows to be conferred on those organs.

However, Member States may provide that the company shall not be bound where such acts are outside the objects of the company, if it proves that the third party knew the act was outside those objects or could not in view of the circumstances have been unaware of it; disclosure of the statute shall not of itself be sufficient proof thereof.

(ii) The limits on the powers of the organs of the company, arising under the statutes from a decision of the competent organ, may never be relied on as against third parties, even if they have been disclosed.

Section 9(1) of the European Communities Act (ECA), passed on the UK becoming a member of what is now the European Union, accordingly provided that

> in favour of a person dealing with a company in good faith any transaction decided on by the directors shall be deemed to be one which it is within the capacity of the company to enter into and the power of the directors to bind the company shall be deemed to be free of any limitation under the memorandum or articles of association, and a party to a transaction so decided on shall not be bound to enquire as to the capacity of the company to enter into it, or as to any such limitation on the power of the directors, and shall be presumed to have acted in good faith unless the contrary is proved.

Several points should be noted in relation to s 9(1) of the ECA 1972 (later re-enacted as s 35 of the Companies Act 1985) and what is now s 40 CA 2006. These are as follows:

(a) The provision only operated in favour of a person dealing with the company. Thus, the company itself could not take advantage of the section to enforce an ultra vires contract.

(b) The section only operated where the person dealing with the company was acting in good faith. The section failed to contain a definition of good faith but, as is stated, there is a presumption of good faith that stands unless the contrary is proved. In *Barclays Bank Ltd v TOSG Trust Fund Ltd* [1984] BCLC 1, Nourse J stated *obiter* that a person acts in good faith if he acts genuinely and honestly in the circumstances of the case and that it is not necessary to show that he acted reasonably to demonstrate that he acted in good faith. In *Wrexham Association Football Club Ltd v Crucialmove Ltd* [2006] NPC 30, it was held that a contractor who did not deal with the board was required to check the authority of the person purporting to act for the company where circumstances suggested that enquiry should be made.

Guterman and Hamilton, who were property developers, planned to relocate Wrexham Football Club to another ground and redevelop the Racecourse Ground for commercial/retail use.

Control of the club was obtained by one of Hamilton's companies. Negotiations to buy the freehold of the stadium from the brewery that owned it were then opened. Guterman, who was a director and chairman of the club, dealt with the purchase and this was completed with funding from Crucialmove and other of Hamilton's companies.

Later the club transferred the freehold to Crucialmove, who held it on trust for Hamilton.

The trial judge in the High Court granted a declaration to the administrators of the club that the club had been wrongfully deprived of the right to acquire the ground for itself. The Court held that as a director, Guterman owed duties to the club not to profit from his position and to avoid a conflict with personal interests. It was further held that Hamilton could not hold the club to the deal as he was aware of Guterman's conflict of interest and the fact that there was no proper authorisation for his actions from the Board.

This decision was upheld by the Court of Appeal.

(c) The transaction had to be decided on by the directors. There was no guidance given as to how this was to be determined but it seems from the decision in *International Sales and Agencies v Marcus* [1982] 3 All ER 551 that, provided a chain of delegation can be traced back to the board of directors, this was sufficient for satisfying the condition in the section.

The claimant company was suing to recover £30,000. This sum of money had been paid to the defendants under the instruction of one Munsey who was the sole effective director of the claimants, the defendants having made a loan of £30,000 to the majority shareholder of the claimant company, Mr Fancy.

The court took the view that the dealings were within the phrase 'decided on by the directors' since Mr Munsey was the sole effective director of the claimant company.

6.11 The Prentice Report and the Companies Act 1989

In the light of the obvious anomalies in the law and the ease with which companies could avoid falling into the ultra vires trap, the government asked Dr Dan Prentice of Oxford University to investigate the area of objects clauses and ultra vires with a view to the possible abolition of the ultra vires doctrine and recommending any necessary safeguards for investors and creditors.

The report recommended the abolition of the doctrine with few provisos, although the resulting Companies Act 1989 provisions did not go as far as some of the more radical recommendations of the Prentice Report.

The Companies Act 1989 did provide for alteration of objects clauses in any circumstances by special resolution and for the adoption of a general objects clause permitting a company to operate as a general commercial company. As has been noted, these provisions have now been overtaken by s 31 CA 2006 providing that companies have unrestricted capacity unless they adopt restricted objects clauses. A provision relating to objects contained in the company's articles is now alterable by special resolution in a similar way to other provisions in a company's articles.

6.12 A company's capacity under the Companies Act 2006

The general thrust of the provisions contained in the Companies Act 1985, as amended by the Companies Act 1989, are retained in the Companies Act 2006.

Section 39 of the Companies Act 2006 provides that the validity of an act done by a company should not be called into question on the ground of lack of capacity by reason of anything in the company's constitution.

This section is therefore wider than merely encompassing provisions relating to the company's objects. In *Re Cleveland Trust* [1991] BCLC 424, the constitution restricted the payment of dividends. The restriction, despite being outside of the objects clause, would be caught by s 39.

Section 40 of the 2006 Act provides that in favour of a person dealing with a company in good faith, the power of the directors to bind the company, or authorise others to do so, is deemed to be free of any limitation under the company's constitution.

A person deals with a company if he is a party to any transaction or other act to which the company is a party. A person dealing with a company is not bound to enquire as to any limitation on the powers of the directors to bind the company or authorise others to do so and is presumed to have acted in good faith unless the contrary is proved, and is not to be regarded as acting in bad faith by reason only of his knowing that an act is beyond the powers of the directors under the company's constitution (s 40(1), (2), (3)).

The section does not, however, affect any right of a member to restrain the company from doing something that is beyond the power of the directors, but no such proceedings lie in respect of an act to be done in fulfilment of a legal obligation arising from a previous act of the company (s 40(4)) (see section 15.2.1).

The section does not affect any liability incurred by the directors or any other person by reason of the directors exceeding their powers (s 40(5)).

6.13 Transactions involving directors or their associates – Companies Act 2006

Section 41 provides that where a company enters into a transaction and the parties to the transaction include:

(i) a director of the company or its holding company, or
(ii) a person connected with any such director

the transaction is voidable at the instance of the company.

Whether or not the contract is voided, any director of the company or of its holding company, or a person connected with any such director, and any director of the company who authorised the transaction, is liable to account to the company for any gain he has made directly or indirectly from the transaction, and to indemnify the company for any loss or damage resulting from the transaction.

However, the transaction ceases to be voidable if:

(a) restitution of any money or other asset which was the subject of the transaction is no longer possible; or
(b) the company is indemnified for any loss or damage resulting from the transaction; or
(c) rights acquired bona fide for value without notice of the directors exceeding their powers by a person who is not a party to the transaction would be affected by the avoidance of the transaction; or
(d) the transaction is affirmed by the company.

It should be noted that transaction in this context includes any act (s 41 CA 2006).

6.14 Directors' power to bind the company – Companies Act 2006

Where a person deals with a company in good faith, the power of the directors to bind the company shall be deemed to be free of any limitation under the company's constitution. The outsider is not to be regarded as in bad faith by reason only of his knowing the act was beyond the directors' powers (s 40).

It should be noted that s 40 protects an outsider who deals with a company and that 'deals' is now defined as where a person is a party to any transaction or other act. This would seemingly encompass gifts and the receipt of cheques (see *International Sales and Agencies Ltd v Marcus* [1982] 3 All ER 551 under the old law).

In *Smith v Henniker-Major & Co* [2003] Ch 182, the question arose of whether a director of a company as opposed to an entirely independent third party could rely on what is now s 40. The section provides that a company may be bound by the actions of its directors in favour of a person dealing with the company in good faith.

A joint venture company (SPDL) was formed to acquire a site with development potential. The claimant held 30 per cent of the shares in the company and was also one of its four directors. Two of the company's directors used another company (SPL) to accomplish the deal with help from SPDL's solicitors, the defendants Henniker-Major & Co. The claimant alleged that the defendant's solicitors had accepted a retainer on behalf of SPL in breach of their fiduciary duties, as SPDL had already instructed them. The claimant, as a creditor of SPDL through guarantees for loans, decided to assign himself the cause of action against the solicitors and to sue them. Notice of a board meeting to carry out this assignment was given to the other remaining director (the other two directors having resigned). The other remaining director, however, did not attend the board meeting. The claimant went ahead with the meeting and, against the articles (as the meeting was not quorate), resolved to assign himself the cause of action. The defendant's firm of solicitors argued the assignment of the cause of action was void as the board was inquorate. The claimant sought to rely on what is now s 40 protecting those dealing with a company by shielding them from the provisions of the company's constitution, i.e. here the provision relating to the quorum.

The Court of Appeal agreed that the claimant could not rely on the section to assign himself the company's cause of action. The policy of the section was to protect somebody from outside of the company and certainly somebody who was not a director who had no reason to doubt the authenticity of a particular act of the company. This could not be said to be the case here, the court said. The court considered that in principle the section was wide enough to include a director as a person dealing with the company, but in this case the claimant was not merely a director, he was also chairman, and as such it was his duty to ensure the constitution was properly applied. He could not, therefore, rely on the section where he, himself, was responsible for the company's constitution not being followed.

6.15 Charities

Sections 39 and 40 relating to corporate capacity and the power of directors to bind the company do not apply to the acts of a company that is a charity except in the following circumstances:

(a)   in favour of a person who does not know, at the time that the act is done, that the company is a charity; or

(b)   a person who gives full consideration in money or money's worth in relation to the act in question and does not know (as the case may be):

(i)   that the act is not permitted by the company's constitution; or
(ii)   that the act is beyond the powers of the directors.

In these two situations, s 39 and s 40 will apply (s 42).

Where a company that is a charity purports to transfer or grant an interest in property, the fact that (as the case may be) the act was not permitted by the company's constitution or that the directors exceeded any limitation on their powers under the constitution, does not affect the title of a person acquiring the property or any interest in it for full consideration without notice of the circumstances affecting the validity of the company's act (s 42(2) CA 2006).

6.16 Capital

As noted, s 10 of the Companies Act 2006 provides that a statement of capital must be delivered at the time of registration. The statement of capital and initial shareholdings must state:

(a)   the total number of shares of the company to be taken on formation by the subscribers to the memorandum;

(b)   the aggregate nominal value of those shares;

(c)   for each class of those shares prescribed particulars of the rights attached to them, the total number of shares of that class and the aggregate nominal value of shares of that class; and

(d)   the amount to be paid up and the amount (if any) unpaid, on each share.

Companies are no longer required to have an authorised share capital, although they may do so and may include such a restriction in their articles.

In consequence of this, whenever a company's share capital changes, whether by reduction or by an allotment of new shares, then in addition to other formalities the company must deliver to the Registrar of Companies a statement of capital. Thus, for example, under s 555 of the Companies Act 2006, when a limited company makes an allotment of shares, there must be delivered to the Registrar for registration a return of the allotment within one month which must be accompanied by a statement of capital. The new statement of capital parallels that set out in s 10 above.

It must therefore state the total number of shares of the company, the aggregate nominal value of the shares and for each class of shares:

(i)   prescribed particulars of the rights attached to the shares;
(ii)   the total number of shares of that class; and
(iii)   the aggregate nominal value of shares of that class.

as well as the amount paid up and the amount (if any) unpaid on each share. This statement of capital should thus provide an up-to-date résumé of the capital of the company at any given time.

Summary

The company's constitution: some vital considerations

The Companies Act 2006 makes a fundamental change to company law in regard to the constitution. Henceforth the memorandum of association is an application to the Registrar for registration. The application will state the company's proposed name, the situate of the registered office, the potential liability of members and whether the company is to be private or public. It will be accompanied by a statement of capital if this is appropriate or a statement of guarantee if this applies. Additionally there will be a statement of the company's proposed officers, together with the application for registration.

Self-test questions

6.1 How does the company register its constitution?

6.2 Is a company free to choose any name it likes as the name of the corporation?

6.3 How may a company change its name?

6.4 Explain the interaction of business names with company names.

6.5 What is the importance of the company's registered office?

6.6 Describe how a company may change from being a private company to a public company.

6.7 What is the importance of the objects clause of a company?

6.8 Describe some of the manoeuvres used by entrepreneurs with the help of their lawyers in drafting objects clauses.

6.9 What used to happen at common law where contracts were ultra vires?

6.10 Explain the impact of the European Communities Act 1972 Section 9(1).

6.11 How did the Companies Act 1989 change the law in this area?

6.12 Describe the current state of the law on ultra vires under the Companies Act 2006.

6.13 What happens where a company enters into a transaction and one of the other parties is a director or someone connected with a director?

6.14 Describe how directors may bind the company, even if the contract is beyond the company's constitution.

6.15 How does the law on ultra vires apply to charitable companies?

6.16 What are the requirements as to capital when a company registers?

Further reading

S de Gay, 'Problems Surrounding Use of the New Single Objects Clause' (1993) 137 SJ 146.

JH Farrar, 'Inquorate Boards, Organs and Section 35A of the Companies Act 1985' [2003] CLJ 45.

E Ferran, 'The Reform of the Law on Corporate Capacity and Directors' and Officers' Authority' (1992) 13 Co Law 124 and 177.

SN Frommel, 'Reform of the *Ultra Vires* Rule: A Personal View' (1987) 8 Co Law 11.

BM Hanningan, 'The Reform of the *Ultra Vires* Rule' [1987] JBL 173.

P Heatherington and J Knapp 'S 35A CA 85' (2003) 153 NLJ 640.

C Howell, 'Companies Act 1985 s 35A and s 322A' (2003) 24 Co Law 264.

BG Pettet, 'Unlimited Objects Clauses?' (1981) 97 LQR 15.

J Poole, 'Abolition of the *Ultra Vires* Doctrine and Agency Problems' (1991) 12 Co Law 43.

H Rajak, 'Judicial Control: Corporations and the Decline of *Ultra Vires*' (1995) CLR 9.

C Schipani and L Talbot, 'A Contextual Analysis of the Demise of the Doctrine of *Ultra Vires* in English Company Law' (2009) 30 Co Law 323.

C Twigg-Flesner, 'Sections 35A and 322A Revisited: Who Is a "Person Dealing With a Company"?' (2005) 26 Co Law 195.

KW Wedderburn, 'Unreformed Company Law' (1969) 32 MLR 563.

KW Wedderburn, '*Ultra Vires* in Modern Company Law' (1983) 46 MLR 204.

Chapter 7

The articles of association

7.1 Introduction

The company has been formed and as noted must have articles prescribing regulations for the company (s 18 CA 2006).

Since the advent of the Companies Act 2006, a company will effectively have a single constitution rather than the two components of memorandum and articles that prevailed before the Companies Act 2006. This will be the articles. As noted in Chapter 5, the new-style memorandum is a document in a prescribed form stating that the subscribers intend to form a company and undertake to become members and to take at least one share each (s 8 CA 2006). The previous chapter considered some of the vital provisions of the constitution and also how a company may change its status.

Since 1856, model articles have been provided for certain types of companies. For example, Companies Act 1985 Table A provides model articles for companies limited by shares. This operates as a 'default' set of articles for all such companies. If a company therefore devises its own articles of association, Table A will not apply except to the extent that the table adopted by the company is not comprehensive. The view was taken that Table A, which has been revised several times over the last 150 years but essentially remains a product of the Victorian era in terms of both language and substance, was in need of a rethink. It is essentially drafted in terms of public rather than private companies and successive revisions have tended to include increasingly complex provisions designed to cover every conceivable event or set of circumstances.

The result is that the vast majority of the provisions in Companies Act 1985 Table A are irrelevant to the vast majority of companies. The 'one size fits all' approach has a number of problems. The 1985 Act Table A is user unfriendly, poorly laid out and often unintelligible to non-specialists. Most of it concerns matters that are remote from the concerns of smaller companies, and it does not take account of relatively recent changes in the law, e.g. the introduction of single-member companies.

Following the recommendations of the Company Law Review, the government considered that reform of Table A was an important part of updating company law for a modern economy. It proposed in future that there should be:

> a radically simplified set of model articles for private companies limited by shares and, for the first time, a full set of model articles for private companies limited by guarantee together with comprehensive, clear and concise guidance for small companies who are using or thinking of using model articles.
>
> Company Law Reform (Cm 6456) March 2005, p. 33)

To companies set up under the new legislation, the default provisions will apply in relation to the new types of model articles in the same way as they did for Companies Act 1985 Table A. Existing companies will be able to replace their current articles with the new model articles if their members pass a special resolution to do so.

Section 19 of the Companies Act 2006 provides that the Secretary of State may, by regulations, prescribe model articles of association for companies.

Table A Model Articles were superseded by the Companies Act 2006 model articles on 1 October 2009.

7.1.1 The Company's (Model Articles) Regulations 2008

These regulations (SI 2008/3229) made under the Companies Act 2006 prescribe model articles for the three most common types of company: private companies limited by shares; private companies limited by guarantee; and public companies.

All three sets of model articles are available electronically on the Companies House website at www.companieshouse.gov.uk/about/tableA/index.shtml.

7.1.2 Changes in the model articles

Private companies in particular are affected by changes to the model articles.

For example, a private company, whether limited by shares or by guarantee, is no longer *required* to hold an annual general meeting under the Companies Act 2006. There is, therefore, no provision made for annual general meetings in the model articles on the assumption that most private companies will take advantage of this change in the law.

However, if the members of a private company incorporated under the Companies Act 2006 wish the company to hold annual general meetings, they may wish to include provisions for annual general meetings similar to those in the model articles for public companies.

Similarly, private companies are no longer required to have a company secretary. They may have one if the members so wish. Model articles for private companies are written permissibly but make it clear there is no requirement for a company secretary.

It is likely that most private companies will wish to take advantage of the *written resolution procedure* (section 16.10.4), and therefore the model articles for private companies do not go as far as those for public companies in setting out detailed rules for general meetings.

Model articles include short permissive articles on indemnity and insurance, giving company directors the power to resolve that the company indemnify directors and/or maintain insurance for directors in accordance with the provisions of the Companies Act 2006 (see section 12.12).

These are just some of the more important changes that have been brought about in the model articles under the Companies Act 2006.

7.1.3 Unlimited companies

There are no model articles provided for unlimited companies and therefore no default provision. The only default provision contained in s 20 of the Companies Act 2006 is for limited companies.

7.1.4 Company checklist

When a company seeks registration it must ensure that, if it does not rely entirely on statutory model articles, its own articles are registered with the Registrar of Companies when it is formed.

Articles must be contained in a single document and divided consecutively in numbered paragraphs.

Where a company changes its articles (by special resolution of its members) an up-to-date copy of the articles must be registered with the Registrar of Companies not later than 15 days after the amendment takes effect.

Companies should also ensure that up-to-date copies of their articles are available for their members on request.

Section 20 applies the default principle to the extent that if a company's registered articles do not cover every situation, the relevant model articles will fill the gap. Additionally, this section makes it clear that the model articles that are in existence at the time a company is formed will be the articles that apply in default (s 20 CA 2006).

7.2 Resolutions or agreements affecting a company's constitution

Section 30 of the Companies Act 2006 provides that copies of resolutions or agreements, or written memoranda setting out the terms of such which affect a company's constitution, must be forwarded to the Registrar within 15 days and recorded by him. Section 29 sets out the resolutions and agreements to which s 30 applies. These are:

(a) any special resolution;

(b) any resolution or agreement agreed to by all the members of a company (which otherwise would only have passed as a special resolution);

(c) any resolution or agreement agreed to by all the members of a class of shareholders (which otherwise would only have passed by resolution with a specified majority);

(d) any resolution or agreement that binds all members of a class of shareholders though not agreed to by all those members;

(e) a resolution to give, vary, revoke or renew authority in relation to the allotment of shares by directors (s 551(9) CA 2006);

(f) a resolution to redenominate share capital or a class of share capital under s 622(8) CA 2006;

(g) a resolution of the directors of a company in connection with re-registration in consequence of a company acquiring its own shares, under s 664(1) CA 2006;

(h) a resolution conferring, varying, revoking or renewing authority under s 701(8) CA 2006 (market purchase of a company's own shares);

(i) a resolution for voluntary winding up (s 84(1)(a) of the Insolvency Act 1986);

(j) a resolution of directors of an old public company that the company should be re-registered as a public company (s 2(1) of the Companies Consolidation (Consequential Provisions) Act 1985); and

(k) a resolution passed by virtue of regulations made under s 790 of the Companies Act 2006 (transfer of title to securities).

Such resolutions and agreements should be embodied in or annexed to the company's articles.

7.3 Companies' objects

Section 31 of the Companies Act 2006 provides that, unless a company's articles specifically restrict the objects of the company, its objects are unrestricted.

Where a company amends its articles so as to add, remove or alter a statement of the company's objects, it must give notice of this to the Registrar (s 31(2)).

The provisions of this section have effect subject to the special position of charities (s 42 CA 2006) (see section 6.15).

7.4 Constitutional documents and members

Section 32 provides that a company must, on request by any member, send him a copy of the up-to-date articles of the company, together with a copy of any resolution or agreement that has been recorded under s 30 as described above.

The provisions of a company's constitution, when registered, bind the company and its members to the same extent as if they were covenants, signed and sealed on behalf of the company and of each member, to observe those provisions (s 33 CA 2006) (see section 7.7).

7.5 Alteration of the articles of association

Section 21 of the Companies Act 2006 provides that a company may amend its articles by special resolution.

Section 22 of the Act provides that a company's articles may provide that specified provisions of the articles may be amended or repealed only if conditions are met or procedures are complied with that are more restrictive than those applicable to the case of a simple special resolution, i.e. provisions in a company's constitution may be entrenched.

If a company's articles on formation contain entrenchment provisions or are subsequently altered to include entrenchment provisions, the company must give notice to the Registrar (s 23 CA 2006). Similarly, if a company removes provisions for entrenchment, the Registrar must be given notice of that fact (s 24 CA 2006).

With regard to existing companies, s 28 provides that the provisions that immediately before the commencement of this part of the Act (Part 3) were contained in a company's memorandum are to be treated after the commencement of this part of the Act as provisions of the company's articles.

This applies not only to substantive provisions but also to provisions relating to entrenchment.

As has been noted, a company may alter its articles of association by special resolution (s 21 CA 2006). Indeed, any article that seeks to restrict a company's freedom to alter its articles is invalid (see *Allen v Gold Reefs of West Africa* [1900] 1 Ch 656), although a separate shareholders' agreement may validly restrict the alterability of the company's articles on the part of shareholders. In *Russell v Northern Bank Development Corporation Ltd* [1992] 1 WLR 588, four shareholders of a company had agreed not to vote in favour of increasing the company share capital unless all the shareholders and the company agreed in writing. The House of Lords held that the company could not be bound by this agreement. However, the agreement could stand as it was valid amongst the shareholders without the company's participation. Had the agreement merely involved the company, this would have been void, whether it had been included in the company's constitution or as part of an external agreement, as it would involve the company fettering its statutory powers.

A company cannot be restricted from altering its articles even if this results in a breach of contract between the company and a third party. In *Southern Foundries (1926) Ltd v Shirlaw* [1940] AC 701, Shirlaw, the respondent, was a director of the appellant company. Later he also became managing director. This was by means of a separate contract and the appointment was to be for ten years. Later the appellant company merged with other companies.

Alterations were made to the articles with each of the companies within the group. One of these was to the effect that if a person ceased to be a director then he would also lose the office of managing director. Shirlaw was removed as a director under the provision in the articles. The effect of this was that he also ceased to be managing director and he sued on his contract for wrongful dismissal.

At first instance, in the Court of Appeal, Shirlaw was successful.

In the House of Lords, by a majority, it was held that his contract contained an implied term that the article that made him a director would not be altered.

The alteration, therefore, resulted in a breach of contract and the company was liable in damages. The company could not be restrained from altering its articles, however.

There are various considerations for a company to bear in mind in relation to changes of articles. Now the minority remedy in ss 994–996 CA 2006 (remedy for unfairly prejudicial conduct) is likely to be used by a party wishing to challenge a change of the company's articles.

The power of a company to alter its articles is subject to certain conditions:

(a) A company cannot alter its articles to contravene the provisions of the Companies Act. Thus, for example, any provision in the articles which would seek to exempt a director from liability for negligence is void by virtue of s 232.

(b) Any alteration of the articles that conflicts with an order of the court is, of course, void. Thus an order of the court under s 996 relating to the remedy for unfairly prejudicial conduct cannot be overridden by a change of articles.

(c) If the alteration of articles involves an alteration or abrogation of class rights, then, in addition to the special resolution required under s 21, the company must follow the regime appropriate to variation of class rights set out in ss 629–634. (This will be considered below – see section 7.6.)

(d) In addition to the statutory restrictions, the power to alter a company's articles is subject to the principle that any alteration must be bona fide for the benefit of the company as a whole. In *Allen v Gold Reefs of West Africa Ltd* (1900), the company's articles of association gave the company a lien upon all partly paid shares held by a member for any debt owed to the company. The defendant's company constitution provided that 'the company would have a first and paramount lien, for all debts, obligations and liabilities of any member ... upon all shares (not being fully paid) held by such member'. One Zuccani owned both fully paid and partly paid shares.

An extraordinary general meeting of shareholders was called to pass a special resolution to alter the article in the company's constitution by omitting the words 'not being fully paid'. The effect of this would have been to extend the company's lien to paid-up as well as partly paid shares. Zuccani's executors (Zuccani having died) sought a declaration that the defendant company had no lien on the fully paid-up shares.

The Court of Appeal concluded that it was open to a company to alter its articles in this way. There was no rule that a company's articles could not be altered retrospectively.

Much of the case law has centred upon a discussion of how it is to be determined whether an alteration is for the benefit of the company as a whole. In *Greenhalgh v Arderne Cinemas Ltd* [1951] Ch 286, it was proposed to delete a provision in the company's articles that gave members a right of pre-emption over shares that a member wanted to sell. It seemed that the majority shareholder, Mr Mallard, was prompted not by what was in the company's best interest but out of malice towards a minority shareholder. The question arose as to whether the alteration was for the benefit of the company as a whole. Lord Evershed MR said that:

> the phrase 'the company as a whole' does not (at any rate in such a case as the present) mean the company as a commercial entity, distinct from the corporators; it means the corporators as a general body. That is to say, the case may be taken of an individual hypothetical member and it may be asked what is proposed, in the honest opinion of those who voted in its favour, for that person's benefit.

In this case, the Court of Appeal held that the alteration was valid.

This analysis does raise difficulties in determining the benefit of the individual hypothetical member. It is clear that hardship to a minority will not of itself invalidate an alteration of articles. In *Sidebottom v Kershaw Leese & Co Ltd* [1920] 1 Ch 154, the claimant company ran mills in competition with the defendant company. It was a member of the defendant company. It was proposed to alter the defendant company's articles to insert a clause whereby a shareholder who competed with the company would be required to transfer his shares at a fair value to the directors. It was held that the alteration was valid even though it was carried out specifically against one particular member. The clause in question, of course, could apply in relation to any member.

By contrast, in *Brown v British Abrasive Wheel Co Ltd* [1919] 1 Ch 290, where 98 per cent majority shareholders wished to insert a provision in the articles requiring the minority who were not prepared to invest further capital to sell their shares as a condition of the majority's providing further capital, the alteration was held invalid. It was noted that such a provision could be used to require a minority to sell its shares at the will of the majority.

The cases do appear to be inconsistent. If the question is not what is for the benefit of the company as a separate corporate entity, it is difficult to conjure up a hypothetical shareholder in whose interest the alteration must be. Malevolence did not prevent Mr Mallard succeeding in *Greenhalgh v Arderne Cinemas*; why should the majority's view be overridden in *Brown v British Abrasive Wheel Co Ltd*? A possible interpretation is offered by Lord Evershed MR in the *Greenhalgh* case where he argues that if the effect of the alteration is to discriminate between the majority shareholders and the minority shareholders to give the majority an advantage, then the alteration should not be permitted.

(e)   It is now the case that ss 994–996 will provide a possible remedy to a shareholder who has been unfairly prejudiced against in the conduct of a company's affairs by the use of majority voting power. This may be in relation to altered articles, see e.g. *Re DR Chemicals* (1988) 5 BCC 39 – dilution of voting power, and *Re a Company (No. 005685 of 1988) ex p Schwarcz* [1989] BCLC 424 – deletion of pre-emption rights.

In addition courts have sometimes been willing to act to protect minority shareholders from the oppressive use of majority voting power. In *Clemens v Clemens Brothers Ltd* [1976] 2 All ER 268, the claimant and her aunt owned the shares in a small family company. The claimant held 45 per cent of the shares and the aunt 55 per cent. The directors of the company, who included the aunt, proposed to increase the company's share capital. The directors, other than the aunt, were to receive 200 shares each, and the remaining 850 shares were to be placed in trust for the company's employees. The claimant objected to the proposed resolution as it would reduce her shareholding to below 25 per cent. Clearly 25 per cent is a strategic amount, giving negative control in many instances.

The aunt voted in favour of the resolutions, which were passed. The claimant sought a declaration setting aside the resolution on the grounds that it was oppressive of the claimant. Judgment was given in favour of the claimant. Foster J held that the aunt was not entitled to use her majority voting power in whatever way she pleased. The case does demonstrate the wide power that exists in equity in relation to restricting the power of majority shareholders.

In the case of *Estmanco (Kilner House) Ltd v Greater London Council* [1982] 1 WLR 2, the Conservative-controlled Greater London Council had formed the Estmanco company to manage a block of flats which it owned. There were 60 flats in the block. The Council entered into an agreement with the company that it would use its best endeavours to sell the flats and indeed it began to sell them to owner-occupiers. Once a flat was sold one of the 60 shares in the company would be transferred to the purchaser.

Voting rights were, however, retained by the Council and would only be transferred to owner-occupiers once all 60 flats had been sold. Local elections intervened after 12 flats had been sold and control of the Council changed. As a consequence so did the Council policy and the new Council adopted a housing policy not to sell the remaining flats. Two directors of the company brought an action against the Council for breach of contract. The Council used its voting control to discontinue the action. One of the owner-occupiers who was a member of the company sought leave to bring a derivative action on behalf of the company against the Council.

Megarry VC held that the action could proceed as a fraud on the minority and was not confined to simple fraud but allowed the intervention of equity where there had been abuse of power or discrimination.

Ways in which disgruntled shareholders can object to alterations of articles are considered by Rixon in 'Competing Interests and Conflicting Principles: An Examination of the Power of Alteration of Articles of Association' [1986] MLR 446.

(f)   A final point should be noted in relation to alteration of the articles.

Notwithstanding that an alteration of the articles may result in a breach of contract by the company, an injunction will not issue to stop the alteration taking place; see *Southern Foundries (1926) Ltd v Shirlaw* (1940). The innocent party will, of course, be able to pursue a remedy in relation to the breach of contract.

7.6 Variation of class rights

Variation of class rights was formerly one of the more complex areas in company law. It was an intricate web of legal technicalities and judicial nuances. The basic principle is that an alteration of rights attached to a particular class of shares involves a special regime, which generally means that separate class consent has to be given. The principle is to protect the holders of those special rights.

The statutory rules are set out in ss 629–634 of the Companies Act 2006. Often, a company may have just one class of shares with uniform rights. In such a situation, questions of class rights obviously do not arise. Sometimes, however, there will be additional classes of shares, such as preference shares or management shares (see section 4.2).

A company may have different classes of shares. This may be done for a variety of reasons. On occasion it is to attract an investor by giving the investor preference shares carrying, for example, a preference on dividend.

Then again, shares may be taken up by family members, who may have superior voting power to keep control of the company.

The interaction between variation of class rights and reduction of capital is important. Clearly if the company only has one class of share, variation of class rights cannot arise where there is a reduction. However, if the company has more than one category of share, and is proposing to reduce its capital, then the potential variation of class rights is an issue and companies need to be aware of this (see section 9.7).

7.6.1 Class rights

Section 629 of the Companies Act 2006 provides that, for the purposes of this part of the Act, shares are of one class if the rights attached to them are in all respects uniform. For this purpose the rights attached to shares are not regarded as different from those attached to other shares by reason only that they do not carry the same rights to dividends in the 12 months immediately following their allotment.

Despite the statutory provision, defining a class of shares remains difficult, Vaisey J offered a workable definition in *Greenhalgh v Arderne Cinemas Ltd* [1946] 1 All ER 512, where he said

> although the word 'class' is not a word of technical art, you cannot put people, whether they be shareholders or policy holders, into the same class if their claims or rights diverge. Rights may well be attached to certain shares such as a right to a preferential dividend or a right to be paid off first in a liquidation.

The traditional view is that the rights must attach to the shares and not to the shareholders. Thus, in *Eley v Positive Government Security Life Assurance Co Ltd* (1876) 1 Ex D 88, where the articles conferred the right to be a company solicitor on a shareholder, the right could not be construed as a class right – it was a personal right attaching to the shareholder. Such a case is a clear example but the rule has hardly been applied uniformly. In the Australian case of *Fischer v Easthaven Ltd* [1964] NSWR 261 (Australia), which concerned a home unit company in which the unit holders were shareholders, the court considered that the relationship between a home unit owner and the company imposed a contractual duty on the company not to alter its articles so as to abrogate their rights, effectively treating them as class rights.

In *Cumbrian Newspapers Group Ltd v Cumberland and Westmorland Herald Newspaper and Printing Co Ltd* [1987] Ch 1, the whole question of class rights was analysed. The case is examined by Polack in a case note on 'Class Rights' [1986] CLJ 399.

The case centred on the claimant's desire to maintain the Cumbrian newspaper's independence from large national chains. The claimant published the *Penrith Observer*, whose circulation, largely confined to that market town, was about 5,500 per week. Their chairman, John Burgess (later Sir John) negotiated with the defendants, who published the *Cumberland and Westmorland Herald* with a circulation throughout Cumbria. The negotiations involved the provision of discounted advertising arrangements for the defendants which would enhance the defendants' ability to attract advertising and could lead to the closure of the *Penrith Observer*. Sir John was anxious to protect the independence of the Cumbrian Press and so it was agreed that his shareholding of 10.67 per cent in the defendant company entitled him to the rights of pre-emption over other ordinary shares, rights over unissued shares and the right to appoint a director. Later, the defendants wanted to cancel these special rights. The claimant contended that they were class rights and therefore subject to the special statutory provisions of the Companies Act 1985.

Scott J held:

> In my judgment, a company which by its articles, confers special rights on one or more of its members in the capacity of member or shareholder, thereby constitutes the share for the time being held by that member or members, a class of shares. The rights are class rights.

The *Eley* case can therefore be distinguished on the basis that the right to be company solicitor did not attach to Eley as shareholder.

7.6.2 Defining 'variation'

The next matter to be considered is whether the company's proposal amounts to a variation of the existing rights. Once again, fine judicial nuances abound in this area.

It should be said at the outset that not every act of a company that adversely affects the interests of a particular class of share amounts to a variation of the class rights of that share. Thus, in *White v The Bristol Aeroplane Co Ltd* [1953] Ch 65, the company proposed to capitalise its profits and distribute them in the form of a bonus issue of ordinary and preference shares.

The court held that the bonus issue would not affect the existing preference shareholders' rights or privileges. These rights might be affected as a matter of business practice because of the new preference stock, but this would relate to the enjoyment of the rights and not the rights themselves. Such fine legalistic reasoning is also apparent in a case decided at about the same time, namely *Re John Smith's Tadcaster Brewery Co Ltd* [1953] Ch 308. In a similar way, it was held in this case that 'variation of rights' provisions on class rights are only affected if they are directly altered.

Another famous case that analysed the concept of variation is *Greenhalgh v Arderne Cinemas Ltd* (1946). Mr Greenhalgh lent money to the company in exchange for 10-pence shares. These shares ranked *pari passu* with the ordinary 50-pence shares. The company later resolved to subdivide the 50-pence shares into 10-pence shares, which effectively quintupled the voting strength of the 50-pence shares.

The Court of Appeal held that the voting rights had not been varied by the resolution. The only voting right was one vote per share and this had remained the same throughout.

Such decisions demonstrate how restrictively the concept of variation of class rights has been interpreted in the cases. The area is riddled with the subtlest of distinctions. Lord Greene MR in *Greenhalgh* even said that:

> If it had been attempted to reduce that voting right [of the 10-pence share], for example, by providing or attempting to provide there should be one vote for every five of such shares, that would have been an interference with the voting rights attached to that class of shares. But nothing of the kind had been done: the right to have one vote per share is left undisturbed.

Nothing could better illustrate the fine legalistic distinctions that are made in the cases. It is clear from Lord Greene's dictum that it is the means rather than the end that is all-important.

Sometimes, the company's constitution will set out clearly when a particular class of shareholders' consent is required. In *Re Northern Engineering Industries plc* [1994] 2 BCLC 709, a company's articles of association stipulated that a reduction of capital required the consent of the company's preference shareholders. The Court of Appeal held that this included the situation where it was proposed to cancel the preference shareholders as a class.

7.6.3 Statutory procedures

If the proposal is clearly to alter the substance of the rights of a class of shareholders, the procedure that is set out in the Act must be followed. It is worth noting that a provision to alter or insert a new procedure relating to class rights is itself a variation of class rights, as is abrogation of rights. Both will involve the statutory procedures (s 630(5), (6) and s 631(5), (6) CA 2006).

In *Re House of Fraser plc* [1987] AC 387, the issue of abrogation of class rights was discussed. In this case, the company applied for a court order to confirm a reduction of capital. The petition to reduce the capital was opposed by two preference shareholders. Capital was to be returned to the preference shareholders. The court confirmed the reduction as it was merely an application of their class rights, the court taking the view that the class rights of the preference shareholders, involving as they did priority in a winding up, had been fulfilled and not varied. The provision in the Act to the effect that an abrogation amounts to a variation does not cover such a case. It was stated in the Court of Session that: 'Abolition or abrogation are not appropriate expressions to describe the situation where a right and its corresponding obligation have been extinguished by performance.' The House of Lords upheld the Court of Session.

Section 630 of the Companies Act 2006 deals with variation of class rights where companies have a share capital.

The rights attached to a class of a company's shares may be varied by the consent in writing of the holders of at least three-quarters in nominal value of the issued shares of that class, or by a special resolution passed at a separate general meeting of the holders of that class.

Where the company has no share capital, s 631 applies. This provides that the consent that is required is the consent in writing of at least three-quarters of the members of the class, or a special resolution passed at a separate general meeting of the members of that class to sanction the variation.

In relation to the right to object to a variation where a company has a share capital, the holders of not less in aggregate than 15 per cent of the issued shares of the class in question, being persons who did not consent to or vote in favour of the resolution, may apply to the court within 21 days to have the variation cancelled (s 633 CA 2006). The variation has no effect then until it is confirmed by the court.

In relation to the right to variation where the company has no share capital, members amounting to not less than 15 per cent of the members of the class in question, being persons who did not consent to or vote in favour of the resolution, may apply to the court within 21 days to have the variation cancelled. Similarly the variation does not take effect unless and until it is confirmed by the court (s 634).

It must be said that, usually, the court will confirm the order, but it will cancel it if it considers that the alteration has been passed by a vote that neglects the interests of the class. This is what occurred in *Re Holders Investment Trust Ltd* [1971] 1 WLR 583.

In this case, Holders Investment Trust Ltd proposed to reduce its capital by cancelling its 5 per cent cumulative preference shares in exchange for an equivalent amount of unsecured loan stock to the shareholders of that class. Almost 90 per cent of the preference shares were vested in trustees and trusts set up by one William Hill. They voted in favour of the resolution. They also held 52 per cent of the ordinary stock and shares. Their vote was clearly influenced by the benefit they would receive as ordinary shareholders from the proposed variation. Megarry J held that the scheme was unfair and refused to sanction the reduction, saying 'it fell substantially below the threshold of anything that can justly be called fair'.

Such cases are exceptional. It is more usual to find that what is acceptable to the majority will have to do for the minority as well.

7.7 Membership contract

Section 33 of the Companies Act 2006 provides that the provisions of a company's constitution bind the company and its members to the same extent as if there were covenants on the part of the company and of each member to observe those provisions. Previous incarnations of this provision were to similar effect, such as s 14 of the Companies Act 1985 and s 20 of the Companies Act 1948. There has been much controversy about the effect of what is now s 33 CA 2006.

In *Hickman v Kent or Romney Marsh Sheep-Breeders' Association* [1915] 1 Ch 881, the Association, which was a registered company, provided in its articles that disputes between the Association and a member of the Association should be referred to arbitration rather than being the subject of litigation in the courts. Mr Hickman, who was in dispute with the Association about his expulsion, started proceedings in the High Court. An injunction was issued to prevent the proceedings in the High Court. Astbury J held that the effect of s 33 was to create a contract between the Association and its members whereby the members agreed not to take a dispute to court.

Another illustration of the same principle is to be found in *Pender v Lushington* (1877) 6 ChD 70. In this case, the articles gave shareholders the right to vote. The articles also fixed a maximum amount of votes that each member could cast, namely 100. To evade this rule, Pender transferred some of his shares into the names of nominees who were bound to vote as directed by him. The shares were registered in their names. At a meeting the chairman refused to count their votes. Pender sued for an injunction to restrain the chairman from declaring the nominees' votes invalid.

He succeeded on the basis of the contract in the articles which bound the company to the shareholder. Shareholders had the right to vote as set out in the articles of association.

Thus far the principle seems straightforward. A member can sue in relation to matters set out in the articles and also can be sued by the company in the same way. However, it seems the matter is not so simple. In *Eley v Positive Government Security Life Assurance Co Ltd* (1876), Eley had been named as company solicitor in the articles of association. He had been appointed as such but was subsequently removed. Eley was a member of the company and he sought to enforce the rights set out in the articles. He was unsuccessful. The court held that he was an outsider and could not enforce the contract in his capacity as a solicitor. The articles only gave him rights in his capacity as a member. It is not clear from the decision whether the position would have been different had he sued as a member. In the later case of *Beattie v E and F Beattie Ltd* [1938] Ch 708, the articles of the company provided for any dispute between a member and the company to be referred to arbitration. A director of the company who also held shares in the company sought to restrain legal proceedings against him on the basis of this article. The Court of Appeal held that he must fail as he was seeking to enforce the terms of the articles as an outsider – that is, as a director rather than as a member. It is thus said that the articles of association cannot be enforced by a member or against a member in relation to outsider rights and obligations.

In *Salmon v Quin and Axtens Ltd* [1909] 1 Ch 311, the company's articles gave the power of management to the board of directors but provided that joint managing directors each had a power of veto over certain key decisions. Salmon, one of the managing directors, sought to enforce this right of veto in relation to a board resolution. He sued the company on behalf of himself and other shareholders to restrain the company from acting on the resolution in breach of the article. The court held that he would succeed. He was thus able to enforce his right as a director by suing upon the membership contract. The case is clearly at odds with the later decision in *Beattie v E and F Beattie Ltd*.

In *Globalink Telecommunications Ltd v Wilmbury Ltd* [2003] 1 BCLC 145, the court held that an indemnity provision for directors contained in the company's articles was ineffective. A separate contract was needed between the company and its directors.

7.7.1 The effect of section 33

There has been much discussion about these cases and the effect of s 33 and its predecessors. Professor Gower took a traditional view that the membership contract is only enforceable in relation to membership rights and obligations in the narrow sense (see Gower and Davies, Principles of Modern Company Law 9th edition (2012), p. 71). Lord Wedderburn ('Shareholders' Rights and the Rule in *Foss v Harbottle*' (1957) 16 CLJ 194 and (1958) 17 CLJ 93), in contrast, took the view that a member always has the right to have the articles and memorandum enforced. He took the view that there is one basic membership right to have the articles and memorandum enforced. Wedderburn's view is endorsed by Drury in 'Relative Nature of the Shareholders Right to Enforce the Company Contract' [1986] CLJ 219. Other academics have joined the fray. GD Goldberg, in 'The Enforcement of Outsider Rights under s 20(1) of the Companies Act 1948' (1972) 35 MLR 362, and then again in 'The Controversy on s 20 Contract Revisited' (1985) 48 MLR 158, and Dr GN Prentice in 'The Enforcement of Outsider Rights' (1980) 1 Co Law 179, have put forward a qualified version of Wedderburn's thesis that a member can sue in respect of a right set out in the articles. Goldberg argues that a member has a contractual right to have the affairs of the company conducted by the appropriate organ while Dr Prentice contends that it is necessary to ask whether the particular provision affects the power of the company to function. These contentions may help to rationalise the decision in *Salmon v Quin and Axtens Ltd*. However, there is no evidence that the judges were thinking in this way.

A different view is put forward by Roger Gregory in 'The s 20 Contract' (1981) 44 MLR 526, who argues cogently that there are two lines of cases supporting different views and that the cases are irreconcilable. This view is probably closest to the truth.

An interesting case that is perhaps consistent with either theory and which illustrates the breakdown that there has been between membership and management rights in small private companies is *Rayfield v Hands* [1958] 2 All ER 194. In this case, a provision in the articles stated that every member who wished to transfer his shares should notify the directors of this and that the directors would be obliged to purchase the shares at a fair value. In this company all of the shareholders were directors.

The claimant informed the directors of his wish to sell his shares and then when they refused to take them as stipulated under the articles, he sought to enforce the article against them. The court held that the article imposed a contractual obligation against the directors in their capacity as members.

On occasion, the company's constitution may form the basis of a quite separate contract. This was the case, for example, in *Re New British Iron Company ex p Beckwith* [1898] 1 Ch 324, where directors were able to imply a contract on the same terms as the articles when suing for their remuneration.

However, if this is the case then the contract incorporating the terms of the company's articles may well be on alterable terms since the articles are freely alterable by the company. Thus, in *Swabey v Port Darwin Gold Mining Company* (1889) 1 Meg 385, the court took the view that the company could alter its articles and so affect the terms of the contract for the future. The company's articles provided that directors should be paid an annual fee of £200. This would later be altered to £5 per month. The Court of Appeal held that this alteration could not be retrospective but could only affect fees for the future.

In some cases, it may be that there is an implied term that the contract is concluded on the basis of the articles as they are at a particular date. Therefore, later variation of the articles will not affect the terms of the contract. Thus, in *Southern Foundries (1926) Ltd v Shirlaw* (1940), both the Court of Appeal and the House of Lords held that it was a breach of contract to alter the articles of the company so as to affect the contract of employment between the appellant and the respondent.

7.7.2 Special features

Quite apart from the controversy concerning the types of rights and obligations that can be enforced via the membership contract, the s 33 contract has other special features. In some respects, it is quite unlike an orthodox contract.

The court has no jurisdiction to rectify the articles even though they do not represent the intention of those signing them, as was held in *Scott v Frank F. Scott (London) Ltd* [1940] Ch 794. In this case the claimant, who was the widow of Frank Stanley Scott, brought an action against the company and her two brothers-in-law. She claimed a declaration that on the construction of the company's constitution she was entitled to be placed on the company's register in relation to the 100 shares that passed to her on her husband's death.

The defendants challenged this right and claimed that she was bound to offer the shares to the two brothers-in-law. They further contended that they were entitled to have the articles of association rectified so as to provide that all ordinary shares of a deceased member should be offered to the principal shareholders, i.e. to the contracting defendant, as this had been the intention of the contracting parties.

The court found the issue of construction in favour of the claimant and further found that there was no room for rectification of a company's constitution.

In a similar way in *Bratton Seymour Service Co Ltd v Oxborough* [1992] BCLC 693, it was urged that the defendant, by virtue of his membership of the claimant company, was under an obligation to pay a reasonable contribution towards expenses incurred in maintaining the utility and amenity areas of the Bratton House development.

At first instance the judge was willing to imply such an obligation into the company's articles of association.

The Court of Appeal noted that the articles of association differ very considerably from a normal contract. The court has no jurisdiction to rectify the articles of association of a company even if they do not accord with what has been the intention of the contracting parties.

In this respect, the contract is quite different from a normal contract. However, if the understanding of the members differs materially from the constitutional arrangements of the company, this may be a basis for winding the company up on the just and equitable ground under s 122(1)(g) of the Insolvency Act 1986. In the New Zealand case of *Re North End Motels (Huntly) Ltd* [1976] 1 NZLR 446 (New Zealand), a retired farmer subscribed for half of the share capital of the company on the basis that he would have an equal say in its management. He found, however, that he was in a minority on the board of directors and he successfully petitioned to wind the company up on the just and equitable ground.

It used to be the case that a member could not sue for damages for breach of his membership contract while remaining a member. This was a rather unusual feature of the membership contract of a company. A member was limited to the remedy of an injunction or a declaration.

This was the rule in *Houldsworth v City of Glasgow Bank* (1880) 5 App Cas 317. However, s 655 CA 2006 now provides that

> a person is not debarred from obtaining damages or other compensation from a company by reason only of his holding or having held shares in the company or any right to apply or subscribe for shares or to be included in the company's register in respect of shares.

The s 33 contract is, of course, subject to the provisions of the Companies Acts and so the articles cannot defeat the provisions of the legislation. Furthermore, the company's articles are alterable by special resolution and so this means that the terms of the s 33 contract can also be altered.

Summary

The articles of association constitute the company's constitution.

Alteration of the articles

Although the articles are said to be freely alterable – in fact, by special resolution under s 21 of the Companies Act 2006 – there are various restrictions that apply:

(a) the alteration must not contravene the companies' legislation;
(b) the alteration must not be 'at odds with' a court order;
(c) a special regime applies if the alteration varies class rights; and
(d) at common law, an alteration of the articles must be put forward bona fide for the benefit of the company as a whole.

Variation of class rights

Where rights are attached to a particular class of share, a special procedure applies for varying those rights.

First, it must be determined that there is a separate class of shares involved. The courts adopt a broad approach to this question as in *Cumbrian Newspapers Group Ltd v Cumberland and Westmorland Herald Newspaper and Printing Co Ltd* (1986).

Second, the question arises as to whether there is a proposed variation of rights attaching to those shares. Here the court adopts a restrictive approach so that if what is to be varied is the enjoyment of rights rather than the rights themselves, then the variation of class rights regime does not apply. For example, a proposed reduction of a preference dividend would be a variation of class rights whereas a proposal to increase the voting strength of management shares as against ordinary shares would not be a variation of the rights of the ordinary shareholders.

Third, if there is a proposed variation of class rights, then in addition to passing a special resolution of all of the shareholders, there needs to be a separate class consent. This may be expressed by special resolution of the class concerned or by three-quarters consent of the class concerned in writing.

Fourth, even if there is a separate class consent given, it is open to a dissentient 15 per cent of the class to apply to the court to seek to stop the variation. They may be able to do so, for example, by demonstrating that the holders of the shares of the class concerned have voted in a particular way as they are also shareholders of another class (see *Re Holders Investment Trust Ltd* (1971)).

Membership contract

The provisions of the articles and also of the memorandum constitute a contract between the company's members and the company and between the members *inter se* (s 33 CA 2006).

There is controversy as to whether the contract is enforceable in relation to all rights and obligations set out in the constitution or merely so-called membership rights and obligations.

There are other special features about the membership contract.

There can be no rectification even if there is a fundamental misunderstanding of the provisions of the company's constitution, although the circumstances may justify a winding-up order.

It is no longer the case that a member cannot sue his company for damages whilst remaining a member.

Self-test questions

7.1　What types of matters are likely to be covered by a company's articles when it registers its constitution?

7.2　What happens in relation to resolutions or agreements affecting a company's constitution after registration?

7.3　What is the legal position in relation to a company's objects in the event that no objects are specified?

7.4 How may members request a copy of the constitution?

7.5 How may a company alter its articles of association?

7.6 What constitutes a class right?

7.7 In what ways is the contract between a member of the company and the company different from an orthodox contract?

Further reading

RR Drury, 'The Relative Nature of a Shareholder's Right to Enforce the Company Contract' [1986] CLJ 219.

E Ferran, 'The Decision of the House of Lords in *Russell v Northern Bank Development Corporation Limited*' [1994] 53 CLJ 343.

GD Goldberg, 'The Enforcement of Outsider Rights Under s20(1) of the Companies Act 1948' (1972) 35 MLR 362.

GD Goldberg, 'The Controversy on the s20 Contract Revisited' (1985) 48 MLR 158.

R Gregory, 'The s20 Contract' (1981) 44 MLR 526.

HH Mason, 'Fraud on the Minority. The Problem of a Single Formulation of the Principle' (1972) 46 ALJ 567.

K Polack, 'Casenote on the Cumbrian Newspapers Group Case' [1986] CLJ 399.

GN Prentice, 'The Enforcement of "Outsider Rights"' (1980) 1 Co Law 179.

B Reynolds, 'Shareholders' Class Rights: A New Approach' [1996] JBL 554.

FG Rixon, 'Competing Interests and Conflicting Principles: An Examination of the Power of Alteration of Articles of Association' (1986) 49 MLR 446.

AP Rutabanzibwa, 'Shareholders' Agreements in Corporate Joint Ventures and the Law' (1996) 17 Co Law 194.

KW Wedderburn, 'Shareholder's Rights and the Rule in *Foss v Harbottle*' [1957] CLJ 194 and [1958] CLJ 93.

PG Xuereb, 'The Limitation on the Exercise of Majority Power' (1985) 6 Co Law 199.

Chapter 8

The payment of dividends

Chapter Contents

When companies distribute their profits to the company's shareholders, they do so by paying dividends on those shares.

8.1 Distributable reserves

The payment of dividends used to be a matter to be decided by commercial prudence and the company's constitution.

8.1.1 The company's constitution

In a company's articles of association it is generally provided that the basic power to pay dividends lies with the company in general meeting. It is granted the power to pay a dividend up to the amount recommended by the directors.

A typical provision would provide that the company may by ordinary resolution declare dividends in accordance with the respective rights of the members, but no dividend shall exceed the amount recommended by the directors.

Generally, directors will be granted the power to declare interim dividends. For example, it may be provided that:

> Subject to the provisions of the Act, the directors may pay interim dividends if it appears to them that they are justified by the profits of the company available for distribution.

If the dividends are to be paid otherwise than in cash, express authority is required. This point was at issue in *Wood v Odessa Waterworks Co* (1889) 42 ChD 636, where the company's articles empowered dividends 'to be paid' by directors. This was interpreted as meaning 'paid in money'. A member was then able to rely on this article in challenging a distribution that was made in a non-cash form by the issue of bonus debentures.

Dividends are payable, in the absence of any provision to the contrary, to those members who are on the register at the time the dividend is declared.

Another question that needs to be considered in relation to provisions in the articles is from which profits are dividends payable. Some articles, for example, specify 'the profits of the business', which is taken to mean that dividends can only be paid out of trading profits and not out of capital profits.

As has been noted previously, preference shareholders are only entitled to a preferential dividend when the dividend is actually declared. However, a preferential dividend is presumed to be cumulative. This means that if the dividend is not paid in one year it must be paid in a later year (see section 4.2.1).

8.1.2 The Stock Exchange

In addition to the requirements set out in the company's constitution, the Stock Exchange provides rules for companies that are listed or are dealt with on the Alternative Investment Market. The Stock Exchange requires that the date of any board meeting at which the declaration or recommendation of payment of a dividend is expected to be decided must be notified to the Stock Exchange in advance; it will then publish the information. The Stock Exchange issues a schedule of suitable dates to assist in settlement of transactions and to permit securities to be traded 'ex-dividend' from a convenient date.

8.1.3 Statutory provisions

If the regime relating to the payment of dividends used to be somewhat lenient, that changed with the Companies Act 1980. Amendments were made by the Companies Act 1981 and the provisions are now contained in the Companies Act 2006.

A company may not make a distribution that includes paying a cash dividend except out of the profits available for distribution (s 830 of the Companies Act 2006).

The statutory provisions of the Companies Act 2006 apply to distributions. These are defined in s 829(1) to include any distribution of the company's assets to its members. The definition is an extremely wide one and covers any benefits in cash or in kind.

However, the following are expressly excluded:

(a) an issue of fully or partly paid bonus shares;
(b) reductions of capital;
(c) the redemption or purchase of any of the company's shares out of capital or out of unrealised profits; and
(d) distributions of assets to members of the company on its winding up (s 829(2)).

The profits available for distribution in both private and public companies are accumulated, realised profits not previously distributed or capitalised, less accumulated, realised losses not previously written off in a reduction or reorganisation of capital (s 830(2)). Two key points about this provision should be noted:

(a) The use of the word 'accumulated' in relation to profits and losses applies to a continuous account. In particular, directors should ensure that previous years' losses are made good before a distribution is made. This reverses the position in *Ammonia Soda Co Ltd v Chamberlain* [1918] 1 Ch 266. In this case, a distribution of revenue profits was made in a trading year even though there was an accumulated deficit from earlier years which had not been made good. The claimant company, which had been incorporated for the purpose of acquiring, developing and working as brineland an estate in Cheshire, sued to recover dividends that the company alleged had been wrongly paid. The Court of Appeal held that there was no law that prohibited a company from distributing the clear net profit of its trading in any year without making good trading losses of previous years. The Court of Appeal considered it was legitimate for companies not to make good past trading losses. Swinfen Eady LJ said:

> The Companies Acts do not impose any obligation upon a limited company, nor does the law require, that it shall not distribute as dividend the clear net profits of its trading unless its paid-up capital is intact or until it has made good all losses incurred in previous years.

This is therefore no longer the case.

(b) Profits must be realised. Directors should ensure that any income whether from trading or from capital must have actually been received by the company. This reverses the decision in *Dimbula Valley (Ceylon) Tea Co Ltd v Laurie* [1961] Ch 353, which permitted the distribution of unrealised capital profits. Article 5 of the company's articles in its constitution permitted the company to pay a dividend to shareholders from an excess of assets on capital account. Buckley J held that this provision was valid and hence the company could pay a dividend based on an unrealised profit. (It is perhaps worth noting that, in a Scottish decision, the opposite result had been reached: see *Westburn Sugar Refineries Ltd v IRC* [1951] AC 625.)

A further restriction in s 831 CA 2006 only applies to public companies. Distributions may only be made so long as the value of the company's net assets does not fall below the aggregate of its called-up share capital plus its undistributable reserves. This requires public companies to maintain the value of their capital.

8.2 Undistributable reserves

Undistributable reserves are defined in s 831(4) as:

(a) the share premium account;
(b) the capital redemption reserve;
(c) the amount by which the accumulated unrealised profits (so far as not previously utilised by capitalisation) exceed its accumulated unrealised losses (so far as not previously written off in a reduction or reorganisation of capital duly made); and
(d) any other reserve that the company is prohibited from distributing by any enactment or by its articles.

This means, in effect, that a public company must maintain its capital and take account of any changes in the value of its fixed assets.

Before the Companies Act 1980 a dividend could be paid out of realised profits without the need to make good any capital loss realised or unrealised, for example, as in *Lee v Neuchatel Asphalte Co* (1889) 41 ChD 1. This is now no longer the case in relation to public companies.

8.3 Investment companies

'Investment companies' was a new category created by the Companies Act 1980, and they are subject to a special regime and may ask for a different basis of distribution of profits. The rules (ss 832–835 CA 2006) are only applicable if the company has a listing, and it must have notified the Registrar of Companies of its status.

An investment company must comply with the following conditions:

(a) its business consists of investing its funds mainly in securities with the aim of spreading investment risk and giving its members the benefit of the results of the management of its funds (s 833(2)(a));

(b) none of its holdings in companies (other than in other investment companies) represents more than 15 per cent by value of its total investment (s 833(2)(b) and s 834);

(c) the distribution of capital profit is prohibited by its articles (s 833(2)(c)); and

(d) the company has not retained during any accounting reference period more than 15 per cent of its investment income from securities (s 833(2)(d)).

The aim of the different rules is to relieve investment companies of the problem they might encounter in connection with the net value test applicable to a public company. Securities, the assets of investment companies, are subject to fluctuation in value which might take the value of assets below the net value level. Yet, since such companies receive considerable income from dividends, due allowance must be made for this fact.

An investment company may make a distribution out of its accumulated realised revenue profits not previously used by distribution or capitalisation, less its accumulated revenue losses, whether realised or not, not previously written off in a reduction or reorganisation of capital if at that time the value of its assets is at least equivalent to one and a half times its total liabilities and to the extent that the distribution does not reduce the value of its assets below that amount (s 832 CA 2006). The advantage of this basis for distribution is that realised and unrealised capital losses do not have to be taken into account in determining the amount available for distribution. However, the company can only distribute realised capital profits on a winding up.

8.4 Insurance companies

Insurance companies (as defined in s 843(7) of the Companies Act 2006 and s 22 of the Financial Services and Markets Act 2000) that carry on a long-term business are also subject to special rules. Any amount that is properly transferred to a company's profit and loss account from a surplus or a deficit on its long-term business funds is to be treated as a realised profit or a realised loss as appropriate (s 843 CA 2006).

8.5 Accumulated realised profits by reference to accounts

It is for the directors of any company, in making a recommendation (if any) to pay a dividend, to ensure that these rules are complied with. A dividend will be based on a company's profits, losses, assets and liabilities as well as provisions (for example, for depreciation) and share capital and reserves. Basically, the directors must determine if there is an accumulated realised profit from which a dividend can be declared. In assessing whether there is such a profit, they should refer to the company's relevant accounts (s 836 CA 2006). Generally, the most recent audited annual accounts will be the relevant ones, and the last annual accounts must have been laid before the company in general meeting. The accounts must have been properly prepared or prepared subject only to matters that are not material, and the auditors must have made a report on the accounts to the members.

If the auditor's report is qualified, then they must state in writing whether, in their opinion, the substance of the qualification is material for determining the legality of the proposed dividend.

If the distribution infringes s 830 or s 831, the directors will need to refer to such 'interim accounts' as are necessary to decide whether a dividend can be paid (s 838). A copy of the accounts must have been delivered to the Registrar in the case of a public company.

If a distribution is to be made during a company's first accounting reference period, or before any accounts have been laid before a general meeting or delivered to the Registrar, 'initial accounts' must be prepared to assess whether there is a profit available for dividend. The 'initial accounts' need not be audited but if the company is a public company, auditors must report on whether the accounts have been properly prepared. Furthermore, a copy of these initial accounts and an auditor's report must be delivered to the Registrar (s 839).

8.6 Distributions in kind

The decision in *Aveling Barford Ltd v Perion Ltd* [1989] BCLC 626, decided by reference to common law rules on distributions and maintenance of capital, is widely considered to have cast doubt on the validity of intragroup asset transfers carried out at book value rather than by reference to market value. The balance sheet of the claimant company (which was now in liquidation) showed that the company had more assets than liabilities but a deficit on its profit and loss account. The claimant sold property valued at £650,000 to the first defendant company, which was controlled by Dr Lee Kin Tat from Singapore. Dr Lee also controlled the claimant company. The property was sold for £350,000; it was then resold within a year for £1.5 million. The claimant company obtained judgment in default on the grounds that the first defendant was a constructive trustee of the proceeds of sale. On appeal it was held to be a breach of Lee's fiduciary duties to arrange to sell the property for £350,000. The first defendant was accountable as constructive trustee.

It is understood that often such transactions are carried out by reference to book value rather than market value for business, administrative or tax reasons. Section 845 of the Companies Act 2006 provides that where the transferring company has distributable profits, its assets can be transferred at book value. This will remove the current uncertainty in the law, and avoid the need for companies to carry out complex asset revaluations requiring considerable professional advice and payment of fees.

8.7 Wrongful payment of dividend

There are various consequences of a wrongful payment of dividend. There are no criminal sanctions for a breach of the rules, but if a shareholder knows or has reasonable grounds for believing at the time of the distribution made to him that the distribution is in contravention of the Companies Act, then he is liable to repay it (or the offending part of it) to the distributing company (s 847 CA 2006). It is necessary to show knowledge of the fact making the payment illegal but not knowledge of the illegality itself. Thus ignorance of the legal position is no defence; see *It's a Wrap (UK) Ltd v Gula* [2006] BCC 626.

In *Precision Dippings Ltd v Precision Dippings Marketing Ltd* [1986] Ch 447, the claimant company, which was a wholly owned subsidiary of the defendant company, paid a cash dividend of £60,000 to the defendant. The relevant accounts, the company's last annual accounts, were qualified. The last annual accounts showed sufficient distributable profits to finance the dividend but no statement on the materiality of the qualification had been made by the auditors as the Act required.

Subsequently, the company went into creditors' voluntary liquidation and the auditors then issued a written statement to the effect that the qualification in their report was not material. The claimant company, through its liquidator, sued to recover the dividend on the ground that it was paid in contravention of the statute and was ultra vires. The Court of Appeal held that the company had paid a dividend in contravention of the statute. The auditors' written statement had to be available before a distribution was made, and the absence of such a statement was not a mere procedural irregularity that could be waived or dispensed with. The dividend payment was ultra vires and, as the defendant company received the money with notice of the facts as a volunteer, it held the money as constructive trustee for the claimant company.

8.7.1 Directors' liability

Section 847 of the Companies Act 2006 does not deal with the position of directors responsible for the payment of dividends. A director who is responsible for an unlawful distribution could be liable to the company for a breach of duty. In *Re Exchange Banking Co, Flitcroft's case* (1882) 21 ChD 519, the question of directors' liability for the wrongful payment of the company's dividends arose. For several years, the directors had presented to the shareholders in general meeting reports and balance sheets in which various debts the directors knew were bad were entered as assets, so that an apparent profit was shown in the company's accounts, although in reality there were no profits. The general meeting relied on the accounts to pass resolutions to declare dividends. The company was wound up and the liquidator sought to have the directors make good the wrongful payment of dividends. The Court of Appeal held that the directors were liable for these wrongful payments and must reimburse the company the full amount of the dividend.

However, this principle only applies where the director knows about the circumstances of the payment. An innocent director is not liable to repay a dividend that has been wrongfully paid.

In *Re Denham & Co* (1883) 25 ChD 752, Crook, a director whose name appeared on the company's reports, never attended board meetings nor took any active part in the preparation or issue of the company's reports or balance sheets, although, at one meeting, he did formally propose the resolution to declare a dividend. It was found that the company had been paying dividends out of capital. The court held, however, that Crook was not personally responsible for the company's reports and balance sheets and the dividends paid under them. He had no reason to suspect any misconduct and was not guilty of negligence. As Chitty J said:

As regards Crook, who acted as a director throughout the period of the four years when the dividends were paid, it is not charged against him that he was guilty of actual fraud, or that he was in fact party or privy to the fraud committed, and I am satisfied, on the evidence, that he had not any suspicion of it ... The auditors are not before me on the present occasion, still I am bound to say that from the evidence, such as it is, it does appear that the auditors themselves were to some extent cognisant of and parties to the fraud. Mr Crook was, however, entitled to trust them, there was nothing at all to arouse his suspicions that they were not doing their duty.

Similarly, in *Dovey v Cory* [1901] AC 477, a director who agreed to the payment of dividends out of capital, and who relied on the advice of a fellow director and general manager of the company by whose statements he was misled and whose integrity, skill and competence he had no reason for suspecting, was held not to be liable in negligence. In the course of his judgment, the Earl of Halsbury LC made it clear that directors are also entitled to trust their auditors:

I cannot think that it can be expected of a director that he should be watching the inferior officers of the bank or verifying the calculations of the auditors themselves. The business of life could not go on if people could not trust those who are put into a position of trust for the express purpose of attending to details of management.

8.7.2 Auditors' liabilities

In addition to directors, the company's auditors may also be liable for the wrongful payment of dividends. The auditors will only be liable to the company if they facilitated the improper payment of a dividend.

As Lindley LJ said of the auditor in *Re London and General Bank Ltd (No 2)* [1895] 2 Ch 673: 'It is nothing to him whether the dividends are properly or improperly declared provided he discharges his own duty to the shareholders.' In that case, dividends had been paid out wrongfully, and the company's assets were overstated in the balance sheet. The court found that the auditors had been negligent in respect of a particular year's report – certain loans which were not realisable were entered in the accounts at face value. The auditor was held liable to repay the dividends in question.

An auditor's liability is generally limited to situations where the auditors are in breach of their contractual duty in relation to the company's annual audit and where this negligence facilitates the payment of a dividend out of capital.

An auditor may be clearly liable to the company for breaches of his contract with the company which has resulted in the wrongful payment of dividends. Lopes LJ spoke of the auditor's contractual duties in those terms in *Re Kingston Cotton Mill Co (No 2)* [1896] 2 Ch 279 (pp. 288–289).

It is the duty of an auditor to bring to bear on the work he has to perform that skill, care and caution which a reasonably competent, careful and cautious auditor would use. What is reasonable skill, care and caution must depend on the circumstances of each case. An auditor is not bound to be a detective or ... to approach his work with suspicion or with foregone conclusion that there is something wrong. He is a watchdog, but not a bloodhound. He is justified in believing hired servants of the company in whom confidence is placed by the company [see also section 18.1.6].

The rules have been made much stricter since 1980. No criminal liability attaches to directors or others simply for the wrongful payment of dividends. Any member knowingly receiving a dividend wrongfully paid is liable to repay it.

Directors may, however, find themselves liable for breach of their duties to the company and auditors may also be in breach of their contractual duty to the company, their client.

Summary

Payment of dividends

The payment of dividends used to be a matter to be decided largely by reference to the company's constitution. The Companies Act 1980 introduced statutory controls for the first time. Since that date, dividends can only be paid out of accumulated realised profits less accumulated realised losses. This applies to private and public companies. Public companies also have to maintain the value of their capital assets before paying any dividend but private companies are also obliged to make provision for depreciation under the accounting rules.

Special rules apply to investment companies and companies carrying on long-term insurance business.

Where dividends are paid wrongfully, recipients will be obliged to pay back the sum where they know of the circumstances. Directors who have recommended payment of an unlawful dividend may be responsible, as may the company's auditor who has facilitated payment of an unlawful dividend.

Self-test questions

8.1   What is the general principle in relation to the payment of dividends?

8.2   What constitutes distributable reserves?

8.3   What special rules apply in relation to dividends paid by investment companies?

8.4   What particular rules apply in relation to the payment of dividends by insurance companies?

8.5   Set out how a dividend may be justified by reference to a particular set of accounts.

8.6   What constitutes a distribution in kind?

8.7   What are the consequences of a wrongful payment of a dividend?

Further reading

N Hutton, 'Declaring Dividends' (1995) 19 CSR 86.

R Instone, 'Realised Profits: Unrealised Consequences' (1985) JBL 106.

D Kershaw, 'Involuntary Creditors and the Case for Accounting-Based Distribution Regulation' (2009) JBL 140.

C Noke, 'Realised Profits: Unrealistic Conclusions' (1989) JBL 37.

Chapter 9

The maintenance of capital

Chapter Contents

9.1 Background

Certain aspects of maintenance of capital have already been considered. The rules relating to the issue of shares and payment for those shares have been considered. It is now proposed to consider certain other rules relating to the maintenance of capital, namely the provision of financial assistance to acquire a company's own shares and the rules relating to a company purchasing its own shares.

9.2 Financial assistance towards the purchase of a company's own shares

The existing statutory prohibition is, in general, removed for private companies by the Companies Act 2006. The 2006 Act retains the prohibition of financial assistance by a public company or by its subsidiaries (which may be private) for the purpose of acquiring the public company's shares (s 678 CA 2006).

A public company is also forbidden from providing financial assistance for the purpose of facilitating the purchase of its holding company shares where that holding company is a private company (s 679).

Although this clearly represents a relaxation of the position in relation to private companies, directors will still need to consider their general duties as directors to the company, and particularly in the context of the company's potential insolvency.

Section 678 CA 2006 provides that where a person is acquiring or proposing to acquire shares in a public company, it is not lawful for that company or any of its subsidiaries to give financial assistance, directly or indirectly, for the purpose of the acquisition before or at the same time as the acquisition takes place.

Section 677 defines financial assistance. It means:

(a) financial assistance given by way of gift;
(b) financial assistance given:

   (i) by way of guarantee, security or indemnity (other than an indemnity in respect of the indemnifier's own neglect or default), or
   (ii) by way of release or waiver;

(c) financial assistance given:

   (i) by way of a loan or any other agreement under which any of the obliga- tions of the person giving the assistance are to be fulfilled at a time when, in accordance with the agreement, any obligation of another party to the agreement remains unfulfilled, or
   (ii) by way of the novation of or the assignment (in Scotland, assignation) of rights arising under a loan or such other agreement; or

(d) any other financial assistance given by a company where:

   (i) the net assets of the company are reduced to a material extent by the giving of the assistance; or
   (ii) the company has no net assets (s 677(1) CA 2006).

Section 678 does not prohibit a company from giving financial assistance for the acquisition of shares if:

(a) the company's principal purpose in giving the assistance is not to give it for the purpose of any such acquisition; or
(b) the giving of the assistance for that purpose is only an incidental part of some larger purpose of the company
and the assistance is given in good faith in the interests of the company (s 678(4) CA2006).

Section 679 deals with assistance by a public company for the acquisition of shares in its private holding company.

In such a situation it is not lawful for a public company that is a subsidiary of the company to give financial assistance directly or indirectly for the purpose of the acquisition before or at the same time as the acquisition takes place. The same exceptions apply as in relation to s 678.

If a company contravenes s 678 or s 679, an offence is committed by the company and every officer in default (s 680 CA 2006).

Section 681 provides that the prohibitions do not cover:

(a) a distribution of the company's assets by way of:

(i)   dividend, or
(ii) distribution in the course of a winding up;

(b) an allotment of bonus shares;
(c) a reduction of capital;
(d) a redemption of shares;
(e) anything done in pursuance of an order of the court under Part 26 (order sanctioning compromise or arrangement with members or creditors);
(f) anything done under an arrangement in pursuance of s 110 of the Insolvency Act 1986 or Art 96 of the Insolvency (Northern Ireland) Order 1989 (liquidator in winding up accepting shares for the company's property); or
(g) anything done under an arrangement made between a company and its creditors binding on the creditors by virtue of Part 1 of the Insolvency Act 1986 or Part 2 of the Insolvency (Northern Ireland) Order 1989.

Section 682 provides that certain transactions are not prohibited:

(a) in the case of a private company; or
(b) in the case of a public company if:

(i)   the company has net assets that are not reduced by the giving of the assistance, or
(ii) to the extent that the assets are so reduced the assistance is provided out of distributable profits.

The transactions to which the section applies are:

(a) the lending of money in the ordinary course of business;

(b)   the provision in good faith in the interests of the company of financial assistance for the purposes of an employee share scheme;

(c)   the provision of financial assistance by the company for the purposes of or in connection with anything done by the company (or another company in the same group) for the purpose of enabling or facilitating transactions in shares in the first-mentioned company or its holding company between and involving the acquisition of beneficial ownership of those shares by:

(i)   bona fide employees or former employees of the company (or of another company in the same group), or

(ii)   spouses or civil partners, widows, widowers or surviving civil partners or minor children or stepchildren of any such employees or former employees; and

(d)   the making by the company of loans to persons other than directors employed in good faith by the company with a view to enabling them to acquire fully paid-up shares in the company or its holding company to be held by them by way of beneficial ownership.

9.2.1 Consequences of breach of the provisions

As has been noted, there are criminal sanctions applying where there is a breach of the sections (s 680). In addition, the transaction itself is unlawful and void. There are various other consequences:

(a)   Any guarantee issued in connection with the transaction is itself void: see *Heald v O'Connor* [1971] 1 WLR 497.

(b)   The company may sue its directors for breach of duty as they are liable in a similar way to trustees in relation to misapplication of trust funds: in *Selangor United Rubber Estates Ltd v Cradock (No 3)* [1968] 1 WLR 1555, an agent acting for Cradock bid for the shares in the claimant company. This was accepted by 79 per cent of the shareholders of the claimant company. The purchase price of £195,000 was borrowed by Cradock from the District Bank. The claimant company's cash balance of £325,000 was transferred to the bank and then loaned through the third party to Cradock. He used it to repay the loan. This was illegal under the Act. The company was able to sue its directors for breach of duty.

In *Belmont Finance Corpn Ltd v Williams Furniture Ltd* [1980] 1 All ER 393, the first defendant, Williams, held all the shares in the second defendant company (City). All the shares in the claimant company were owned by City. James was the chairman of all three companies. One Grosscurth, who was the controlling shareholder of Maximum, wished to acquire the claimant company. James believed that this would be beneficial to the Williams Group. The following negotiations were concluded: Maximum was sold to Belmont Finance for £500,000, and Grosscurth bought the share capital of Belmont for £489,000. No independent valuation of Maximum was carried out.

The claimant company went into insolvent liquidation and the receiver then obtained a valuation of Maximum placing its value at around £60,000.

Proceedings were then commenced against the defendants as constructive trustees of the money received in trust for Belmont and for damages.

In the Court of Appeal it was held that Belmont had provided financial assistance to Grosscurth and his associates in relation to the purchase of Belmont share capital and that this was illegal and therefore the money was held on constructive trust for Belmont.

(c) Furthermore, other persons receiving corporate property with knowledge that it is being applied for a wrongful purpose are liable to the company on the basis of constructive trust: see *Selangor United Rubber Estates Ltd Co v Cradock* and *Belmont Finance v Williams Furniture*.

(d) There is also the possibility that the company can sue for conspiracy if two or more persons have got together to accomplish the unlawful act: see *Belmont Finance v Williams Furniture*.

9.2.2 Financial assistance

It should be recalled that prior to the 2006 Act, private companies were also, in general, subject to a prohibition on the provision of financial assistance. While this is no longer the case generally, unless they are facilitating the acquisition of shares in a public company, some of the earlier case law provides useful guidance on what constitutes financial assistance and may, therefore, cause public companies in the future to fall foul of the law.

The question of the provision of financial assistance arose in *Parlett v Guppys (Bridport) Ltd* [1996] BCC 299. Mr and Mrs Parlett, and their two sons, agreed that four companies controlled by them should provide Parlett with salary, bonus and pension in return for Parlett transferring his shares in Estates, one of the four companies, into the joint names of himself and his sons. The sons subsequently challenged the agreement alleging that it was unenforceable as it gave financial assistance in breach of the Companies Act.

The court took the view that the agreement did not have to be performed in breach of the Act. It could reasonably have been believed that other companies in the group would bear the costs and there was accordingly no reduction in the net assets of Estates and no financial assistance given within the section.

In *Brady v Brady* [1989] AC 755, a scheme had been devised to break deadlock within a family business. The scheme was challenged on the basis that Brady was providing financial assistance for the purchase of its own shares. The two shareholders in Brady were two brothers, Jack and Bob, whose discord had led to the scheme. The brothers agreed to divide the business. Brady became a subsidiary of a new company called Motoreal, which issued to a new company Actavista loan stock equal to half the asset value of Brady. This debt was to be discharged by the transfer to Motoreal of half of Brady's asset value. It was accepted that this infringed the Act in that Motoreal had acquired shares in its subsidiary Brady and had incurred liability for the purchase of that acquisition. Brady had given financial assistance to discharge that liability.

A crucial issue in the case was whether the transaction was saved by what is now s 678(4) CA 2006 in that the company's principal purpose in giving the assistance was not to reduce or discharge liability but to end the deadlock. The House of Lords took the view that there was no larger purpose. As Lord Oliver said: 'The acquisition was not a mere incident of the scheme devised to break the deadlock. It was the essence of the scheme itself and the object which the scheme set out to achieve.' Note that the scheme was not illegal as the company was private and therefore fell within the private company exception under the Companies Act 1985.

9.3 A company's purchase of its own shares and the issue of redeemable shares

Section 684 provides that a limited company with a share capital may issue shares that are to be redeemed or are liable to be redeemed at the option of the company or the shareholder ('redeemable shares') subject to the following provisions.

(a)   The articles of a private limited company can exclude or restrict the issue of redeemable shares.
(b)   A public limited company may only issue redeemable shares if it is authorised to do so by its articles.
(c)   No redeemable shares may be issued at a time when there are no issued shares of the company that are not redeemable.

Section 685 provides that the directors of a limited company may determine the terms, conditions and manner of redemption of shares if they are authorised to do so:

(a)   by the company's articles, or
(b)   by a resolution of the company (s 685(1) CA 2006).

A resolution may be by ordinary resolution even though it amends the company's articles.

Where the directors are so authorised to determine the terms, conditions and manner of redemption of shares, they must do so before the shares are allotted and any obligation of the company to state, in a statement of capital, the rights attached to the shares extends to the terms, conditions and manner of redemption.

If the directors are not so authorised, the terms, conditions and manner of redemption of any redeemable shares must be stated in the company's articles.

Section 686 provides that redeemable shares may not be redeemed unless they are fully paid. The terms of redemption of shares in a limited company may provide the amount repayable on redemption, and may, by agreement between the company and the holder of the shares, be paid on a day later than the redemption date.

Section 687 provides for the financing of redemption. A private limited company may redeem redeemable shares out of capital in accordance with Chapter 5 of Part 18 of the Act (see section 9.4), but subject to that, redeemable shares in a limited company may only be redeemed out of distributable profits of the company or the proceeds of a fresh issue of shares made for the purposes of the redemption.

Section 688 provides that redeemed shares are to be treated as 'cancelled', and the amount of the company's issue share capital is diminished accordingly.

Section 689 provides that where a limited company redeems any redeemable shares, it must within one month of doing so give notice to the Registrar specifying the shares redeemed, and the notice must be accompanied by a statement of capital.

Although a company is prohibited subject to the provisions of the Act from purchasing its own shares, the company may, in certain circumstances, acquire its own shares. Thus, a company may acquire its shares as a gift. Furthermore, the company's articles may provide for the forfeiture of shares or the acceptance of shares in lieu of forfeiture where sums are owed to the company.

In addition to the rules that allow a company to purchase or redeem its shares in certain circumstances, a company may acquire its shares in a reduction of capital or in pursuance of a court order under, for example, ss 994–996 in relation to the remedy for unfairly prejudicial conduct.

9.4 The purchase by a company of its own shares

Section 690 provides that a limited company with a share capital may purchase its own shares including any redeemable shares subject to the provisions of the Act and any restriction or prohibition in the company's articles.

A limited company may not purchase its own shares if, as a result of the purchase, there would no longer be any issued shares of the company other than redeemable shares or shares held as treasury shares.

Section 691 provides that a limited company may not purchase its own shares unless they are fully paid, and where a limited company purchases its own shares, the shares must be paid for upon purchase.

Section 692 provides that a private limited company may purchase its own shares out of capital in accordance with Chapter 5 of Part 18 of the Act. Subject to that, a limited company may only purchase its own shares out of:

(i)   distributable profits; or
(ii)   the proceeds of a fresh issue of shares made for the purpose of financing the purchase.

Any premium payable on the purchase by a limited company of its own shares must be paid out of distributable profits of the company.

Section 693 provides that a limited company may only purchase its own shares:

(a)   by an off-market purchase in pursuance of a contract approved in advance in accordance with s 694; or
(b)   by a market purchase authorised in accordance with s 701.

Section 694 deals with off-market purchases. Either the terms of the proposed contract must be authorised by special resolution of the company before the contract is entered into, or the contract must provide that no shares may be purchased in pursuance of the contract until its terms have been authorised by a special resolution of the company.

Section 701 deals with authority for a market purchase. A company may only make a market purchase of its own shares if the purchase has first been authorised by resolution of the company. That authority may be general or limited to the purchase of shares of a particular class or description, and may be unconditional or subject to conditions. The authority must specify the maximum number of shares authorised to be acquired, and determine both the maximum and minimum prices that may be paid for the shares.

Section 706 deals with the treatment of shares where purchased. Where a limited company makes a purchase of its own shares in accordance with this chapter (Chapter 4 of Part 18 of the Act), then:

(a) if s 724 (treasury shares) applies, the shares may be held and dealt with in accordance with Chapter 6 of this part of the Act; or

(b) if that section does not apply, the shares are treated as cancelled and the amount of the company's issued share capital is diminished accordingly.

Section 707 deals with a return to the Registrar of a purchase of a company's own shares. Where a company purchases shares it must deliver a return to the Registrar within the period of 28 days beginning with the date on which the shares are delivered to it.

9.5 Redemption or purchase by a private company out of capital

Section 709 provides that a private limited company may, subject to any restriction or prohibition in the company's articles, make a payment in respect of redemption or purchase of its own shares otherwise than out of distributable profits or the proceeds of a fresh issue of shares.

Section 710 sets out the permissible capital payment. The payment that may, in accordance with these provisions, be made by a company out of capital is such amount as, after applying for that purpose:

(a) any available profits of the company; and

(b) the proceeds of any fresh issue of shares made for the purposes of the redemption or purchase.

This is required to meet the price of redemption or purchase.

Section 711 provides that any available profits mean any profits that are available for distribution and s 712 sets out whether profits are available for distribution in accordance with this part of the Act.

Section 712 provides that profits should be determined by reference to the following items in the relevant accounts:

(a) profits, losses, assets and liabilities;

(b)   provisions:

    (i)   where the relevant company accounts are Companies Act accounts pro-
          visions of a kind specified for the purposes of this subsection by regula-
          tions under s 396, and

    (ii)   where the relevant accounts are, IAS accounts, provisions of any
          kind, and

(c)   share capital and reserves (including undistributable reserves).

Having determined the profits, the amount should then be reduced by the amount of
any distribution lawfully made by the company and any other payment lawfully
made by the company out of distributable profits after the date of the relevant
accounts and before the end of the relevant period. The resulting figure is the amount
of available profits.

Section 713 provides that the following actions are necessary if there is to be a
payment out of capital by a private company:

s 714 (directors' statement and auditor's report);
s 716 (approval by special resolution);
s 719 (public notice of proposed payment); and
s 720 (directors' statement and auditor's report to be available for inspection).

Section 714 provides for the directors' statement and the auditor's report. These must
state that in their opinion the company will be able to continue to carry on business
as a going concern and be able to pay its debts as they fall due throughout the year.

Section 715 provides that if the directors have no reasonable grounds for that
opinion, then their actions constitute an offence.

Section 716 provides that the payments are to be approved by special resolution
to be passed on or within a week immediately following the date on which the directors make their statement (under s 714 above).

Section 721 provides that where a private company passes the special resolution
approving a payment out of capital for the redemption or purchase of its shares, then
any member of the company, other than one who assented to or voted in favour of
the resolution, or any creditor of the company, may apply to the court for cancellation of the resolution. The application must be made within five weeks after the
passing of the resolution. The court may order an arrangement for the purchase of
dissentient members' interests or for the protection of dissentient creditors. In
general, it may cancel or confirm the resolution and may do so on such terms as it
thinks fit.

9.6 Treasury shares

Section 724 provides that a limited company, where it makes a purchase of its own
shares, may, subject to conditions, hold the shares or deal with them. Where shares
are held by the company, the company must be entered in its register of members as
the member holding the shares. These are treasury shares.

Section 725 provides that where a company has shares of only one class, the aggregate nominal value of shares held as treasury shares must not at any time exceed 10 per cent of the nominal value of the issued share capital.

Where the share capital of a company is divided into different classes, the aggregate nominal value of each class of shares held as treasury shares must not exceed 10 per cent of the nominal value of the relevant class.

Section 726 provides that a company must not exercise any right in respect of the treasury shares, and any purported exercise of such a right is void. This would apply in particular to the right to attend or vote at meetings, for example.

Section 727 deals with the disposal of treasury shares. A company may sell the shares for a cash consideration or transfer the shares into an employees' share scheme.

Section 728 provides that where shares that are held by a company as treasury shares are sold or transferred, the company must deliver a return to the Registrar not later than 28 days after the disposal. Failure to comply with this section is an offence committed by every officer of the company who is in default.

Section 729 provides that a company may cancel treasury shares and where there is such a cancellation, the amount of the company's share capital is reduced accordingly by the nominal amount of the shares cancelled.

The company must deliver a return to the Registrar not later than 28 days after the shares are cancelled (s 730).

Section 731 provides for the treatment of proceeds of sale of treasury shares. If the proceeds of sale are equal to or less than the purchase price paid by the company for the shares, then the proceeds are treated as a realised profit of the company. If the proceeds of the sale exceed the purchase price paid by the company, then an amount equal to the purchase price is treated as realised profit and the excess must be transferred to the company's share premium account.

9.7 The capital redemption reserve

Where shares of a limited company are redeemed or purchased wholly out of the company's profits, the amount by which the company's issued share capital is diminished on cancellation of the shares redeemed or purchased, or on cancellation of shares held as treasury shares, must be transferred to a reserve called the capital redemption reserve (s 733 CA 2006).

The company may use the capital redemption reserve to pay up new shares to be allotted to members as fully paid bonus shares (s 733(5)). Subject to that the capital redemption reserve is treated as capital.

9.8 Reduction of capital

It used to be the case that a company's articles had to authorise a reduction of capital before this was allowed. This is no longer necessary, although the articles may prohibit or restrict such a reduction (s 641(6) CA 2006).

In the case of a private company, it is possible to reduce the company's share capital by special resolution supported by a solvency statement. In the case of a public company, a special resolution confirmed by the court is necessary.

There are three types of capital reduction:

(a) to extinguish or reduce liability on any of the company's shares in respect of share capital not paid up;
(b) to cancel any paid-up share capital that is lost or unrepresented by available assets; or
(c) to repay any paid-up share capital in excess of the company's needs (s 641(4) CA 2006).

In cases (a) and (c), the company is actually giving something back to the shareholders, either an actual return of capital or cancelling an existing liability. In case (b), nothing is being returned to the shareholders; there is merely a recognition of the fact that the company's paid-up share capital is unrepresented by the company's assets.

A company may wish to reduce capital in order to buy out a retiring member of the company or to pay money over to the personal representatives of a deceased member where there are insufficient profits available for distribution. In the case of a private company, this can be accomplished by purchasing the company's own shares out of capital (see section 9.4), but, in the case of a public company, a formal reduction of capital will often be used in such circumstances.

Where a company with no more than one class of share is proposing to reduce its capital, the issue of variation of class rights must be considered (see section 7.6).

9.8.1 Reduction of capital by a private company

The procedure for private companies reducing their share capital is set out in ss 642–644 CA 2006.

A resolution for reducing the share capital is still needed. This needs to be a special resolution, although it may be passed as a written resolution (s 642 CA 2006).

A solvency statement must be made available to every eligible member at the time that a proposed written resolution is sent out and, where the resolution is passed at a general meeting, a copy of the solvency statement must be made available for inspection by members of the company throughout the meeting (s 642(2) and (3) CA 2006).

The solvency statement is a statement that each of the directors has formed the opinion as regards the company's position, that there is no ground on which the company could be found unable to pay its debts, and has also formed the opinion:

(a) if it is intended to commence the winding up of the company within 12 months of that date, that the company will be able to pay its debts in full within 12 months of the commencement of the winding up; or
(b) in any other case, that the company will be able to pay its debts as they fall due during the year immediately following that date.

If the directors make a solvency statement without having reasonable grounds, and the company is insolvent, then an offence is committed by every director in default.

The solvency statement should be made no more than 15 days before the date of the resolution to reduce the company's capital.

9.8.2 Reduction of capital by a public company

A reduction of capital in a public company is carried out in accordance with ss 645–651 CA 2006.

A special resolution must be passed and then the company must apply to the court for an order confirming the reduction.

If the proposed reduction involves either:

(a)   a diminution of liability in respect of unpaid share capital; or

(b)   the payment to a shareholder of any paid-up share capital

then s 646 (creditors entitled to object to a reduction) applies unless the court orders otherwise.

In the case of s 646 applying, every creditor of the company who would be entitled to any debt or claim, that if the company were winding up would be admissible in proof against the company, is entitled to object to the reduction of capital.

The court will then consider objections and may refuse or order a reduction of capital. Any order confirming a reduction of capital may be on such terms and conditions as the court thinks fit (s 648(1)).

The court must not confirm the reduction unless it is satisfied with respect to every creditor of the company who is entitled to object to the reduction of capital that either:

(a)   his consent to the reduction has been obtained; or

(b)   his debt or claim has been discharged or has been determined or has been secured (s 648(2)).

Where the court confirms the reduction, it may order the company to publish the reasons for the reduction of capital or such other information as the court thinks expedient (s 648(3) CA 2006).

The court may, if for any special reason it thinks it proper to do so, make an order requiring the company to add at the end of the company name, the words 'and reduced' for a specified period of time (s 648(4) CA 2006).

It should be noted that where a proposed reduction of capital of a public company would mean that the company will no longer have the authorised minimum capital, the registrar must not register the order unless either:

(a)   the court so directs; or

(b)   the company is first re-registered as a private company (ss 650–651 CA 2006).

Summary

Financial assistance towards the purchase of a company's own shares

There are restrictions on the provision of financial assistance for the purpose of acquiring shares in the company or of its holding company, particularly in the case of public companies. There are various exceptions to this prohibition, for example, private companies are exempt in most cases.

Purchase of a company's own shares and the issue of redeemable shares

All companies may, subject to satisfying certain conditions, issue redeemable shares and may also purchase their own shares. In the case of public companies, this can only be financed out of distributable profits or out of the proceeds of a fresh issue. In the case of private companies, the purchase may be financed out of capital.

Reduction of capital

Companies may reduce their issued capital by special resolution followed, in the case of public companies, by application to the court. The court will consider the position of creditors in deciding whether to approve the reduction.

Self-test questions

9.1 In what circumstances is it not permissible to provide financial assistance towards the purchase of a company's own shares?

9.2 How may a company issue redeemable shares?

9.3 Other than redeemable shares, in what circumstances may a company purchase its own shares?

9.4 How may a private company redeem or purchase its own shares out of capital?

9.5 Explain the concept of treasury shares.

9.6 What is the capital redemption reserve?

9.7 How may a company reduce its issued share capital?

Further reading

R Drury, 'The Delaware Syndrome: European Fears and Reactions' [2005] JBL 709.
P Leyte, 'The Regime of Capital Maintenance Pertaining to Public Companies, Its Reform and Alternatives' (2004) 25 Business LR 84.
G Morse, 'The Introduction of Treasury Shares Into English Law and Practice' [2004] JBL 303.
BG Pettet, 'Developments in the Law of Financial Assistance for the Purchase of Shares' (1988) 3 JIBL 96.
BG Pettet, 'Financial Assistance for the Acquisition of Shares: Further Developments' (1995) 10 JIBL 388.
MJ Sterling, 'Financial Assistance by a Company for the Purchase of Its Shares' (1987) 8 Co Law 99.

Chapter 10

Directors

Chapter Contents

10.1 Management of the company

The company is not a natural person. Therefore, someone needs to act on behalf of the company. The division of powers between the shareholders in general meetings and the directors will be considered later (see section 11.2, control of the directors). Suffice it to state at this juncture that the power of management is largely left with the directors. The purpose of this section of the textbook is to consider the role of directors, the appointment of directors, the removal of directors, the powers of directors and directors' duties. There is no precise definition of a director. Section 250 of the Companies Act 2006 merely states that a director 'includes any person occupying the position of director, by whatever name called'.

10.2 The appointment of directors

Section 7 of the 2006 Act provides that subscribers may form a company. In order to do so, they must submit registration documents which include a statement of the company's proposed officers (s 9(4)(c) CA 2006).

Section 12, which deals with the statement of the proposed officers, provides that the statement of the company's proposed officers required to be disclosed to the Registrar must contain the required particulars of:

(a) the person who is, or persons who are, to be the first director or directors of the company, together with

(b) details of any secretary or joint secretaries of a private company, if there is to be one, and

(c) in the case of a public company the person who is, or the persons who are, to be the first secretary or joint secretaries of the public company.

The statement must also contain a consent by each of the persons named to act in the relevant capacity.

Section 154 of the Companies Act 2006 provides that a private company must have at least one director, and a public company must have at least two directors. Section 155 goes on to provide that a company must have at least one director who is a natural person.

This requirement is met if the office of director is held by a natural person as a corporation sole or otherwise by virtue of an office. If it appears to the Secretary of State that a company is in breach of either s 154 or s 155, the Secretary of State may give the company a direction under s 156 indicating what the company must do in order to comply, and the period within which it must do so.

A minimum age is introduced for directors by s 157 CA 2006. A person may not be appointed a director of a company unless he has attained the age of 16 years. Section 158 provides that the Secretary of State may make provision by regulation for cases in which a person who has not attained the age of 16 may be appointed as a director of a company.

With regard to existing underage directors before the Companies Act 2006, any person who is under age will cease to be a director on s 157 coming into force (s 159).

Section 160 provides that in a public company the appointment of each individual as a director must be by a separate resolution, unless a resolution that the votes may be composite is agreed to by the general meeting without any vote given against it (s 160 CA 2006).

Section 161 provides that the acts of a person acting as a director are valid, notwithstanding that it is afterwards discovered that there is a defect in the appointment, or that the person is disqualified from holding office, or that the person has ceased to hold office, or that he was not entitled to vote on the matter in question. This applies too even if the resolution is void under s 160 (appointment of directors of a public company to be voted on individually).

Every company must keep a register of its directors (s 162 CA 2006). The register must be kept available for inspection either at the company's registered office or at a place specified in the regulations under s 1136. The company must give notice to the Registrar of the address at which the register is kept available for inspection and of any change in that place unless it has, at all times, been kept at the company's registered office (s 162(3), (4) CA 2006).

The company's register of directors should contain details of each director including a service address. It was formerly necessary for a private address to be given but this is no longer the case. The service address that the director has to give may be stated as the company's registered office (s 163(5) CA 2006).

A company is also obliged to keep a register of directors' residential addresses and to notify Companies House of its contents (s 165 CA 2006). The contents of this, however, are, with few exceptions, kept private (see s 240 CA 2006). The protection of privacy, however, ceases to apply if the director's service address is ineffective (s 245 CA 2006).

These provisions do not apply to directors' residential addresses already on the public register at Companies House. However, the Act does enable regulations to be made requiring the Registrar to make a specific address unavailable to public view if an application is made specifying the address that is to be removed, and its location on the register (s 1088 CA 2006).

Subsequent directors may be appointed in accordance with the articles. The board of directors may generally appoint people to casual vacancies between annual general meetings, but where this is done the people appointed to such vacancies must stand down at the next annual general meeting and be subject to re-election by ordinary resolution.

Changes in directors and registered details of directors (for example, a change of address) must be notified to the companies registry within 14 days of the change (s 167).

10.2.1 Shadow director

Section 251 (as amended by Section 90 of the Small Business, Enterprise and Employment Act 2015) defines a shadow director. In the Companies Act 'shadow director', in relation to a company, means a person in accordance with whose directions or instructions the directors of the company are accustomed to act.

It is provided that a person is not to be regarded as a shadow director by reason only that the directors act on advice given by him in a professional capacity.

It is further provided that a body corporate is not to be regarded as a shadow director of any of its subsidiary companies for the purposes of:

Chapter 2 (general duties of directors),
Chapter 4 (transactions requiring members' approval), and
Chapter 6 (contract with sole member who is also a director)

by reason only that the directors of the subsidiary are accustomed to act in accordance with its directions or instructions.

The overriding intention of the definition is to prevent controllers of the company from escaping legal responsibilities and liabilities.

Section 223 provides that in certain situations a shadow director is treated as a director. These are:

(a)   ss 188 and 189 (directors' service contracts) (see section 10.5.3);
(b)   ss 190–196 (property transactions) (see section 12.14);
(c)   ss 197–214 (loans etc.) (see section 10.9);
(d)   ss 215–222 (payments for loss of office) (see section 10.8).

It is further provided in s 223 that any reference in these provisions to loss of office as a director does not apply in relation to loss of a person's status as a shadow director.

It is important to stress that a person is a shadow director of a company only if 'the directors of the company' are accustomed to act in accordance with that person's directions or instructions. The shadow director must be 'the puppet master controlling the actions of the board' whilst the directors 'must be the "cat's-paw" of the shadow director'. Furthermore, the reference to 'accustomed to act' indicates that the acts must be done not on one individual occasion but over a period of time and as a regular course of conduct (see *Re Unisoft Group Ltd (No 3)* [1994] BCC 766 per Harman J at p. 775). Furthermore, if only a minority of the board follows the instructions then the person will not be regarded as a shadow director (see *Kuwait Asia Bank EC v National Mutual Life Nominees Ltd* [1990] 3 All ER 404) and more recently *Lord v Sinai Securities Ltd* [2004] EWHC 1764 (Ch) [2005] 1BCLC 295.

The Court of Appeal considered the definition of shadow director in *Secretary of State for Trade and Industry v Deverell* [2001] Ch 340 and restated the following principles and provided more elucidation:

(a)   it is not necessary to show that the person gives directions or instructions on every matter but to show that the person must have real influence;
(b)   any particular communication is for the court to determine objectively whether it is considered a direction or instruction;
(c)   advice (provided it is not professional advice) may be a direction or instruction;
(d)   it is not necessary to demonstrate that the directors adopted a subservient role or surrendered their discretion;
(e)   it is not necessary for the shadow director to lurk in the shadows but it is possible for a person to be a shadow director quite openly.

It seems clear from the judicial interpretation of s 251 that a high degree of control of a company's business is necessary for a person to be adjudged to be a shadow director. In *Re PFTZM Ltd* [1995] 2 BCLC 354, PFTZM ran a hotel. The hotel had financial difficulties and the hotel's landlord company permitted the company to continue trading on the basis that a director and a manager of the landlord company attended the company's management meetings and decided which of the company's creditors would be paid. The court held that there was no prima facie case for deciding that the landlord company's director and manager were shadow directors.

Judge Paul Baker QC said, speaking of the term 'shadow director' ([1995] 2 BCLC 354, at p. 367):

> This definition is directed to the case where the nominees are put up but in fact behind them their strings are being pulled by some other persons who do not put themselves forward as appointed directors. In this case, the involvement of the applicants here was thrust upon them by the insolvency of the company. They were not accustomed to give directions. The actions they took, as I see it, were simply directed to trying to rescue what they could out of the company using their undoubted rights as secured creditors.

There is a distinction between shadow directors and those acting as directors but who have not been formally appointed – de facto directors. In *Re Moorgate Metals Ltd* [1995] 1 BCLC 503, Warner J held that a Mr Rawlinson, who was acting as a director of Moorgate, was a de facto director. He was in sole charge of the company's trading and had brought the company into being.

In *Re Mumtaz Properties Ltd* [2011] EWCA Civ 610, the Court of Appeal provided guidance on the criteria as to whether an individual is to be taken to be a de facto director of a company in relation to s 212 of the Insolvency Act 1986.

Liability will be imposed on people who act as directors or exercise the powers of directors and discharge the tasks and functions of directors. This is irrespective of whether or not there has been a valid appointment as a director. See also *Re Sykes (Butchers) Ltd* [1998] 1 BCLC 110.

In *Revenue and Customs Commissioners v Holland* [2010] UKSC 51, decided on 24 November 2010, the Supreme Court held that a human director of a corporate director of a company is not thereby a de facto director of the company and liable for the misuse of any assets where he has acted appropriately as a director of the corporate director.

More recent case law has established that a person can be both a shadow director and a de facto director: see *Re Mea Corporation* [2006] EWHC 1846 (Ch) [2007] 1 BCLC 618 and *Commissioners of HM Revenue and Customs v Holland* [2010] UKSC 51, [2010] 1 WLR 2793.

Section 89(1) of the Small Business, Enterprise and Employment Act 2015 provides that the general duties of directors will apply to shadow directors where and to the extent that they are so capable of applying and applicable to shadow directors and s 89(2) enables the Secretary of State to make regulations concerning the application of general duties of directors to shadow directors subject to such adaptations as may be prescribed in s 89(3).

10.3 Executive and non-executive directors

A distinction is often made between executive and non-executive directors. A non-executive director is a director who is employed under a contract for services and is not working full time for the company and will receive, in exchange for his work for the company, a director's fee. By contrast, an executive director is a director who is employed under a contract of service, i.e. an employment contract, and will be generally working full time for the company and will be receiving a salary in exchange for his work.

There is no great significance in the distinction between the two in company law. For example, they are subject to the same regime of directors' duties (see in particular section 12.6.1). However, in relation to corporate governance, discussed below (Chapter 13), non-executive directors have an important role to play in seeking to ensure that the board of a company acts in the interests of the company rather than of individual members of the board. The Combined Code on Corporate Governance 2003 provides for a balance of executive and non-executive directors, and in particular independent non-executive directors. It is their task to control the executive directors. At least half of the board of companies in the FTSE 350 should be independent, while smaller quoted companies should have at least two independent directors. Independent non-executive directors should form the majority on the nomination committee which recommends appointments of directors, and the remuneration and audit committees should consist entirely of independent non-executive directors. The role of non-executive directors (and particularly independent non-executive directors, as defined in the Combined Code – see section 13.9) is therefore vital in ensuring appropriate corporate governance.

10.4 Qualification of directors

Unlike company secretaries, directors do not need to have any particular qualification to serve even in a public company. However, there are some negative conditions that must be considered.

Articles generally provide that a person may be disqualified from office if he becomes insane or bankrupt; also the articles may provide that the board may remove a director who has been voluntarily absent from board meetings for a period of six months or more.

In addition, there are statutory disqualifications from office. By virtue of the Company Directors Disqualification Act of 1986, both undischarged bankrupts and those disqualified by the court are ineligible to serve. Disqualification of directors will be considered below, in section 10.7. In addition, persons aged over 70 can only be elected or re-elected as directors of public companies or private companies that are subsidiaries of public companies if special notice is given before the meeting in accordance with CA 2006 (special notice is considered below, in section 16.4.1).

10.5 Removal from office

Section 168 of the Companies Act 2006 provides that a company may by ordinary resolution at a meeting remove a director before the expiration of his period of office, notwithstanding any agreement between the company and him.

This provision was first introduced in the Companies Act 1948 in response to the recommendations of the Cohen Committee of 1945. At first sight it seems to be a very powerful weapon in the hands of shareholders but its apparent power is subject to certain very real restrictions.

10.5.1 Weighted voting provisions

Although the section prohibits the exclusion of the right to remove a director by ordinary resolution, it does nothing to counteract normal principles of company law that may make that power very difficult to exercise. Thus, in British company law, it has always been possible to weight votes attaching to shares. This may, therefore, be used to give a minority shareholder who is a director the power to block his removal. In *Bushell v Faith* [1970] AC 1099, the House of Lords held that a weighted voting provision was valid in this context. Shares were held in a property company that owned a block of flats in Southgate, North London, by two sisters and a brother. The shares were held equally. The sisters wished to remove the brother from the board of directors. In normal circumstances, they would have had no problem as they had more than half of the shares. However, there was a provision in the articles of association that stated that on a resolution to remove a director, his shares would carry three votes each. The House of Lords held by a majority of four to one that this provision was valid. The effect of this was sufficient to block the brother's removal as a director. It is perhaps worth noting that the senior Law Lord, Lord Morris of Borthy-Gest, dissented in this case. He said the effect of finding that weighted voting was permissible in such circumstances was to drive a coach and horses through the intention of the legislature. It is possible that a shareholder could, in appropriate circumstances, use such a weighted voting provision against the petitioner as the basis of a petition under ss 994–996 of the Companies Act 2006.

10.5.2 Quorum provisions

By the same token, it would seem that other devices may be used. For example, a quorum provision that stated that the meeting was inquorate in the absence of the director threatened with removal would not be contrary to the Companies Act 2006. However, it may well be that a shareholder wishing to remove a director may be able to use such a provision as the basis of a petition under ss 994–996 CA 2006 as being unfairly prejudicial (see section 15.3). In *Harman v BML Group Ltd* [1994] 1 WLR 893, there was a shareholders' agreement which contained a provision that the meeting was only quorate if Blumenthal or his proxy was present. Blumenthal was removed as a director in his absence and he issued proceedings under s 994 contesting his removal. The Court of Appeal held that those wishing to remove the director could not use s 168 as the section could not be used to override class rights. The shareholders' agreement attached rights to shares and this has the same effect as if the class rights were contained in the company's articles.

In *Smith v Butler* [2012] EWCA Civ 314, the issue involved the holding of a corporate meeting with the quorum fixed at one by the court. Butler, as the managing director of Contract Holdings Ltd, purported to suspend Smith, the majority shareholder and chairman of the company. The reason for the purported suspension was in relation to an alleged fraud. This alleged fraud had been committed several years previously and had been known about by Butler for some time, but he had taken no action in relation to it until after Smith had declared that he wished to appoint a chief executive for the company as he was concerned about how Butler was running the company.

After the purported suspension, Smith was denied any role in the company's business. He subsequently attempted to hold a company meeting to consider the removal of Butler as a director of the company. Butler refused to attend such a meeting and, in consequence, under the company's articles, the meeting could not be quorate.

Smith then applied for relief from the court. He sought a declaration that his suspension was void as it was not consistent with the company's articles of association, and also sought an order under s 306 CA 2006, authorising a company meeting to be ordered with the quorum fixed at one.

The court held that Smith was entitled to the relief sought and that he was entitled to have a meeting ordered with the quorum fixed at one. He was a majority shareholder and was entitled to exercise his appropriate voting rights to appoint and remove directors.

10.5.3 Compensation provisions

Section 168(5)(a) provides that a person who is removed under s 168 is not deprived of compensation or damages payable to him in respect of the termination of his appointment as director or of any appointment terminating with that as director thereby. The section is therefore without prejudice to the removed director's rights to compensation for breach of contract. It was formerly the case that directors would have lengthy service contracts at high remuneration and therefore, at least in private companies, it would be extremely expensive to remove them. Section 188 provides that directors' long-term service agreements need the approval of the members (see also section 10.2.1).

This is in relation to any term of a director's employment that is longer than two years. The company must agree to any provision longer than two years and must do so by resolution of the members of the company and, in the case of a director or a holding company, by resolution of the members of that company too.

A resolution cannot be passed unless a memorandum setting out the proposed contract incorporating the provision is made available to members:

(a)   in the case of a written resolution by being sent to every eligible member; and
(b)   in the case of a resolution at a meeting by being made available for inspection by members of the company, both:

    (i)   at the company's registered office for not fewer than 15 days ending with the date of the meeting, and
    (ii)   at the meeting itself.

Removal may still prove expensive for the company: see *Shindler v Northern Raincoat Co Ltd* [1960] 1 WLR 1038 and *Southern Foundries Ltd v Shirlaw* [1940] AC 701. It may be that the company has concluded a service agreement with the director in which there is a liquidated damages provision specifying how much is payable to the director in the event of breach of the service agreement. In such an instance, the director may sue for the sum as a debt provided it is not a penalty; see *Taupo Totara Timber Co Ltd v Rowe* [1977] 3 All ER 123, a Privy Council decision on appeal from New Zealand.

10.5.4 Voting agreements

A director may have entered into voting agreements with other shareholders whereby they agree to vote as directed by him in specific instances. If this is the case, the director may ensure that they vote as promised: see *Stewart v Schwab* (1956) 4 SA 791 (South Africa) and see, on voting agreements in a different context, *Russell v Northern Bank Development Corporation Ltd* [1992] 1 WLR 588 (see also section 7.5).

10.5.5 Petition to complain of a removal

If the company is a quasi-partnership company, it may be that the director, if he is also a member, can petition under ss 994–996 CA 2006 on the grounds that his removal from office is unfairly prejudicial to his interests as a shareholder. This was one of the successful grounds for the petition in *Re a Company (No 00477 of 1986)* [1986] BCLC 376, for example. In *Re Bovey Hotel Ventures Ltd* (1981) (31 July unreported), an excluded director succeeded in a petition to purchase the shares of the excluding director. In *Re Bird Precision Bellows Ltd* [1984] Ch 419, it was accepted by the parties concerned that the company was a quasi-partnership. The petitioning shareholders had been excluded from office as directors. The court held that in the circumstances of the case the conduct amounted to unfair prejudice and it was ordered that the petitioner's shares be purchased by the respondents at a fair value.

In order to pre-empt a removal under s 168, the director concerned could threaten that, if removed, he would seek a remedy under ss 994–996 (see also section 15.3).

10.5.6 Petition for a winding-up order

In a similar way, under s 122(1)(g) of the Insolvency Act 1986, a director-member who is removed from a quasi-partnership company may seek to wind the company up on the just and equitable ground. Such a petition was successful in *Ebrahimi v Westbourne Galleries Ltd* [1973] AC 360. In this case, Ebrahimi and Nazar had run a successful partnership business selling carpets and tapestries. They decided to incorporate. The business flourished. Later Nazar sought the entry of his son, George, into the business and this was agreed. Some shares were transferred from Ebrahimi and some from Nazar. Discord soon followed and Nazar and George excluded Ebrahimi from the business and removed him as a director. Furthermore, the considerable profits of the business were paid out as directors' salaries rather than in the form of dividends. Exclusion as a director therefore kept Ebrahimi away from the profits. He sought a winding-up order under the Act. The House of Lords held unanimously that his petition would be granted.

In most circumstances, director-members in such a situation will now petition under ss 994–996. The just and equitable winding-up remedy is after all a 'sledgehammer' remedy. Furthermore, s 125(2) of the Insolvency Act 1986 requires the court, if it is of the opinion that the petitioner is entitled to relief, to decide whether it is just and equitable that the company should be wound up, bearing in mind the possibility of other forms of relief. The court, if it comes to the conclusion that it would be just and equitable that the company should be wound up in the absence of any other remedy, must make a winding-up order unless it is of the opinion that the petitioner is acting unreasonably in not pursuing that other remedy. In most circumstances, it will be unreasonable for a petitioner not to seek a remedy in such a situation, under ss 994–996 of the Companies Act 2006. However, in *Virdi v Abbey Leisure Ltd* [1990] BCLC 342, the court considered that a refusal by the shareholder to accept an offer to buy his shares, where he feared that the valuation would be wrong, was not unreasonable (see also section 15.6).

10.6 Special notice

Special notice is required in two situations in company law. The removal of a director is one of these circumstances (s 168(2)). The other is the removal of the company's auditors (ss 510–511 CA 2006) (see also section 16.4.1).

If the resolution concerns the removal of a director, the resolution must be forwarded forthwith to the director in question (s 169(1)). He may make representations in writing which must then be circulated to every member of the company to whom notice of the meeting is to be sent. If for some reason it is not possible to circulate his representations, they must be read out at the meeting. An exception to this situation is where the representations are considered to amount to an abuse of the section, in which case application may be made to the court, which would then decide if circulation was inappropriate.

Notice of the resolution to remove the director would then be included in the notice of the meeting that is to be called. The director who is threatened with removal would be allowed to speak in his defence at the meeting (s 169).

In both situations where special notice is appropriate, the resolution that is needed is an ordinary resolution.

In general, if the requirements of special notice are not complied with, the meeting and the removal of the director at such a meeting will be void. However, this gives way to the principle that the court will not interfere with the decision that is reached at such a meeting if it is clear that, had the correct procedures been followed, the decision would have been the same. In *Bentley-Stevens v Jones* [1974] 1 WLR 638, the claimant was seeking an injunction to restrain the defendants, one of which was a company of which the claimant was a director, from acting on a resolution passed at a general meeting of the company removing the claimant as a director.

The meeting had been convened by the company's holding company following a resolution of the holding company's board. The claimant, who was a director of the holding company, had had no notice of the board meeting.

Plowman J held that even if the claimant's complaint of irregularities was borne out, the court would not interfere to force the companies to conduct their business according to the strictest rules where the irregularity complained of could be put right at any moment.

The mere serving of special notice by a member who wishes to propose a resolution to remove a director will not of itself entitle that member to have the resolution circulated. Were it otherwise, any vexatious member (perhaps planted by a rival company) could embarrass the company by requiring meetings to be held to discuss his proposed resolution. In *Pedley v Inland Waterways Association Ltd* [1977] 1 All ER 209, Pedley, who was a solicitor (and so should arguably have known better), proposed the removal of the entire board of the company. He served special notice. Not surprisingly, the board did not wish to call the meeting. They did not do so. Pedley argued that this was a contravention of the provisions of the Act. He was unsuccessful. In order to ensure that a meeting is held, a person serving special notice will need to fit within one of the categories of those able to call meetings. These circumstances will be considered subsequently in Chapter 16.

The Companies Act 1989 introduced a regime whereby private companies did not need to call meetings if members otherwise agreed on a particular course of conduct. These situations will be considered subsequently in section 16.10.4. At this stage, suffice it to say that there are certain exceptions where meetings will need to be held and these include the proposed removal of a director and the proposal to remove an auditor. The director (and auditor) has, after all, the right to speak in his own defence, a right that can only properly be secured if a meeting is held.

10.7 Statutory disqualification of directors

The Company Directors Disqualification Act 1986 governs the position on disqualification. Section 1 of the Act sets out the basic thesis whereby a person may be disqualified from being:

(a) a director;
(b) a liquidator or administrator;
(c) a receiver or manager; or
(d) in any way directly or indirectly concerned or taking part in the promotion, formation or management of a company.

Thus the effect of a disqualification order extends beyond disqualification as a director. In fact the disqualification extends to similar management roles in friendly societies, NHS trusts, building societies, charitable trusts and limited liability partnerships.

There are various periods of disqualification which may be meted out depending upon the ground of disqualification. The period of disqualification runs from the date of the disqualification order.

10.7.1 Disqualification for general misconduct

Sections 2 to 5 of the Company Directors Disqualification Act 1986 deal with disqualification for general misconduct in connection with companies.

Section 2 provides for disqualification upon the conviction of an indictable offence in connection with the promotion, formation, management or liquidation of a company or with the receivership or management of a company's property.

The disqualification order may be passed by a court winding up the company or by a court before or upon a person being convicted of an offence. The maximum period of disqualification is five years in the case of a court of summary jurisdiction and 15 years in any other case.

Sections 3 and 5 of the Act permit disqualification for persistent breaches of companies' legislation. A person is to be taken to be persistent in default if it is conclusively proved that in the five years ending with the date of the application he has been adjudged guilty of three or more defaults in relation to Companies Act provisions.

The default may either involve conviction resulting from a particular provision or a default order being made against the person in question under one of the following:

(a)   s 242(4) – failure to deliver company accounts;
(b)   s 713 – failure to make returns;
(c)   s 41 of the Insolvency Act 1986 – failure of a receiver or manager to make returns; or
(d)   s 170 of the Insolvency Act 1986 – failure of a liquidator to make returns.

The maximum period of the disqualification under s 3 is five years.

Section 4 allows the court to disqualify for fraudulent trading (see section 25.3) or for fraud in relation to the company by an officer, liquidator, receiver or manager or breach of duty by such officer, liquidator, receiver or manager.

The maximum period of the disqualification under s 4 is 15 years.

10.7.2 Disqualification for unfitness

Sections 6 to 9 of the Act provide for disqualification for unfitness.

It is provided that the court must make a disqualification order against a person when application has been made if it is satisfied that a person has been a director of a company that has become insolvent and that his conduct as a director of that company (either taken on its own or together with his conduct as a director of any other company or companies) makes him unfit to be concerned in the management of a company. Application under s 6 is made by the Secretary of State for Trade and Industry or, if the Secretary of State so directs, by the official receiver.

A company is taken to be insolvent if:

(a)   the company goes into liquidation at a time when its assets are insufficient to pay its debts and liabilities and the expenses of the winding up;
(b)   an administration order is made in relation to the company; or
(c)   an administrative receiver of the company is appointed.

There is a duty upon the official receiver, the liquidator, the administrator or a receiver as is appropriate to inform the Secretary of State for Business, Innovation and Skills if any of them consider that a director is within the section. Schedule 1 of the Act provides the matters that are relevant for determining the unfitness of directors.

These are:

(a) any misfeasance or breach of any fiduciary or other duty by the director;

(b) misapplication or retention of property by the director or any conduct by the director giving rise to an obligation to account for money or other property;

(c) the extent of the director's responsibility for the company entering into any transaction that is liable to be set aside under Part XVI of the Insolvency Act 1986 which deals with provisions relating to debt avoidance;

(d) the extent of the director's responsibility for failure by the company to comply with one of the various provisions that are set out relating to the keeping of records and the making of an annual return;

(e) failure to approve and sign the company accounts;

(f) the director's responsibility for the company's insolvency;

(g) the extent of the director's responsibility for the company entering into a transaction or giving a preference which is liable to be set aside under s 127 of the Insolvency Act 1986 (as a disposition after the commencement of winding up) or a transaction which may be set aside as a transaction at an undervalue or a preference (see ss 238–240 of the Insolvency Act 1986); and

(h) failure to comply with one or more of the obligations under the Insolvency Act relating to the provision of a statement of affairs, cooperation with the liquidator, delivering up company property or calling or attending a creditors' meeting.

Note: The matters set out in (f), (g) and (h) above relate specifically to where the company has become insolvent. The other matters are applicable in all cases and may thus arise where the director's conduct in another (possibly solvent) company is being examined.

The maximum period of disqualification under the section is 15 years and the minimum period is two years.

Section 8 provides for disqualification of a director after an investigation of a company (see Chapter 23). If it appears to the Secretary of State from a report made by inspectors that it is expedient in the public interest that a disqualification order should be made against a person who is or has been a director or shadow director, he may apply to the court for such an order to be made against that person. The court may make such an order if it is felt that the director is unfit.

The disqualification period here is subject to a maximum of 15 years.

In *Re Sevenoaks Stationers (Retail) Ltd* [1991] BCLC 325, the Court of Appeal set out certain principles on disqualification for unfitness. Dillon LJ said at p. 328:

> I would for my part endorse the division of the potential 15-year disqualification period into three brackets, which was put forward by Mr Keenan for the Official Receiver to Harman J in the present case and has been put forward by Mr Charles for the Official Receivers in other cases, viz:
>
> (i) the top bracket of disqualification for periods over ten years should be reserved for particularly serious cases. These may include cases where a director who has already had one period of disqualification imposed on him falls to be disqualified yet again;

(ii)   the minimum bracket of two to five years' disqualification should be applied where, though disqualification is mandatory, the case is relatively not very serious;

(iii)   the middle bracket of disqualification for from six to ten years should apply for serious cases which do not merit the top bracket.

These are, of course, just general guidelines. Each case will turn on its own particular facts. The prime purpose of the provision is to protect the public and to raise standards. See *Re Blackspur Group plc* [1998] 1 WLR 422.

In *Secretary of State for Trade and Industry v Gray* [1995] Ch 421, the Court of Appeal allowed an appeal where the first-instance judge had considered that the future protection of the public did not merit a period of disqualification. The Court of Appeal stated that if the respondents' conduct fell below the standard appropriate for persons considered fit to be directors, then it was the judge's duty to make a disqualification order.

An example of a disqualification for unfitness is provided by *Re Firedart Ltd* [1994] 2 BCLC 340, where Fairall, the director, had continued trading through the medium of the company when it was insolvent, had received excessive remuneration and had failed to keep proper accounting records. The appropriate period of disqualification was held to be six years. See also *Re Park House Properties Ltd* [1997] 2 BCLC 530.

Further examples of unfitness include failure to exercise independent judgement (*Re Bradcrown Ltd, Official Receiver v Ireland* [2001] BCLC 547), trading when knowing a company is insolvent (*Re Ipcon Fashions Ltd* (1989) 5 BCC 773) and failure to pay tax due and financial irregularities (*Official Receiver v Doshi* [2001] 2 BCLC 235).

10.7.3 Disqualification in other cases

Sections 10 to 12 deal with other cases of disqualification. Section 10 provides that where there has been participation in wrongful trading or fraudulent trading such that a person is held liable to make a contribution to a company's assets, then whether or not an application for an order is made, the court may if it thinks fit make a disqualification order against the person to whom the declaration of liability relates. The maximum period of the disqualification is 15 years.

Section 11 of the Act provides that it is an offence for a person who is an undischarged bankrupt to act as a director. Section 12 provides that where a person fails to make a payment as provided for in an administration order of the county court, the court may make a disqualification order against the person concerned in revoking the administration order. The period may not exceed two years.

10.7.4 Consequences of disqualification

Section 13 provides that a person who acts in contravention of a disqualification order is guilty of an offence which on conviction on indictment is punishable by up to two years' imprisonment and/or a fine, and is punishable on summary conviction by imprisonment of not more than six months and/or a fine up to the statutory maximum. Section 14 of the Act provides that where a company is guilty of an offence of acting in contravention of a disqualification order and it is shown that the offence occurred with the consent or connivance or is attributable to any neglect on the part of any director, manager, secretary or other officer of the body corporate or any person purporting to act as such, he shall be guilty of an offence as well as the body corporate.

Section 15 provides that a person who is disqualified and continues to act is personally responsible for all the relevant debts of the company.

There is a register of disqualification orders which is kept by the Secretary of State in pursuance of s 18 of the Act.

10.7.5 Summary disqualification procedure

Sometimes, there is the possibility of a summary procedure for dealing with applications for disqualification of directors being utilised. This procedure, as set out in *Re Carecraft Construction Co Ltd* [1993] 4 All ER 499, was reviewed in *Secretary of State for Trade and Industry v Rogers* [1997] BCC 155 by Scott VC.

Scott VC said that the Carecraft summary procedure can be used where:

(a)   the facts regarding the director's conduct are not disputed;
(b)   the Secretary of State for Trade and Industry is willing for the case to be dealt with by the judge on those undisputed facts;
(c)   the director is willing for the case to be dealt with by the judge on those facts; and
(d)   the Secretary of State and the director have reached agreement either on the length of the disqualification period or at least on the parameters within which it should fall.

This process enables disqualification to proceed expeditiously and with reduced costs.

10.8 Directors' loss of office and compensation payments

Where a director loses office, he may, nevertheless, be awarded a golden handshake sum. Sections 215 to 222 of the Companies Act 2006 deal with this area (see also section 10.2.1).

Section 217 provides that a company may not make a payment for loss of office to a director unless the payment has been approved by a resolution of the members of the company. The section further provides that it cannot make payment for loss of office to a director of its holding company unless the payment has been approved by a resolution of the members of each of those companies.

Under s 218 no payment for loss of office may be made by any person to a director of a company in connection with the transfer of the whole or any part of the undertaking or property of the company unless the payment has been approved by a resolution of the members of the company.

Further, no payment for loss of office may be made by any person to a director of a company in connection with the transfer of the whole or any part of the undertaking or property of a subsidiary of the company unless the payment has been approved by a resolution of the members of each of the companies.

Section 219 provides that, if a payment is proposed to be made to a director by any person in connection with the transfer of shares in the company or in a subsidiary of the company resulting from the takeover bid, it may not be made unless the payment has been approved by a resolution of the relevant shareholders. The shareholders who need to approve the payment are the holders of the shares to which the bid relates, and any holders of shares of the same class as any of those shares.

Section 222 deals with the consequences of payments in contravention of the golden handshake sections.

If a payment is made in contravention of s 217 (payment by a company), the payment is held by the recipient on trust for the company making the payment, and any director who authorised the payment is jointly and severally liable to indemnify the company that made the payment for any loss resulting from it.

If a payment is made in contravention of s 218 (payment in connection with the transfer of undertaking, etc.), it is held by the recipient on trust for the company whose undertaking or property is proposed to be transferred.

If a payment is made in contravention of s 219 (payment in connection with share transfer):

(a)   it is held by the recipient on trust for the persons who have sold their shares as a result of the offer made; and

(b)   the expenses incurred by the recipients in distributing that sum amongst those persons shall be borne by him and not retained out of that sum.

It should be noted that the provisions on golden handshakes do not apply to payment of compensation for breach of a contract of service by court order (s 168(5)(a)) or to a bona fide settlement of a claim under s 168, or where a director sues for a liquidated sum set out in the contract as payable in the event of breach: see *Taupo Totara Timber Co Ltd v Rowe* (1977), a Privy Council decision on appeal from New Zealand (see s 220).

There is also an exception for small payments in relation to the golden handshake provisions where approval is not required if:

(a)   the payment in question is made by the company or any of its subsidiaries; and

(b)   the amount or value of the payment, together with the amount or value of any other relevant payments, does not exceed £200 (s 221).

10.9 Loans, quasi-loans and credit transactions in favour of directors

The law in this area is not likely to set the pulse racing. The 2006 Act removed former prohibitions on loans etc. to directors and connected persons (see also section 10.2.1). There is now a general position where such loans etc. may be made subject to the requirement of the shareholders' approval, which must be obtained before the particular transaction with the director etc. is entered into (ss 197–214 CA 2006). In general for a private limited company, shareholder approval is required for loans in excess of £10,000 with a limit of £50,000 if the loan is to meet expenditure on company business. A tax charge is imposed under the Corporation Tax Act 2010 for loans to directors of a close company (under the control of five or fewer members or participators) exceeding a prescribed limit and after a prescribed period so it is important to consider the tax ramifications for a company.

Section 197 of the Companies Act 2006 provides that a company may not make a loan to a director or give a guarantee or provide security in connection with a loan made by any person to a director unless the transaction has been approved by a resolution of the members of the company.

If the director is a director of the company's holding company, the transaction must also have been approved by a resolution of the members of the holding company.

Section 198 deals with quasi-loans. These are defined in s 199 to mean transactions where one party (the creditor) agrees to pay or pays otherwise than in pursuance of an agreement, a sum for another (the borrower) or agrees to reimburse that other in relation to expenditure incurred by another party for the borrower.

In relation to quasi-loans to directors, s 198 provides that if the company is a public company or a company associated with a public company, then the company may not make a quasi-loan to a director of the company or of its holding company, or give a guarantee or provide security in connection with such a quasi-loan, unless the transaction has been approved by a resolution of the members of the company. If the director is a director of the company's holding company, the transaction must also have been approved by a resolution of the members of the holding company.

Section 256 CA 2006 and the definition of an associated company are relevant here. Section 256(b) provides that companies are associated if one is a subsidiary of the other or both are subsidiaries of the same body corporate.

Section 200 CA 2006 deals with loans or quasi-loans to persons connected with directors.

The section applies to a company that is a public company or a company associated with a public company. In these circumstances a company may not make a loan or quasi-loan to a person connected with a director of the company or of its holding company, or give a guarantee or provide security in connection with such a loan or quasi-loan unless the transaction has been approved by a resolution of the members of the company. If the connected person is a person connected with a director of the company's holding company, the transaction must also have been approved by a resolution of the members of the holding company.

Sections 201 and 202 deal with credit transactions. A credit transaction is a transaction under which one party, the creditor, supplies goods or sells land under a hire purchase agreement or conditional sale agreement, or leases or hires land or goods in return for periodical payments, or otherwise disposes of land or supplies goods or services on the understanding that payment is to be deferred (s 202 CA 2006).

Section 201 provides that in relation to a public company or a company associated with a public company, the company cannot enter into a credit transaction as creditor for the benefit of a director of the company or of its holding company or a person connected with such a director, or give a guarantee or provide security in connection with a credit transaction, unless the transaction or the giving of the guarantee or the provision of security has been approved by a resolution of the members of the company.

If the director or connected person is a director of its holding company, or a person connected with such a director, the transaction must also have been approved by a resolution of the members of the holding company.

Section 203 CA 2006 is a provision designed to plug a loophole such that the company may not enter into an arrangement with somebody else which would have required approval under ss 197, 198, 200 or 201, where the other person entering the arrangement obtains a benefit from the company or a body corporate associated with it, or where the company arranges for the assignment to it or assumption by it of any rights, obligations or liabilities under a transaction that if it had been entered into by the company would have required such approval.

In such situations the arrangement must be approved by a resolution of the members of the company, and of its holding company (if appropriate).

There are certain exceptions to these general rules:

(a) expenditure in connection with regulatory action or investigation (s 206 CA 2006);
(b) expenditure, de minimis (s 207 CA 2006);
(c) intragroup transactions (s 208 CA 2006); and
(d) expenditure by moneylending companies made on the normal terms of business (s 209 CA 2006).

Section 213 deals with the civil consequences of contravention.

The transaction or arrangement in question is voidable at the instance of the company unless restitution is no longer possible, or the company has been indemnified for any loss or damage, or rights acquired in good faith for value and without notice of the contravention by a person who is not a party to the transaction would be affected by the avoidance.

It is to be noted that the categories of a person 'connected' with a director for these provisions have been extended from spouse and children and stepchildren to include civil partners, cohabitants, infant children of the cohabitant living with the director, the director's adult children and his parents (ss 252–253 CA 2006).

It should be noted that certain transactions remain outside of the scope of the prohibition, thus quasi-loans to and credit transactions with a director or connected persons by a private company that is not associated with a public company do not require approval.

Summary

Appointment of directors

The appointment of directors is a matter that is generally settled by the articles of association.

Public companies must have at least two directors and private companies must have at least one director.

There are various categorisations of directors; particularly important is the distinction between executive and non-executive directors. Shadow directors, those in accordance with whose directions and instructions directors are accustomed to act, are subject to many of the same rules and principles as directors.

Removal of directors

Section 168 CA 2006 provides for the removal of directors from the board of directors by ordinary resolution in general meeting.

There are various provisos which may affect the exercise of this power:

(a)   the possibility of weighted voting shares;
(b)   a carefully drawn quorum provision;
(c)   compensation payable for breach of contract;
(d)   voting agreements;
(e)   a ss 994–996 petition by a shareholder/director;
(f)   a winding-up petition on the just and equitable ground (s 122(1)(g) of the Insolvency Act 1986) by a shareholder/director; and
(g)   the procedural niceties of the special notice procedure.

Statutory disqualification

The Company Directors Disqualification Act 1986 provides for disqualification from office as:

(a)   a director;
(b)   a liquidator or administrator;
(c)   a receiver or manager; or
(d)   a person concerned in the promotion, formation or management of a company.

Disqualification may arise on various grounds. It may be from conviction of an indictable offence connected with the running of a company, persistent breach of filing provisions of the companies legislation or for fraudulent trading.

In addition, directors may be disqualified on the ground of unfitness following the insolvency of their company or following a company investigation. There are various guidelines that are set out in a schedule to the Act which are relevant in determining unfitness.

An undischarged bankrupt cannot act as a director.

Directors' loss of office and compensation payments

Golden handshake payments for directors have to be disclosed to members and assented to.

Loans, quasi-loans, etc.

There are strict rules restricting loans, quasi-loans and credit transactions in favour of directors and connected persons. Transactions in breach of the provisions are void and civil consequences may result.

Self-test questions

10.1 Who is responsible for the management of the company?

10.2 Explain how directors may be appointed.

10.3 Explain the distinction between executive and non-executive directors.

10.4 What is the age restriction on directors in public companies?

10.5 How may directors be removed from office?

10.6 Explain the concept of special notice.

10.7 On what grounds may a director be disqualified from office? Give examples of decided cases illustrating different circumstances of disqualification.

10.8 Set out the rules in relation to compensation payments for directors' loss of office.

10.9 What are the rules in relation to loans, quasi-loans and credit transactions in favour of directors?

Further reading

PV Baker, 'A Casenote on *Bushell v Faith*' (1970) 86 LQR 155.

S Griffin, 'The Disqualification of Unfit Directors and the Protection of the Public Interest' (2002) NILQ 207.

A Hicks, 'Disqualification of Directors – Forty Years On' (1988) JBL 27.

A Hicks, 'Director Disqualification – The National Audit Office Follows Up', ILP, 15 (1999) 112.

A Hoey, 'Disqualifying Delinquent Directors' (1997) 18 Co Law 130.

D Millman, 'Personal Liability and Disqualification of Company Directors: Something Old, Something New' (1992) 43 NILQ 1.

C Noonan and S Watson, 'The Nature of Shadow Directorship: Ad Hoc Statutory Intervention or Core Company Law Principle?' [2006] JBL 763.

KTW Ong, 'Disqualification of Directors: A Faulty Regime?' (1998) 19 Co Law 7.

K Wardman, 'Directors and Employee Status: An Examination of Relevant Company Law and Employment Law Principles' (2003) 24 Co Law 139.

S Wheeler, 'Directors' Disqualification: Insolvency Practitioners and the Decision-Making Process' (1995) 15 LS 283.

Chapter 11

Powers of directors

Chapter Contents

11.1 Introduction

Generally, companies will delegate considerable powers of management to the directors of the company. Table A of the Companies Act 1985, Article 70 (SI 1985/805), for example, provided:

> Subject to the provisions of the Act, the memorandum and the articles and to any directions given by special resolution, the business of the company shall be managed by the directors who may exercise all the powers of the company. No alteration of the memorandum or articles and no such direction shall invalidate any prior act of the directors which would have been valid if that alteration had not been made or that direction had not been given.

The model articles for private companies limited by shares under the Companies Act 2006 provide in Article 3 – Directors' General Authority – 'Subject to the articles, the directors are responsible for the management of the company's business, for which purpose they may exercise all the powers of the company' (The Companies (Model Articles) Regulations 2008 (SI 2008/3229)).

Article 4 of the model articles for private companies, as well as Article 4 of the model articles for public companies (both under the 2006 Act), provide that the members of a company may give instructions to the board by special resolution.

The company will obviously delegate only such powers as it itself has. Thus, the directors are not competent to engage in ultra vires transactions. As has been seen, however, ultra vires transactions may be ratified and the breach of directors' duties may be ratified by a separate special resolution. Furthermore, the directors can only validly act in the interests of the company and for the purposes for which the powers are conferred upon them: see *Hogg v Cramphorn Ltd* [1967] Ch 254 and *Bamford v Bamford* [1970] Ch 212 (see section 12.5.1).

The powers delegated to the directors are delegated to them collectively. It is open to the directors, of course, to subdelegate powers to individual directors or, indeed, to others.

11.2 Control of the directors

In general, the directors are vested with management by the members. Their removal from office is by an ordinary resolution passed in general meeting following special notice: see s 168 of the Companies Act 2006. Directors may exercise their powers of management while they are in office: see *Salmon v Quin and Axtens Ltd* [1909] 1 Ch 311. Where companies have articles like Article 3 of the Private Company Model Regulations 2008 (see section 11.1), however, this permits directions to be given by special resolution to the directors.

In *John Shaw & Sons (Salford) Ltd v Shaw* [1935] 2 KB 113, the Court of Appeal refused to allow the members to override the decision of the directors to commence legal proceedings. In *Breckland Group Holdings Ltd v London and Suffolk Properties Ltd* [1989] BCLC 100, the company attempted to commence legal proceedings. The company had two members, Breckland Ltd and Crompton Ltd. It had been agreed that Crompton Ltd would appoint two directors and Breckland Ltd one director. It had further been agreed that for legal proceedings to be commenced, both Breckland Ltd and Crompton Ltd would have to agree. The High Court restrained the parties from taking any further steps until a board meeting of the company could be held. The matter was one for the board of directors to determine under the equivalent of Table A, Art 70. Previously, in *Marshalls Valve Gear v Manning Wardle & Company* [1909] 1 Ch 267, it had been held that the board of directors could be overridden by the company in general meeting in relation to potential litigation involving one of the directors.

In other circumstances, the members may have to act to fill a void.

The House of Lords, in *Alexander Ward & Co v Samyang Navigation Co* [1975] 1 WLR 673, allowed two members to act to protect the interests of the company when the company had no directors. In this case before the House of Lords on appeal from Scotland, the claimant company brought the action at the instance of two shareholders of a company having no board of directors.

The House of Lords accepted that in such circumstances it was open to the general meeting to assume the powers of management of the company.

In *Re Argentum Reductions (UK) Ltd* [1975] 1 WLR 186, Megarry J declined to decide whether the members had reserve powers where the directors were unable to act, stating at p. 189 that 'there are deep waters here'. There was an application under the provisions of the Companies Act to obtain leave of the court to allow a company, against which a winding-up petition had been filed, to pay certain debts.

Megarry J held that in his judgment the shareholder had a sufficient *locus standi* to make the application.

The cases are far from consistent. On occasion, the courts have permitted the members to act where there is deadlock on the board of directors. Thus in *Barron v Potter* [1914] 1 Ch 895, the company had two directors who were not on speaking terms. It was impossible to hold constructive board meetings. Canon Barron refused to attend board meetings with Potter. Potter tried to call a general meeting. Barron intended to boycott this meeting but his train was met at Paddington by Potter, who proceeded to try to hold a meeting on the platform. He proposed Charles Herbert, William George Walter Barnard and John Tolhurst Musgrave as additional directors. Barron objected and Potter purported to use his casting vote as chairman. The court held that this was an ineffective meeting. In the circumstances, it was held that in view of the deadlock on the board of directors, the powers were exercisable by the members in general meeting. In a similar way, in *Foster v Foster* [1916] 1 Ch 532, there was a dispute over which of the two directors should be appointed as managing director of the company. There were three directors in all. The articles gave the power to appoint a managing director to the board of directors. However, directors could not vote on a matter in which they had a personal interest. It was, accordingly, not possible to pass the resolution. The general meeting accordingly could fill the vacuum.

It is open to the members of the company in general meeting to ratify matters that have been performed by the directors. It is possible to use this power of ratification in relation to ultra vires acts by special resolution. It is possible to use the power of ratification in relation to acts that are beyond the directors' authority by ordinary resolution provided that the directors are not acting fraudulently: see *Hogg v Cramphorn Ltd* (1967), *Bamford v Bamford* (1970) and *Grant v United Kingdom Switchback Railways Co* (1888) 40 ChD 135.

11.3 Managing director

The articles, such as Art 72 of Table A of the 1985 Act, permit the appointment of a managing director. Article 5 of the Private Company Model Articles and Public Company Model Articles, under the 2006 Act, permits delegation by the directors to any person or committee. The appointment of a managing director, however, is not a legal requirement.

The appointment of a managing director will cease if he ceases to be a director. If he has a separate service agreement and is removed as a director, he may, of course, sue upon this contract: see s 168(5)(a) CA 2006.

11.4 Validity of the acts of directors

If matters are delegated to the board of directors, this, of course, means directors who are properly appointed. On occasion, directors may be invalidly appointed and questions arise as to whether those dealing with them may hold the company bound. There are certain rules of law that tend to validate the acts of a director in spite of any irregularities in his appointment in such circumstances.

There is a statutory principle contained in s 161 CA 2006 that the acts of a person acting as a director are valid, notwithstanding that it is afterwards discovered:

(a)   that there was a defect in his appointment;
(b)   that he was disqualified from holding office;
(c)   that he had ceased to hold office;
(d)   that he was not entitled to vote on the matter in question.

It should be noted that s 161 covers defects of appointment or qualification, but, as is made clear by *Morris v Kanssen* [1946] AC 459, the principle cannot apply where there has been a fraudulent attempt to appoint a director. It can only apply where there is a bona fide attempt to appoint a director, etc. It does not cover cases of fraud.

A quite separate principle is an application of the rule in *Turquand's case, Royal British Bank v Turquand* (1856) 6 E1 & B1 327, which is considered more fully below (section 11.5). If a person deals with a company through persons who are purporting to act as directors, even though they have not been properly appointed, he may be entitled to assume that they are in fact directors and to hold the company bound by their acts: see *Mahony v East Holyford Mining Co* (1875) LR 7 HL 869, where the persons purporting to act as secretaries and directors who had concluded the transaction had not, in fact, been appointed.

The principles of agency law dictate that an agent can only act within his actual or ostensible authority in binding the company. If an agent acts beyond his actual and ostensible authority and contracts with another, the company is not bound. The remedy for the other party contracting with the non-agent in these circumstances will be for breach of warranty of authority.

The outsider may be able to hold the company bound on the basis of actual authority or on the basis of ostensible authority (sometimes called 'apparent' authority, holding out or agency by estoppel).

Diplock LJ in *Freeman and Lockyer v Buckhurst Park Properties (Mangal Ltd)* [1964] 2 QB 480, at p. 505, said:

> The commones t form of representation by a principal creating an 'apparent' authority of an agent is by conduct, namely, by permitting the agent to act in the management or conduct of the principal's business. Thus, if in the case of a company, the board of directors who have 'actual' authority under the memorandum and articles of association to manage the company's business, permit the agent to act in the management or conduct of the company's business, they thereby represent to all persons dealing with such agent that he has authority to enter on behalf of the corporation into contracts of a kind which an agent authorised to do acts of the kind which he is in fact permitted to do, normally enters into in the ordinary course of such business.

Thus, if the company makes it appear that an individual director or person has authority to conclude a particular transaction, an outsider can hold the company bound. A director simply by virtue of holding the office of director has no implied authority as agent of the company to conclude contracts. Yet, if the company allows the director to act as if he had such authority, then the company may be estopped from denying that he has the authority. It is no longer the case that the mere fact that the company's constitution makes it clear that there is no such authority is sufficient to render the authority non-existent (see section 6.10). There is no constructive notice of such restrictions (see s 40 CA 2006). The question of agency by estoppel was discussed in *Freeman and Lockyer v Buckhurst Park Properties (Mangal)* (1964). Diplock LJ said that there must have been a representation that a person had authority and that representation must have been made by those who had authority within the company. The other party must have relied on the representation in entering into the contract. He went on to say that there must be nothing in the constitution to countermand that authority. This last point of Diplock LJ is, of course, no longer applicable. In *Freeman and Lockyer* itself, the board of directors had permitted one director to act as if he had been appointed managing director. In fact he had not been appointed as managing director but the articles of association made provision for such an appointment. Accordingly the company was held liable. On occasion problems may arise as identified by Lord Pearson in *Hely-Hutchinson v Brayhead Ltd* [1968] 1 QB 549 at p. 593:

> now there is not usually any direct communication in such cases between the board of directors and the outside contractor. The actual communication is made immediately and directly, whether it be expressed or implied by the agent to the outside contractor. It is, therefore, necessary in order to make a case of ostensible authority to show in some way as such communication which is made directly by the agent is made ultimately by the responsible parties, the board of directors. That may be shown by inference from the conduct of the board of directors in the particular case by, for instance, placing the agent in a position where he can hold himself out as their agent and acquiescing in his activities, so that it can be said that they have in effect caused the representation to be made.

In this case the claimant loaned money to the defendant and guaranteed other loans. There were cross undertakings indemnifying the claimant made by the defendant in writing and signed by one Richards. In fact Richards had never been appointed as managing director of the defendant.

The Court of Appeal held that since Richards was actually authorised to act for the company, the company was bound.

In *Armagas Ltd v Mundogas SA* [1986] AC 717, Lord Keith of Kinkel said (p. 777):

> Ostensible authority comes about where the principal, by words or conduct, has represented that the agent has the requisite actual authority, and the party dealing with the agent has entered into a contract with him in reliance on that representation.

Thus, in *First Energy (UK) Ltd v Hungarian International Bank Ltd* [1993] BCLC 1409, the manager of a branch of the bank made an offer of facilities to First Energy. He did not have authority to make such offers himself, but it was held that he had ostensible authority to communicate such offers. The bank was, therefore, held liable.

If there is a representation by the principal (the directors) that the agent has the necessary authority, then the principal is estopped from asserting that the agent did not have authority. Of course, the principal may withdraw a representation of authority but this is only effective when communicated.

11.5 The rule in *Turquand's case*

In *Turquand's case* (*Royal British Bank v Turquand* (1856)), the company's articles authorised the directors to borrow money if this had been sanctioned by ordinary resolution. A resolution was passed but it did not specify the amount that the directors could borrow. The directors borrowed money and the company became insolvent. Turquand was sued as the liquidator. It was held that the claimant's bank was deemed to be aware that the directors could only borrow up to the amount of the resolution as the articles were available at Companies House and, therefore, there was constructive notice of the contents of the articles of association. Yet an outsider had no means of knowing whether an ordinary resolution had been passed. Ordinary resolutions were not registrable. In the circumstances, the bank was entitled to assume the fact of a resolution being passed and was not required (indeed not entitled) to investigate the internal workings of the company. The rule is sometimes called 'the indoor management rule'.

The rule does not apply in all circumstances. Thus, if the outsider actually knew or had strong grounds for suspecting that the act was not authorised, the rule cannot be relied upon: see *Underwood v Bank of Liverpool and Martins* [1924] 1 KB 775. In this case the director of a company kept his own personal bank account at the bank. It was held that the bank was put on enquiry where he paid cheques made out to the company into his own private bank account.

Furthermore, if the person dealing with the company is himself one of its directors, then it is reasonable to assume that he will know of the internal operations of the company and may therefore not be able to rely upon the principle: see *Hely-Hutchinson v Brayhead Ltd* (1968).

Furthermore, it seems that the principle in *Royal British Bank v Turquand* cannot be relied upon if the document that is presented is a forgery: see *Ruben v Great Fingall Consolidated* [1906] AC 439. The principle of indoor management is therefore useful to bind the company to acts of directors (or apparent directors) who are acting beyond their capacity.

Those dealing with the company no longer have constructive notice of the articles whether or not they contain restrictions on the capacity of persons to act.

The rule is seemingly restricted to situations where the board as a whole is presumed to have authority rather than individual directors.

The area of agents' authority clearly overlaps with the area of corporate capacity and powers. Section 40 of the Companies Act 2006 will generally afford more protection to an outsider as even knowledge of the act being beyond the authority of the board will not, of itself, amount to bad faith (s 40(2)(iii)). On the other hand, *Turquand* probably applies where there is not a properly constituted board and so the principle in *Turquand's case* therefore remains of importance. Furthermore, s 40 does not apply to charitable companies and the rule in *Turquand's case* is also applicable here.

Summary
Introduction
Articles such as Companies Act 1985 Table A Art 70 and Art 3 of the Private Company Model Articles under the Companies Act 2006 provide for the management of the company's business by the directors and most companies follow this format.

It is rarely open to the shareholders in general meeting to take on the functions of the directors. There are certain exceptions to this general rule, however. If the directors are unable to act for some reason, such as deadlock or if there are no directors, then the shareholders may act.

Validation of directors' acts
If a person acts as director but there is some defect in his initial appointment, nevertheless, his acts are to be treated as valid.

Furthermore, where a person is held out as a director or as having authority to the outside world and this is relied upon where there is nothing to indicate the lack of actual authority, the outsider will be able to hold the company responsible on agency principles.

A further rule, called the indoor management rule or the rule in *Turquand's case*, provides that, if to an outsider the correct procedures appear to have been adhered to, then the outsider can hold the company responsible notwithstanding that there is some internal irregularity. An outsider is not bound, indeed not entitled, to enquire into the internal workings of the company.

Self-test questions
11.1 How does a company exercise powers?

11.2 How are the directors of a company controlled?

11.3 Must a company have a managing director?

11.4 What happens where somebody acting as a director has not been properly appointed?

11.5 What is the rule in *Turquand's case* – is it still important today?

Further reading

E Ferran, 'The Reform of the Law on Corporate Capacity and Directors' and Officers' Authority' (1992) 13 Co Law 124.

J Flynn, 'The Power to Direct' (1991) 13 DULJ 101.

H Hirt, 'The Company's Decision to Litigate Against Its Directors: Legal Strategies to Deal With the Board of Directors' Conflict of Interest' [2005] JBL 159.

J MacKenzie, 'Who Controls the Company? The Interpretation of Table A' (1983) 4 Co Law 99.

LS Sealy, 'Agency Principles and the Rule in Turquand's Case' (1990) 49 CLJ 406.

G Sullivan, 'The Relationship Between the Board of Directors and the General Meeting in Limited Companies' (1977) 93 LQR 569.

Chapter 12

Directors' duties

Chapter Contents

12.1 Introduction

One of the most significant changes brought about by the Companies Act 2006 is in relation to the statutory code of duties that a director owes to a company (ss 170–177 CA 2006).

A person who ceases to be a director continues to be subject:

(a) to the duty in s 175 (duty to avoid conflicts of interest) as regards the exploitation of any property, information or opportunity of which he became aware at a time when he was a director; and

(b) to the duty in s 176 (duty not to accept benefits from third parties) in relation to things that were done or omitted by the director before he ceased to be a director.

Section 170(4) provides that the general duties shall be interpreted and applied in the same way as the common law rules or equitable principles and regard should be had to the corresponding common law rules and equitable principles in interpreting and applying those general duties.

It is therefore proposed to consider pre-existing case law that impacts on the interpretation of these duties.

After the passage of the Companies Act 2006, the minister responsible for steering the legislation through the House of Commons, the Rt Hon Margaret Hodge MP, the Minister of State for Industry and the Regions, issued guidance on the statutory duties of directors in the Act.

She noted that she and other ministers were questioned about the meaning of provisions. Some of the responses and statements she considered may be helpful to those interested in what the provisions meant and a structured collection of them was therefore issued. Some of them are reproduced here as guidance and to indicate the scope of the duties under the Act.

Guidance for company directors

1 Act in the company's best interests, taking everything you think relevant into account.

2 Obey the company's constitution and decisions taken under it.

3 Be honest, and remember that the company's property belongs to it and not to you or to its shareholders.

4 Be diligent, careful and well informed about the company's affairs. If you have any special skills or experience, use them.

5 Make sure the company keeps records of your decisions.

6 Remember that you remain responsible for the work you give to others.

7 Avoid situations where your interests conflict with those of the company. When in doubt, disclose potential conflicts quickly.

8 Seek external advice where necessary, particularly if the company is in financial difficulty.

The minister noted that there are two ways of looking at the statutory statement of directors' duties: on the one hand it simply codifies the existing common law obligations of company directors; on the other – especially in s 172, the duty to act in the interests of the company – it marks a radical departure in articulating the connection between what is good for a company and what is good for society at large.

It is noted that the statutory expression of the duties is essentially the same as the existing duties established by case law, the only major exception being the new procedures for dealing with conflicts of interest.

It is noted also that for most directors, who are working hard and put the interests of their company before their own, there will be no need to change their behaviour.

Compared with the pre-existing definitions of the common law duties of directors, however, the new statutory statement captures a cultural change in the way in which companies conduct their business.

12.2 The nature of the duty owed

The traditional view in British company law was that directors owed their duties to the company, which was interpreted as the provider of capital – that is to say, to the shareholders. This duty was owed to the shareholders as a body and not to individual shareholders. Thus, in *Percival v Wright* [1902] 2 Ch 421, where certain shareholders approached the directors asking them to purchase their shares at a time when secret takeover negotiations were going on, the directors failed to mention this to the shareholders. In subsequent litigation, it was held that the directors were not in breach of duty to the shareholders. The directors owed their duty to the shareholders as a body and the court took the view that premature disclosure of the takeover negotiations would have been detrimental to the shareholders. Section 170(1) specifies that the codified duties are owed to the company and consequently, only the company will be able to enforce them although in certain circumstances shareholders may be able to bring a derivative action on the company's behalf.

The position is different if the approach is made by the directors to the shareholders. In such a situation, the directors constitute themselves as fiduciaries vis-à-vis the shareholders: see *Briess v Woolley* [1954] AC 333. In *Allen v Hyatt* (1914) 30 TLR 444, the appellants contacted the respondents with a view to obtaining options from the respondent shareholders so that they could deal with representatives of the company. The appellants did not disclose to the respondents that they were buying their shares on their own account and had entered into a secret arrangement to conceal from the other shareholders information that they should disclose as directors. The Privy Council upheld the Court of Appeal to the effect that the appellants were trustees for the respondents. In *Peskin v Anderson* [2000] 1 BCLC 372, the Court of Appeal confirmed that there need to be special circumstances to justify the imposition of fiduciary duties on directors to particular shareholders.

The case involved the demutualisation of the RAC club in Pall Mall with payouts to members. Former members of the club who retired prior to the cut-off date argued that the directors were in breach of fiduciary duty for not disclosing the plans. The Court held that there were no special circumstances requiring particular attention to those former members.

In contrast, in *Platt v Platt* [1999] 2 BCLC 745, the court ruled that a fiduciary relationship existed between a director (Keith) and his two brother shareholders (Colin and Denis), who had been duped into transferring shares to the brother director in their BMW franchise which was later sold at a considerable profit.

Other jurisdictions take a more liberal view of the duty owed to individual shareholders. Thus, in *Coleman v Myers* [1977] 2 NZLR 225, the New Zealand Court of Appeal held that the managing director and chairman of a company owed fiduciary duties to the shareholders of the company in a takeover situation. Indeed, even in Great Britain, it seems that in certain situations the courts are willing to hold that a duty is owed to individual shareholders. This seems to be the case in takeover situations: see *Gething v Kilner* [1972] 1 WLR 337. This case concerned a takeover bid by Town Centre Securities Ltd for the stock of the Rochdale Canal Company.

Shareholders of Rochdale complained that the Rochdale board was recommending the takeover offer to its shareholders without disclosing that they had received some contrary advice. Town Centre was also implicated in the supportive action of the Rochdale board, so it was claimed.

Brightman J accepted that the directors of an offeree company owe a duty to their shareholders to be honest and not to mislead. On the facts of this case the judge considered that there had not been any wrongdoing.

Note that the decision in *Percival v Wright* in relation to the purchase of shares by directors is obviously now subject to legislative provisions on insider dealing; and indeed the proposition that directors of a company may purchase the shares of other shareholders without disclosing pending negotiations for the purchase of the company has been doubted by Browne-Wilkinson VC in *Re Chez Nico (Restaurants) Ltd* [1992] BCLC 192. In this case a letter had been sent by the largest shareholder in the company to other shareholders. The intention was to purchase their shares and then to transform the company from a public company to a private one.

In this case, Browne-Wilkinson VC doubted the proposition in *Percival v Wright* to the effect that there was no legal requirement to disclose the circumstances of the acquisition to the shareholders.

Particular problems may arise in relation to nominee directors. In *Hawkes v Cuddy & Others* [2009] 2 BCLC 427 (also called *Re Neath Rugby Club Ltd*), Neath and the Ospreys were two rugby clubs. Neath formed part of the region in which the Ospreys were the regional team. Hawkes and Cuddy formed a joint venture. They set up Neath Rugby Club Ltd. Hawkes was a director of Neath, as was Cuddy's wife. They had 50 per cent each of the shares. Cuddy was a nominee director for Neath Rugby Club on Ospreys' board. Neath Rugby Club held 50 per cent of the shares of Ospreys; Swansea Rugby Club held the other 50 per cent.

The relationship between Hawkes and Cuddy broke down. Hawkes presented a petition under s 459 of the Companies Act 1985 (s 994 CA 2006). He alleged that Cuddy, as a nominee director, failed to represent Neath Rugby Club and, indeed, had acted against its interests on the board of Ospreys. Cuddy and his wife presented a cross petition based on the breakdown of trust and confidence and the deadlock that resulted.

At first instance the judge held that Cuddy, as a director of Ospreys, owed a duty to Hawkes to consult him and Neath, as well as a duty to Ospreys. He held that Cuddy had fulfilled the duty. He also held that deadlock would allow a petitioner to wind up on the just and equitable ground, and so it did also under s 994 of the Companies Act 2006 (formerly s 459 CA 1985).

On appeal in the Court of Appeal it was held that the duty owed by Cuddy was to Ospreys Ltd, although he could take account of Neath Rugby Club Ltd and of Hawkes, but his overriding duty was to Ospreys Ltd.

It was also held that facts sufficient for justifying a winding-up order on the just and equitable ground did not necessarily mean that an order would similarly be given under s 994, as although there was an overlap, the two were not coterminous and the conduct may not amount to unfair prejudice.

The courts are notoriously reluctant to interfere with directors' thinking. In *R (People and Planet) v HM Treasury* [2009] EWHC 3020 the government was the majority shareholder: the Royal Bank of Scotland. The government was accused of breaking undertakings relating to climate change and human rights. The court held that the Treasury was entitled to adopt a commercial approach in the exercise of its powers.

12.3 Duty to promote the success of the company

Section 172(1) of the Companies Act 2006 now provides that a director of a company must act in the way that he considers, in good faith, would be most likely to promote the success of the company for the benefit of its members as a whole. This clearly preserves the principle in *Percival v Wright* in statutory form.

In a debate during the passage of the Bill through Parliament in the House of Lords, Lord Goldsmith spoke, as follows, about the 'success of the company':

> What is success? The starting point is that it is essentially for the members of the company to define the objective they wish to achieve. Success means what the members collectively want the company to achieve. For a commercial company, success will usually mean long-term increase in value. For certain companies, such as charities and community interest companies, it will mean the attainment of the objectives for which the company has been established.
>
> (Lord Goldsmith, Lords Grand Committee, 6 February 2006, column 255)

He continued:

> for a commercial company, success will normally mean long-term increase in value, but the company's constitution and decisions made under it may also lay down the appropriate success model for the company ... it is essentially for the members of a company to define the objectives they wish to achieve. The normal way for that to be done – the traditional way – is that the members do it at the time the company is established. In the old style, it would have been set down in the company's memorandum. That is changing ... but the principle does not change that those who establish the company will start off by setting out what they hope to achieve. For most people who invest in companies, there is never any doubt about it – money. That is what they want. They want a long-term increase in the company. It is not a snap poll to be taken at any point in time.
>
> (Lord Goldsmith, Lords Grand Committee, 6 February 2006, column 258)

Section 172(1) goes on to provide that in promoting the success of the company the director must have regard amongst other matters to:

(a) the likely consequences of any decision in the long term;
(b) the interests of the company's employees;
(c) the need to foster the company's business relationships with suppliers, customers and others;
(d) the impact of the company's operations on the community and the environment;
(e) the desirability of the company maintaining a reputation for high standards of business conduct; and
(f) the need to act fairly as between members of the company.

The previous common law rule in *Percival v Wright*, with regard to a duty being owed to the providers of capital, had previously been extended by statute to include the interests of employees by the Companies Act 1980, s 46. This was then consolidated in the Companies Act 1985, s 309. Previously it was inappropriate for directors to take account of the interests of employees. The point was exemplified, for example, in *Parke v Daily News Ltd* [1962] Ch 927, where a single shareholder succeeded in obtaining an injunction to restrain directors from making payments to employees in excess of their legal entitlements where a business was ceasing to exist.

Since the introduction of the new duty in 1980 there have been few examples of the extended duty being demonstrated in decided cases. In *Re Saul D Harrison & Sons plc* [1995] 1 BCLC 14, the directors justified their decision to carry on running the company inter alia in terms of protecting the interests of employees. This was therefore regarded by the judge as appropriate.

However, this was the extent of the existing duty by directors when the new provisions in the Companies Act 2006 came into being.

There were certain dicta in decided cases indicating a wider range of interests that directors should take account of, even prior to the Companies Act 2006. In *Lonrho Ltd v Shell Petroleum Co Ltd* [1980] 1 WLR 627, Lord Diplock had referred to the interests of creditors as something that directors should take account of.

That said, there was, for example, considerable doubt in common law as to whether a duty was owed to creditors. Thus in *Liquidator of West Mercia Safetywear Ltd v Dodd* [1988] BCLC 250, while the Court of Appeal held that a director of an insolvent company must have regard to the interests of its creditors, there was no wider principle invoked. Similarly, in *Colin Gwyer & Associates Ltd v London Wharf (Limehouse) Ltd* [2003] 2 BCLC 153, the judge spoke of the need for a company that was insolvent or of dubious solvency to take account of the interests of creditors. Section 172(3) has provided some clarification to this aspect of the law by displacing the duty when the company is insolvent by the obligation to have regard to the interests of the creditors as the company nears insolvency.

In addition, s 214 of the Insolvency Act 1986 makes it clear that a duty is owed to creditors of the company in the event of the company's insolvency by directors and shadow directors.

Furthermore, an insolvent company can sue its directors for breach of directors' duties where they have used the company to defraud creditors, *Bilta (UK) Ltd (in liquidation) v Nazir (No. 2)* [2012] EWHC 2163 (Ch) [2013] EWCA Civ 968, upheld by the Supreme Court in *Jetivia SA v Bilta (Uk) Ltd (in liquidation)* [2015] UKSC 23.

When considering whether to enter into a transaction (e.g. giving security), the directors must act in a way they believe to be in the best interests and benefit of the company and not just in the best interests of and for the benefit of the group as a whole: *Rolled Steel Products (Holdings) Ltd v British Steel Corporation* [1986] Ch 246.

If an intention of corporate benefit cannot be established then the directors will be in breach of their duties and the company may not have the capacity to enter into the transaction. This could lead to the security being unenforceable if the security holder is on actual or constructive notice of this breach.

Section 172(1) has been stated to enshrine in statutory form the principle of 'enlightened shareholder value'. There was much discussion of 'enlightened shareholder value' during the passage of the legislation. In the House of Lords, Lord Goldsmith said:

> The Company Law Review considered and consulted on two main options. The first was 'enlightened shareholder value', under which a director must first act in the way that he or she considers, in good faith, would be most likely to promote the success of the company for its members ... The Government agrees this is the right approach. It resolves any confusion in the mind of directors as to what the interests of the company are, and prevents any inclination to identify those interests with their own. It also prevents confusion between the interests of those who depend on the company and those of the members.
>
> (Lord Goldsmith, Lords Grand Committee, 6 February 2006, column 255)

In the House of Commons, meanwhile, the Rt Hon Alistair Darling, MP, the Secretary of State for Trade and Industry, spoke as follows:

> For the first time the Bill includes a statutory statement of directors' general duties. It provides a code of conduct that sets out how directors are expected to behave. That enshrines in statute what the law review called 'enlightened shareholder value'. It recognises that directors will be more likely to achieve long-term sustainable success for the benefit of their shareholders if their companies pay attention to a wider range of matters ... Directors will be required to promote the success of the company in the collective best interest of the shareholders, but in doing so they will have to have regard to a wider range of factors, including the interests of employees and the environment.
>
> (Alistair Darling, Commons Second Reading, 6 June 2006, column 125)

As can be seen from the above, s 172 has been the subject of numerous comments. In *Re Southern Counties Fresh Foods Ltd* [2008] EWHC 2810, the court compared the new form of word 'success' in s 172 with the old 'bona fide in the interests of the company' and they concluded that they came to the same thing. In the same case, the court also confirmed that the test under the first limb remains subjective in nature i.e. whether the director honestly believed that he acted in a way most likely to promote the company's success reflecting the pre-2006 position as set out in *Re Smith and Fawcett Ltd* [1942] Ch 304.

12.4 Duty to exercise independent judgement

Section 173 of the Companies Act 2006 provides that a director of a company must exercise independent judgement. This puts it beyond doubt that a director who is placed on a board as a nominee of a substantial shareholder or otherwise must act in accordance with the interests of the company that he is serving rather than the interests of the nominator.

In the House of Lords, Lord Goldsmith, in interpreting independent judgement, spoke as follows:

> the clause does not mean that a director has to form his judgement totally independently from anyone or anything. It does not actually mean that the director has to be independent himself. He can have an interest in the matter ... It is the exercise of the judgement of a director that must be independent in the sense of it being his own judgement ... The duty does not prevent a director from relying on the advice or work of others, but the final judgement must be his responsibility. He clearly cannot be expected to do everything himself. Indeed, in certain circumstances directors may be in breach of duty if they fail to take appropriate advice – for example, legal advice. As with all advice, slavish reliance is not acceptable, and the obtaining of outside advice does not absolve directors from exercising their judgement on the basis of such advice.
>
> (Lord Goldsmith, Lords Grand Committee, 6 February 2006, column 282)

Thus while a director may enter into an agreement to act in a particular way where he believes in good faith that this is in the company's interest, he may not enter into a contract to vote in a particular way regardless of whether this is in the best interests of the company or not; see *Fulham Football Club Ltd v Cabra Estates plc* [1992] BCC 863.

12.5 Directors' exercise of powers for a proper purpose

Section 171 of the Companies Act 2006 provides that a director of a company must:

(a) act in accordance with the company's constitution; and
(b) only exercise powers for the purposes for which they are conferred.

This statement of duty reflects the pre-existing position in case law.

On occasion, the question of whether directors have exercised their powers for a proper purpose has arisen in decided cases. The most common example of the exercise of directors' powers in decided cases is the power to issue shares.

12.5.1 Power to issue shares

It is no longer necessary for private companies with one class of share to obtain authority from the company's shareholders before allotting shares. The Act permits directors of such companies to allot shares unless the articles provide otherwise (s 550 CA 2006). This does not, however, apply to companies with more than one class of share, or to public companies. In such cases there must be authorisation for the exercise of the power of allotment in the company's constitution.

The power to issue shares is given for the purpose of raising necessary capital for the company. Any other purpose is not prima facie a legitimate exercise of that power. However, the courts have recognised that other purposes may be validated by the company in general meeting. Thus, for example, it is an improper purpose to issue shares to defeat a takeover bid, but the exercise of the issue of shares for this purpose may be validated by the company in general meeting. In *Hogg v Cramphorn Ltd* (1967), a takeover bid was proposed which the directors genuinely believed not to be in the best interests of the company. To block the takeover bid, the directors issued 5,000 additional shares which were to be held on trust for the employees of the company. The court held that the issue was not a proper exercise of the directors' powers and was therefore invalid. However, the court ordered that a meeting of the members should be held which could, if it considered it appropriate, validate the issue. At this company meeting, the new shares would not be able to vote. In the event, the issue was ratified.

A similar conclusion was reached in *Bamford v Bamford* (1970). It is not every issue of shares for extraneous purposes that can be validated, however. If the purpose of the issue of shares is clearly to further the directors' or majority shareholders' own personal interests, the issue cannot be validated by the company in general meeting; see *Howard Smith Ltd v Ampol Petroleum Ltd* [1974] AC 821 (a Privy Council case from Australia). In this case, there were rival bids for the share capital of a company. The majority shareholders favoured one bid. The directors who favoured a different bid issued additional shares to the bidding company to place the majority shareholders in a minority position. The Privy Council held that the issue was an improper exercise of their powers as it was designed to thwart the wishes of the majority shareholders.

In *Clemens v Clemens Brothers Ltd* [1976] 2 All ER 268, two shareholders held the entire share capital of a company and the majority shareholder used her voting power to pass a resolution authorising the issue of new shares to an employee trust scheme. This was held to be invalid. The effect of the new issue of shares was to reduce the other shareholder's holding (that of her niece) to less than the 25 per cent stake where she had been able to block a special resolution. Foster J considered that the exercise of the majority's voting power in this case was being used inequitably against the minority shareholder and this was therefore held to be invalid.

In an earlier unreported decision, *Pennell, Sutton and Moraybell Securities Ltd v Venida Investments Ltd* (1974) (unreported, but noted in (1981) 44 MLR 40 by Burridge), the majority proposed to increase the share capital of the company. The minority had sought a declaration that this constituted a fraud on the minority and asked for an interlocutory injunction. The minority succeeded. Templeman J held that there was a prima facie case of abuse of powers by the company's directors and the judge considered that the company was a quasi-partnership company based on mutual trust and confidence.

In *Criterion Properties plc v Stratford UK Properties* [2004] 1 WLR 1846, a director of the claimant company caused it to enter into an agreement whereby an excessive payment had to be made if control of the company changed or if some of the management team left. It was said in the case to be excessive and it was questioned as to whether the director in question could conclude the contract.

12.5.2 Power to refuse to register a transfer of shares

There are, however, other examples of the exercise of directors' powers that are subject to the same fiduciary duty. In *Re Smith and Fawcett Ltd* (1942), the question arose as to the exercise of the directors' power to refuse to register a transfer of shares. By the articles of association, the directors had unlimited discretion to refuse to register a transfer. The appellant sought to register 4,001 shares in his name after the death of his father, who had previously held the shares. The directors refused to register the transfer but offered to register a transfer of 2,001 shares, provided that the applicant sold the other shares to one of the directors at a price proposed by the directors of the company. The High Court held that the directors were acting within their discretion and this was upheld by the Court of Appeal.

12.5.3 Power to enter into a management agreement

In a similar way, the question of the exercise of directors' powers arose in *Lee Panavision Ltd v Lee Lighting Ltd* [1992] BCLC 22. In this case, the claimants had acquired an option to purchase the defendants. The claimants also had a management agreement by which they ran the defendants' business and they also nominated the company's directors. It was clear that the option to purchase the business was not to be exercised and that the management agreement would therefore be terminated. Since the claimants wished to continue managing the business, they ensured that the directors of the defendants voted in favour of a second management agreement perpetuating the claimants' control of the company. Subsequently, the directors of the defendants were removed from office and the defendants announced that they did not consider themselves bound by the second management agreement. The claimants sought an injunction to prevent breach of the second agreement. The defendants alleged that the directors had not disclosed their interest in the agreement. Harman J held that the agreement was void at the instance of the defendants and that the agreement had not been entered into in the interests of the defendants. This was upheld by the Court of Appeal. Harman J had also held that it was voidable on the basis of the failure of the directors to declare their interests to a board meeting. The Court of Appeal took the view that there was no breach of what is now s 177, since the interest of the directors was known to all members of the board.

12.5.4 Other powers

The powers of directors that are subject to directors' fiduciary duties also extend to other areas including:

(a)   the power to borrow money and grant securities: see *Rolled Steel Products (Holdings) Ltd v British Steel Corporation* (1986);

(b)   the power to call general meetings;

(c) the power to provide information to shareholders; and

(d) the power to make calls on partly paid shares.

Even where there is no breach of duty in relation to the exercise of powers by directors, there is the possibility of a petition alleging unfair prejudice under ss 994–996 of the Companies Act 2006.

12.6 The duty of care and skill

This duty is now provided for in statute by s 174 CA 2006.

It is provided that a director of a company must exercise reasonable care, skill and diligence. This means the care, skill and diligence that would be exercised by a reasonably diligent person with:

(a) the general knowledge, skill and experience that may reasonably be expected of a person carrying out the functions carried out by the director; and

(b) the general knowledge, skill and experience that the director has.

This provides for an objective standard but one raised by the actual knowledge, skill and experience of a particular director if this is greater.

The old law was set out in *Re City Equitable Fire and Insurance Co Ltd* [1925] Ch 407. The company had experienced a serious depletion of funds and the managing director, Mr Bevan, was convicted of fraud. The liquidator, however, sought to make other directors liable in negligence for failing to detect the frauds. Romer J, in what has become the classic exposition of the director's duties of care and skill, set out three propositions. There are, in addition, one or two other general propositions that seem to be warranted by the reported cases:

1 A director need not exhibit in the performance of his duties a greater degree of skill than may reasonably be expected from a person of his knowledge and experience. A director of a life insurance company, for instance, does not guarantee that he has the skill of an actuary or of a physician. In the words of Lindley MR,

> if the directors act within their powers, if they act with such care as is reasonably to be expected from them, having regard to their knowledge and experience, and if they act honestly for the benefit of the company they represent, they discharge both their equitable as well as their legal duty to the company.

See *Lagunas Nitrate Co v Lagunas Syndicate* [1899] 2 Ch 392. It is perhaps only another way of stating the same proposition to say that the directors are not liable for mere errors of judgement.

2 A director is not bound to give continuous attention to the affairs of his company. His duties are of an intermittent nature to be performed at periodic board meetings and at meetings of any committee of the board upon which he

happens to be placed. He is not, however, bound to attend all such meetings, though he ought to attend whenever, in the circumstances, he is reasonably able to do so.

3   In respect of all duties that, having regard to the exigencies of business, and the articles of association, may properly be left to some other official, a director is, in the absence of grounds for suspicion, justified in trusting that official to perform such duties honestly.

12.6.1 Standard of care and skill

In relation to the first principle set out by Romer J, the decision in *Re Denham & Co.* (1883) 25 ChD 752 is illustrative. In this case a director recommended the payment of a dividend out of capital. As has been seen (Chapter 8), this is not something that is permissible. The director was held not liable in negligence. As was stated in the case, the director was 'a country gentleman and not an accountant!' Although such cases resound with Victorian echoes, it was probably the case that little changed until the Companies Act 2006. Section 13 of the Supply of Goods and Services Act 1982 introduced a statutorily imposed implied term that the supplier of services would provide services of a reasonable standard. Directors were exempted from this provision before it even came into force by Statutory Instrument 1982/1771. In *Dorchester Finance Co Ltd v Stebbing* [1989] BCLC 498 (a decision that was reached some ten years before it was fully reported), Foster J held that the duties owed by non-executive directors were the same as those owed by executive directors. In this case, an executive director and two non-executive directors all had relevant accounting experience. The two non-executive directors signed blind blank cheques which the executive director then used to further his own ends and those of companies that he controlled. It was held that all three directors had been negligent.

Foster J in delivering his judgment stated, at p. 505:

> For a chartered accountant and an experienced accountant to put forward the proposition that a non-executive director has no duties to perform I find quite alarming. It would be an argument which, if put forward by a director with no accounting experience, would involve total disregard of many sections of the Companies Act 1948 [see in particular ss 176–204]. The signing of blank cheques by Hamilton and Parsons [the two non-executive directors] was, in my judgment, negligent, as it allowed Stebbing [the executive director] to do as he pleased.

There is some reason for believing that some movement in the law occurred prior to 2006. In s 214 of the Insolvency Act 1986, an objective standard of care was introduced in relation to directors and shadow directors where the company was insolvent (see section 25.3). Disqualification cases also demonstrate a move to an objective standard of care and skill for directors.

In *Norman v Theodore Goddard* [1991] BCLC 1028, Hoffmann J accepted that the standard in s 214 applied generally in relation to directors and that the relevant yardstick was what could be expected of a person in the position of the director carrying out those functions. The standard may well be different from what could be expected of that particular director. In the event, Hoffmann J held that the director of the property development company acted reasonably in accepting information from a senior partner in the city solicitors, Theodore Goddard.

In *Re D'Jan of London Ltd* [1994] 1 BCLC 561, a director signed an insurance proposal without checking it. The information provided turned out to be wrong and the insurance company refused to pay up when the company's premises burnt down. It was held that the director had been negligent.

In both *Norman v Theodore Goddard* and *Re D'Jan of London Ltd*, Hoffmann J (later LJ) accepted that s 214 set out the modern law regarding the duty of care and skill of directors.

Interestingly the position, as set out by Hoffmann J in *Norman v Theodore Goddard* and *Re D'Jan of London Ltd*, was adopted by Lord Goldsmith in the House of Lords when he said:

> the standard of care which a director owes is enormously important … it is now accepted that the duty of care … is accurately stated in Section 214(4) of the Insolvency Act 1986 … Under the clause you take account both of the general knowledge, skills and experience that may be reasonably expected of a person carrying out those functions and the general knowledge, skills and experience that the director has. It is a cumulative requirement … I want to emphasise the point that it is not making a change from what is already in the common law.
>
> (Lord Goldsmith, Lords Grand Committee, 6 February 2006, column 284)

In *Bishopsgate Investment Management Ltd v Maxwell (No 2)* [1993] Ch 1, it was held that, where Ian Maxwell as a director of the company signed an instrument of transfer of shares in a pension fund which was for the company's employees and ex-employees, he could not rely on the opinion of fellow directors that the transfer was a proper one nor avoid liability by demonstrating that the transfer would have gone ahead without his concurrence.

In *Re Continental Assurance Co of London plc* [1997] 1 BCLC 48, a leading disqualification case, a senior bank official was a non-executive director of the company and also its parent company. Both companies collapsed. The wholly owned subsidiary had made a number of cash advances to the parent company which were in breach of the provisions prohibiting financial assistance towards the purchase of shares.

The Secretary of State sought and obtained an order disqualifying him as his conduct rendered him unfit to hold office.

It was accepted that the director did not realise that there was indebtedness between the subsidiary and its holding company. However, it was reasonable that, given his background, he should have read and understood the company's statutory accounts. He was disqualified for three years.

In many disqualification cases there has been a movement towards a more rigorous standard. Thus in *Re Barings plc (No 5)* [1999] 1 BCLC 433 at p. 489, Jonathan Parker J, in a dictum endorsed by Morritt LJ in the Court of Appeal [2000] 1 BCLC 523 at pp. 535–536, spoke of a 'continuing duty to acquire and maintain a sufficient knowledge and understanding of the company's business' to enable them properly to discharge their duties as directors. Furthermore, he stated that:

> whilst directors are entitled (subject to the Articles of Association of the company) to delegate particular functions to those below the management chain, and to trust their competence and integrity to a reasonable extent, the exercise of the power of delegation does not absolve the director from the duty to supervise the discharge of the delegated function.

The judge further stated that there was no rule of universal application that could be formulated as to the duty in relation to supervision. The extent of the duty and the question whether it has been discharged must depend on the facts of each particular case, including the director's role in the management of the company.

As noted, the objective standard upheld in some cases is now of general effect, although it may be enhanced if the subjective knowledge etc. of the particular director is higher. It should be noted that many cases on disqualification of directors are relevant here and underline the move to an objective standard of care and skill backed up by a higher subjective standard where appropriate. See *Re Landhurst Leasing plc* [1999] 1 BCLC 286, p. 344.

In *Gregson v HAE Trustees Ltd* [2008] EWHC 1006, the High Court expressed the view that s 174 merely codified the existing law.

In law there is no difference in the status of executive and non-executive directors. In *Equitable Life Assurance Society v Bowley* [2004] 1 BCLC 180 at p. 188, Langley J stated that the duty owed by a non-executive director 'does not differ from the duty owed by an executive director but in application it may and usually will do so'. The case was part of the saga of Equitable Life and the sale of guaranteed annuity rates. It involved the issue of whether Equitable's non-executive directors were liable in negligence and for breach of fiduciary duty. The judge considered the extent to which non-executive directors could rely on executive directors. He considered non-executive directors were expected to come up to a higher standard than formerly.

The point is underlined in *Mond v Bowles* (unreported, 21 October 2011), where the Registrar stated that the term 'non-executive' was not one recognised in English law. The two non-executive directors were held not liable under s 214 IA 86, but this was on the specific facts of the case and not because of their status as non-executive directors, i.e. it was not the label 'non-executive' that prevented liability here but the fact that the liquidator had not established liability on the facts of the case.

12.6.2 Continuous attention

In relation to Romer J's second proposition, *Re Cardiff Savings Bank, Marquis of Bute's Case* [1892] 2 Ch 100 provides a stark example of this principle at play. In this case the Marquis of Bute was appointed president and director of the Cardiff Savings Bank when he was only six months old. At this age, clearly little could be expected from him in terms of corporate control! In the next 38 years, the Marquis only attended one board meeting and, during this time, massive frauds were perpetrated by another director. The court held that the Marquis was not liable for breach of duty in failing to attend board meetings as he had not undertaken to do so. This proposition would not now stand.

12.6.3 Delegation

The third proposition set out by Romer J seems unexceptionable. It permits delegation to experts. Thus, in *Dovey v Cory* [1901] AC 477, where a director, John Cory, had delegated the task of drawing up the accounts to others, it was held that he was entitled to rely on those accounts in recommending the payment of a dividend that subsequently turned out to be illegal. This would stand under the new law.

It is now clear that *Re City Equitable* no longer represents good law. The statute makes it clear that a director must exercise the standard of care, skill and diligence of a reasonably diligent person in the director's position. This, therefore, introduces an objective standard, although as has been noted the law was probably moving in this direction in any event.

In addition, the section ensures that if the director's particular knowledge, skill and experience is greater than that of a reasonably diligent person in his position, then that higher standard of care will apply.

12.7 Fiduciary duties

In addition to the duty to act to promote the success of the company and to exercise reasonable care, skill and diligence, the Act provides for certain fiduciary duties that must be adhered to by a director.

12.7.1 Conflicts

Thus a director must avoid actual or possible conflicts of interest or duties (other than a conflict arising in relation to a transaction or arrangement with the company) unless the matter has been authorised by the independent directors, i.e. without interested directors counting for the vote or in the quorum (s 175(6) CA 2006).

In a private company, directors may authorise the matter unless there is a provision in the company's constitution preventing it. In the case of a public company there must be a permissive provision in the constitution.

As Lord Goldsmith said in the House of Lords during the passage of the legislation:

> So far as private companies are concerned, the default position is that the directors may authorise the matter unless there is a provision in the company's constitution saying otherwise. In the case of a public company ... directors may authorise the matter only if the company's constitution includes provisions saying they can do so. It must follow that if the constitution does not do so, steps will have to be taken to amend it to that effect and the members of the company will be able to take a view about whether they think that is a good move.
>
> (Lord Goldsmith, Lords Grand Committee, 6 February 2006, column 294)

When the law was passing through the House of Lords, Lord Goldsmith stated that:

> the law already recognises that potential conflicts in certain circumstances are to be avoided ... there is currently no absolute rule prohibiting directors from holding

multiple directorships or even from engaging in business that competes with the company of which they are a director, but obviously a tension results from that degree of tolerance and the fiduciary duties which the director owes. The solution to it is ... there is no prohibition of a conflict or potential conflict as long as it has been authorised by the directors in accordance with the requirements set out in [the Act].

(Lord Goldsmith, Lords Grand Committee, 6 February 2006, column 288)

He went on to say:

We do not say that this should happen just because in the mind of a director it is all right; there should be a process for the company, through its members or directors, to make that decision, and that is what these new regulations permit.

(Lord Goldsmith, Lords Grand Committee, 6 February 2006, column 289)

In addition, it should be noted that the duty is not infringed if the situation cannot reasonably be regarded as likely to give rise to a conflict of interest (s 175(4)(a)). Lord Goldsmith said:

Following consultation, the Government have already adjusted the provision ... to use instead the expression 'if the situation cannot reasonably be regarded as likely to give rise to a conflict of interest'. This introduces the concept of reasonableness which makes the situation easier from the point of view of a director and avoids a very harsh test, although it is still a heavy duty and intended to be so.

(Lord Goldsmith, Lords Grand Committee, 6 February 2006, column 293)

Additionally, a director must not accept benefits from a third party conferred by reason of his directorship unless the acceptance cannot reasonably be regarded as likely to give rise to a conflict (s 176 CA 2006).

As was said in the House of Lords during the passage of the Bill:

the purpose of the clause ... is to impose on a director a duty not to accept benefits from third parties. It applies only to benefits conferred because the director is a director of the company or because of something that the director does or doesn't do as director. The word 'benefit' ... includes benefits of any description, including non-financial benefits.

The clause codifies ... [the] long-standing rule, prohibiting the exploitation of the position of director for personal benefit. It does not apply to benefits that the director receives from the company, or from the associated company, or from any person acting on behalf of any of those companies ... I ... draw attention to the fact that benefits are prohibited by the duty only if their acceptance is likely to give rise to a conflict of interest.

(Lord Goldsmith, Lords Grand Committee, 6 February 2006, column 330)

Section 177 provides that a director needs to declare the nature and extent of his interest to the other directors in a proposed transaction or arrangement with the company if he is in any way directly or indirectly interested in that transaction or arrangement. The director need not be a party to the transaction for the rule to apply. An interest of another person in a contract with the company may require the director to make a disclosure, if the other person's interest amounts to a direct or indirect interest on the part of the director. This must be done before the company enters into that transaction or arrangement. This declaration is backed up by s 182 which requires a declaration to the extent that the interest has not been declared under s 177. Criminal sanctions exist for failure to declare an existing interest: s 183.

There are a few exceptions to the declaration of interest. Section 177(5) provides that a director need not declare an interest if he is not aware of the interest or unaware of the transaction or arrangement by the company. However he is treated as being aware of matters of which he ought reasonably to have been aware.

Under s 177(6), a director need not declare an interest if it cannot be reasonably be regarded as likely to give rise to a conflict, or to the extent that the other directors are aware (or ought reasonably to be aware of) the interest or to the extent that it concerns terms of the director's service contract which have been or are being considered by a meeting of the directors or a committee of directors appointed for this purpose.

Obviously in a situation of a sole directorship, no disclosure is required.

12.8 Use of corporate opportunities

Where directors place themselves in a position where their personal interest conflicts with their duty to the company, then obviously this brings the new duty in s 175 into play.

The leading case in this area is the House of Lords' decision in *Regal (Hastings) Ltd v Gulliver* [1942] 1 All ER 378. Regal owned a cinema in Hastings. The company's solicitor considered that it would be a sound business move to acquire two other cinemas in the town. He suggested this to the directors. The company had insufficient funds. However, a scheme was hatched and a subsidiary was created for the purpose of acquiring the two other cinemas.

The directors of Regal put up some money to subscribe for shares, as did the company solicitor. The move proved to be a successful one and, ultimately, the shares of Regal and its subsidiary were sold to a purchaser. The directors made a profit on the sale as did the company solicitor. The company under its new management then proceeded to start an action against the former directors for damages in respect of the secret profit made on the sale of the shares. It was proved that the directors had acted from sound motives and there was no mala fides. The House of Lords held that the directors who acquired a beneficial interest in the shares were liable to disgorge their profits back to the company (that is, back to the purchaser who willingly paid the asking price for the business!) as this profit had been made at the expense of the company. The company's solicitor, as he was not a director, was not subject to any fiduciary duties and was therefore not liable to disgorge. It had, of course, been his idea in the first place!

The decision is in many ways a horrendous one. It is the triumph of form over substance. If the directors had obtained the consent of the company in general meeting to what they were doing, no complaint would have been possible. Further-more, had the directors sold the business as a going concern rather than sold the shares, the purchaser would not have been in a position to bring the action as the company. The decision is a comedy – or rather tragedy – of errors. However, it does establish the very clear principle that directors should not let their personal positions conflict with their duties to the company.

Later cases illustrate the same point. In *Industrial Development Consultants Ltd v Cooley* [1972] 1 WLR 443, Cooley was an architect with the East Midlands Gas Board. He left to become a director of IDC. He was subsequently approached by the Eastern Gas Board. They wished him to do some work for them by designing a gas holder at Ponders End. They did not wish to deal with IDC and made it quite clear that the offer was only applicable to Cooley in his personal capacity. Because Cooley was tied to IDC by contract, he went to his management and told them that he was desperately ill and sought leave to terminate his contract. This was agreed to. Where-upon Cooley convalesced by designing the gas holder! IDC then brought this action for disgorgement of profit. IDC was successful. One can in some ways sympathise with IDC. Clearly, Cooley was dishonest and the prospect of his profiting from his dishonesty is not an attractive one. The decision, though, must be questionable as it is unlikely that Cooley had here taken a corporate opportunity, as the Eastern Gas Board made it clear it did not wish to deal with IDC but only with Cooley. The judge, Roskill J, said that Cooley should have stayed with IDC and sought to con-vince the Eastern Gas Board to change its mind.

This approach was followed in *Re Bhullar* [2003] 2 BCLC 241. The case con-cerned a grocery business run as a quasi-partnership. Following a breakdown of the relationship of mutual trust, some directors seized an opportunity to buy property for themselves. This was at a time when the other directors had made it clear they were against further company expansion. Nevertheless, it was held that the directors were in breach of fiduciary duty in that they took an opportunity personally which was that of the company. They did not disclose the opportunity to the company, still less seek permission to take that opportunity.

Another interesting decision in this same line of cases is *Horcal Ltd v Gatland* [1984] BCLC 549. In this case, Gatland, who was a director, was nearing retire-ment. The board of directors other than Gatland had just decided to make a golden handshake payment to him on his retirement. Gatland subsequently, when a person rang up to arrange for some building work, diverted the contract to himself and undertook to execute it on his own account without putting it through the company books. Later, when the customer rang up to complain that the work was faulty after Gatland had retired from the company, it became obvious what he had done. Horcal Ltd then brought this action to (1) obtain disgorgement of the profit on the contract, and (2) obtain reimbursement of the golden handshake. The company was successful in obtaining disgorgement of the profit. That much is clear. However, the company was not successful in obtaining a return of the golden handshake. The judge said that at the time when the golden handshake payment was agreed to by the board, Gatland had evil thoughts but there had been no evil deeds! The decision on this point seems surprising. Surely, had the board known of these evil intentions, the golden handshake payment would not have been made.

In *Re Allied Business and Financial Consultants Ltd, O'Donnell v Shanahan* [2009] 2 BCLC 666, the petitioner and the two respondents were directors of Allied, a company that was set up to give advice on mortgages, loans, insurance, etc. It was a quasi-partnership company. The petitioner was aware that the two respondents were engaged in property development on their own account, and acquiesced in this.

A businessman, Suleiman, approached one of the two respondents to find somebody to acquire Aria House, a property owned by Suleiman. The respondents approached a client of the company to see if the client was interested. This failed. They then asked Holleran and his brother. Holleran was another client of the company. He was asked if he could take 50 per cent, with the respondents taking the other 50 per cent. This was agreed. The petitioner was at the meeting but was not asked to participate in the shareholding arrangements.

Subsequently Allied Business failed and the petitioner petitioned under s 459 of the Companies Act 1985 (now s 994 CA 2006), alleging that the respondents were in breach of their fiduciary duties to the company.

At first instance the judge held that the opportunity came to them as directors but it was outside the company's business and would need extra funding. The petitioner would not have been prepared to participate even if she had been asked, and there was no breach of directors' duties.

The Court of Appeal reversed this. It held that the rule was that there should be no conflict between duty and self-interest.

The company is run on the basis of trust and confidence between shareholders, so the respondents could not simply take up the opportunity for their own benefit. The company's informed consent was needed and they held that the petitioner, O'Donnell, did not know all the circumstances of the acquisition.

Some cases present much simpler legal questions. In *Cranleigh Precision Engineering v Bryant* [1964] 3 All ER 289, the director concerned had been working on a revolutionary above-ground swimming pool. He left the company, taking the plans and designs with him, and developed the swimming pool on his own. The company later brought this action to seek disgorgement of profits he had made from developing the swimming pool for his own purposes. It is clear that the company should succeed, as indeed it did.

In *Ball v Eden Project Ltd* [2001] 1 BCLC 313, Ball applied to register the name Eden Project as a trademark. He was a founder and director of the company. It was held that the trademark was that of the company. There was a breach of director's fiduciary duty as he was trying to hold the company to ransom.

As noted under s 175 CA 2006, the director's action may be authorised by the independent directors in the case of a private company if there is nothing in the company's constitution that invalidates such authorisation, and in the case of a public company if the constitution includes provision for such authorisation.

By the same approach some breaches of directors' fiduciary duties are ratifiable (see s 239 CA 2006). In *Regal (Hastings) Ltd v Gulliver* (1942), it was open to the company as a matter of law to ratify what the directors had done. This did not happen as a matter of fact because control had passed to others. In other cases where fraud is involved, clearly ratification is not possible. Fraud cannot be ratified. Thus, in *Cook v Deeks* [1916] 1 AC 554, where directors had diverted corporate opportunities to themselves, contracts which they should have taken up on behalf of the company, ratification was not possible because it involved misappropriation of the company's property.

Questions of criminal law may also arise in such cases. Directors may well be guilty of theft in instances where they are appropriating company property to themselves (s 1 of the Theft Act 1968).

The duty to avoid conflicts will continue to apply as regards the exploitation of any property, information or opportunity known to him when he was a director despite ceasing to be a director.

If the board of directors considers a proposed activity or transaction and turns it down bona fide and then an individual director takes it up and exploits it, it is clear that this is not exploitation of a corporate opportunity. It has ceased to be a corporate opportunity when turned down by the company, provided that the matter is decided independently of the directors with an interest in the matter (s 175(4), (5), (6) CA 2006). See *Peso Silver Mines Ltd v Cropper* [1966] 58 DLR (2d) 1, from the Supreme Court of Canada. In *Island Export Finance Ltd v Umunna* [1986] BCLC 460, Hutchinson J said that the question of whether a director was liable to disgorge a profit to his former company from a corporate opportunity was to some extent a question of timing. Umunna had been managing director of the company and when he resigned, the company had some hopes of doing business with the Cameroon authorities. Umunna resigned hoping to do business with the Cameroon authorities. At this time there were no specific corporate opportunities. It was held that Umunna could take them on his own account when such opportunities did arise some two years later.

12.9 Competing with the company

In a similar way, a director who competes with his company, either through the medium of another company or through another form of trading, either as an individual or in a partnership, is in a conflict position and this will involve a breach of his duties as set out in s 175 CA 2006, unless it is sanctioned by the independent directors in the same way as in relation to the use of corporate opportunities.

Strangely, the position in the case law is somewhat confused. From the position of strict logic it would seem that directors should not be directors of competing companies, nor should they compete on their own account or through a partnership. They would be placed in invidious positions, where corporate opportunities arose, as to which of the two companies they should favour with the opportunity. As is so often predictably the case, the only British authority on the point flies in the face of logic. It indicates that there is no principle of law that prevents a director from being a director of two competing businesses: see *London and Mashonaland Exploration Co Ltd v New Mashonaland Exploration Co Ltd* [1891] WN 165. The decision is an old one and is open to question. Yet the decision was approved by Lord Blanesburgh *obiter* in *Bell v Lever Brothers Ltd* [1932] AC 161. Commonwealth authority is inconsistent on the point. Some cases follow the *Mashonaland* case; others indicate that directors may not be directors of competing companies: see *Abbey Glen Property Corporation v Stumborg* [1976] 65 DLR (3d) 235 (Canada), from Canada. In a related area of the law, it seems that it is not possible for senior employees to compete by holding two employments in similar lines of business. Thus, in *Hivac*

Ltd v Park Royal Scientific Instruments Ltd [1946] Ch 169, senior employees engaged on sensitive work in wartime were prohibited from working for competing employers. They were normally engaged in work on miniature valves for hearing aids. During the war, the work had wartime applications.

In partnership law, partners may not compete with their partnerships. The logical position should be that directors should not be able to compete with their company, either as directors of other competing businesses or as partners within a firm or indeed acting on their own account. The *Mashonaland* case is reviewed and criticised by Michael Christie in 'The Director's Fiduciary Duty Not to Compete' (1992) 55 MLR 506.

In *Plus Group Ltd v Pyke* [2002] 2 BCLC 201, the Court of Appeal missed the opportunity to overrule the *Mashonaland* decision.

Pyke and Plank each held 50 per cent of the shares in the Plus Group. They were the only directors and also the only directors of three subsidiaries. Constructive Interiors had an excellent relationship with Mr Pyke. They were the company's main customer. In 1996, Pyke suffered a stroke. He subsequently fell out with Plank and there was a complete rupture in the business relationship. Pyke was excluded from management of the company and denied remuneration and not allowed to draw on a loan account of the company. Pyke then incorporated John Pyke Interiors Ltd and carried out £200,000 worth of contractual work for Constructive. The question was whether Pyke had breached his duties. He had set up in competition and courted Plus's chief customer and used knowledge acquired as a director. The Court of Appeal unanimously held there was no breach of duty. It is not a breach of fiduciary duty, according to the court, for a director to work for a competing company where he has been excluded effectively from the company of which he is a director. The clear implication is that had the circumstances been different, there would have been a breach of duty.

Now it is clear that in competing with the company, unless this is agreed to by directors independent of the competing director, there will be a breach of duty under s 175 CA 2006.

12.10 Benefits from third parties

Clearly, where directors accept benefits from third parties, conferred by reason of the directorship, these actions will involve a breach of the duty under s 176. Thus, in *Attorney General for Hong Kong v Reid* [1994] 1 AC 324, an appeal to the Privy Council from Hong Kong, in an analogous situation a solicitor who joined the legal service in Hong Kong and who accepted bribes to stifle prosecutions was ordered to pay 12.4 million Hong Kong dollars to the Crown.

Lord Templeman said that in law a gift from bribery belonged to the fiduciary and he became debtor to the person to whom he owed his duties.

If the acceptance cannot reasonably be regarded as likely to give rise to a conflict, there is no breach. The exception would cover the donation of small gifts at Christmas time, or on other occasions, for example. Benefits conferred by the company, its holding company or subsidiaries and benefits received from a person who provides director's services to the company, are excluded.

Members of a company to authorise the acceptance of benefits that would otherwise be a breach of this duty is preserved by s 180(4) and the company's articles may contain provisions for dealing with these eventualities.

As stated earlier, s 170(2)(b) makes it clear that a director who ceases to be a director is still subject to the duty not to accept third party benefits as regards things done or omitted to be done before cessation as a director.

The conduct of directors in this area may also involve criminal sanctions under the Bribery Act 2010 (see section 1.3.1).

12.11 Personal liability of directors

In addition to liability to the company, directors may be directly liable to outsiders.

12.11.1 Contractual liability

Directors may be contractually liable as follows:

Breach of warranty of authority. If directors indicate to outsiders that they have authority to conclude a particular transaction on behalf of the company and no such authority exists, then the director (or indeed other person) is liable for breach of the warranty of authority.

Collateral guarantee. Often, when directors conclude a contract on behalf of their company, they will also give a collateral guarantee. This is particularly the case where a company borrows money from its bank and the bank requires security from the company's officers. In such a situation, if the primary liability fails, the outsider may sue the guarantor on the collateral guarantee.

Pre-incorporation contracts. As has already been examined (see section 3.5), where a person (perhaps a future director) concludes an agreement on behalf of an as yet unformed company, that person will be liable on the agreement unless there is an express contrary intention (s 51(1) CA 2006).

12.11.2 Tortious liability

Directors may be tortiously liable as follows:

Fraud. A director may be liable in fraud to subscribers and even purchasers on the open market in relation to statements made in a company prospectus under the principle in *Derry v Peek* (1889) 14 App Cas 337 (see section 5.13.2).

Negligent misstatement. In a similar way, a director may be liable in tort for the tort of negligent misstatement to subscribers and purchasers under the principle in *Hedley Byrne & Co Ltd v Heller & Partners Ltd* [1964] AC 465 for misstatements in a prospectus (see section 5.13.3).

Personal skill and care of directors. In rare circumstances, where a director has warranted his own personal skill and care, he may be liable to the outsider notwithstanding that the contract has been concluded with the company rather than with the director. Thus, in *Fairline Shipping Corporation v Adamson* [1975] QB 180, where the claimants agreed in writing with Game & Meat Products Ltd's managing director, Adamson, to store perishable goods in their refrigeration store in Southampton, the machinery failed and a large part of the consignment of meat, vegetables and fat went bad. Game & Meat Products were in financial difficulties and went into voluntary liquidation shortly after the discovery of the damage to the consignment.

The director, Adamson, had known of Game & Meat Products' financial difficulties and had not expected them to recover from these since the beginning of 1972. The contract for the storage of the goods was concluded in March 1972 and the company went into liquidation in April 1972.

The judge (Kerr J) said that, on the special facts of the case, Adamson owed a duty of care. He noted that the letter sent by Adamson was written in the first person singular, indicating the personal nature of his dealing, and this was crucial in the finding in the case.

A similar position was initially reached in *Williams v Natural Life Health Foods Ltd* [1998] 1 WLR 830. The company admitted that it had made negligent misstatements which had induced the claimants to enter into a franchise agreement with the company, and to purchase a health food shop in Rugby. The figures produced for future sales were too optimistic and the business failed. The court at first instance held that the company was liable for the negligent misstatement and that the managing director was also personally liable. The company itself was insolvent.

On appeal, the Court of Appeal took the view that the director must have assumed personal responsibility for personal liability to result. The director in Williams had played a pivotal role in the production of the projections. By a majority of two to one, the Court of Appeal found the director personally liable.

However, the Court of Appeal decision was unanimously reversed by the House of Lords. The House of Lords held that a director of a limited company would only be personally liable for loss suffered as a result of negligent advice given by the company if the director had assumed personal responsibility for the advice, and if the other party had relied on that assumption of responsibility. The House of Lords took the view that the director, Richard Mistlin, did not assume personal responsibility for the representations relating to the business. The House of Lords further considered that there was no evidence that the claimants believed that Mr Mistlin was undertaking such personal responsibility.

The normal rule remains that, when carrying out company business, directors are presumed to be acting for their company.

12.11.3 Statutory liability

Personal liability to outsiders may also arise under statute. For example, under s 90(1) of the Financial Services and Markets Act 2000, compensation for any untrue or misleading statement or omission from a prospectus or supplementary prospectus is payable by any person responsible, which includes every director of the company.

12.11.4 Other liability

There are, of course, other areas where there may be personal liability of directors in relation to company debts, but these areas generally involve a contribution to the company's assets in liquidation rather than a direct payment to the outsider. Thus directors may be liable for fraudulent trading under s 213 of the Insolvency Act 1986, for wrongful trading under s 214 of the Insolvency Act 1986 and for acting in contravention of a disqualification order under s 15 of the Company Directors Disqualification Act 1986.

12.12 Limiting the liability of directors

Section 232 of the Companies Act 2006 provides that any provision purporting to exempt a director of a company from any liability that would otherwise attach to him in connection with any negligence, default, breach of duty or breach of trust in relation to the company is void.

The section further provides that any provision by which a company directly or indirectly provides an indemnity for a director of the company, or of an associated company against any liability, attaching to him in connection with any negligence, default, breach of duty or breach of trust, is void except as permitted by ss 233, 234 and 235 CA 2006.

12.12.1 Provision of insurance

Section 233 provides that it is permissible for a company to purchase and maintain for a director of a company, or an associated company, insurance against any such liability, as is mentioned in s 232.

12.12.2 Qualifying third party indemnity provision

Section 234 provides that third party indemnity provision against liability incurred by a director to a person other than the company or an associated company is permitted, although it cannot cover any liability of the director to pay a fine in criminal proceedings, to pay a sum to a regulatory authority by way of penalty, or any liability incurred by a director in defending criminal proceedings in which he is convicted, or in defending civil proceedings where judgment is given against him or in connection with an application for relief in which the court refuses to grant him relief.

12.12.3 Qualifying pension scheme indemnity provision

Section 235 provides for pension scheme indemnity provision whereby a director of a company that is a trustee of an occupational pension scheme is indemnified against liability incurred in connection with the company's activities as trustee of the scheme. Once again this cannot extend to an indemnity against fines, sums payable to regulatory authorities or liabilities incurred in defending criminal proceedings.

12.12.4 Relief from the court

Notwithstanding s 232, it is open to the court to grant relief to an officer if it is proved that the officer acted honestly and reasonably and ought in all the circumstances to be excused in whole, or in part (s 1157 CA 2006). This matter was discussed in *Re Duomatic Ltd* [1969] 2 Ch 365. The company in this case had three directors. The articles of the company required directors' remuneration to be determined by the general meeting. One director, Elvins, drew a salary without the approval of the company in general meeting, assuming that it would be agreed at the subsequent annual general meeting. In fact, the company went into liquidation before the annual general meeting could be held. He also made a gratuitous payment to Hanley, another director, without complying with Companies Act provisions that require disclosure of golden handshakes and approval of the payment by the company in general meeting, and in addition he drew in excess of the agreed limit on his drawings from the company.

It was held that Elvins would be relieved from liability for drawing the unauthorised salary as it was reasonable for him to follow the established practice. He was not relieved from liability in relation to the payment of the compensation payment as he should have sought legal advice in relation to this matter and he was also liable for the excessive drawings from the company. In relation to this last matter he had been neither honest nor reasonable.

An alternative course of action for the company where a director has acted in breach of duties (provided the breach of duty is not fraudulent) is to ratify what the director has done. This has the effect of negating any breach of duty. This is what occurred in *Hogg v Cramphorn* and *Bamford v Bamford* (see section 12.5.1). In relation to matters that are ultra vires the company, the possibility of ratification is now open to the company. The act itself must first be ratified and then the unauthorised act of the director must also be ratified.

In dealing with directors' liability, a sensible balance needs to be struck between, on the one hand, dealing robustly with cases of gross negligence and dishonesty, and on the other, ensuring that Britain has a diverse pool of high-quality individuals assuming the role of company director to take informed and rational risks.

12.12.5 Negating a breach of duty

Shareholders will be able to give authority by ordinary resolution after full disclosure of relevant details to an act that would otherwise be a breach of duty in circumstances where the common law already allows directors to do that (s 180(4)(a) CA 2006).

Section 180(4)(b) CA 2006 provides that where a company's articles contain provisions for dealing with conflicts of interest, then there is no breach of a director's duties if the director acts in accordance with these provisions.

Ratification of directors' acts is allowed by s 239 CA 2006. Where the company ratifies the conduct of a director that amounts to negligence, default, breach of duty or breach of trust, then this must be conducted by resolution of the members of the company by way of ordinary resolution. If the resolution is proposed as a written resolution, neither the director (if a member of the company), nor any member connected with him is an eligible member and similarly the director and connected persons' votes are ignored in any meeting where a resolution is proposed.

Section 239(7) stipulates that the requirements imposed by s 239 are in addition to any other limitations or restrictions imposed by law as to what may or may not be ratified and when. *Franbar Holdings Ltd v Patel* [2008] EWHC 1534 Ch) confirmed that restrictions in the old cases developed by the court largely in response to wrong-doing directors being permitted to vote their shares on a ratification resolution are still good law.

12.13 Directors' contracts

Section 177 provides that it is the duty of a director to declare an interest in any pro-posed transaction or arrangement with his company, whether the interest is direct or indirect. He must declare the nature and extent of his interest to the other directors at a meeting of the directors or by notice to all of the directors either by notice in writing or by a general notice. The declaration must be made before the company enters into the transaction or arrangement.

A declaration is not required where the director is not aware of his interest or the transaction or arrangement but directors will be deemed aware of matters of which they reasonably ought to be aware. If the interest cannot reasonably be regarded as likely to give rise to a conflict of interest or if the other directors are aware of it, no declaration is required. Similarly if the company has only one director, no declaration is necessary.

Section 182 requires a director to declare an interest in an existing transaction or arrangement in the same way. Thus, if an existing transaction or arrangement gives rise at a later stage to an interest of the director, then he must, at that stage, declare his interest to a meeting of the directors or by notice in writing or by general notice. It is a breach of duty giving rise to criminal consequences for a director to fail to make a dec-laration of interest in an existing transaction or arrangement (s 183 CA 2006).

Section 182 CA 2006 applies to shadow directors just as the other provisions contained in ss 170–181 apply to shadow directors.

12.14 Substantial transactions

In addition to compliance with ss 177 and 182, substantial property transactions requiring the approval of members are dealt with in s 190 CA 2006 (see also section 10.2.1).

The section provides that a company may not enter into an arrangement under which a director of the company, or of its holding company, or a person connected with such a director, acquires or is to acquire from the company substantial non-cash assets, or where the company acquires or is to acquire substantial non-cash assets from such a director or other person so connected. In both cases the arrangement must have been approved by a resolution of the members of the company or be con-ditional on such approval being obtained.

Section 191 defines a substantial asset as an asset whose value:

(a)   exceeds 10% of the company's asset value and is more than £5,000, or
(b)   exceeds £100,000 (s 191(2) CA 2006).

Section 195 provides for the consequences of contravention. Section 195(2) states that the arrangement or transaction is voidable at the instance of the company unless:

(a)   restitution is no longer possible;
(b)   the company has been indemnified in pursuance of the loss or damage suffered; or
(c)   rights acquired in good faith for value and without actual notice of the contravention by a person who is not a party to the arrangement or transaction have intervened.

If the director or connected person is a director of the company's holding company, or a person connected with such a director, the arrangement must also have been approved by resolution of the members of the holding company or be conditional on such approval being obtained.

Whether or not the arrangement or transaction has been avoided, the following people will be liable to account to the company for any gain that has been made directly or indirectly by the arrangement or transaction, and jointly and severally with any other person to indemnify the company for any loss or damage resulting from the arrangement or transaction. The people liable are the director of the company or its holding company and any person who is connected with such a director and any other director of the company who authorised the arrangement or transaction entered into in pursuance of such an arrangement.

Re Duckwari plc (No 2) [1999] Ch 253 demonstrates the severity of the section, applying, as it does, to direct and indirect gains.

It should be noted that the section applies to shadow directors in the same way as it applies to directors (s 223 CA 2006).

Note that solicitors who fail to advise of a potential s 195 situation in advising clients on arrangements may well be held to be negligent (see *British Racing Drivers Club Ltd v Hextall, Erskine and Co (a firm)* [1996] 3 All ER 667).

12.15 Control of political donations and expenditure

Section 362 makes provision in relation to political donations made by companies to political parties, to other political organisations and to independent election candidates, and to political expenditure incurred by companies. Trade unions are expressly excluded (s 374 CA 2006).

Section 363 provides that this part of the Act (Part 14) applies to political parties that are registered under Part II of the Political Parties, Elections and Referendums Act 2000, or if the political party carries on or proposes to carry on activities for the purposes of or in connection with the participation of the party in any elections to public office held in a Member State other than the United Kingdom. Section 364 defines a political donation adopting the definition contained in ss 50–52 of the Political Parties, Elections and Referendums Act 2000, and s 53 of that Act applies in the same way for the purpose of determining the value of the donation. Donation is defined widely to include gifts, sponsorship, subscriptions, loans at uncommercial rates, and the provision of property, services, facilities or personnel at uncommercial rates.

Section 365 defines political expenditure. In relation to a company this means expenditure incurred by a company on:

(a) the preparation, publication or dissemination of advertising or other promotional or publicity material:

   (i) of whatever nature, and
   (ii) however published or otherwise disseminated

   that, at the time of publication or dissemination, is capable of being reasonably regarded as intended to affect public support for a political party or other political organisation or an independent election candidate; or

(b) activities on the part of the company that are capable of being reasonably regarded as intended:

   (i) to affect public support for a political party or other political organisation or independent election candidate, or
   (ii) to influence voters in relation to any national or regional referendum held under the law of a Member State.

Section 366 provides for authorisation required for donations or expenditure. A company must not make a political donation to a political party or organisation or to an independent election candidate, or incur any political expenditure unless the donation or expenditure is authorised in accordance with this section.

The donation or expenditure must be authorised:

(a) in the case of a company that is not a subsidiary of another company by a resolution of the members of the company;
(b) in the case of the company that is a subsidiary of another company by:

   (i) a resolution of the members of the company, and
   (ii) a resolution of the members of any relevant holding company.

It is further provided, however, that no resolution is required on the part of a company that is a wholly owned subsidiary of a UK company.

Section 367 provides that a resolution conferring authorisation with regard to political donations and political expenditure may relate to the company passing a resolution, one or more subsidiaries of that company, or the company passing the resolution and one or more subsidiaries of that company, and the resolution may authorise donations for expenditure under one or more of the following heads:

(a) donations to political parties or independent election candidates;
(b) donations to political organisations other than political parties;
(c) political expenditure (s 367(3) CA 2006).

For each of the specified heads, the resolution must authorise donations or, as the case may be, expenditure up to a specified amount in the period for which the resolution has effect (s 367).

Section 368 provides that a resolution conferring authority has effect for a period of four years from the date the resolution is passed unless the directors determine, or the articles require, a shorter period of time.

Section 369 provides that where a company makes political donations or incurs political expenditure without authorisation, the directors in default are jointly and severally liable.

Section 370 provides that any liability of a person under s 369 is enforceable by proceedings brought under this section in the name of the company by an authorised group of members of the company. This is in addition to being enforceable by proceedings brought by the company.

Those who may bring the proceedings as an 'authorised' group means:

(a)   the holders of not less than 5 per cent in nominal value of the company's issued share capital;
(b)   if the company is not limited by shares, not less than 5 per cent of its members; or
(c)   not fewer than 50 of the company's members.

Section 371 provides that the group may apply to the court for an order directing the company to indemnify the group in respect of costs.

In addition to trade unions that are exempt under s 374, as they are not considered to be political organisations, trade associations are also exempt under s 375, and all-party parliamentary groups are exempt under s 376.

Section 377 provides that political expenditure may be exempted by order of the Secretary of State under the section. The order under the section is subject to affirmative resolution procedure.

Section 378 further provides that donations not amounting to more than £5,000 in any 12-month period are exempt from the requirement for authority.

Summary

Introduction

The law on directors' duties has now been codified, although the 2006 Act makes it clear that existing case law exemplifying common law and equitable principles is still relevant in interpreting directors' duties.

Traditionally, directors owed duties to the providers of capital (the shareholders) although the directors had to take account of the interests of employees (reforms introduced by the Companies Act 1980), and some cases suggested that directors should take account of the interests of creditors.

This has now been extended by statute in s 172 CA 2006 so that directors must take account of the likely consequences of any decision in the long term. They must take account of the interests of the company's employees and the need to foster the company's business relationships with suppliers, customers and others. They must take account of the community and the environment, and of the desirability of the company maintaining a reputation for high standards of business conduct. The directors must also take account of the need to act fairly between members of the company.

This provision is said to reflect the 'enlightened shareholder value' approach to directors' duties.

Duty of care and skill

The previous law in this area resounded with Victorian echoes. Little was expected of directors in terms of care and skill in the past: see *Re City Equitable Fire and Insurance Company Ltd* (1925). More recently some cases have suggested a movement towards an objective standard of care – see interpretation of s 214 of the Insolvency Act 1986, and cases such as *Norman v Theodore Goddard* (1991).

Section 174 CA 2006 now introduces an objective standard of care geared up by the actual knowledge, skill and experience of a particular director if this is greater than the norm.

Fiduciary duties

Traditionally, the standard expected of directors in relation to honesty, integrity and good faith is in stark contrast to the old approach in relation to care and skill. Now the rules are statutory.

Directors must avoid actual or possible conflicts of interest or duties (s 175). A director must not accept benefits from a third party conferred by reason of his directorship in general terms (s 176 CA 2006).

Nominee directors must exercise independent judgement (s 173 CA 2006). Directors must exercise their powers for the purposes for which they are conferred and act in accordance with the company's constitution (s 171 CA 2006).

Directors must declare an interest in any proposed transaction or arrangement (s 177). Additionally they must declare an interest in any existing transaction or arrangement that arises (s 182).

Personal liability of directors to outsiders

Directors may, on occasion, be liable to outsiders in contract, in tort or by statute.

Limiting directors' liability

Section 232 provides that any purported exemption of a director in a company's constitution from liability for negligence, default, breach of duty or breach of trust is void.

However, insurance is permissible under s 233, as is qualifying third party indemnity provision under s 234. Furthermore, s 235 provides for qualifying pension scheme indemnity provision in appropriate circumstances. Additionally, s 1157 permits the court, in appropriate circumstances, to grant relief to an officer if it is proved that the officer acted honestly and reasonably, and ought in all the circumstances to be excused in whole or in part.

Political donations and expenditure

The Companies Act 2006 sets out restrictions on political donations and expenditure.

Self-test questions

12.1   Is the Companies Act 2006 significant in relation to directors' duties?

12.2   To whom do directors owe duties?

12.3   What is the scope of s 172 of the Companies Act 2006?

12.4   Explain what is meant by the duty to exercise independent judgement.

12.5   Give examples of how directors must exercise powers for a proper purpose.

12.6   Explain the evolution of the duty of care and skill.

12.7   What is the scope of directors' fiduciary duties?

12.8   Can a director ever legitimately take a corporate opportunity?

12.9   Can a director ever compete with a company of which he is a director?

12.10   Can a director ever take a benefit from a third party conferred by reason of the directorship?

12.11   Can directors ever be personally liable in relation to contracts undertaken by the company through the agency of a director?

12.12   How may directors' liability be limited?

12.13   What must a director do in relation to any contract with a company in which the director has a personal interest?

12.14   What is a substantial transaction?

12.15   What are the statutory rules in relation to political donations made by companies?

Further reading

D Ahern, 'Nominee Directors' Duty to Promote the Success of the Company: Commercial Pragmatism and Legal Orthodoxy' (2011) 127 LQR 118.

D Ahern, 'Guiding Principles for Directorial Conflicts of Interest: Re Allied Business and Financial Consultants Ltd; O'Donnell v Shanahan' (2011) 74 MLR.

D Ahern, 'Directors' Duties, Dry Ink and the Accessibility Agenda' (2012) 128 LQR 114.

A Alcock, 'An Accidental Change to Directors' Duties' (2009) 30 Co Law 362.

GMD Bean, 'Corporate Governance and Corporate Opportunities' (1994) 15 Co Law 266.

S Beck, 'Saga of Peso Silver Mines: Corporate Opportunity Reconsidered' (1971) 49 Can Bar Rev 80.

A Berg, 'Company Law Review: Legislating Directors' Duties' (2000) JBL 472.

A Boyle, 'The Common Law Duty of Care and Enforcement Under s459' (1996) 17 Co Law 83.

S Burridge, 'Wrongful Rights Issues' (1981) 44 MLR 40.

M Christie, 'The Director's Fiduciary Duty Not to Compete' (1992) 55 MLR 506.

M Conaglen, 'The Nature and Function of Fiduciary Loyalty' (2005) 121 LQR 452.

W Day, 'Attributing Illegalities' (2015) 74 CLJ 409.

R Edmunds and J Lowry, 'The Continuing Value of Relief for Directors' Breach of Duty' (2000) MLR 195.

V Finch, 'Company Directors – Who Cares About Skill and Care?' (1992) 55 MLR 179.

R Grantham, 'Can Directors Compete With the Company?' (2003) MLR 109.

N Hawke, 'Creditors' Interests in Solvent and Insolvent Companies' [1989] JBL 54.

L Herzel and DE Colling, 'The Chinese Wall' (1983) 4 Co Law 14.

A Hicks, 'Directors' Liability for Management Errors' (1994) LQR 390.

H Hirt, 'The Law on Corporate Opportunities in the Court of Appeal' [2005] JBL 669.

The Honourable Justice Ipp, 'The Diligent Director' (1997) 18 Co Law 162.

A Keay, 'Directors' Duties to Creditors, Contractors, or Concerns Relating to Efficiency and Over-Protection of Creditors' (2003) MLR 665.

A Keay, 'Directors' Duties and Creditors' Interests' (2014) 130 LQR 443.

P Koh, 'Directors' Fiduciary Obligations – A Fresh Look' [2003] CLJ 42.

P Koh, 'Once a Director Always a Fiduciary' [2003] CLJ 403.

E Lim, 'Directors' Fiduciary Duties: A New Analytical Framework' (2013) 129 LQR 242.

E Lim, 'Attribution in Company Law' (2014) 77 MLR 794.

J Lowry, 'Regal (Hastings) 50 Years On: Breaking the Bonds of the Ancient Regime?' (1994) 45 NILQ 1.

J Lowry, 'Directorial Self-Dealing: Constructing a Regime of Accountability' (1997) 48 NILQ 211.

J Lowry, 'The Duty of Loyalty of Company Directors: Bridging the Accountability Gap Through Efficient Disclosure' [2009] 68 CLJ 607.

J Lowry and R Edmund, 'The Corporate Opportunity Doctrine: Shifting Boundaries of the Duty and Its Remedies' (1998) 61 MLR 515.

D Milman, 'Strategies for Regulating Managerial Performance in the "Twilight Zone" – Familiar Dilemmas: New Considerations' [2004] JBL 493.

C Nakajima, 'Signing Without Reading' (1994) 15 Co Law 123.

RC Nolan, 'Controlling Fiduciary Power' [2010] 68 CLJ 29.

B Pettet, 'Duties in Respect of Employees Under the Companies Act 1980' (1981) 34 CLP 199.

D Prentice, 'The Corporate Opportunity Doctrine' (1974) MLR 464.

D Prentice, 'Creditors' Interests and Directors' Duties' (1990) OJLS 265.

H Rajak, 'Company Directors – The End of an Era' (1989) NLJ 1374, 1458.

C Riley, 'Directors' Duties and the Interests of Creditors' (1989) 10 Co Law 87.

L Roach, 'Equitable Life and Non-Executive Directors: Clarification from the High Court?' (2005) 26 Co Law 253.

S Scott, 'The Corporate Opportunity Doctrine and Impossibility' (2003) MLR 852.

L Sealy, 'Bona Fides and Proper Purposes in Corporate Decisions' (1989) Mon LR 265.

L Sealy, 'Reforming the Law on Directors' Duties' (1991) 12 Co Law 175.

P Watts, 'Corrupt Company Controllers, Their Companies and Their Companies' Creditors: Dealing With Ex Turpi Causa' (2014) JBL 161.

Lord Wedderburn, 'Companies and Employees: Common Law or Social Dimension?' (1993) 109 LQR 220.

PG Xuereb, 'The Limitation on the Exercise of Majority Power' (1985) 6 Co Law 199.

PG Xuereb, 'Remedies for Abuse of Majority Power' (1986) 7 Co Law 53.

PG Xuereb, 'Voting Rights: A Comparative Review' (1987) Co Law 16.

P Yeoh, 'Who'd Be a Director?' [2012] 33 Business LR 174.

Chapter 13

Corporate governance

Chapter Contents

13.1 Introduction

Until the twentieth century the separation of ownership and control in companies was not a major issue in company law. Increasingly with the growth of corporate activity it was identified as problematic (see e.g. *The Modern Corporation and Private Property* (1932) by Adolf A. Berle and Gardner C. Means). Shareholdings were often diffuse and directors exercised massive economic muscle.

In response to the increasing tendency for economic power to be vested in the boards of directors of public companies, company law took account of newly identified interests and new forms of governance emerged.

Corporate governance developments in the United Kingdom are of relatively recent date. As has been seen in company law in the UK, the interests of shareholders have generally predominated until the first statutory intervention in the Companies Act 1980, to broaden the duties of directors to include a duty to employees.

Increasingly, however, it has been recognised that other stakeholders have an interest in the governance of companies. Particular concern was attached to larger companies and specifically to listed companies. Companies' scandals at the end of the last century such as BCCI, Polly Peck and Maxwell heightened concerns.

Current thinking on corporate governance recognises a corporation's obligations to society generally in the form of stakeholders. Corporate governance is concerned with issues such as:

the effectiveness of a company's operations;
the reliability of a company's financial reporting compliance with laws and regulations; and
the safeguarding of corporate assets.

Corporate governance has recently become increasingly focused on corporate failures, auditor independence, excessive remuneration for directors and other executives, ineffective non-executive directors and the representation of large investors in public companies.

The origins of the corporate governance debate are in the need to respond to the problems that are caused by the separation of ownership and control in companies dating back to the formation of joint stock companies in the middle of the nineteenth century. Then, as now, the owners of companies were not necessarily involved in day-to-day operational matters. That is why shareholders were originally centre stage in the corporate governance debate. Now, however, as noted, it is recognised that a corporation's obligations run more widely to society generally in the form of stakeholders.

It is widely recognised in the United Kingdom that a large number of financial failures have been caused by breakdowns in internal control. This is true also in the United States. The Tredway Commission in the USA found that in nearly 50 per cent of cases of corporate breakdown, fraudulent financial reporting was a contributory issue.

13.2 The Cadbury Committee

The Committee on the Financial Aspects of Corporate Governance (the Cadbury Committee) published its final report in December 1992. This report contained a

Code of Practice which aimed at achieving the very highest standards of corporate behaviour.

The Committee was set up in May 1991 by the Financial Reporting Council, the London Stock Exchange and the accountancy profession. It adopted as its terms of reference: to consider the following in relation to financial issues arising from financial reporting and accountability, and to make recommendations on good practice:

(a) the responsibilities of executive and non-executive directors for reviewing and reporting on performance to shareholders and other financially interested parties, and the frequency, clarity and form in which information should be provided;

(b) the case for audit committees of the board, including their composition and role;

(c) the principal responsibilities of auditors and the extent and value of the audit;

(d) the links between shareholders, boards and auditors; and

(e) any other relevant matters.

The Cadbury Report in December 1992 attracted considerable attention. The concern about financial reporting and accountability was no doubt heightened by the then recent company scandals.

The Committee's recommendations are for the most part centred upon the control and reporting functions of boards and the role of auditors. This reflects the Committee's main aim, which was to review those aspects of corporate governance related to financial reporting and accountability.

At the core of the Committee's recommendations was a Code of Best Practice which was designed to achieve the necessary high standards of corporate behaviour. The London Stock Exchange required all listed companies registered in the United Kingdom, as a continuing obligation of listing, to state whether they were complying with the Code and to give reasons for any points of non-compliance.

The Code was thus directed to listed companies. The principles upon which the code was based were principles of openness, integrity and accountability.

Many of the key recommendations of the Committee were incorporated into the code. Some of the key recommendations were as follows:

(a) There should be a clearly defined split of responsibilities at the head of a company to ensure a balance of power and authority between executive and independent non-executive directors.

(b) There should be a schedule of matters specifically reserved for board decision so that it is clear that the company's control and direction are firmly in its hands.

(c) There should be an agreed procedure for directors in the furtherance of their duties to take independent professional advice if necessary, at the company's expense.

(d) Ideally, the posts of Chairman and Chief Executive should be kept separate.

(e) Executive directors' service contracts should not exceed three years.

(f) Executive directors' pay should be subject to the recommendations of a remuneration committee made up wholly or mainly of non-executive directors.

(g) Non-executive directors should be appointed for specified terms and reappointment should not be automatic.

(h) Non-executive directors should be selected through a formal process and this should be a matter for the board as a whole.

(i) The board should establish an audit committee of at least three non-executive directors with written terms of reference.

(j) The directors should report on the effectiveness of the company's internal controls.

(k) There should be full disclosure of fees paid to audit firms for non-audit work.

13.2.1 Critique

Various criticisms were made of the Cadbury Committee report. Some people criticised the lack of statutory teeth. This criticism was rejected by Sir Adrian Cadbury, who felt that the report had given companies a checklist and shareholders an agenda to improve the effectiveness of corporate governance in Britain. Yet some of the recommendations did not 'go the whole hog'. Thus, the report urged, generally, there should be a split of the chairmanship and post of chief executive between different people.

Another criticism levelled at the Cadbury Report was that it failed to address itself to long-term solutions encouraging long-term incentives for management and a long-term view of the investment by investment institutions, despite its statement in the opening paragraph of the report: 'The country's economy depends on the drive and efficiency of its companies.'

13.3 The Greenbury Committee

The governance of companies remained a favourite topic of debate. Following the Cadbury Committee report, a further committee was set up by the CBI under the chairmanship of Sir Richard Greenbury. The aim of this committee was to consider issues relating to directors' remuneration and emoluments. The committee's report, which was published in 1995, once again set out a Code of Best Practice. This Code was annexed to the listing rules and every listed company had to state, in its annual report and accounts, whether it had secured compliance with the Code. If it had failed to comply with the Code, it must explain why this was so.

Basically, the Code requires that directors of a listed company should establish a remuneration committee made up of non-executive directors to determine policy on remuneration packages for executive directors. The remuneration committee should have access to independent professional advice and the committee chairman, or alternatively another member of the committee, should attend the company's AGM to be available to answer questions on remuneration.

13.4 The Hampel Committee

A further committee on corporate governance, this time under the chairmanship of Sir Ronald Hampel, was set up in November 1995. This was at the behest of the Financial Reporting Council.

The Hampel Committee was asked:

(a) to review the Cadbury Code and its implementation to ensure that its purposes were being achieved and to suggest amendments to the code as necessary;
(b) to review the role of directors;
(c) to pursue any relevant matters arising from the report of the Greenbury Committee;
(d) to address, as necessary, the role of shareholders and auditors in corporate governance issues; and
(e) to deal with any other relevant matters.

The Hampel Committee published its preliminary report on 5 August 1997. The Committee:

(a) rejected the principle of stakeholder democracy and a two-tier board system;
(b) rejected the government's idea for a standing panel on governance;
(c) asserted that companies are more concerned with accountability than business prosperity – the Committee indicated that it wanted to see this imbalance corrected;
(d) proposed a set of general principles rather than a detailed corporate governance blueprint and rejected what it termed the 'tick-box' attitude to compliance pursued by Cadbury and Greenbury; and
(e) stated that companies should include a statement in the annual report on compliance with broad corporate governance principles.

Following consultation, the Committee resisted pressure from the government to 'beef up' its proposals.

Sir Ronald Hampel, Chairman of the Committee and Chairman of ICI, indicated that the Committee had stuck to the fundamental principle of corporate prosperity before accountability.

Some criticisms have been made that the report dilutes the Cadbury guidelines in that, for example, it concludes that companies need not separate the roles of chairman and chief executive, although this goes against a key principle of the Cadbury guidelines.

The Hampel Committee report (1998) considered that, in the debate on corporate governance, too much stress had been laid on accountability and not enough on business prosperity.

The report urged that companies should include in their annual report a description of how corporate governance is being applied in relation to their business. The Hampel Committee produced a set of principles and a Code which comprehends the work of the Cadbury, Greenbury and Hampel Committees – the Combined Code.

Companies should have a Nomination Committee to make recommendations for appointments to the board. Remuneration Committees should be made up of independent directors to consider remuneration packages and their application. Institutional investors are said to have a responsibility to use their vote sensibly and the key role of shareholders at the AGM is acknowledged.

Every company should establish an Audit Committee made up of at least three non-executive directors.

The final Hampel report contained a proposal that each board should have a lead non-executive director. He would be a focal point of contact for shareholders.

Some critics (for example, CA Riley in 'Whither UK Corporate Governance?' *Amicus Curiae*, October 1997) argue that the approach to corporate governance raises a deeper and more troubling problem. This is that the debate on corporate governance has been semi-privatised and carried out through the medium of relatively small and unrepresentative committees championing a narrow range of interests.

The Secretary of State announced that she did not intend to legislate on the Hampel recommendations, but preferred that they should be established by best practice:

> There are those who would say the government has a responsibility to legislate for good corporate governance. However, while the legal system can be used to enforce aspects of best practice, I believe that the very best will adopt even better practice because they see its value, and will do so more readily of their own accord than if it is forced on them. That is why I would prefer to see many of the recommendations ... embodied in good practice rather than enshrined in legislation.
>
> (the Rt Hon Margaret Beckett, MP, the President of the Board of Trade, in a speech to the Pensions and Investment Research Consultants on 4 March 1998)

13.5 The Turnbull Report

The Turnbull Committee was set up by the Institute of Chartered Accountants in England and Wales. The report of the committee – *Internal Control: Guidance for Directors on the Combined Code* – was published in 1999 and sets out how directors of listed companies should comply with the UK's Combined Code requirements in respect of internal controls. The guidance was supported and endorsed by the London Stock Exchange.

13.6 The Higgs Report

In April 2002, the Secretary of State for Trade and Industry and the Chancellor of the Exchequer appointed Derek Higgs to lead a short independent review of the role and effectiveness of non-executive directors. Derek Higgs published his report in January 2003.

The Higgs Report considered the position of non-executive directors. Among its recommendations were the need for a fuller discussion of the role and responsibilities of non-executives, a requirement to disclose attendance at board meetings, the need for the provision of training, and the need for non-executives to meet major investors as part of their induction and for the senior independent director to meet shareholders regularly.

13.7 The Smith Report

The Smith Review, chaired by Sir Robert Smith and set up by the Financial Reporting Council, considered the guidance for audit committees. The Smith Report was published in January 2003. The committee recognised that the main role and responsibility of audit committees should be to monitor the integrity of the company's financial statements and to review its internal financial controls.

The audit committee should be given written terms of reference by the board of directors tailored to the particular circumstances of the company. It should review annually its terms of reference and its effectiveness, and recommend any necessary changes to the board.

The audit committee should be comprised solely of independent non-executive directors; the term independent is defined by the Higgs Report as a director who is independent in character and judgement and has no relationships or circumstances that affect his judgement. It is stipulated that the chairman of the company should not be an audit committee member.

The audit committee should, at least annually, meet the external and internal auditors without management being present to discuss issues arising from the audit. The audit committee should be provided with sufficient resources to undertake its duties.

Appropriate training should be given to members of the audit committee.

The chairman of the audit committee should be present at the annual general meeting to answer questions through the chairman of the board on the audit committee's activities and matters within the scope of the audit committee's responsibilities.

13.8 The Tyson Report

Following a recommendation contained in the Higgs Review, Professor Laura Tyson, Dean of the London Business School, was asked to consider how companies might draw on broader pools of experience and talent to enhance board effectiveness. The Tyson Report on The Recruitment and Development of Non-Executive Directors (June 2003) accordingly added another piece to the jigsaw by highlighting how a range of different backgrounds and experiences among board members can enhance board effectiveness.

The report made recommendations about diversity and background, skills and experience of non-executive directors, the need for foreign national directors, particularly in view of the increasing globalisation of business, the role of executive search firms in identifying potential non-executive directors, and the importance of continuing board training for directors.

The report noted that optimising board membership is vital for the company's performance and competitiveness. It also noted that this can play an important role in restoring shareholder and public trust in UK boardrooms.

13.9 The Combined Code on Corporate Governance 2003

In July 2003, a new version of the Combined Code on Corporate Governance was issued. This code superseded and replaced the Combined Code issued by the Hampel Committee on Corporate Governance in 1998. The code derived from a review of the role and effectiveness of non-executive directors by Derek Higgs (January 2003) and a review of audit committees by a group led by Sir Robert Smith (January 2003), as well as provisions on internal control derived from the Turnbull Committee (September 1999).

The Combined Code applied to reporting years beginning on or after 1 November 2003. The Financial Services Authority (succeeded by the Financial Conduct Authority) annexed the code to the listing rules and made consequential rule changes.

All companies incorporated in the UK and listed on the London Stock Exchange are required under the Listing Rules to report on how they have applied the Combined Code in their annual report and accounts. This requirement does not apply to Alternative Investment Market (AIM) companies.

The code contains both main and supporting principles and provisions. Listed companies have to make a disclosure statement in two parts in relation to the code. In the first part of the statement, companies need to report on how they apply the principles and provisions of the code. Companies should set out their governance policies and any special circumstances that apply to them. In the second part of the statement, companies have to confirm that they comply with the code's provisions or, if they depart from them, to provide an explanation. This 'comply or explain' approach has been in operation since the Cadbury Code was adopted and has been generally welcomed by companies and investors.

While it is recognised that most listed companies will comply with the code's provisions most of the time, it is recognised that sometimes departure from the provisions of the code may be justified. Every company must review every provision carefully and provide an explanation if it departs from the code's provisions. Smaller listed companies, especially those that are new to listing, may feel that some of the provisions are disproportionate or less relevant in their case. Some of the provisions do not apply to companies below FTSE 350. Such companies may, however, feel that it is right to adopt the general approach of the code and are encouraged to consider this option.

The 2003 code does not include material from the previous code on the disclosure of directors' remuneration. This is because the Directors' Remuneration Report Regulations 2002 (SI 2002/1986) are now in force and supersede the earlier code provisions.

The code, as has been noted, is made up of main principles together with supporting principles and provisions.

The Financial Reporting Council (FRC) reviewed the present code in 2005. Some minor amendments were proposed and these came into force in November 2006. A further review was conducted in 2007.

13.10 The Walker Report

In February 2009 Sir David Walker was asked by the then Prime Minister (Gordon Brown) to review corporate governance in UK banks in the light of the experience of critical loss and failure throughout the banking system.

The terms of reference were as follows:

> To examine corporate governance in the UK banking industry and make recommendations, including in the following areas: the effectiveness of risk management at board level, including the incentives in remuneration policy to manage risk effectively; the balance of skills, experience and independence required on the boards of UK banking institutions; the effectiveness of board practices and the performance of audit, risk, remuneration and nomination committees; the role of institutional shareholders in engaging effectively with companies and monitoring of boards; whether the UK approach is consistent with international practice and how national and international best practice can be promulgated.

Later the terms of reference were extended so the review should also identify where its recommendations were applicable to other financial institutions.

Sir David made preliminary conclusions and recommendations in July 2009 with a request for comments by 1 October. The final report was made on 26 November 2009.

Many of the recommendations, where applicable to listed companies generally, were incorporated into the Code on Corporate Governance.

13.10.1 Main themes of the review

Five key themes of the review were identified thus:

1   Both the UK unitary board structure and the combined code of the FRC remain fit for purpose. It is also noted that the 'comply or explain' approach to guidance and provisions under the Combined Code provides the surest route to better corporate governance.
2   The principal deficiencies in boards and other financial institutions relate much more to patterns of behaviour than to organisations. The most critical need is identified as an environment in which effective challenge of the executive is expected and achieved.
3   Given that the overriding strategic objective of a bank or other financial institution is the successful management of financial risk, board-level engagement in risk oversight should be materially increased.
4   There is need for better engagement between fund managers acting on behalf of their clients as beneficial owners and the boards of investee companies.
5   Against a background of inadequate control, unduly narrow focus and serious excess in some instances, substantial enhancement is needed in board-level oversight of remuneration policies. It is also recommended that the remit and responsibility of board remuneration committees should be extended beyond executive board members to senior employees.

13.10.2 Recommendations

Board size, composition and qualification

1   In order to ensure that non-executive directors have the knowledge and understanding of the business, personalised induction, training and development are needed and should be reviewed annually with the chairman.

2 A bank or other financial institution board should provide for dedicated support for non-executive directors.

3 The overall time commitment of non-executive directors on a FTSE 100 listed bank or life assurance company board should be greater than has been the norm in the past. For example: a minimum expected time commitment of 30 to 36 days in a major bank board should be clearly indicated in letters of appointment.

4 The then Financial Services Authority's (now succeeded by the Financial Conduct Authority) ongoing supervisory process should give closer attention to the overall balance of the board in relation to the risk strategy of the business, taking into account the experience, behavioural and other qualities of individual directors and their access to adequate induction and development programmes.

5 The Financial Services Authority's (now the Financial Conduct Authority) interview process for non-executive directors proposed for FTSE 100 listed bank and life assurance company boards should involve questioning and assessment by one or more senior advisers with relevant experience.

Functioning of the board and evaluation of performance

6 As part of their role as members of the unitary board of a bank or other financial institution, non-executive directors should be ready, able and encouraged to challenge and test proposals on strategy.

7 The chairman of a major bank should be expected to commit a substantial proportion of his time, probably around two-thirds, to the business of the entity with clear understanding from the outset that in the event of need, the chairmanship role would have priority over any other business time commitment.

8 The chairman of a bank or other financial institution board should bring a combination of relevant financial industry experience and a track record of successful leadership capability in a significant board position.

9 The chairman is responsible for leadership of the board.

10 The chairman of a bank or other financial institution board should be proposed for election on an annual basis.

11 The role of the senior independent director should be to provide a sounding board for the evaluation of the chairman and to serve as a trusted intermediary for the non-executive directors.

12 The board should undertake a formal and rigorous evaluation of its performance and that of committees of the board with external facilitation of the process every second or third year.

13 The evaluation statement on board performance and governance should confirm that a rigorous evaluation process has been undertaken.

The role of institutional shareholders: communication and engagement

14 The board should ensure that they are made aware of any material cumulative changes in the share register as soon as possible. Where material cumulative changes take place over a short period, the Financial Services Authority (now Financial Conduct Authority) should be promptly informed.

15 This recommendation was deleted.

16 The remit of the Financial Reporting Council should be explicitly extended to cover the development and encouragement of the adherence to principles of best practice in stewardship by institutional investors and fund managers.

17 The code on responsibility of institutional investors prepared by the Institutional Shareholders Committee should be ratified by the Financial Reporting Council and become the Stewardship Code. Its status should be akin to the Combined Code as a statement of best practice. (This code is annexed to the Walker Report.)

18 The Financial Reporting Council should oversee a review of the Stewardship Code on a regular basis.

18B All fund managers that indicate commitment to engagement should participate in a survey to monitor adherence to the Stewardship Code.

19 Fund managers and other institutions authorised by the Financial Services Authority (now the Financial Conduct Authority) to undertake investment business should signify on their websites or in other accessible form whether they commit to the Stewardship Code.

20 The Financial Services Authority (now the Financial Conduct Authority) should require institutions that are authorised to manage assets for others to disclose clearly on their websites or in other accessible form the nature of their commitment to the Stewardship Code or their alternative business model.

20B In view of the importance of facilitating enhanced engagement between shareholders and investee companies, the Financial Services Authority (now the Financial Conduct Authority), in consultation with the Financial Reporting Council and Takeover Panel, should keep under review the adequacy of what is in effect 'safe harbour' interpretation and guidance that has been provided as a means of minimising regulatory impediments to such engagement.

21 Institutional investors and fund managers should actively seek opportunities for collective engagement where this has the potential to enhance their ownership influence.

22 Voting power should be exercised, fund managers and other institutional investors should disclose their voting record, and their policies in respect of voting should be described in statements on their websites or in another publicly accessible form.

Governance of risk

23 The board of a FTSE 100 listed bank or life insurance company should establish a board risk committee separately from the audit committee. The board risk committee should have responsibility for oversight and advice to the board on the risk exposures of the entity and future strategy.

24 In support of board-level risk governance, a bank or other financial institution board should be served by a Chief Risk Officer who should participate in the risk management and oversight process at the highest level on an enterprise-wide basis. The remuneration of the Chief Risk Officer should be subject to approval by the chairman or chairmen of the board remuneration committee.

25 The board risk committee should be attentive to the potential added value from seeking external input to its work as a means of taking full account of relevant experience elsewhere and in challenging its analysis and assessment.

26   In respect of a proposed strategic transaction it should, as a matter of good practice, be for the board risk committee in advising the board to ensure that a due diligence appraisal of the proposition is undertaken.

27   The board risk committee (or board) risk report should be included as a separate report within the annual report and accounts.

Remuneration

28   The remuneration committee should have a sufficient understanding of the company's approach to pay and employment conditions to ensure that it is adopting a coherent approach to remuneration.

29   The terms of reference of the remuneration committee should be extended to oversight of remuneration policy and outcomes in respect of all 'high end' employees.

30   In relation to 'high end' employees, the remuneration committee report should confirm that the committee is satisfied with the way in which performance objectives and risk adjustments are reflected in the compensation structures for this group and explain the principles underlying the performance objectives, risk adjustments and the related compensation structure if these differ from those for the executive board members.

31   For FTSE 100 listed banks and comparable unlisted entities such as the largest building societies, the remuneration committee report for the 2010 year of account and thereafter should disclose in bands the number of 'high end' employees. These bands should be ranging from £1 million to £2.5 million, from £2.5 million to £5 million, and from £5 million upwards, and within each band should be the main elements of salary, cash bonus, deferred shares, performance-related long-term awards and pensions contributions. These bands cover 'high end' employees including executive board members.

32   Financial Services Authority (succeeded by the Financial Conduct Authority) authorised banks that are UK domiciled subsidiaries of non-resident entities should disclose for the 2010 year of account and thereafter details of total remuneration bands (including remuneration received outside the UK) and the principal elements within such remuneration for their 'high end' employees on a comparable basis and timescale to that required for UK listed banks.

33   Deferral of incentive payment should provide the primary risk adjustment mechanism to align rewards with performance for executive board members and 'high end' employees.

34   Executive board members and 'high end' employees should be expected to maintain a shareholding or retain a portion of vested awards in an amount in line with their total compensation on historic or expected basis.

35   The remuneration committee should seek advice from the board risk committee on specific risk adjustments.

36   If the non-binding resolution on a remuneration committee report attracts less than 75 per cent of the total votes cast, the chairman of the committee should stand for re-election in the following year irrespective of his or her normal appointment term.

37   The remuneration committee report should state whether any executive board member or 'high end' employee has the right or opportunity to receive enhanced

benefits whether while in continued employment or on termination, resignation, retirement or in the wake of any other event such as a change of control.

38/9   Remuneration consultants should put in place a formal constitution for the professional group that has now been formed with provision for independent oversight and review of the remuneration consultant's code. This code should be lodged on the Financial Reporting Council website.

13.11 UK Corporate Governance Code 2014

The first version of the UK Code on Corporate Governance was produced by the Cadbury Committee in 1992. The Code applies to listed companies. It supplements statutory law and case law. Corporate governance is identified as what the board of a company does and how it sets out the company's values and standards as opposed to the day-to-day operational matters of the company.

Prior to the code, there were earlier substantial reviews conducted in 2003, 2005, 2007, 2010 and 2012. The code is not therefore unchanging.

Sir David Walker conducted a review of the governance of banks and financial institutions. Many of the recommendations of Sir David's committee are incorporated into the current code on corporate governance (see 13.10).

The current code applies to accounting periods starting on or after 1 October 2014. The 2003 code remains the main building block within the current code on corporate governance.

Additionally, the FRC publishes a series of guidance notes to help companies on specific issues of governance and accountability. These cover board effectiveness, the role of audit committees, risk management, internal control and assessing and reporting on whether the business is a going concern.

Investors are encouraged to commit to the UK Stewardship Code. This sets out standards for investors to help improve the dialogue between investors and directors. The Financial Conduct Authority requires asset managers to report on compliance with the code. The most recent stewardship code was published in September 2012.

More information on the codes and annual reports on the impact and implementation of the codes is to be found via the FRC's website and www.frc.org.uk.

Much of the recent work on corporate governance has been informed by attempts to counter perceived (and indeed actual) short termism in British investment and corporate life see: *A Long-Term Focus for Corporate Britain* (Department for Business, Innovation and Skills, October 2010) and *The Kay Review of UK Makers and Long-Term Decision Making* (July 2012).

13.11.1 Key principles

Two fundamental conclusions in conducting the review were made by the Financial Reporting Council. The first was the importance of adherence to the spirit of the code as well as the letter of the code.

The second major conclusion was that the nexus between shareholders and the board of directors was of key significance in this area. In recognition of this the Financial Reporting Council has assumed responsibility for a Stewardship Code which provides guidance to shareholders.

The Code on Corporate Governance gives considerable freedom of manoeuvre to boards as to how they should act. It sets out a framework.

The aim of the code is to help companies and their boards to discharge their obligations. Thus chairmen are encouraged to report personally on the performance of their companies in their annual statements.

In addition, board directors of FTSE 350 companies should be subject to annual re-election, the code states.

13.11.2 'Comply or explain'

The traditional approach of 'comply or explain' is retained in the 2014 code. This is consistent with the flexibility of the code.

The code is not rigid. It is made up of principles (main and supporting) as well as provisions. The principles are the core of the code.

Smaller listed companies, particularly if they are new to listing, may feel that some of the obligations set out in the code are inappropriate to them. Here the importance of 'comply or explain' is particularly clear. It should be borne in mind also that some of the content of the code does not apply to companies outside the FTSE 350.

13.11.3 The contents of the code

The code is divided into sections.

Section A – Leadership

Companies should have effective boards. No single individual should have unrestricted power. The chairman is responsible for leadership on the board. Non-executive directors should challenge the executive arm of the board.

Section B – Effectiveness

The board should contain the right mixture of skills and expertise. It should be an appropriate size. It should contain an appropriate number of non-executive directors. It should also have committees of nomination (nominating directors), audit and remuneration.

Non-executive directors should be identified as independent, if appropriate, and at least half the board should normally comprise non-executive directors.

Measures should be taken to ensure proper development for directors.

Re-election should occur at regular and frequent intervals, with directors of FTSE 350 companies being subject to annual election.

Section C – Accountability

The board should present an appropriate analysis of the company's state and its future potential.

There should be appropriate risk management and internal management control systems. There should, in addition, be an audit committee of non-executive directors monitoring the performance of the company and its audit function.

The audit committee should recommend the external auditors of the company.

Section D – Remuneration

Appropriate remuneration should be paid to directors and there should be a performance-related element to directors' remuneration. This should be overseen by the remuneration committee of the board made up of non-executive directors.

Section E – Relations with shareholders

The interaction between the board and shareholders is crucial. This is primarily the responsibility of the board of directors.

The chairman of the company should draw to the attention of the board concerns raised by major shareholders.

The company's annual general meeting should be used effectively to communicate with investors and measures taken to encourage the participation of investors.

The chairman of the board should ensure that the chairs of the audit, nomination and remuneration committees are available at the annual general meeting to answer questions from investors.

13.12 Alternative Investment Market companies

The Corporate Governance Code does not apply to companies quoted on the Alternative Investment Market. To fill this lacuna the Quoted Companies Alliance has published guidelines for AIM companies. The guidelines are made up of a code of best practice.

13.13 International corporate governance

In recent times, many well-known global companies have experienced financial collapses and this has eroded global confidence in them – most notably Enron and WorldCom.

Multilateral bodies such as the World Bank and the Organisation for Economic Co-operation and Development (OECD) have contributed to the corporate governance debate on an international basis.

The World Bank and the OECD established a global governance forum in 2001 to contribute to governance reform on an international basis. This forum has helped develop initiatives in emerging economies and identified areas for the reform of corporate governance. The OECD has developed Principles of Corporate Governance to help develop frameworks for corporate governance rules. The principles are non-binding and are broadly drawn but they have helped in the promotion of appropriate standards of corporate governance worldwide. They provide guidance on the basis of an effective framework for corporate governance, the treatment of shareholders and their rights, the role of stakeholders in corporate governance, and board responsibilities. The principles were first released in 1999 and revised in 2004 and reviewed again in 2015.

13.14 European Commission

At the same time the European Commission has set up a European Corporate Governance Forum to encourage the coordination of national codes. This could well lead to harmonisation of corporate governance rules and accordingly the Companies Act 2006 by Part 43 gives the Financial Conduct Authority the power to make rules to implement any such Directive. It is not intended to introduce a European Corporate Governance Code; however, it considers that the EU should adopt a common approach to governance.

13.15 The United States

In the United States, the Sarbanes-Oxley Act 2002 applies to companies that have a listing in the US. It was introduced following the Enron and WorldCom collapses (the so-called 'pinstripe plunder'), and imposes criminal liabilities on officers of companies who knowingly sign off false financial statements.

The Sarbanes-Oxley reforms have led to improvements in the corporate governance performance of large companies in the US. However, the reforms have had their critics too. The costs of compliance, especially with regard to s 404 requiring outside audit of a company's internal control systems, have often been severely criticised as being disproportionate.

The principles of the Sarbanes-Oxley Act supplements the workings of the Securities and Exchange Commission and guidelines of the stock exchanges like NASDAQ, NYSE etc.

Summary

Since the early 1990s, increased attention has been paid to corporate governance, particularly in the case of listed companies in the United Kingdom.

In 1992, the Cadbury Committee on the Financial Aspects of Corporate Governance published its final report. It was looking at the responsibilities of executive and non-executive directors, the case for audit committees, principal responsibilities of auditors, and the links between shareholders, board and auditors, as well as other relevant matters. The report contained a Code of Practice. Listed companies were required to comply with the Code of Practice.

The Greenbury Committee looked at directors' remuneration. Once again, it published a Code of Best Practice which was annexed to the listing rules. It reported in 1995.

The Hampel Committee was set up in November 1995 to review the Cadbury code, to review the role of directors, to pursue any matters arising from the Greenbury Committee, and to address, as necessary, the role of shareholders and auditors in relation to corporate governance. It published its preliminary report in 1997 and its final report in 1998. It put forward a code for compliance for listed companies.

The Turnbull Committee published a report in 1999 setting out how directors of listed companies should comply with the code, and this guidance was endorsed by the London Stock Exchange.

In April 2002, Derek Higgs was asked to lead a review into the role and effectiveness of non-executive directors. He published his report in 2003.

The Smith Review, chaired by Sir Robert Smith, looking at the position of audit committees, also published its report in 2003.

In July 2003, a new version of the Combined Code on Corporate Governance was issued. This replaced the Combined Code issued by the Hampel Committee in 1998. There were two later revisions of this combined code. There then followed a report into the banking system, the Walker Report. This report was made on 26 November 2009. Further revisions to the existing code recommended by the Financial Reporting Council (FRC) are contained in the UK Corporate Governance Code 2014. This is the latest version of regulations on corporate governance annexed to the listing rules while still largely based on the 2003 code.

In 2005, 2007, 2010, 2012 and 2014, reviews of the implementation of the 2003 version of the combined code were effected. Investors are encouraged to commit to the UK Stewardship Code. The latest version was published in September 2012.

Self-test questions

13.1   Set out in brief the matters with which corporate governance is concerned.

13.2   Describe the importance of the Cadbury Committee's report.

13.3   What did the Greenbury Committee consider?

13.4   Set out the importance of the Hampel Committee's report.

13.5   What did the Turnbull Report consider?

13.6   What did the Higgs Report consider?

13.7   Set out the matters that were considered by the Smith Report.

13.8   What was the importance of the Tyson Report?

13.9   Set out the main areas with which the UK Code on Corporate Governance is concerned.

13.10 How are Alternative Investment Market companies governed in relation to corporate governance?

13.11 Describe the impact of international developments in relation to corporate governance.

13.12 What European developments are worthy of note in relation to corporate governance in the EU?

13.13 Describe in brief US developments in relation to corporate governance.

Further reading

A Alcock, 'Corporate Governance: A Defence of the Status Quo' (1995) 58 MLR 898.

A Belcher, 'Regulation by the Market: The Case of the Cadbury Code and Compliance Statement' [1995] JBL 321.

C Chambers, 'Another Day Another Culprit: Corporate Governance – Is It to blame for the Banking Crisis?' (2009) 30 Business LR 264.

I Chiu, 'The Role of a Company's Constitution in Corporate Governance' [2009] JBL 697.

A Dignam, 'A Principled Approach to Self-Regulation? The Report of the Hampel Committee on Corporate Governance' (1988) 9 Co Law 140.

J Dine, 'The Governance of Governance' (1994) 15 Co Law 73.

V Finch, 'Board Performance and Cadbury on Corporate Governance' [1992] JBL 581.

P Goldenberg, 'Reforming Corporate Governance – A Very British Solution' (2003) 24 Bus Law Review 82.

A Keay, 'Assessing Accountability of Boards Under the UK Corporate Governance Code' (2015) JBL 551.

M Hemraj, 'Corporate Governance: Rationalising Stakeholder Doctrine in Corporate Accountability' (2005) 26 Co Law 211.

CA Riley, 'Corporate Management – UK and US Initiatives' [1994] LS 244.

C Villiers, 'Draft Report by the Cadbury Committee on the Financial Aspects of Corporate Governance' (1992) 13 Co Law 214.

KW Wedderburn, 'The Social Responsibilities of Companies' (1982) Melbourne University LR1.

KW Wedderburn, 'Companies and Employees: Common Law and Social Dimension' [1993] LQR 220.

P Yeoh, 'The Sarbanes-Oxley Act 2002: Time for Some Tinkering' (2007) 28 Business LR 90.

Chapter 14

Insider dealing and market abuse

14.1 Introduction

Insider dealing is essentially the trading in company securities on a recognised stock exchange, with a view to making a profit or avoiding a loss, by someone who has confidential information about those securities that if that information were widely known would affect their price.

It was only with the Companies Act 1980 that there was the first legislative intervention in the United Kingdom to combat insider dealing. Other jurisdictions came to this problem much earlier on, for example, the USA in the Securities Exchange Act 1934. Previously, the relevant UK legislation was contained in the Companies Securities (Insider Dealing) Act 1985 and the Financial Services Act 1986.

Legislation has altered the law on insider dealing to take account of the EC Directive on Insider Dealing (89/592). The law is now contained in Part V of the Criminal Justice Act 1993 and Schedule 1 of that Act.

The securities covered by the legislation are set out in Schedule 2. They include shares and gilts. The law for the most part only covers dealings on a regulated market so that the law does not generally extend to unlisted companies. Certain off-market deals are caught.

There are two categories of insiders caught by the legislation – primary insiders and secondary insiders or tipees.

Primary insiders are persons who have information as an insider obtained through:

(a) being a director, employee or shareholder or an issuer of securities; or
(b) having access to the information by virtue of employment, profession or office.

Secondary insiders are those who have received or obtained information from a person who is an insider either directly or indirectly.

A person is not a secondary insider or tipee merely by virtue of being procured to deal in securities. He must have inside information and must know that it is inside information and he must know that it is from an inside source (s 57).

The legislation prohibits dealing in securities by a person whether by himself or as an agent for another person. There is also a prohibition on encouraging or procuring another person to deal and also of disclosing information except in the performance of one's duties or on showing one did not expect the person to act upon the disclosure. Inside information is defined as specific information that is not in the public domain and that is unpublished. It must be information which, if published, would have an effect on the price of the securities (s 56).

The legislation requires that there should be an intention to make a profit or to avoid a loss. The new law, however, tilts the balance towards the prosecution in that it is presumed that persons who deal in securities with the relevant knowledge have the intention to make a profit or avoid a loss. Thus the legislation places the burden on the defendant of disproving the intention. There are certain limited defences (s 53 and Sch 1).

There is no civil remedy for insider dealing. The contract itself remains intact. The maximum criminal sanction that applies on indictment is seven years' imprisonment and/or an unlimited fine. On summary conviction, the maximum penalty is a fine and/or six months' imprisonment (s 61).

Investigations may be set up under the Financial Services and Markets Act 2000 to investigate possible insider dealing (see section 23.5).

The law in relation to insider dealing and market abuse is now largely contained in the Financial Services and Markets Act 2000, the Criminal Justice Act 1993 and the Financial Services Act 2012.

14.2 Criticisms

Various criticisms have been made of the UK law on insider dealing.

14.2.1 No civil remedy

The fact that there was no civil remedy was often the subject of criticism. By contrast, in the USA there has been a civil remedy ever since the Securities and Exchange Act 1934 whereby the person who has sold shares to an insider (or possibly bought from an insider) is able to sue for the profit made by the other or the loss avoided by the other. There was no civil remedy in the United Kingdom. It is possible that there may be an indirect remedy. Under the Powers of the Criminal Courts Act 1973 and, in Scotland, the Criminal Justice (Scotland) Act 1980, any victim of a criminal offence may be awarded compensation under the Act. This occurred, for example, in Scotland in *Procurator Fiscal v Bryce* in 1981 (unreported).

The market abuse provisions of the Financial Services and Markets Act 2000 provide for civil penalties in the form of injunctions and restriction orders.

Insofar as directors profit from their use of inside information, there may be a remedy available to the company against the directors for breach of duty.

It must be borne in mind, however, that the term 'insiders' encompasses more than directors and also that there may be difficulties with the company suing directors where the directors are in control of the company. In any event, as Suter notes, in *The Regulation of Insider Dealing in Britain* (1989, London: Butterworths), p. 122: 'There is no reported decision in Britain on a claim by a company to recover insider dealing profits from an insider. Hence, the issue of whether insiders are accountable to their companies for such profits is unresolved.'

14.2.2 No insider trading agency

A second major criticism made of the legislation in the United Kingdom is that there is no institution that has been set up specifically to deal with the matter of insider dealing. There is such an institution in the USA, namely the Securities and Exchange Commission. There have been calls from the Stock Exchange for an insider trading agency. At present most prosecutions are carried out by the Department for Business, Innovation and Skills on the basis of evidence gathered by the Stock Exchange.

14.2.3 Legislation only applies to quoted companies

A third criticism that is made is that the legislation only applies to quoted companies, with one or two minor exceptions. There seems no real reason why the legislation should not apply to non-quoted companies as well. Clearly, the problem is more severe in relation to quoted companies, as in other cases a person would generally know that he is selling to or buying from an insider. However, it does seem that in circumstances where it can be shown that an insider has acted in contravention of the basic principle that influences the legislation, even in a non-quoted company, that person should be subject to some sanction.

14.2.4 Enforcement is haphazard

A fourth criticism made of the Act is that enforcement is haphazard. There have been few prosecutions and very few convictions. Yet there is still evidence of widespread insider dealing. This is of some significance when it is the case that there is inter-national competition between different stock exchanges and there are few sentences of imprisonment in relation to insider dealing in the United Kingdom. Although the maximum penalty was increased in 1988 from two years' imprisonment to seven years' imprisonment, at that stage there had been very few convictions and there have been very few sentences of imprisonment imposed. This may be contrasted with the United States enforcement where early on Richard Whitney, the Head of the New York Stock Exchange, was despatched for a stay in Sing Sing in 1934.

In *R v Calvert* (unreported, 11 March 2010), Malcolm Calvert, a former partner of the Queen's stockbroker Cazenove, was sentenced to 21 months' imprisonment after being found guilty of insider dealing contrary to s 52 of the Criminal Justice Act 1993.

There were various counts with which Calvert was charged relating to inside information inter alia in HP Bulmer plc, MacDonald Hotels plc, British Biotech plc, RAC plc and South Staffordshire plc.

Judge Peter Testar said that insider dealing was not a victimless crime: 'It leads to the dishonest enrichment of a few at the expense of the public interest and of con-fidence in a clean and fair market.'

14.3 Insider dealing as market abuse

The stock market can only work effectively where there is a level playing field in terms of those dealing, i.e. buying and selling shares and securities. Public confi-dence in the reliability of the Stock Exchange and the open nature of dealing will mean that the fairer the Stock Exchange is seen to be and the more reliable the market system, the more people will be inclined to use the relevant stock exchange.

In addition to laws combating insider dealing, there are laws to combat market abuse.

Section 118 of the Financial Services and Markets Act 2000, as amended by SI 2005/381, deals with insider dealing as market abuse, and market manipulation as market abuse. This amendment was undertaken to implement the Insider Dealing and Market Manipulation Directive (Market Abuse) (2003/6/EC) (known as 'MAD' – the Market Abuse Directive) in the UK.

Market abuse in relation to insider dealing is defined as behaviour, whether by one person alone or two or more persons jointly or in concert, that occurs in relation to qualifying investments admitted to trading on the prescribed market or qualifying investments in respect of which a request for admission to trading on such a market has been made, or certain behaviour in relation to related investments to such qualifying investments. This behaviour is where an insider deals or attempts to deal in a qualifying investment or related investment on the basis of inside information relating to the investment in question (insider dealing), or where an insider discloses inside information to another person other than in the proper course of the exercise of his employment profession or duties (improper disclosure).

A further example of insider dealing as market abuse is where the behaviour of any person

> is based on information not generally available to those using the market but which, if available to a regular user of the market, would be or would be likely to be regarded by him as relevant when deciding the terms on which transactions in qualifying investments should be effected.
>
> (s 118(4)(a) Financial Services and Markets Act 2000)

Behaviour that is based on such information will be market abuse if it does not pass the regular user test. It is likely to be regarded by a regular user of the market as a market abuse if there is a failure on the part of the person concerned to observe the standard of behaviour reasonably expected of a person in his position in relation to the market (s 118(4)(b)) (misuse of information).

Further, under Part 7 of the Financial Services Act 2012, there are criminal offences of making false or misleading statements, creating false or misleading impressions, and making false or misleading statements or creating a false or misleading impression in relation to specified benchmarks. These are all contained in s 89, s 90 and s 91 of the Financial Services Act 2012 respectively.

On 20 October 2011, the European Commission published proposals to replace MAD with a Regulation on insider dealing and market manipulation and a directive on criminal sanctions to deal with market abuse. Both were subsequently published and Member States have until 3 July 2016 to transpose them into national law; MAD would from this date be repealed and replaced by these new Regulations. The UK, however, has decided to opt out of these new provisions.

14.4 Insiders

Insiders are defined in s 118B as any person who has inside information:

(a) as a result of his membership of an administrative, management or supervisory body of an issuer of qualifying investments;

(b) as a result of his holding shares in the capital of an issuer of qualifying investments;

(c) as a result of having access to the information through the exercise of his employment, profession or duties;

(d) as a result of his criminal activities; or

(e) which the person has obtained by other means, and which he knows, or could reasonably be expected to know, is inside information.

14.5 Inside information

Section 118C defines inside information in relation to qualifying investments or related investments that are not commodity derivatives as information of a precise nature that:

(a)   is not generally available;
(b)   relates directly or indirectly to one or more issuers of the qualifying invest-ments or to one or more of the qualifying investments; and
(c)   would, if generally available, be likely to have a significant effect on the price of the qualifying investments or on the price of related investments.

(s 118C(2) Financial Services and Markets Act 2000)

In relation to commodity derivatives, the third condition is that users of the markets on which the derivatives are traded would expect to receive the information in accordance with any accepted market practices on those markets. The other two con-ditions apply *mutatis mutandis*.

For a person charged with the execution of orders concerning any qualifying investments or related investments, inside information includes information con-veyed by a client and related to the client's pending orders that:

(a)   is of a precise nature;
(b)   is not generally available;
(c)   relates directly or indirectly to one or more issuers of qualifying investments or to one or more qualifying investments; and
(d)   would, if generally available, be likely to have a significant effect on the price of those qualifying investments or on the price of related investments.

(s 118C(4) Financial Services and Markets Act 2000)

Information is precise if it:

(a)   indicates circumstances that exist or may reasonably be expected to come into existence or an event that has occurred or may reasonably be expected to occur; and
(b)   is specific enough to enable a conclusion to be drawn as to the possible effect of those circumstances or that event on the price of qualifying investments or related investments.

(s 118C(5) Financial Services and Markets Act 2000)

It should be noted that the market abuse provisions depend upon information that is not generally available to those using the market, but which if available to a regular user of the market would be or would be likely to be regarded by him as relevant when deciding the terms on which transactions in qualifying investments should be effected.

14.6 Market manipulation as market abuse

The remaining courses of behaviour in s 118 relate to market manipulation:

(a) Where the behaviour consists of effecting transactions or orders to trade, which give, or are likely to give, a false or misleading impression as to the supply of, or demand for, or the price of, one or more qualifying investments.
(b) Where the behaviour consists of effecting transactions or orders to trade, which secure the price of one or more such investments at a normal or artificial level (manipulating transactions).
(c) Where the behaviour consists of effecting transactions or orders to trade which employ fictitious devices or any other form of deception or contrivance (manipulating transactions).
(d) Where the behaviour consists of the dissemination of information by any means which gives, or is likely to give, a false or misleading impression as to the qualifying investment by a person who knew or who could reasonably be expected to have known that the information was false or misleading (dissemination).
(e) Where the behaviour is likely to give a regular user of the market a false or misleading impression as to the supply of, demand for or price or value of, qualifying investments (misleading information).
(f) Where the behaviour would be likely to be regarded by a regular user of the market as behaviour that would distort, or would be likely to distort, the market in a qualifying investment (distortion), and the behaviour is likely to be regarded by a regular user of the market as a failure on the part of the person concerned to observe the standard of behaviour reasonably expected of a person in his position in relation to the market.

14.7 Exceptions

Certain categories of behaviour are exempted by s 118A(5) as follows:

(i) If it conforms with a rule that includes a provision to the effect that behaviour of conforming with the rule does not amount to market abuse.
(ii) That it conforms with the relevant provisions of Commission Regulations (EC) 227/2003, 22 December 2003, implementing Directive 2003/6/EC, regarding exemptions to buy-back programmes and stabilisation of financial instruments.
(iii) If it is done by a person acting on behalf of a public authority in pursuit of monetary policies or policies with respect to exchange rates for the management of public debt or foreign exchange reserves.

14.8 Sanctions

Section 123(1)(a) of the Financial Services and Markets Act 2000 provides that if the Financial Conduct Authority is satisfied that a person is or has engaged in market abuse, it may impose a financial penalty or publish a statement to the effect that a person has engaged in market abuse. Similarly, if the Financial Conduct Authority is satisfied that a person has required or encouraged others to do something that would amount to market abuse, it may apply the relevant sanctions.

The standard of proof that is appropriate is on a balance of probabilities. The relevant transaction is not rendered void or unenforceable by reason of a penalty being imposed (s 131 of the Financial Services and Markets Act 2000).

Section 381 of the Financial Services and Markets Act empowers the High Court to issue an injunction regarding continuing market abuse. It may also order a person to take steps to remedy or mitigate market abuse (s 381(2) and (6)). The Financial Conduct Authority may make a restitution order against a person who has engaged in market abuse or encouraged another to do so (s 384), or may apply to the High Court for it to make an order (s 383).

Defences are available in relation to a financial penalty or restitution order if the Financial Conduct Authority or the court is satisfied that:

(a)   the person concerned believed on reasonable grounds that his behaviour was not market abuse (or requirement or encouragement of market abuse); or

(b)   the person took all reasonable precautions and exercised all due diligence to avoid engaging in market abuse or requiring or encouraging others to do so.

14.9 Financial institutions and fraud

The Fraud Act 2006, although strictly not part of the UK market abuse or insider dealing regime, provides that a general offence of fraud may be committed by providing false representations, or a failure to disclose pertinent information and an abuse of position. This general offence focuses on the offender's intentions as opposed to the consequences of their actions (such as the victim being deceived) and therefore in some circumstances, this legislation could be used in preference to or alongside other specialist legislation. The fact that this legislation packs a powerful punch, penalty for breach is punishable up to a maximum of ten years' imprisonment or a fine or both may mean that we may see more prosecutions under this Act.

Summary

Legislation on insider dealing was not introduced in the United Kingdom until 1980. The law is currently set out in the Criminal Justice Act 1993 which implements the EC Directive on Insider Dealing (89/592).

Criminal sanctions including imprisonment may be applied where an insider deals in securities of a quoted company on the basis of inside information. The law also prohibits secondary insiders (tipees) with insider information from dealing in the securities of quoted companies.

Various criticisms are levelled at the legislation:

(a)   no civil remedy is provided;

(b)   there is no institution specifically charged with investigating insider dealing;

(c) the legislation does not generally extend to unquoted companies; and

(d) the enforcement of the law on insider dealing is haphazard.

The Financial Services and Markets Act 2000 also prohibits 'market abuse' by insider dealing, manipulation, use of fictitious devices, dissemination of misleading information and distortion. There are financial penalties that attach to breaches of the relevant provisions and the High Court can impose an injunction to prevent further abuse; a restitution order may also be made.

Self-test questions

14.1 What is insider dealing?

14.2 Set out some of the problems with the current law on insider dealing.

14.3 What does s 118 of the Financial Services and Markets Act 2000 and Part 7 of the Financial Services Act 2012 provide in relation to market abuse?

14.4 Who constitute insiders in s 118 of the Financial Services and Markets Act 2000?

14.5 What does s 118 provide in relation to inside information?

14.6 What does s 118 provide in relation to market manipulation as market abuse?

14.7 What exemptions apply in relation to conduct that would otherwise amount to market abuse?

14.8 What are the sanctions that apply in relation to s 118 of the Financial Services and Markets Act 2000 and s 89, s 90 and s 91 of the Financial Services Act 2012?

Further reading

A Alcock, 'Insider Dealing – How Did We Get Here?' (1994) 15 Co Law 67.
N Jain, 'Significance of Mens Rea in Insider Trading' (2004) 25 Co Law 132.
H McVea, 'What's Wrong With Insider Dealing?' (1995) 15 LS 390.
H McVea, 'Fashioning a System of Civil Penalties for Insider Dealing: ss 61 and 62 of the Financial Services Act 1986' [1996] JBL 344.
M White, 'The Implications for Securities Regulation of New Insider Dealing Provisions in the Criminal Justice Act 1993' (1995) 16 Co Law 163.

Chapter 15

Minority protection

15.1 The rule in *Foss v Harbottle*

Historically, the rule in *Foss v Harbottle* (1843) 2 Hare 461 has been of the utmost significance in governing when shareholders can take action on behalf of the company in which they hold shares. The facts of the case were as follows.

Certain burghers in Manchester had got together to purchase parkland to dedicate to the then heiress to the throne, Princess Victoria. The park opened to great acclamation but difficulties soon followed. It was alleged by some of the company's members that some directors had misapplied company property. The case was heard by Wigwram VC. He held that the action could not proceed as the individual shareholders were not the proper claimants. If a wrong had been committed, the wrong had been committed against the company and the company was therefore the proper claimant. The rule in *Foss v Harbottle* has acted like a dead hand on minority protection in British company law. The rule is, to some extent, justifiable. It has sometimes been justified as preventing a multiplicity of actions and sometimes by the argument that the company can ratify what directors have done and that, therefore, litigation might well be pointless.

In *Stein v Blake* [1998] 1 All ER 724, the claimant and the defendant each owned 50 per cent of the shares of the company. The defendant, who was the sole director of the company, transferred assets at an undervalue to companies under his control.

The claimant brought an action in his personal capacity, alleging that the defendant had breached his director's duties. The Court of Appeal upheld the decision of the trial judge. Millet LJ quoted from the judgment of the Court of Appeal in *Prudential Assurance Co Ltd v Newman Industries (No 2)* [1982] Ch 204: 'what [a shareholder] cannot do is to recover damages merely because the company in which he is interested has suffered damage'.

The rule in *Foss v Harbottle*, however, quickly gave way to certain exceptions where a minority action may be brought by a member arguing that a wrong has been done to the company. Historically at common law, these exceptions were:

(a)   ultra vires acts;
(b)   where a special majority is needed;
(c)   the personal rights exception; or
(d)   fraud by those in control of the company.

15.2 Exceptions to the rule

Historically it has not been possible to bring an action as an exception to the principle in *Foss v Harbottle* as a derivative claim where the claim is one of negligence – at least where the directors have not profited from the negligence in question.

It is proposed to examine each of these exceptions to the principle in *Foss v Harbottle* and then to examine the change brought about by s 260 of the Companies Act 2006, which introduces a new statutory procedure for a 'derivative claim'.

15.2.1 Ultra vires acts

The principle that the company can ratify what had been done, converting an initial wrong into action that was legitimate, could not formerly apply to ultra vires activities. Ultra vires acts could not be ratified: see *Parke v The Daily News Ltd* [1962] Ch 927 and *Simpson v Westminster Palace Hotel Co* (1860) 8 HL Cas 712. Despite virtual abolition of the doctrine of ultra vires, it is still possible for shareholders to restrain companies from acting in an ultra vires way before a transaction has been concluded. The exception, therefore, to this extent remains (s 40(4) CA 2006) (see also section 6.9).

15.2.2 Where a special majority is needed

If the company's constitution stipulates that a special majority is needed before a particular course of conduct can be accomplished then, if the company seeks to fly in the face of this provision and not obtain the particular majority, a single shareholder may maintain an action as an exception to *Foss v Harbottle*. This is the basis of the decision in *Edwards v Halliwell* [1950] 2 All ER 1064.

In fact, the case involves a trade union rather than a company. The law in this particular area is the same in both categories of law. The National Union of Vehicle Builders was seeking to increase its subscriptions and it was alleged that this was in contravention of the union rule book without obtaining the consent of the union members to the increase. Members of the Cricklewood branch of the union complained about this and were successful. The same principle operates in company law.

The case is an interesting one and the judgment of Jenkins LJ is particularly helpful in setting out lucidly the law in this area.

15.2.3 The personal rights exception

If the company denies a shareholder rights that are set out in the company's constitution, the shareholder can bring an action on behalf of himself and all other shareholders denied the right to enforce the rights that have been negated. Thus, in *Pender v Lushington* (1877) 6 ChD 70, a shareholder was able to enforce his right and that of other shareholders that they should be able to cast their votes. The action was brought by a Mr Pender on behalf of himself and all shareholders who voted against an amendment, and on behalf of the Direct United States Cable Company Ltd as claimants. The defendants, EH Lushington and other gentlemen, had rejected the votes on the contention that the shares were held in trust for others.

The judge held that the rights accorded to members were the rights accorded to registered members and therefore their votes were wrongly rejected.

In *Wood v Odessa Waterworks Co* (1889) 42 ChD 636, a shareholder was able to enforce his right to a dividend in cash rather than a dividend *in specie* (in the form of property) as provided for under the company's articles. The company's articles of association provided for the payment of a dividend. The general meeting had approved a resolution that dividends be paid by way of a distribution of debentures. The judge, Stirling J, held that the implication of the article of association was that a dividend must be paid in cash and could not be paid in kind, i.e. by a distribution of property such as debentures. The company was accordingly restrained from acting upon the resolution.

15.2.4 Fraud by those in control

One reason for restricting derivative claims to fraud was to prevent a multiplicity of claims where it was possible that the action complained of would be ratified by the company. The exception of fraud enabled a shareholder to bring an action on behalf of the company (a derivative action deriving from the company's right to sue) for a fraud perpetrated by somebody in control. Fraud can never be ratified so the ratification objection does not arise. In *Cook v Deeks* [1916] 1 AC 554, a Privy Council case on appeal from Ontario, a shareholder was able to bring an action under this head complaining that directors had diverted corporate opportunities to themselves. The exception does not extend to cases of negligence: see *Pavlides v Jensen* [1956] 2 All ER 518, where the complaint was that the directors had been negligent in selling an asbestos mine in Cyprus at an undervaluation. The exception did not extend either to negligence tantamount to expropriation, which was the way that the cause of action was pleaded in *Heyting v Dupont* [1964] 1 WLR 843, which concerned a Jersey company formed to exploit an invention of the defendant consisting of a machine for the manufacture of plastic pipes. A particularly difficult case arose in *Daniels v Daniels* [1978] Ch 406. In this case a director had purchased property from a company for £4,250 and then resold it shortly afterwards for £120,000. The allegation was pleaded as one of negligence. The judge, Templeman J, allowed the action to proceed. This has sometimes been misinterpreted. The case is not authority for the proposition that where there has been gross negligence, an action is possible as an exception to *Foss v Harbottle*. The judge specifically stated: 'To put up with foolish directors is one thing; to put up with directors who are so foolish they make a profit of £115,000 odd at the expense of the company is something entirely different' (p. 414). Clearly, the decision is exceptional. Templeman J is indicating that there is more to the case than meets the eye.

Another important decision in the area of fraud is that of *Prudential Assurance Co Ltd v Newman Industries Ltd* [1980] 2 All ER 341. The case dealt, inter alia, with the question of control. In this case, Vinelott J held that management control was sufficient and seemed to accept that the directors were in management control. The Court of Appeal took a different view as it considered it would need a trial to see if management control actually existed. Voting control, on the other hand, is easy to demonstrate. Vinelott J had erred in not considering as a preliminary issue whether the claimants could bring a derivative action. A derivative action should be permitted, according to the view of the Court of Appeal, where the board of the company was shown to be under the control of the fraudsters; only then could the issue of fraud be considered.

15.2.5 Statutory derivative claims

Section 260 of the Companies Act 2006 now allows a derivative claim to be brought in respect of a cause of action arising from an actual or proposed act or omission involving negligence, default, breach of duty or breach of trust by a director of a company.

The range of this remedy is clearly much wider than the pre-existing common law derivative action procedure, which required at least that the director should have profited from the negligence or breach. The cause of action may arise before the plaintiff seeking to bring the derivative action became a member of the company. This accords with the common law position.

It may be that this new procedure will increase claims against directors but the provisions do encompass some safeguards.

The safeguard is that a member of a company who brings a derivative claim must apply to the court for permission to continue with the claim (s 261 CA 2006). The same applies where a member applies to take over an action that has been brought by a company where it is appropriate for the member to continue the claim as a derivative claim (s 262 CA 2006).

If it appears to the court in either case that the evidence filed by the applicant does not disclose a prima facie case for giving permission for the continuation of the derivative claim, then the court should dismiss the application and make any consequential order that it considers appropriate.

The matters that are to be considered in determining whether permission is to be given or not are set out in s 263 CA 2006.

Permission must be refused if the court is satisfied:

(a) that a person acting in accordance with s 172 (duty to promote the success of the company) would not seek to continue the claim; or
(b) where the cause of action arises from an act or omission that is yet to occur, that the act or omission has been authorised by the company; or
(c) where the cause of action arises from an act or omission that has already occurred that the act or omission:

    (i) was authorised by the company before it occurred, or
    (ii) has been ratified by the company since it occurred (s 263(2) CA 2006).

In general, in considering whether to give permission the court must take into account, in particular, the following:

(a) whether the member is acting in good faith in seeking to continue the claim;
(b) the importance that a person acting in accordance with s 172 (duty to promote the success of the company) would attach to continuing;
(c) where the cause of action results from an act or omission that is yet to occur, whether the act or omission could be, and in the circumstances would be likely to be:

    (i) authorised by the company before it occurs, or
    (ii) ratified by the company after it occurs;

(d) where the cause of action arises from an act or omission that has already occurred, whether the act or omission could be, and in the circumstances would be likely to be, ratified by the company;
(e) whether the company has decided not to pursue the claim; and
(f) whether the act or omission in respect of which the claim is brought gives rise to a cause of action that the member could pursue in his own right rather than on behalf of the company (s 263(3) CA 2006).

In considering whether to give permission, the court will have particular regard to evidence before it as to the views of members of the company who have no personal interest, whether direct or indirect, in the matter.

It seems a multiple derivative action can still be brought at common law. Thus in *Universal Project Management Services Ltd v Fort Kilkicker Ltd* [2013] EWHC 348 Ch where a wrong was done to a subsidiary company and the subsidiary's directors refused to act and those same directors controlled the holding company, a member of the holding company was able to sue on behalf of the subsidiary.

There are practical deterrents in bringing a derivative action as the relief is awarded to the company if the claim is successful rather than to the claimant. Further costs are normally awarded against unsuccessful claimants.

In *Franbar Holdings Ltd v Patel* [2008] BCC 885, the appellant company Franbar applied for permission to continue a derivative claim against the respondents on behalf of the third respondent company (Medicentres (UK) Ltd).

Medicentres's business was in providing healthcare. It was at one stage wholly owned by Franbar but Franbar had sold 75 per cent of the shares to another company (Casualty Plus Ltd). Casualty Plus appointed two directors who were the first and second respondents.

Franbar claimed under s 260 CA 2006 that the first and second respondents were liable for neglect, default and breach of the duty of care to Medicentres. They claimed that the respondents had driven down the share price of Medicentres by driving business away and by failing to provide adequate financial information.

They also made a claim for breach of a shareholders' agreement with Casualty Plus and also under s 994 CA 2006 in relation to unfairly prejudicial conduct.

The court refused Franbar leave to continue with the derivative claim as they had the shareholders' agreement action and the petition under s 994.

The court took the view that a hypothetical director would be more likely to regard the pursuit of the derivative claim as less important in the light of the fact that several of the complaints were more naturally formulated as claims in relation to the breach of the shareholders' agreement.

In *Mission Capital plc v Sinclair* [2008] BCC 866, former directors (Sinclair) sought permission to continue a derivative action against the company (Mission Capital). Mission Capital had terminated Sinclair's employment and required them to resign as it was alleged they had failed to meet financial forecasts and submit important financial information to the board. Mission Capital obtained an injunction to exclude Sinclair from the company's premises and requiring them to deliver up documents. Sinclair counterclaimed and brought a derivative action against Mission Capital, the non-executive directors and Phillips, a replacement director.

It was argued that the company would be liable to a substantial claim for wrongful dismissal.

The court took the view that there was a two-stage process under s 260. The first stage under s 263(2)(a) requires the court to consider whether a notional director would continue with the action. The court took the view that it was possible that a notional director would continue with the action because of the impact of a wrongful dismissal claim.

The second stage requires the court to exercise discretion under s 263(3). Here the court took the view that a notional director would not attach much significance to the liability for wrongful dismissal and it would be more likely to replace Sinclair than to take action against those responsible. It was further noted that Sinclair might succeed under s 994 and this was a factor in the decision too.

In *Kleanthous v Paphitis* [2011] All ER 33, the court had to consider the possibility of the success or otherwise of the derivative claim. Kleanthous, the applicant, was seeking permission to continue a derivative action in relation to an alleged breach of duty by Paphitis and three other directors. Theodore Paphitis was well known, of course, as one of the 'dragons' in the popular enterprise-promoting TV programme *Dragons' Den*. The company was the office stationery company, Ryman Group Ltd.

All four parties were directors of the relevant company. The company had had the opportunity to purchase a majority shareholding in another company. It had failed to do so and subsequently Paphitis had decided to buy the shareholding in a personal capacity. The other directors had loaned money to a company set up for the purpose of purchasing the shareholding. They subsequently became directors of that company. Considerable profits were made by this company, both in terms of dividends and in terms of its later sale to a third party.

The court dismissed the applicant's claim in relation to breach of duty by Paphitis and the other directors. It found that there was the possibility of success and the award of a significant sum of money, but held that a director acting in accordance with s 172 CA 2006 – that is to say in a way which would be most likely to promote the success of the company – would not continue with such a claim.

15.2.6 Shareholders' collateral actions

In *Johnson v Gore Wood & Co* [2002] 2 AC 1, the House of Lords had to consider the extent to which a shareholder could bring a collateral claim where the company had already sued.

The case concerned an allegation that the defendant firm of solicitors had failed in its undertaking to serve efficaciously a notice to exercise an option to purchase land. The company that held the option had already sued the firm and obtained satisfaction of a large part of its claim. Before the settlement agreement was concluded the claimant, who owned all but two of the shares in the company, notified the firm that he too would be suing on the basis that the firm had contracted with, or otherwise assumed responsibility to him, as well as to the company. The settlement agreement contemplated the claimant retaining his right of action against the firm. The House of Lords struck out the claimant's claims to the extent that they reflected the loss suffered by the company. They left in place claims for consequential loss that the claimant may have suffered that were not so reflected.

This principle is entirely reasonable. A shareholder should not be able to reopen a case by seeking to pursue the defendant in a personal capacity where the company has already sued if his loss is merely reflective of the company's loss. As Lord Millett said in *Johnson* at p. 66, 'Mr Johnson cannot be permitted to challenge in one capacity the adequacy of the terms he agreed to in another.'

The issue of reflective loss arose in *Giles v Rhind* [2003] Ch 618. Giles and Rhind were both shareholders, employees and directors of SHS Ltd. Rhind left the company and diverted business away in breach of a shareholders' agreement. The company started proceedings against him but the proceedings were discontinued by the administrator as the company could not afford to continue. Giles then started an action in his personal capacity. Could he proceed as the company had a right of action against Rhind? Waller LJ, in the Court of Appeal, said it hardly seems right that a wrongdoer in breach of contract to a company and to a shareholder should be able to block an action by a shareholder where he had prevented the company pursuing an action by demanding costs from the company. The shareholder's action was allowed to proceed.

Thus, as seems entirely reasonable, the defendant cannot shelter behind the no reflective loss principle where the defendant's wrongdoing has caused the company to be unable to sue.

15.3 The statutory remedy

Minority protection is now one of the most active areas of company law. Until the Companies Act 1980 and s 75 of that Act, now ss 994–996 CA 2006, minority protection was arguably the most stagnant area.

Section 210 of the Companies Act 1948, which provided relief where a minority was oppressed, was introduced in response to the recommendations of the Cohen Committee in 1945. The section was used very rarely in its 32 years of operation between 1948 and 1980. It was used successfully in *Scottish CWS v Meyer* [1959] AC 324, where a shareholder complained that the company's business was diverted away to another company in which the petitioning shareholder had no interest. The petition was successful. In another case, *Re HR Harmer Ltd* [1959] 1 WLR 62, the founding father of a stamp-dealing company was ordered not to interfere in the affairs of the company. The petition was presented by his sons. The father, aged 88 at the time of the action, was running the business as if it was his own personal business. He was tyrannical and dictatorial. He defied board resolutions and appointed a private detective to spy on some of his staff whom he wrongly suspected of stealing company assets. The petition was successful.

15.3.1 Drawbacks of s 210 of the Companies Act 1948

The old minority remedy section had various drawbacks. These were highlighted by the Jenkins Committee in 1962. The drawbacks were as follows:

(a) An order could only be made if the facts could be the basis for a winding-up order on the just and equitable ground. This meant that the section was very closely allied to the rules relating to winding up.

(b) A single act was insufficient to justify a petition under s 210. A course of conduct had to be shown to found a petition.

(c) The petitioner had to show that the conduct was oppressive. This meant 'burdensome, harsh and wrongful' (*Scottish CWS v Meyer* (1959) *per* Viscount Simonds).

(d) A petition could not be based on omissions or on proposed future conduct.

(e) It was generally thought that the old minority section could not encompass personal representatives; however, Plowman J, in *Re Jermyn Street Turkish Baths Ltd* [1971] 1 WLR 1042, took the view that personal representatives could petition.

15.3.2 The remedy post 1980

These shortcomings were all remedied by s 75 of the Companies Act 1980 (now ss 994–996 CA 2006). The link with winding up was swept away. A single act or omission or threatened future conduct can be the basis for a petition although in some circumstances it is impossible for the unfairly prejudicial conduct to recur by virtue of the fact that the wronged party was in control, thus there is no scope for the court to grant relief and a petition cannot be brought. See Peter Gibson LJ in *Re Legal Costs Negotiators Ltd* [1999] BCC 547 at p. 551 where a minority shareholder and director was dismissed as an employer because of his conduct. The majority were not entitled to an order to purchase the minority shares as they had remedied the prejudicial conduct and there could be no continuing unfair conduct as they were in control. Personal representatives can now sue (see s 994(2) CA 2006). Most importantly, the new remedy applies in cases of unfair prejudice. This is obviously far easier to demonstrate than oppression, which requires a course of deliberate conduct. The section now provides as follows:

> A member of a company may apply to the court by petition for an order ... on the ground that the company's affairs are being or have been conducted in a manner which is unfairly prejudicial to the interests of its members generally or of some part of its members (including at least himself) or that any actual or proposed act or omission of the company (including an act or omission on its behalf) is or would be so prejudicial.

15.3.3 Exclusion from management

The most common example of the minority seeking relief is where an undertaking to a member that he would have a say in the management of a company has been breached, usually by his removal from the board of directors. Under the old law, it was essential that the oppression was suffered qua member in the narrow sense. This requirement was strictly applied, so that a member complaining of exclusion from management would not have succeeded. The requirement of petitioning qua member has now, at least, been more broadly construed so that, for example, a founder member could well argue that a right to participate in the management of the company was a membership right.

Early on, it seemed that the old rule still applied, even under the reformed section. In *Re a Company (No 004475 of 1982)* [1983] Ch 178, Lord Grantchester QC held that prejudice had to be suffered qua member in the narrow sense. However, in an earlier unreported decision, *Re Bovey Hotel Ventures Ltd* (1981, unreported), there had been a successful petition on the basis of exclusion from management. A husband and wife had operated a hotel company. They split up. The erstwhile husband excluded the former wife from participating in the management of the company. She successfully petitioned under the section and indeed was able to purchase the husband's shareholding as her remedy.

Another case involving exclusion from management is *Re RA Noble & Sons (Clothing) Ltd* [1983] BCLC 273. Here, the court accepted that exclusion from management could be the basis of a petition. However, it found that on the facts of the case the petitioner had brought the exclusion on himself by his lack of interest.

Re London School of Electronics [1986] Ch 211 provides a further example of exclusion from management. This case concerned a North London tutorial college where the petitioner complained of his de facto dismissal as a director. The other directors argued that the petitioning director, Lytton, had brought the exclusion upon himself by his own conduct. Nourse J held that the petitioner's conduct did not prevent him from bringing the petition. The alleged conduct, if proven, would be a factor in determining what relief should be available to the petitioning shareholder. It might also serve to demonstrate that the prejudice was not unfair.

In *Re a Company (No 002567 of 1982)* [1983] 1 WLR 927, Vinelott J took the view that the section would apply in an *Ebrahimi*-type situation where a shareholder was wrongly excluded from management in a company. In *Re Bird Precision Bellows Ltd* [1986] Ch 658, the petitioners, who were minority shareholders in Bird Precision Bellows Ltd, had been removed from the board of directors by the respondents. It was ordered by consent, without any admission of liability on the part of the respondents that they had been responsible for unfairly prejudicial conduct, that the respondents should purchase the petitioners' shares at a price to be determined. Nourse J subsequently held that the exclusion was wrongful.

In *Richards v Lundy* [2000] 1 BCLC 376, a remedy was granted where Richards was removed as an employee but remained a director of the Apollo Cleaning Services Company. The judge held he had expected to play an active management role.

In *Foster Bryant Surveying Ltd v Bryant* [2007] 2 BCLC 239, the first defendant Bryant and Foster were surveyors. Alliance Leisure Services, whose managing director was Mrs Watts, was a client of the firm where Foster was employed. Foster then set up his own company, Foster Bryant Surveyors Ltd, and approached Bryant to join him, which he did. Bryant had 40 per cent of the shares, Foster 60 per cent. Mrs Bryant joined as an employee as she was also a surveyor.

Fallout followed. Foster set out certain complaints in an email and announced that he wanted to make Mrs Bryant redundant. Bryant then resigned.

Mrs Watts then took Bryant on in his own right after the notice period with Foster Bryant had ended as she had to make alternative arrangements. Bryant then incorporated a new company, Savernake Property Consultants Ltd, the second defendant.

The judge found that Bryant had been excluded as a director and the resignation was forced upon him. He held there was no breach of directors' duties. This was upheld in the Court of Appeal, where it was held that he had not diverted business opportunities to himself but had acquiesced in Alliance's solution to the problem caused to this business by the departure of Bryant and Mrs Bryant from Foster Bryant Surveying Ltd.

The need to apply the rules of honesty and integrity and to avoid any conflict of interest with any duty was emphasised. A pragmatic and common-sense approach was needed. Bryant's resignation had no ulterior purpose.

The pattern is not absolutely uniform. Clearly, not every exclusion from management in a small private company is wrongful. In *Coulson, Sanderson and Ward Ltd v Ward* (1986) 2 BCC 99, Slade LJ considered that exclusion from management would not necessarily found a petition under s 994. Furthermore, in *Re XYZ Ltd* (also under the name *Re a Company (No 004377 of 1986)* [1987] 1 WLR 102), it was similarly held that not every exclusion from management in a quasi-partnership company would ground a petition. It did not necessarily follow that there was always a legitimate expectation of management in such companies.

While it is extremely unlikely that a petition can be presented under s 994 for exclusion from a public company, still less a quoted company, the door does not seem absolutely closed on this possibility. In *Re Blue Arrow plc* [1987] BCLC 585, the court held that although there was generally no room for implying a legitimate expectation of continued employment in the management of a public company, special situations could arise where exclusion from management could be the basis for a petition in respect of a public company. However, on the facts of this particular case, Vinelott J held that the petition was so hopeless on its face that the right course of action was to strike it out.

Re Tottenham Hotspur plc [1994] 1 BCLC 655 provides the type of situation where a director may be able to argue successfully that there has been an understanding that there should be a role for him in the management in a public company situation, although Terry Venables, the chief executive, failed to establish that in this case. He went on to become manager of the England team, so it did not hold him back. For a more recent example, see *Re I Fit Global Ltd* [2013] EWHC 2090 (Ch) also known as *Blunt v Jackson* [2013] EWHC 2090 (Ch) where the petitioner was dismissed as director where the parties had agreed on the basis of a partnership to establish the company.

There must, however, be some membership nexus. Thus, in *Re JE Cade & Son Ltd* [1992] BCLC 213, the petitioning member was seeking to protect his interests as a landowner and failed as protecting such interests was held to be outside of the scope of the remedy; while in quasi-partnership situations a shareholder will be able to demonstrate that there was a clear understanding of a management role, this clearly went well beyond such a claim.

15.3.4 Other grounds on which petitions have been based

There are various other grounds on which petitions have been based. Petitions might therefore include the following:

(a) The company failing to purchase the shares of a minority – *Re a Company (No 004475 of 1982)* (1983), before Lord Grantchester QC. This petition was unsuccessful.

(b) The company changing its business. This was another ground for complaint in *Re a Company (No 004475 of 1982)* (1983), before Lord Grantchester QC. This argument was also unsuccessful. The company had set up as an advertising agency and later diversified to become a wine bar and restaurant.

(c) A shareholder voting his shares in breach of an undertaking to the government – *Re Carrington Viyella plc* (1983) 1 BCC 98, 951. This was an unsuccessful petition.

(d) The provision of inadequate information and advice in recommending acceptance of a takeover bid. In *Re a Company (No 008699 of 1985)* [1986] BCLC 382, Hoffmann J held that circulars containing inadequate information in a takeover situation may ground a petition.

(e) Calling a meeting to replace a director by a nominee of another company. This petition was successful in *Re Whyte Petitioner* [1984] SLT 330.

(f) Making a rights issue. This was a successful ground in *Re a Company (No 002612 of 1984)* [1986] BCLC 430, where Harman J granted an injunction to restrain a rights issue that would have reduced the petitioner's holding from one-third to less than 5 per cent, but unsuccessful in *Re a Company (No 007623 of 1984)* [1986] BCLC 362, where there had been no refusal by the respondents to buy the petitioner's shares at a fair valuation. If the directors fail to properly consider the price that could (and should) be fixed for the rights issue in breach of their fiduciary duty, especially when the board are in a position to benefit from the rights issue as shareholders, this could constitute unfair prejudice. See *Re Sunrise Radio Ltd* [2009] EHC 2893 (Ch).

(g) A proposal to sell property belonging to the company. This was unsuccessful in *Re Gorwyn Holdings* (1985) 1 BCC 99.

(h) A proposal to sell the company's business substantially undervalued to connected persons. This allegation was not proven and the petition was unsuccessful in *Re Posgate and Denby (Agencies) Ltd* [1987] BCLC 8. An important feature of this case was that Hoffmann J, in the course of his judgment, said that the statutory shareholder remedy enabled the court to take account not just of the interests of members under the company's constitution but also their 'legitimate expectations' arising from agreements or understandings of the members *inter se*.

(i) Delay in holding a meeting. This was the basis of a successful petition in *McGuinness* [1988] BCLC 673. This petition was successful notwithstanding that the delay in holding the meeting was not contrary to the provisions of the Companies Act. The loophole was closed by para 9 of Sch 19 of the Companies Act 1989 (now s 304 CA 2006).

(j) Failure to lay accounts. This was a successful ground for the petition in *Re Nuneaton Borough AFC Ltd* [1989] BCLC 454. Note too that s 994(1A) deems the removal of a company's auditors as unfair prejudice if effected merely on grounds of divergence of view on accounting treatments or audit processes.

(k) Failure to pay dividends. There was previously some doubt as to whether this could be a ground for a petition because of the former requirement that some part of the membership be prejudiced. See *Re a Company (No 00370 of 1987) ex p Glossop* [1988] 1 WLR 1068 and *Re Sam Weller Ltd* [1990] Ch 682. This difficulty has now been remedied by the amendment in para 11 of Sch 19 of the Companies Act 1989, which provided that the conduct must be unfairly prejudicial to the interest of the company's members generally or some part of the members. This is now incorporated into the Act (now s 994 CA 2006). However note that the non-payment of dividends or the setting of the rate of the dividends are commercial decisions and depend on the affordability for the company, and courts are generally unwilling to interfere. But if the only reason dividends have not been paid is because all distributable profits have been exhausted through drawing of excessive remuneration, this could constitute a basis for successful petition, see *Irvine v Irvine (no. 1)* [2006] EWHC 406 (Ch). In *Re Gate of India (Tynemouth) Ltd* [2008] EWHC 959, it was held that the lower or non-payment of an agreed level of dividend where it was part of the basis on which the petitioner became a member of a company could be unfair prejudice. This was, however, subject to showing that the company's financial position could justify such agreed payments.

(l) Deletion of pre-emption rights. It was recognised that this may be a reason for a petition in *Re a Company (No 005685 of 1988) ex p Schwarcz (No 2)* [1989] BCLC 427.

(m) Dilution of voting power. This was a successful ground for the petition *in Re DR Chemicals* (1989) 5 BCC 39, where the controlling shareholder in a chemical company based in Swansea sought to dilute the voting power of his fellow director. In *Re Coloursource Ltd* [2004] EWHC3078 (Ch), allotting further shares in the company for the improper purpose of diluting a minority shareholder's shareholding was considered unfairly prejudicial conduct.

(n) Use of company assets for the family and friends of the controller of the company. This was the basis of the successful petition in *Re Elgindata Ltd* [1991] BCLC 949.

(o) The company operating at a loss with the directors taking excessive remuneration. Such a petition failed on the facts in *Re Saul D Harrison & Sons plc* [1995] 1 BCLC 14, as there was not excessive remuneration. The company's main business had been the production of J Cloths and cleaning products. It also sold second-hand clothing, mostly to Africa.

The company's premises in West Ham had been acquired by London and Regional Transport and compensation had been paid to the company.

The petitioner's complaint alleged that the company, although it had substantial assets, was in decline. It was alleged that a reasonable board of directors would close the business down and distribute the assets. It was further alleged that the directors were taking excessive remuneration. The court did not believe that this allegation had been made out.

(p) Mismanagement of the company. In *Re Elginata* (1991), the court said that it would refuse to intervene in relation to allegedly poor managerial decisions, accepting that there was a commercial risk of bad management. However, in *Re Macro (Ipswich) Ltd* [1994] 2 BCLC 354, the court considered the mismanagement so serious that it granted a remedy to the petitioning shareholder. The companies concerned were in the business of letting residential properties and garages in the Ipswich area. The mismanagement involved inter alia failure to maximise rental income and paying too much for repairs and improvements.

(q) Failure to hold general meetings, provide accounts and to disclose interests in a transaction with the company. This was the basis of a successful petition in *Re Woven Rugs* [2010] EWHC 230 (Ch).

(r) Failure to abide by the company's articles which prohibit transfers to non-members. This was the basis of a successful petition in *Re Piccadilly Radio plc* (1989) 5 BCC 692.

(s) The level of director's remuneration is also a commercial decision where the courts will not intervene. However, the drawing of any remuneration will be a basis for successful petition if done contrary to the understanding that the directors will not be remunerated. See *Fisher v Cadman* [2005] EWHC 377 (Ch) and in *Re Halt Garage* [1982] 3 All ER 1016 where the remuneration paid to the directors in control of the company is not calculated by reference to the value of services provided but instead was a dressed up return of capital constituted unfair prejudice.

(t) Failure to consult or provide information where it was agreed that the petitioner would be provided such information or would be consulted. See *Hawkes v Cuddy* [2009] EWCA Civ 291.

(u) Amending Articles of Association to include compulsory transfer mechanisms. In *Arbuthnott v Bonnyman* [2015] EWCA Civ 536, the Court of Appeal held that amendments to articles to include drag-along rights were not necessarily invalid (see the case for a list of principles derived from common law cases for circumstances where alterations could be held invalid) or involve unfairly prejudicial conduct. The judge found that there was no evidence of bad faith or improper motive and the amendment was nothing more than a tidying-up exercise. A significant point was that the judge noted that the alterations in this case did not introduce any major change from the compulsory transfer provisions that existed before the alteration.

15.4 The section in operation

In determining if a person can bring a petition, it is not necessary that he comes to court with clean hands, i.e. without any wrongdoing on his part; see *Re London School of Electronics* (1986). However, if a petitioner has to some extent brought the conduct upon himself, this may be relevant in determining whether the prejudice is unfair and also in determining what remedy is available to the petitioner.

The question of unfair prejudice is an objective question and does not depend upon the intention of the respondents. See *Re RA Noble & Sons (Clothing) Ltd* (1983). This was confirmed *in Re Sunrise Radio Ltd* (2009) which established that whilst the prejudice must be unfair, bad faith is not required and the petitioner does not need to establish the existence of a conscious intention to cause prejudice to the petitioner.

In *Re Macro (Ipswich) Ltd* (1994), Arden J considered that the question of prejudice was an objective one. If the prejudice was established, it then had to be demonstrated that there was unfairness. This was a matter of balancing different interests. The case involved allegations of exclusion from management and corporate mismanagement leading to a loss of value in the petitioner's shareholding. Unfair prejudice was made out.

The starting point in any case involving s 994 is to focus upon the terms of the company's articles to determine whether the conduct of which the claimant complains is in contravention of the terms of the articles (see the judgment of Hoffmann LJ in *Re Saul D Harrison & Sons plc* (1995)).

Hoffmann LJ in *Re Saul D Harrison* went on to state that there are situations where the company's articles do not reflect all of the understandings on which the business is run. The section protects the 'legitimate expectations' of shareholders. However, trivial or technical infringements that do not give rise to real prejudice would not suffice.

The case concerned a petition presented by a minority shareholder seeking compulsory winding up of the company under s 994 or an order that the petitioner's shares be purchased by the other shareholders. The company was in the business of converting waste textiles into cleaning and wiping cloths. The Court of Appeal held that there were no grounds for saying that it would be unfair for the board to act in accordance with the company's articles. Her legitimate expectations amounted to no more than that the board would run the company in compliance with their fiduciary obligations.

The first case on what is now s 994 in the House of Lords was *O'Neill v Phillips* [1999] 1 WLR 1092. Phillips was originally the sole director and shareholder of the company, which stripped asbestos from buildings. O'Neill was originally a manual worker and was very talented. During the construction boom of the 1980s, O'Neill proved invaluable. Phillips promised him 50 per cent of the profits but only transferred 25 per cent of the shares to him. He did, indeed, pay him 50 per cent of the profits.

Phillips retired, effectively making O'Neill managing director. Phillips also said, in principle, that he would transfer 50 per cent of the shares to O'Neill when the company's net asset value reached half a million pounds. There was no formal agreement to this effect.

Later there was a downturn in the business and O'Neill was effectively removed as managing director, and Phillips resumed a managerial role. O'Neill remained on the board. He severed links later and brought a s 994 petition, where he failed at first instance. The Court of Appeal, however, held that O'Neill had been forced out because of Phillips' action. The House of Lords, however, unanimously upheld Phillips' appeal. Lord Hoffmann said that legal rights were subject to equitable considerations but retreated from the 'legitimate expectations' phrase that he himself had used in *Re Saul D Harrison & Sons plc*.

The decision also makes it clear that unfairness may be negated by a reasonable offer such as to purchase the shares of the party who has suffered the unfairness. The decision in *O'Neill v Phillips* has sometimes been misinterpreted as limiting claims by disenchanted minorities where there has been a breach of an understanding or agreement by the majority. It is clear Lord Hoffmann did not intend this, as was made clear, for example, in *Arrow Nominees Inc v Blackledge* [2000] 2 BCLC 167.

The section does not, however, provide a right for a disenchanted minority to ask to be bought out. In *Phoenix Office Supplies Ltd v Larvin* [2003] 1 BCLC 76, the claimant was an employee and director of the company. He held a third of the shares, as did two other directors. He resigned as an employee for personal reasons and said he would resign as a director on agreed terms. The other two shareholders offered to buy his shares at a substantial discount. He refused the offer and brought a s 994 petition.

The judge held that the company was a quasi-partnership company and that the claimant director was entitled to have his shares purchased for a third of the value of the company.

It was held on appeal in the Court of Appeal that s 994 did not provide a shareholder who wished voluntarily to sever connections with a company the means of having his shares purchased (see Taylor, 'No Such Thing as a No-Fault Corporate Divorce' (2003) NLJ 502).

In *Exeter City AFC v The Football Conference Ltd* [2004] 1 WLR 2910, the question involved was whether a minority petition could be stayed where the dispute was covered by an arbitration agreement. Judge Weeks QC believed that such an agreement could not preclude the section.

In *Fisher v Cadman* [2006] 1 BCLC 499, Mrs Fisher was a minority shareholder and acquiesced in informality within the company. Later her attitude changed and she insisted on annual general meetings being held. The judge held, following *Anderson v Hogg* (2002) SC 190, that a shareholder could acquiesce in informality and that this would not then constitute unfairness against that shareholder. Here, however, Mrs Fisher was able to 'revive' provisions in the articles and the judge found inter alia that the subsequent failure to hold AGMs was unfair to her.

It seems that a shareholder may petition on the grounds of unfair prejudice and recover as a creditor and not as a shareholder in limited circumstances. The Privy Council took the view that to preclude this where the terms of a joint venture required shareholders to provide working capital would be inconsistent with the purpose of the section. See *Gamlestaden Fastigheter AB v Baltic Partners Ltd* [2007] UK PC 26 (on appeal to the Privy Council from Jersey).

Whilst s 994(1)(b) CA 2006 expressly contemplates future conduct, any potential conduct needs to be judged in the light of imminence and actual occurrence. In *Re a Company (No 004475 of 1982)* where a majority shareholder indicated a desire to carry out an act which may be unfairly prejudicial but where the board has not yet decided to effect such a direction, the courts would be unlikely to consider the act as sufficiently imminent. Likewise, in *Re Ringtower Holdings plc* [1989] 5 BCC 82, a public company was re-registered as a private company. The court declined to infer that this was done to facilitate the provision of financial assistance for the purchase of the company's shares and judged that a petition was premature. Any such act required a special resolution which could then be the subject of a petition.

Where a group of minority shareholders had attempted to act in a prejudicial manner, the concern being that a future act would likewise occur when the shareholders obtain a majority is insufficient, the petitioner has to adduce evidence that such an act or omission is imminent. See *Re Astec (BSR) plc* [1998] BCC 59.

For a successful claim, the prejudice must be suffered and must be unfair. Therefore, if the claimant is no worse off as the result of the conduct complained of, a petition will be unsuccessful. In *Rock (Nominees) Ltd v RCO (Holdings) plc* [2004] EWCA Civ 118, the directors, in breach of their fiduciary duty, sold a wholly owned subsidiary to its majority shareholder. No prejudice was found in this case when it was established that the sale was at the best reasonably available price.

15.5 Remedies

The court has power to make such order as it thinks fit for giving relief in respect of the matters complained of (s 996(1) CA 2006). Some examples are set out in the Act. The court may make an order to regulate the conduct of the company's affairs in the future. It may require the company to refrain from doing or continuing to do an act complained of, or to do an act that the petitioner has complained it has omitted to do. The court may authorise civil proceedings to be brought in the name of the company. It may require the company not to make any, or any specified, alterations to its articles without the leave of the court. A very common remedy is where the court orders the purchase of the petitioners' shares. As noted, the court has the power to award whatever relief it considers fit (s 996(1)), and make an order to regulate the company's affairs or to restrict the company from acting in a particular way. It may order the company to do something or it may order civil proceedings to be brought in the name of the company.

The court is not constrained by the type of order sought by the petitioner although it will take this and a host of other factors into account including the interests of creditors and other relevant third parties and the need to regulate the future affairs of the company. See *Hawkes v Cuddy* [2007] EWCA 2999 (Ch) where the interests of a third party joint venture was taken into consideration. In *Grace v Biagioli* [2005] EWCA Civ 1222, the court went so far as to say that the reality and practicalities of the overall situation, past, present or future would be taken into account. In this case, the court assessed the appropriateness of the remedy as at the date of hearing and not the date of the petition and said it may even take into account conduct that occurred between those two days!

On occasion, it may be ordered that the respondent sell his shares to the petitioner, as in *Re Bovey Hotel Ventures Ltd* (1981). It is rare, however, for the court to order that the minority buy out the majority. Such an order was made in *Re Brenfield Squash Racquets Club Ltd* [1996] 2 BCLC 184, where the petitioners only held 14 per cent of the shares in the Brentwood-based squash business. If the court does order the purchase of shares, problems of valuation arise. There is no rule in s 996 regarding share valuation. As Oliver LJ said in *Re Bird Precision Bellows Ltd* [1986] Ch 658, at p. 669: 'It seems to me that the whole framework of the section ... is to confer on the court a very wide discretion to do what is considered fair and equitable in all the circumstances of the case'. Generally, where a minority shareholding is sold, there is a discount applied as a percentage of the company's value. This rule only applies, however, if a sale is a willing sale; see dicta of Nourse J in *Re Bird Precision Bellows Ltd* [1984] Ch 419.

What has become the classic situation of exclusion from management in a quasi-partnership company arose in *Quinlan v Essex Hinge Co Ltd* [1997] BCC 53. The petitioner had been working for the company, which manufactured hinges, in excess of 30 years. For 27 years he had been production director. The managing director had joined the company in 1936 and was extremely autocratic. The company did not pay dividends but, instead, paid bonuses to the company's directors. After a dispute, the managing director dismissed the petitioner.

The court held that this amounted to exclusion from management and that the petitioner was entitled to have his shares bought with no discount being made for their being a minority holding. (See also *Richards v Lundy* (2000).)

On the other hand, a discounted valuation might be appropriate if the petitioner brought the exclusion upon himself.

Another moot point is the date of the valuation. Once again, there is no fixed rule to apply. If the petitioner refused a reasonable offer for his shares, the date of valuation may well be the date of the hearing; see *Re a Company (No 002567 of 1982)* (1983).

On the other hand, if a fair offer is not made and the conduct of the majority causes the value of the company's shares to fall, the court may order a valuation at the date the unreasonable conduct began: see *Re OC (Transport) Services Ltd* [1984] BCLC 251.

This seems to be the most logical date for valuing the shares.

In *Thomas v Dawson* [2015] EWCA Civ 706, an option for the remaining shareholder to purchase the other shareholder's single share in the company for a price of £55,000 despite expert valuation evidence that the company was insolvent was upheld by the Court of Appeal. The first-instance judge was entitled and correct to take into account the significant positive value of the shares to the option holder and that its acquisition would mean obtaining control of the company.

There is no limitation period for an unfair prejudice petition but the court has a discretion to refuse to entertain a petition brought after a period of inordinate and unexplained delay, see *Re Grandactual* [2005] EWHC 1415. However where the conduct has been ongoing for several years and is continuing at the date of the petition, and the petitioner has not acquiesced, a petition may still be presented in relation to the historical acts and omissions, see *Southern Counties Fresh Foods Ltd* [2008] EWHC 2810.

The old minority remedy was very much a fly swatter or pea-shooter of a remedy compared to the blunderbuss of the present remedy. It consistently failed to meet the needs of wronged minorities and prompted the Jenkins Committee on Company Law to recommend in 1962 that a broader remedy of unfair prejudice should be introduced (Cmnd 1749, para 205). Under the present remedy, companies must consider carefully the effect that their actions and inactions will have on all of their members. The possibility is that the pendulum now has swung too far in the opposite direction and that, from a position of too little protection for shareholders, we have now moved to a position of too much.

That said, the scope of s 994 is not unlimited.

In *Fulham Football Club (1987) Ltd v Richards* [2011] EWCA Civ 855 a clash arose between arbitration and the scope of the unfair prejudice remedy.

The case concerned a contest between Fulham Football Club and Tottenham Hotspur for a signing of Peter Crouch, the England striker from Portsmouth.

Fulham sought to bring an unfair prejudice claim under s 994 alleging that as a member of the Football Association Premier League, they had been unfairly prejudiced by the preferring of Tottenham by the chairman of the League, Sir David Richards.

The League and Richards successfully argued that the Arbitration Act 1996 applied as it was a matter covered by an arbitration agreement.

The High Court and the Court of Appeal on appeal granted a stay of proceedings.

This decision restricts the ambit of s 994.

15.6 Just and equitable winding up

A company may be wound up by the court if the court is of the opinion that it is just and equitable that the company should be wound up (s 122(1)(g) of the Insolvency Act 1986). (The procedure on a winding up will be considered in Chapter 25.) Before the advent of ss 459–61 of the Companies Act 1985, just and equitable winding up was sometimes the only possible statutory remedy for a disenchanted minority shareholder. It was this remedy that was sought and obtained in *Ebrahimi v Westbourne Galleries Ltd* [1973] AC 360. The remedy is a sledgehammer remedy. Since the advent of what is now ss 994–996, it has been less common. Indeed, s 125(2) of the Insolvency Act 1986 provides that, if the court is of the opinion that there is some other remedy that is available to the petitioners, and that they are acting unreasonably in seeking to have the company wound up instead of pursuing that other remedy, then the court should refuse the petition. Yet in *Virdi v Abbey Leisure Ltd* [1990] BCLC 342, the Court of Appeal considered that, where a minority shareholder sought a winding-up order rather than utilising the mechanism under the articles to have his shares purchased at a fair valuation, the minority was not acting unreasonably. The Court of Appeal took the view, reversing Hoffmann J at first instance, that the minority might legitimately object to the mode of valuation for valuing his shares.

In *Ebrahimi v Westbourne Galleries* (1973), the House of Lords made the point that the categories of conduct where just and equitable winding up might be ordered were not closed. It will be attempted here to classify the cases into certain areas. There is nothing magic in this categorisation.

Jonathan Parker J held in *Re Guidezone Ltd* [2000] 2 BCLC 321 that a petition to wind up on the just and equitable ground could only be granted if a petition based on unfairly prejudicial conduct would have been successful. This view is highly questionable and at odds with *Re RA Noble (Clothing) Ltd*. The decision in *Re Guidezone Ltd* is criticised by Acton in 'Just and Equitable Winding Up: The Strange Case of the Disappearing Jurisdiction' (2001) 22 Co Law 134.

15.6.1 Exclusion from management

Apart from *Ebrahimi* itself, exclusion from management has featured in other cases. In *Re A & BC Chewing Gum Ltd* [1975] 1 All ER 1017, the petitioning shareholder had put up a third of the capital of the company and had been promised a say in the management of the company. The court granted the petitioning shareholder's petition where he had been excluded from management. In *Tay Bok Choon v Tahansan Sdn Bhd* [1987] 1 WLR 413 (Privy Council from Malaysia), in similar circumstances, a shareholder who had put up a considerable amount of capital and who was excluded from management was held entitled to wind the company up. The company, based in Kuala Lumpur, was in the business of manufacturing window louvres.

15.6.2 Destruction of the substratum of the company

If the main and overriding purpose for which the company has been formed is destroyed so that the company cannot achieve its main objective, then a petition to wind the company up on the just and equitable ground will be successful. In *Re German Date Coffee Co* (1882) 20 ChD 169, the company had been formed to obtain a German patent to manufacture coffee from dates. A request for a patent was refused. It was held that a petition to wind the company up would be successful. It must be that all of the company's main activities are incapable of achievement before such a petition can succeed. In *Re Kitson & Co Ltd* [1946] 1 All ER 435, the company's engineering business had ceased when it was sold. The company had other activities, however, that were still capable of achievement. A petition to wind the company up was therefore not granted.

It is interesting to note that a petition will not succeed merely because a company is making a loss. In order to succeed, it must be demonstrated that the company is incapable of making a profit: see *Re Suburban Hotel Co* (1867) 2 Ch App 737. Here the company ran the Hampstead Heath Hotel. It was making a loss year on year but the court took the view that this was not inevitable and that under different management it might make a profit.

15.6.3 Deadlock

If there is deadlock within the company and there is no way of breaking that dead-lock by some mechanism in the articles or by the shareholders resolving the problem by appointing a director or removing a director, then a petition will be granted. In *Re Yenidje Tobacco Co Ltd* [1916] 2 Ch 426, the company had two shareholders with an equal number of shares who were each directors. They could not agree on how the company should be managed. There was no provision for breaking the deadlock and a petition to wind the company up on the just and equitable ground was granted.

15.6.4 Lack of probity of the directors

If a petitioning shareholder can demonstrate a lack of probity and integrity on the part of directors, this will be sufficient ground for winding up the company. In *Re Bleriot Manufacturing Aircraft Co* (1916) 32 TLR 253, the court held that where directors had misappropriated company property, a winding-up order could be made. In *Loch v John Blackwood Ltd* [1924] AC 783, a Privy Council decision on appeal from the Court of Appeal of the West Indies (Barbados), where directors had failed to supply corporate information to shareholders and to hold company meetings and in general ran the company as if it was their own property, a winding-up order was granted. Similarly, in *Re Lundie Brothers Ltd* [1965] 1 WLR 1051, Plowman J granted a winding-up petition in a situation where the directors ran the printing company as if it was their own business without taking any account of the interests of shareholders. In addition, the petitioner had been excluded from management.

15.6.5 Breakdown of trust and confidence

This category overlaps with exclusion from management; indeed, in many of the cases, some of the factors set out in the different areas may be present. In *Re Zinotty Properties Ltd* [1984] 1 WLR 1249, it was held that one of the founding shareholders of a business set up to acquire land and build upon it was entitled to assume he would participate in the management. He was excluded from the management. Furthermore, it had been understood that once the company had developed a particular site, the company would be dissolved. This did not happen. Some of the company's money was lent to another business in which one of the directors had an interest. The petition brought by the excluded shareholder was successful.

It may thus be seen that the remedy of just and equitable winding up is available in a variety of circumstances, although its popularity has decreased since the remedy in ss 994–996 has been on the scene as selling company property in a liquidation generally means obtaining a discounted price for the company's assets, which is not in the interests of any of the shareholders.

15.6.6 Self-help

A company may provide for shares to be bought out by provision in its articles. This is a possible exit route for a shareholder, exercisable by notice to the company. The exit route could be exercisable, for example, where there is a removal of a shareholder/director from office.

Summary

The rule in *Foss v Harbottle* and s 260 CA 2006

Historically, the decision in *Foss v Harbottle* has meant that, where the company suffers harm, the company is the proper claimant so that shareholders cannot generally sue for wrongs done to the company.

Exceptions

There are certain exceptions:

(a)   where there is an ultra vires act;
(b)   where a special majority is needed;
(c)   where personal rights are infringed; or
(d)   where fraud had been committed by those in control.

Section 260 CA 2006 now provides that a derivative claim may be brought in respect of a cause of action arising from an actual or proposed act or omission involving negligence, default, breach of duty or breach of trust by a director of a company.

This is a broader remedy but there are certain safeguards that apply, so that permission to bring proceedings must be refused if there has been authorisation or ratification and may be refused if this is likely, for example.

The statutory remedy

Before ss 994–996 CA 2006, the old remedy, s 210 of the Companies Act 1948, had certain serious defects:

(a)   an order could only be made if a winding-up order could have been made on the just and equitable ground;
(b)   a single act was insufficient to found a petition;
(c)   the petitioner had to show that the conduct was oppressive;
(d)   a petition could not be based on omissions or on future conduct; or
(e)   probably personal representatives could not present petitions.

Under what is now ss 994–996, all of these defects are remedied. In particular, a petitioner needs now to demonstrate unfair prejudice and does not need to show oppression.

The 2006 Act remedy covers a wide range of situations. The courts have interpreted the remedy liberally and it is not necessary for a petitioner to confine his petition to membership matters in the narrow sense and he may, for example, in appropriate circumstances complain of exclusion from management. The court has a total discretion as to what remedy to award a successful petitioner, although the usual remedy is a purchase of the petitioner's shares.

Just and equitable winding up

'Just and equitable' winding up may not look like a membership remedy at first sight but it is.

A disenchanted member will usually only seek this remedy where all other possibilities have been exhausted. Just and equitable winding up under s 122(1)(g) of the Insolvency Act 1986 is a sledgehammer remedy and the court should refuse it if there is some other remedy, that is appropriate, that the petitioner is unreasonable in not seeking.

Just and equitable winding up may be granted in various situations and the categories are not closed. The situations include:

(a) exclusion from management;
(b) destruction of the substratum of the company;
(c) deadlock;
(d) lack of probity of management; and
(e) breakdown of trust and confidence.

Self-test questions

15.1 What is the significance of the decision in *Foss v Harbottle*?

15.2 What are the exceptions to the rule in *Foss v Harbottle*?

15.3 Discuss the scope of the statutory remedy in ss 994–996 CA 2006.

15.4 How is unfair prejudice determined under the statutory remedy in s 994 CA 2006?

15.5 What remedies are available to a court under s 996 CA 2006 in relation to unfair prejudice?

15.6 Discuss the scope of the just and equitable winding-up remedy.

Further reading

A Acton, 'Just and Equitable Winding Up: The Strange Case of the Disappearing Jurisdiction' (2001) 22 Co Law 134.

AJ Boyle, 'The New Derivative Action' (1997) 18 Co Law 256.

B Cheffins and J Dine, 'The Statutory Protection of Minority Shareholders: Section 459 of the Companies Act 1985' (1992) 13 Co Law 83.

MR Chesterman, 'The "Just and Equitable" Winding Up of Small Private Companies' (1973) 36 MLR 129.

R Cheung, 'Shareholders' Agreements: Shareholders' Contractual Freedom in Company Law' (2012) JBL 504.

E Ferran, 'Litigation by Shareholders and Reflective Loss' (2001) CLJ 245.

S Griffin, 'Defining the Scope of a Membership Interest' (A Casenote on *Re J E Cade & Son Ltd* [1992] BCLC 213) (1993) 14 Co Law 64.

S Griffin, 'Shareholder Remedies and the No Reflective Loss Principle: Problems Surrounding the Identification of a Membership Interest' [2010] JBL 461.

B Hannegan, 'Drawing Boundaries Between Derivative Claims and Unfairly Prejudicial Petitions' [2009] JBL 606.

H Hirt, 'In What Circumstances Should Breaches of Directors' Duties Give Rise to a Remedy Under ss 459–461 of the Companies Act 1985?' (2003) Co Law 100.

A Keay and J Loughrey, 'Derivative Proceedings in a Brave New World for Company Management and Shareholders' [2010] JBL 151.

D Kershaw, 'The Rule in Foss v Harbottle is Dead: Long Live the Rule in Foss v Harbottle' (2015) JBL 274.

P Koh, 'Derivative Actions Once Removed' [2010] JBL 101.

J Lowry, 'The Elasticity of Unfair Prejudice: Stretching the Ambit of Companies Act 1985 s 459' [1995] LMCLQ 337.

J Lowry, 'Reconstructing Shareholder Actions: A Response to the Law Commission's Consultation Paper' No 142 (1997) 18 Co Law 247.

H McVea, 'Section 994 of the Companies Act and the Primacy of Contract' (2012) 75 MLR1123.

LJ Moran, 'Missing Links and Missed Opportunities' (1997) 18 Co Law 264.

J Mukwiri, 'Section 459 on Parent and Subsidiary Companies' (2005) 26 Co Law 75.

J Mukwiri, 'The No Reflective Loss Principle' (2005) 26 Co Law 304.

J Payne, 'Section 459 and Public Companies' (1999) 114 LQR 368.

J Payne, 'Clean Hands in Derivative Actions' [2002] CLJ 76.

J Payne and DD Prentice, 'Section 459 and the House of Lords' View' (1999) 114 LQR 587.

DD Prentice, 'Winding Up on the Just and Equitable Ground: The Partnership Analogy' (1973) 89 LQR 107.

DD Prentice, 'The Theory of the Firm: Minority Shareholder Oppression and ss 459–61 of the Companies Act 1985' (1988) OJLS 55.

DD Prentice, 'Shareholder Actions: The Rule in Foss v Harbottle' (1988) 104 LQR 341.

BAK Rider, 'Partnership and Its Impact on Domestic Companies' [1979] CLJ 148.

CA Riley, 'Contracting Out of Company Law: s 459 of the Companies Act and the Role of the Courts' (1992) 55 MLR 782.

CA Riley, 'The Values Behind the Law Commission's Consultation Paper' (1997) 18 Co Law 260.

P Roberts and J Poole, 'Shareholder Remedies – Efficient Litigation and the Unfair Prejudice Remedy' [1999] JBL 38.

P Rolls and M Warwick, 'Unfair Prejudice – How Buyout Offers Can Be Used to End Petitions Based on Unfairly Prejudicial Conduct' (2003) Sol Jo 735.

L Sealy, 'The Rule in Foss v Harbottle: The Australian Experience' (1989) 10 Co Law 52.

G Simm, 'Shareholders in Dispute' (2003) NLJ 876.

D Sugarman, 'Reconceptualising Company Law: Reflections on the Law Commission's Consultation Paper on Shareholder Remedies' (1997) 18 Co Law 226 and 274.

B Taylor, 'No Such Thing as a No-Fault Corporate Divorce' (2003) NLJ 502.

S Watkins, 'The Common Law Derivative Action: An Outmoded Relic?' 30 Camb LR 40.

P Watts, 'The Shareholder as Co-promisee' (2001) 117 LQR 388.

Chapter 16

Company meetings

Chapter Contents

16.1 Annual general meetings

There are two types of members' meetings: annual general meetings and general meetings.

Section 336 of the Companies Act 2006 provides that every public company must hold a general meeting as its annual general meeting within six months of the day following the accounting reference date. Failure to comply with this requirement is an offence committed by every officer of the company who is in default.

Section 337 provides that a notice calling an annual general meeting of a public company must state that the meeting is an annual general meeting.

Section 338 of the 2006 Act provides that the members of a public company may require the company to give to members of the company entitled to receive a notice of the next annual general meeting notice of a resolution which it is intended to be moved at that meeting. The company is required to give notice of a resolution once it has received a request to do so:

(a)   from members representing at least 5 per cent of the total voting rights of the members who have a right to vote on a resolution at the AGM to which the requests relate; or

(b)   from at least 100 members who have a right to vote on the resolution at the AGM to which the request relates, and hold shares in the company on which there has been paid up an average sum per member of at least £100 (s 338(3) CA 2006).

Section 339 provides that public companies must circulate resolutions that are submitted in accordance with the above conditions, and s 340 provides that the expenses in complying with the section are to be borne by the company if the resolution is submitted to the company before the end of the financial year preceding the meeting. Otherwise, the expenses in complying with the section must be paid by the members unless the company resolves otherwise and, unless the company has previously so resolved, it is not bound to comply with the section unless there is deposited with it not later than six weeks before the AGM to which the request relates, or if later, the time at which notice is given of that meeting, a sum reasonably sufficient to meet the expenses in complying with the section.

Prior to the 2006 Act, private companies could opt out of the requirement to hold AGMs if their members unanimously agreed. Since the 2006 Act, private companies are not required to hold AGMs at all, although they may do so if they wish.

16.2 General meetings

16.2.1 Members

Section 303 provides for the members' power to require directors to call meetings. The directors are required to do so if members who hold at least 10 per cent of the paid-up capital of the company carrying voting rights at general meetings, except in the case of a private company where more than 12 months has elapsed since the end of the last general meeting, in which case the required percentage is 5 per cent.

Section 304 provides that it is the directors' duty to call meetings that are required by members under s 303. They must call the meeting within 21 days of receiving the request and the meeting must be held not more than 28 days after the date of the notice convening the meeting (s 304(1) (a), (b) CA 2006).

Section 305 provides that the members may call a meeting at the company's expense if the directors are required under s 303 to call a meeting and have not done so in accordance with s 304 CA 2006. The meeting must be called for a date not more than three months after the date on which the directors become subject to the requirement to call a meeting (s 305(3)). Any reasonable expenses incurred by the members requesting the meeting by reason of the failure of the directors duly to call a meeting must be reimbursed by the company (s 305(6)).

It should be noted that s 303 requires 'members' in the plural: one member will not satisfy the section; see *Morgan v Morgan Insurance Brokers Ltd* [1993] BCC 145.

16.2.2 The court

Section 306 provides for the court to order a meeting. The section applies if, for any reason, it is impracticable:

(a) to call a meeting of the company in any manner in which meetings of that company may be called; or
(b) to conduct the meeting in the manner prescribed by the company's articles or the Act (s 306(1) CA 2006).

The court may either, of its own motion or on the application:

(a) of a director of the company; or
(b) of a member of the company who would be entitled to vote at a meeting, order a meeting to be called, held and conducted in any manner the court thinks fit (s 306(2) CA 2006).

A previous similar provision was often used in the case of deadlock where a company perhaps has two members and one member is refusing to attend a meeting; for example, see *Re Sticky Fingers Restaurant Ltd* [1992] BCLC 84. In this case, one member of the company had presented a petition claiming unfairly prejudicial conduct. The other member, Bill Wyman of the Rolling Stones, was allowed to hold a meeting with the quorum fixed at one for the purpose of appointing additional directors, provided that any such directors would not act to the prejudice of the other shareholder pending the outcome of the minority protection proceedings. The section was used in a similar way in *Re Whitchurch Insurance Consultants Ltd* [1993] BCLC 1359, where Mr Rudd wished to remove the other member, Mrs Rudd, as a director. In *Re the British Union for the Abolition of Vivisection* [1995] 2 BCLC 1, application was made to the court under the precursor of s 306 to give directions for the calling of a meeting to avoid anticipated disruption. There had been disorder at a previous meeting and what was therefore sought was the convening of a small meeting consisting only of members of the committee, with no other members being entitled to attend in person but those absent to vote by postal means. This was so ordered.

Section 306 cannot be used to affect substantive voting rights or to shift the balance of power between different shareholders.

The Court of Appeal allowed an appeal in *Ross v Telford* [1998] 1 BCLC 82, where the judge had ordered a meeting which would have had the effect of enabling one 50 per cent shareholder and his solicitor to outvote the other 50 per cent shareholder. Ross and Telford, during the course of their marriage, had carried on business as electrical contractors through the medium of a small group of companies. They had equal shareholdings in one company (PLB), although Ross had effectively more shares in another company (Linkside Development Co Ltd). The shareholdings in (Linkside) were held as to 50 per cent by Ross and as to 50 per cent by PLB.

Ross alleged that Telford had forged his (Ross's) name on company cheques. He caused the company (Linkside) to start proceedings against Telford. He applied for, and obtained, an order under s 371 that a meeting of the board of Linkside (Ross and Telford were the only directors) could be called, and that one member should be deemed to be a quorum. This was granted by court order, the judge ordering that a meeting be held for the purpose of considering and voting upon a resolution for the appointment of a representative of Ross's solicitors as a third director of the company, and that the representative of the solicitors might attend at the meeting and vote on behalf of PLB.

The effect of the order made by the judge was to regulate the affairs of PLB by authorising a representative of Mr Ross's solicitors to be appointed to represent the company at a general meeting of Linkside. Such an appointment would normally be made at a board meeting of PLB. The effect of the order was to break the deadlock in PLB.

The Court of Appeal held that what is now s 306 did not empower the court to break a deadlock in this way at either a board or a general meeting of a company.

The court cannot make an order so as to permit a 50 per cent shareholder to override the wishes of the other 50 per cent shareholder.

This case is clearly distinguishable from cases such as *Re Sticky Fingers Restaurant Ltd* (1992), where the court was determined to prevent the quorum provisions from being abused by minority shareholders.

16.2.3 Directors

Section 302 provides that the directors may call general meetings.

16.2.4 Auditors

Section 518 CA 2006 provides that an auditor may deposit with a notice of resignation a signed requisition calling on the directors of the company forthwith duly to convene a general meeting of the company for the purpose of receiving and considering such explanation of the circumstances connected with the resignation as the auditor may wish to place before the meeting.

16.2.5 Serious loss of capital

The directors of a public company are obliged to call an extraordinary general meeting where the net assets of the company are half or less of its called-up share capital (s 656 CA 2006).

The directors must call a general meeting of the company to consider what steps, if any, should be taken to deal with the situation. They must do so not later than 28 days from the earliest day on which that fact is known to a director of the company. The meeting must be convened for a date not later than 56 days from that date.

Failure to convene a meeting as required constitutes an offence by any director who knowingly authorises or permits the failure, or after the relevant period knowingly authorises or permits the failure to continue.

16.3 Class meetings

In addition to meetings of the company, meetings may also be held of different classes of shareholders. Such meetings may be necessary, for example, to consider a proposed variation of class rights (see section 7.6). Most of the rules that apply in relation to company meetings also apply in relation to class meetings (ss 334–335 CA 2006).

16.4 Notice

The Companies Act 2006 lays down periods of notice required for general meetings.

Section 307 provides that the notice required for a general meeting of a private company is at least 14 days' notice.

In relation to a public company, the notice required is in the case of an annual general meeting at least 21 days and in any other case at least 14 days (s 307(2) CA 2006).

Shorter notice may be agreed to by the members (s 307(4)), though this does not apply to an annual general meeting of a public company. In the case of an annual general meeting of a public company, all of the members must agree to the giving of short notice (s 337(2) CA 2006).

The waiving of full notice must be done purposefully and cannot be done simply by all of the members turning up to the meeting without realising that there should have been a longer period of notice provided to the members: see *Re Pearce Duff* [1960] 1 WLR 1014. Thus precedent was not cited in *Re a Company (No 004377 of 1986)* [1987] 1 WLR 102, where it was held attendance indicated acceptance of short notice.

In *Schofield v Schofield* [2011] EWCA Civ 154, on 25 February 2011, the Court of Appeal held that shareholders can treat a meeting as valid despite irregularities in the notice.

The shorter notice period must be agreed to by a majority in number of the members having the right to attend and vote at the meeting, being a majority who together hold not less than the requisite percentage in nominal value of the shares with a right to attend and vote, or, in the case of a company not having a share capital, together represent not less than the requisite percentage of the total voting rights at that meeting. The requisite percentage is:

(a)   in the case of a private company, 90 per cent or such higher percentage (not exceeding 95 per cent) as may be specified in the articles; and
(b)   in the case of a public company, 95 per cent (s 307(5) and (6) CA 2006).

Notice may be given in hard copy form, in electronic form or by means of a website (s 308 CA 2006). In relation to a website notice, s 309 provides as follows.
    The website notification must:

(a)   state that it concerns a notice of a company meeting;
(b)   specify the place, time and date of the meeting; and
(c)   in the case of a public company, state whether the meeting will be an annual general meeting.

The notice must be available on the website throughout the period, beginning with the date of the notification and ending with the conclusion of the meeting (s 309(3) CA 2006).
    Notices must be sent to every member of the company and every director (s 310(1) CA 2006).
    In relation to members this includes any person entitled to a share in consequence of death or bankruptcy of a member (s 310(2) CA 2006).
    The notice of a general meeting of a company must state:

(a)   the time and date of the meeting; and
(b)   the place of the meeting.

Notice of a general meeting of a company must state the general nature of the business to be dealt with at the meeting (s 311 CA 2006).
    S311A (inserted by the Companies (Shareholder's Rights) Regulations 2009 (SI 2009/1632)) obliges a traded company to have the following information in relation to a general meeting made available on a website. The information is:

(a)   the matters set out in the notice of the meeting (s311(A) (1)(a));
(b)   the total number of shares in the company and in each class in respect of which members are entitled to exercise voting rights at the meeting (s311(A) (1)(b));
(c)   the totals of the voting rights that shareholders are entitled to exercise at the meeting in respect of the shares of each section (s311(A)(1)(c));
(d)   shareholders' statement, shareholders' resolutions and shareholders' matters of business received by the company after the first date on which notice of the meeting is given (s311(A)(1)(d)).

S311(A)(4) specifies when the above information is to be made available and s311(A)(5) requires the information to be kept available for a period of two years from the date on which the information is to be made available on the website.

The website must be maintained by or on behalf of the company, and identify the company (s311(A)(2)). Access to information on the website and the ability to obtain hard copies must not be subject to any fees or be restricted in any way (s311(A)(3)).

Failure to comply with s311(A), does not affect the validity or anything done at a meeting but an offence is committed by every officer of the company who is in default and is liable to a fine.

16.4.1 Special notice

Where, by any provision of the Companies Act, special notice is required of a resolution, the resolution is not effective unless notice of the intention to move it has been given to the company at least 28 days before the meeting at which it is moved (s 312(1) CA 2006).

The company must, where practicable, give its members notice of any such resolution in the same manner and at the same time as it gives notice of the meeting. If that is not practicable, the company must give its members notice at least 14 days before that meeting:

(a) by advertisement in a newspaper having appropriate circulation; or
(b) in any other manner allowed by the company's articles (s 312(2) and (3) CA 2006).

It is provided that if after notice of the intention to move such a resolution has been given to the company, a meeting is called for a date 28 days or fewer after the notice has been given, the notice is deemed to have been properly given though not given within the time required (s 312(4) CA 2006) (see also section 10.6).

16.4.2 Accidental failure to give notice

Section 320 CA 2006 deals with the accidental failure to give notice of a resolution or meeting.

Where a company gives notice of:

(a) a general meeting; or
(b) a resolution intended to be moved at a general meeting,

any accidental failure to give notice to one or more persons shall be disregarded for the purpose of determining whether notice of the meeting or resolution (as the case may be) is duly given.

It is important to realise the effect of this provision. The accidental failure to send a notice where there was an oversight did not render the meeting invalid in *Re West Canadian Collieries Ltd* [1962] Ch 370. The error arose here because the dividend payment had been made separately to certain members and their addressograph plates had therefore been kept in a separate place. They were, therefore, omitted when notices were sent out. By contrast, the failure to send notice in

Musselwhite v Musselwhite & Son Ltd [1962] Ch 964 was quite deliberate. It was considered that the members concerned did not have a right to vote at the meeting as they had agreed to sell their shares. This was a genuine mistake but the failure to send notice was deliberate and therefore the meeting was invalid.

16.4.3 Members may require statements to be circulated

Section 314(1) provides that the members of a company may require the company to circulate to members of the company entitled to receive notice of the general meeting a statement of not more than 1,000 words with respect to:

(a)   a matter referred to in a proposed resolution to be dealt with at that meeting, or
(b)   other business to be dealt with at that meeting.

A company is required to circulate a statement if it receives a request to do so from:

(a)   members representing at least 5 per cent of the total voting rights of all members who have a relevant right to vote; or
(b)   at least 100 members who have a relevant right to vote and hold shares in the company on which there has been paid up an average sum per member of at least £100.

If a company fails to circulate a member's statement under s 314, then an offence is committed by every officer of the company who is in default (s 315 CA 2006).

The expenses of circulating members' statements need not be paid by the members who requested the circulation of the statement if:

(a)   the meeting to which the requests relate is an annual general meeting of a public company, and
(b)   requests sufficient to require the company to circulate the statement are received before the end of the financial year preceding the meeting (s 316(1) CA 2006).

Otherwise the expenses of the company in complying with the section must be paid by the members who requested the circulation unless the company resolves otherwise. Unless the company has previously so resolved, it is not bound to comply with that section unless there is deposited with it, or tendered to it, not later than one week before the meeting a sum reasonably sufficient to meet its expenses in doing so (s 316(2) CA 2006).

A company is not required to circulate a statement under s 322 if, on an application by the company or another person who claims to be aggrieved, the court is satisfied that the rights conferred are being abused (s 317(1)).

The court may order the members who requested the circulation of the statement to pay the whole or part of the company's costs on such an application, even if they are not parties to the application (s 317(2) CA 2006).

16.5 Quorum at meetings

Section 318 provides that in the case of a company limited by shares or guarantee, and having only one member, one qualifying person present at a meeting is a quorum (s 318(1) CA 2006).

In any other case, subject to the company's articles, two qualifying persons present at a meeting are a quorum, unless:

(a)   each is a qualifying person only because he is authorised under s 323 to act as the representative of the corporation in relation to the meeting, and they are representatives of the same corporation; or

(b)   each is a qualifying person only because he is appointed as proxy of a member in relation to the meeting and they are proxies of the same member (s 318(2) CA 2006).

Problems sometimes arise over the matter of a quorum. The *Concise Oxford English Dictionary* defines a meeting as 'an assembly of people for a purpose'. This implies that there should be more than one person present and that they should be in each other's physical presence. Each of these features tends to cause problems.

At common law, a meeting must be made up of more than one person. In *Sharp v Dawes* (1876) 2 QBD 26, a meeting of a stannary mining company governed under the Stannaries Acts (which governed tin-mining companies set up in Cornwall) was called for the purpose of making a call on shares. Only one member, Silversides, turned up at the meeting, together with the company secretary, who was not a member. Lord Coleridge CJ said in the Court of Appeal, 'the word "meeting" prima facie means a coming together of more than one person' (p. 29). The court held that there was no meeting here. Lord Coleridge CJ did acknowledge that on occasion the word 'meeting' could have a different meaning but found there was nothing here to indicate that that was the case.

The same principle applies where one member present has proxies for the other company members: see *Re Sanitary Carbon Company* [1877] WN 223. This was also applied in *Re London Flats Ltd* [1969] 1 WLR 711, where all but one member had left the room when the vote was taken. The court held that there could be no meeting. Plowman J considered that there would need to be special circumstances present to displace the usual rule. In *MJ Shanley Contracting Ltd (in voluntary liquidation)* (1979) 124 SJ 239, the court held there was no meeting where the chairman present at the meeting held a proxy for his wife and had the consent of the other member to vote in favour of voluntary liquidation (although there was no meeting, the decision to put the company into liquidation was upheld on the basis of the assent principle, which is discussed below at section 16.10.5). In the Scottish case of *James Prain & Sons Ltd, petitioners* (1947) SC 325, the Court of Session declined to confirm a reduction of capital that had been authorised at a meeting where only one person was present.

This principle that one person cannot constitute a meeting has to give way to certain exceptions.

Sometimes, as has been noted, it is necessary to hold a class meeting, for example, to consider a proposed variation of class rights. It may be that there is only one shareholder of the class in question. In these circumstances clearly the quorum for the class meeting cannot be set higher than one: see *East v Bennett Bros* [1911] 1 Ch 163.

This now also applies in relation to companies that have only one member (s 318(1) CA 2006).

As noted above (section 16.2.2), under s 306 CA 2006 the court may order an extraordinary general meeting to be held and may fix the quorum at one. In *Re El Sombrero Ltd* [1958] Ch 900, the company had three members. The applicant had 90 per cent of the shares and he wished to remove the other two shareholders as directors. They held 5 per cent of the shares each. They refused to attend meetings where this was to be proposed. The applicant, therefore, applied to the court for a meeting to be ordered under s 306 and for the quorum to be fixed at one. This was done. The decision in *Re El Sombrero Ltd* was followed in *Re HR Paul & Son* (1973) 118 SJ 166. In this case, the matter at issue was not the removal of directors but the alteration of the articles where the majority shareholder wished to alter the articles and the minority shareholders were blocking his wishes. In *Re Sticky Fingers Restaurant Ltd* (1992) (see 16.2.2 above), deadlock in a small private company was again featured. A member sought an order under s 306 of the Act requiring a meeting to be convened at which the quorum could be fixed at one. The court ordered this, subject to the proviso that any outcome of such a meeting would be stayed until a s 994 matter being pursued by the other member had been resolved.

Problems relating to quorum abound. On occasion, the acquiescence of those entitled to attend a meeting is sufficient to validate the action taken.

Hood Sailmakers v Axford [1996] 4 All ER 830 involved a board meeting that purported to make pension arrangements for the company. Axford and Bainbridge, two directors, sought their share of a pension fund from the company following their dismissal. The company resisted on the ground that Axford had changed the pension arrangements by written resolution following a board meeting of which no notice had been given to the then only other director, Hood (Hood was succeeded by Woodhouse and Bainbridge). Hood resided in the USA and played no part in the management of the company.

The Pensions Ombudsman held that the resolutions were valid under reg 106, Table A of the Companies Act 1948, since they were in writing and all directors entitled to receive notice had done so (Hood was not so entitled as he was abroad). The Pensions Ombudsman so held despite the fact that reg 99 provides for a quorum of two directors.

The Queen's Bench Division dismissed the appeal. Written resolutions made at board meetings that did not meet the quorum requirements were invalid. However, Woodhouse had acquiesced in the new pension scheme so that it was unconscionable for the company to deny the validity of the resolutions.

A second problem referred to in relation to a quorum at a meeting is the matter of whether a meeting can be held where members are not in each other's physical presence. This becomes a very real problem in a time of technological change and given the possibility of video and audio link-ups. In *Re Associated Color Laboratories* (1970) 12 DLR (3d) 338, a Canadian decision held that it was not possible to hold a meeting by telephone link between California and Vancouver. McDonald J took the view that a meeting meant that the participants were in each other's presence. The decision was, however, reversed by s 109(9) of the Canada Business Corporations Act. In Britain, *Byng v London Life Association Ltd* [1990] Ch 170 considered the matter of the audio and visual link system of holding meetings. The court held that a meeting may be validly held even though people at the meeting are not together in the same room where there is some audiovisual link-up. The decision seems a sensible one.

16.6 Chairman

A member may be elected to be chairman of a general meeting by a resolution of the company passed at the meeting (s 319(1) CA 2006).

On a vote on a resolution at a meeting on a show of hands, a declaration by the chairman that the resolution:

(a)   has or has not been passed, or

(b)   passed with a particular majority

is conclusive evidence of that fact without proof of the number or proportion of the votes recorded in favour of or against the resolution (s 320(1) CA 2006).

The Chairman is responsible for keeping order: see *John v Rees* [1969] 2 All ER 274. In this case there was a meeting of the Pembroke Constituency Labour Party. There was strong disagreement, a good deal of noise and some minor violence.

It was held that, in these circumstances, it was appropriate for the Chairman to adjourn the meeting.

In *Byng v London Life Association Ltd* (1990), the Court of Appeal held that it was appropriate to adjourn a meeting that was being held in the Barbican Centre in London. As a single room was not large enough to accommodate the meeting, there was an audiovisual linking system between rooms. The system broke down and the Chairman adjourned the meeting.

It was held that the adjournment was valid at common law because of the difficult circumstances of the meeting. However, it was not reasonable to reconvene the meeting for the afternoon of the same day as the notice was too short.

16.7 Polls

A provision in a company's articles is void insofar as it would have the effect of excluding the right to demand a poll at a general meeting on any question other than:

(a)   the election of the chairman of the meeting, or

(b)   the adjournment of the meeting (s 321(1) CA 2006).

A provision of a company's articles is void insofar as it would have the effect of making ineffective a demand for a poll on any such question that is made:

(a)   by not fewer than five members having the right to vote on the resolution;
(b)   by a member or members representing not less than 10 per cent of the total voting rights of all the members having the right to vote on the resolution; or
(c)   by a member or members holding shares in the company conferring a right to vote on the resolution being shares on which an aggregate sum has been paid up equal to not less than 10 per cent of the total sum paid up on all the shares conferring that right (s 321(2) CA 2006).

Section 322 provides for voting on a poll. On a poll taken at a general meeting of a company, a member entitled to more than one vote need not, if he votes, use all his votes or cast all the votes he uses in the same way.

Section 323 CA 2006 provides for the representation of corporations at meetings.

If a poll is conducted by a traded or quoted company, the resolution and the result of the voting have to be published on a website (s 341 CA 2006) (see below 16.11).

16.8 Proxies

Section 324 provides for the right to appoint proxies. A member of a company is entitled to appoint another person as his proxy to exercise all or any of his rights to attend, speak and vote at a meeting of the company.

In the case of a company with share capital, a member may appoint more than one proxy in relation to a meeting, provided that each proxy is appointed to exercise the rights attached to a different share or shares held by him or (as the case may be) to a different £10 or multiples of £10 of stock held by him (s 324(2) CA 2006).

In every notice calling a meeting of a company there must appear, with reasonable prominence, a statement informing a member of his rights under s 324, and any more extensive rights conferred by the company's articles to appoint more than one proxy (s 325 CA 2006).

Section 326 CA 2006 provides that if there are issued at the company's expense invitations to members to appoint as proxy a specified person or a number of specified persons, the invitations must be issued to all members entitled to vote at the meeting.

The notice required of the appointment of a proxy is dealt with in s 327. Any provision in the company's articles is void in so far as it would have the effect of requiring any such appointment or document to be received by the company or another person earlier than the following time:

(a)   in the case of a meeting or adjourned meeting, 48 hours before the time for the holding of the meeting or adjourned meeting;
(b)   in the case of a poll taken more than 48 hours after it was demanded, 24 hours before the time appointed for the taking of the poll; or
(c)   in the case of a poll taken not more than 48 hours after it was demanded, the time at which it was demanded (s 327(2) CA 2006).

In calculating the periods, no account should be taken of any part of a day that is not a working day (s 327(3)).

Section 328 provides that a proxy may be elected to be the chairman of the general meeting by a resolution of the company passed at the meeting, subject to any provision of the company's articles which states who may or may not be chairman.

The appointment of a proxy to vote on a matter at a meeting of a company authorises the proxy to demand or join in demanding a poll on that matter (s 329 CA 2006).

In relation to termination of a proxy's authority, unless the company receives notice of the termination before the commencement of the meeting it does not affect:

(a)   whether he counts in deciding whether there is a quorum at a meeting;
(b)   the validity of anything he does as chairman of the meeting; or
(c)   the validity of a poll demanded by him at a meeting.

The termination of authority does not affect the validity of a vote given by that person unless the company receives notice of the termination:

(a)   before the commencement of the meeting or adjourned meeting at which the vote is given; or
(b)   in the case of a poll taken more than 48 hours after it was demanded, before the time appointed for taking the poll (s 330 CA 2006).

Section 331 provides that nothing in the Act prevents a company's articles from conferring more extensive rights on members or proxies than are conferred by the Act.

16.9 Electronic communications

Section 340 provides that where a company has given an electronic address in a notice calling a meeting, it is deemed to have agreed that any document or information relating to proceedings at the meeting may be sent by electronic means to that address.

16.10 Resolutions

The Companies Act lays down stringent rules in relation to resolutions. Section 281 CA 2006 deals with resolutions.

Section 281(1) provides that a resolution of the members or a class of members of a private company must be passed:

(a)   as a written resolution in accordance with Chapter 2 of Part 13 of the Act; or
(b)   at a meeting of the members (see Chapter 3 of Part 13 of the Act).

Section 281(2) provides that a resolution of the members or a class of members of a public company must be passed at a meeting of the members.

16.10.1 Ordinary resolutions

Section 282 CA 2006 deals with ordinary resolutions. An ordinary resolution is defined as one that is passed by a simple majority.

Section 282(2) provides that a written resolution is passed by a simple majority if it is passed by members representing a simple majority of the total voting rights of eligible members. This is not available to public companies (see section 16.10.4).

Section 282(3) provides that a resolution is passed at a meeting on a show of hands if it is passed by a simple majority of:

(a)   the members who, being entitled to do so, vote in person on the resolution; and
(b)   the persons who vote on the resolution as duly appointed proxies of members entitled to vote on it.

Section 282(4) provides that a resolution passed on a poll taken at a meeting is passed by a simple majority if it is passed by members representing a simple majority of the total voting rights of members who vote in person or by proxy on the resolution.

16.10.2 Special resolutions

Section 283 provides that a special resolution of the members or a class of members of a company means a resolution passed by a majority of not less than 75 per cent.

Section 283(2) provides that a written resolution is passed by a majority of not less than 75 per cent if it is passed by members representing not less than 75 per cent of the total voting rights of eligible members. (As noted below in section 16.10.4, this is not available to public companies.)

Section 283(3) provides that where a resolution of a private company is passed as a written resolution:

(a)   the resolution is not a special resolution unless it stated that it was proposed as a special resolution; and
(b)   if the resolution so stated, it may only be passed as a special resolution.

Section 283(4) provides that a resolution passed at a meeting on a show of hands is passed by a majority of not less than 75 per cent if it is passed by not less than 75 per cent of:

(a)   the members who, being entitled to do so, vote in person on the resolution; and
(b)   the persons who vote on the resolution as duly appointed proxies of members entitled to vote on it.

Section 283(5) provides that a resolution passed on a poll taken at a meeting is passed by a majority of not less than 75 per cent if it is passed by members representing not less than 75 per cent of the total voting rights of the members who (being entitled to do so) vote in person or by proxy on the resolution.

Extraordinary resolutions have been abolished by the Companies Act 2006. It should also be noted that special resolutions no longer require 21 days' notice (s 283 CA 2006).

16.10.3 Votes on resolutions

Section 284 CA 2006 provides for the position in relation to the general legal position on votes.

Section 284(1) provides that on a vote on a written resolution:

(a)   in the case of a company having a share capital, every member has one vote in respect of each share or each £10 worth of stock held by him; and
(b)   in any other case, every member has one vote.

Section 284(2) provides that on a vote on a resolution on a show of hands at a meeting:

(a)   every member present in person has one vote; and
(b)   every proxy present who has been duly appointed by a member entitled to vote on a resolution also has one vote.

Section 284(3) provides that on a vote on a resolution on a poll taken at a meeting:

(a)   in the case of a company having a share capital, every member has one vote in respect of each share or each £10 of stock held by him; and
(b)   in any other case, every member has one vote.

Section 284(4) provides that this is all subject to any provision of the company's articles (which could provide for weighted voting). On a poll, a member with more than one vote is not obliged to use all his votes or cast them in the same way.

Section 285(1) provides that where a member entitled to vote on a resolution has appointed one proxy only, and the company's articles provide that the proxy has fewer votes in a vote on a resolution on a show of hands taken at a meeting than the member would have if he were present in person:

(a)   the provision about how many votes the proxy has on a show of hands is void; and
(b)   the proxy has the same number of votes on a show of hands as the member who appointed him would have if he were present at the meeting.

Section 285(2) provides that where a member has appointed more than one proxy, subsection (1) above applies as if the references to the proxy were references to the proxies taken together.

In a similar fashion, in relation to a resolution required or authorised by an enactment, if a private company's articles provide that a member has a different number of votes in relation to a resolution, when it is passed as a written resolution, and when it is passed on a poll taken at a meeting:

(a)   the provision about how many votes a member has in relation to the resolution passed on a poll is void; and
(b)   a member has the same number of votes in relation to the resolution when it is passed on a poll as he has when it is passed as a written resolution (s 285(3)).

Listed companies have to ensure that all valid proxy appointments received for general meetings are properly recorded and counted. Where a vote has been taken on a show of hands, the company should give information (at the meeting as well as on a website maintained by the company).

The chairman's declaration of the result on a show of hands is conclusive evidence without proof of the number or proportion of votes in favour for or against the resolution (s 320).

16.10.4 Written resolutions

Section 288 CA 2006 provides in relation to written resolutions of private companies. Certain resolutions may not be passed as written resolutions:

(a)   a resolution under s 168 removing a director before the expiration of his period of office; and
(b)   a resolution under s 510 removing an auditor before the expiration of his term of office (s 288(2)).

Section 288(3) provides a resolution may be proposed as a written resolution:

(a)   by the directors of a private company (s 291); or
(b)   by the members of a private company (ss 292–295).

Eligible members are those in relation to a resolution proposed as a written resolution, who would have been entitled to vote on the resolution on the circulation date of the resolution (s 289).

Section 291 provides in relation to circulation of written resolutions proposed by directors.

Section 291(2) provides that the company must send or submit a copy of the resolution to every eligible member.

The copy of the resolution must be accompanied by a statement informing the member:

(a)   how to signify agreement to the resolution (s 296); and
(b)   as to the date by which the resolution must be passed if it is not to lapse (s 297).

In the event of default in complying with this section, an offence is committed by every officer who is in default (s 291(5)).

Section 292 provides that members of a private company may require the company to circulate a resolution that may properly be moved and is proposed to be moved as a written resolution (s 292(1)).

A resolution may be moved as a written resolution unless:

(a)   it would, if passed, be ineffective whether by reason of inconsistency with any enactment or the company's constitution or otherwise;
(b)   it is defamatory of any person; or
(c)   it is frivolous or vexatious (s 292(2)).

Where the members require a company to circulate a resolution, they may require the company to circulate with it a statement of not more than 1,000 words on the subject matter of the resolution (s 292(3)).

A company is required to circulate the resolution and any accompanying statement once it has received requests that it is to do so from members representing not less than the requisite percentage of the total voting rights of all members entitled to vote on the resolution (s 292(4)).

The requisite percentage is 5 per cent or such lower percentage as is specified for this purpose in the company's articles (s 292(5)).

Section 293 provides that a company that is required under s 292 to circulate a resolution must send or submit to every eligible member:

(a) a copy of the resolution; and
(b) a copy of any accompanying statements.

Section 295(1) provides that a company is not required to circulate a member's statement under s 293 if, on an application by the company or another person who claims to be aggrieved, the court is satisfied that the rights conferred by s 292 and that section are being abused.

Section 296 provides the procedure for signifying agreement to a written resolution. A member signifies agreement when the company receives from him an authenticated document:

(a) identifying the resolution to which it relates; and
(b) indicating his agreement to the resolution.

The document must be sent to the company in hard copy form or in electronic form. A member's agreement to a written resolution, once signified, may not be revoked (s 296(3)).

Section 297 provides that the period for agreeing to a written resolution proposed as a written resolution lapses if it is not passed before the end of:

(a) the period specified for this purpose in the company's articles; or
(b) if none is specified, the period of 28 days beginning with the circulation date.

The agreement of a member to a written resolution is ineffective if signified after the expiry of that period (s 297).

Section 298 provides for the sending of documents relating to written resolutions by electronic means.

Section 299 provides for the publication of a written resolution on a website. The section applies where a company sends:

(a) a written resolution; or
(b) a statement relating to a written resolution to a person by means of a website.

Section 299(2) provides that the resolution or statement is not validly sent for the purposes of this part of the Act unless the resolution is available on the website throughout the period, beginning with the circulation date and ending on the date on which the resolution lapses under s 297.

It is now possible for private though not public companies to pass written resolutions by the same majority required at actual meetings. Thus written resolutions will require only a simple majority in the case of an ordinary resolution, or 75 per cent if a special resolution is required.

16.10.5 De facto resolutions – the assent principle

Quite independently of the Companies Act 2006, on occasion the courts have been willing to recognise certain acts, irrespective of the fact that no proper meeting has been called on the basis of the company's unanimous consent. Thus, in *Re Express Engineering Works Ltd* [1920] 1 Ch 466, where all the members agreed at a board meeting rather than at a general meeting, the assent principle was applied.

The same principle was applied in *Cane v Jones* [1980] 1 WLR 1451. Kingsway Petrol Station Limited was the company at issue here. It was set up by two brothers, Percy and Harold Jones, in 1946. Percy and his descendants held half the shares, and Harold and his descendants the other half. The articles gave the chairman a casting vote on the board as well as in general meetings. A written agreement signed by all shareholders in 1967 stated that the chairman should not exercise the casting vote. This was done to preserve equity within the two parts of the family.

After a family dispute, Percy's side claimed that the 1967 agreement overrode the articles and restricted the use of the chairman's casting vote.

Michael Wheeler QC, sitting as a Deputy High Court Judge, agreed that the agreement signed by all shareholders overrode the articles indicating unanimous consent to a course of action.

The principle has also been applied in *Parker and Cooper Ltd v Reading* [1926] Ch 975.

The position has not been uniform, though, and in some cases the courts have been unwilling to recognise the unanimous assent of members as a substitute for a resolution at a meeting: see *Re Barry Artist Ltd* [1985] 1 WLR 1305. The written resolution procedure makes this principle of less significance but it may remain important, particularly for public companies which cannot avail themselves of the written resolution procedure. In this case Nourse J stated that a resolution adopted unanimously without a meeting would not satisfy the statutory definition of a special resolution. It is clear that it would not normally have been acceptable to the Court to proceed without the appropriate resolution.

16.10.6 Records of resolutions and meetings, etc.

Section 355 CA 2006 provides that every company must keep records comprising copies of all resolutions, minutes of all proceedings of general meetings and details provided to the company in accordance with s 357 (decision of the sole member). The records must be kept for at least ten years from the date of the resolution, meeting or decision as appropriate (s 355(2) CA 2006).

It is provided in s 356 that where there is a record of a resolution or of minutes of proceedings of a general meeting, then the record of a resolution passed otherwise than at a general meeting, if purported to be signed by a director of the company or by the company secretary, is evidence of the passing of the resolution.

Where there is a record of a written resolution of a private company, the requirements of the Act with respect to the passing of the resolution are deemed to be complied with unless the contrary is proved, and the minutes of proceedings of the general meeting, if purported to be signed by the chairman of that meeting or by the chairman of the next general meeting, are evidence of the proceedings at the meeting.

Where there is a record of proceedings of a general meeting, then until the contrary is proved, the meeting is deemed duly held and convened, the proceedings are deemed to have duly taken place and all appointments at the meeting are deemed valid (s 356).

Section 357 deals with records of decisions by a sole member. Where the member takes any decision that may be taken by the company in a general meeting and has effect as if agreed by the company in a general meeting, then he must provide the company with details of the decision. Failure to do so is an offence (s 357(4) CA 2006).

The company must, at all times, keep available for inspection records of resolutions etc. relating to the previous ten years and open those records to inspection by any member without charge. Any member is entitled, on payment of such fee as may be prescribed, to be furnished with a copy of any of those records (s 358 CA 2006).

16.10.7 Amendments

Resolutions may be amended at the meeting provided that the amendment is within the general notice of the business that has been sent out to members, it is no more onerous on the company than the existing resolution and it does not have the effect of negating the substantive resolution. This principle does not apply if the resolution has to be set out verbatim. In the case of special resolutions, no amendment can be permitted that alters the substance of the resolution contained in the notice: see *Re Moorgate Mercantile Holdings Ltd* [1980] 1 WLR 227 and applied in *Re Peninsular and Oriental Steam Navigation Co* [2006] AER(D) 36. In the *Moorgate* case, notice had been given of a special resolution to cancel the share premium account. At the meeting an amendment was put forward to the resolution and this was passed.

It was held that the amendment and the consequent resolution was not validly passed as it differed in substance from the one for which notice had been given.

An amendment to a resolution would be permitted to resolve an ambiguity or to correct a grammatical mistake without the notice usually necessary e.g. *Re Uniq plc* [2011] EWHC 749 (Ch), where there was a numerical error in the text of a special resolution set out in the notice circulated to shareholders.

If the chairman improperly rejects an amendment and the unamended resolution is then passed, that resolution is then invalid: see *Henderson v Bank of Australasia* (1888) 40 ChD 170.

Where amendments are proposed, the amendment is first put to the vote. If that is passed the amended resolution is then voted upon.

16.11 Additional requirements for quoted companies

There are additional requirements for quoted companies.

Section 341 provides that where a poll is taken at a general meeting of a quoted company, the company must ensure that the following information is made available on a website:

(a) the date of the meeting;
(b) the text of the resolution or, as the case may be, a description of the subject matter of the poll;
(c) the number of votes cast in favour; and
(d) the number of votes cast against.

Section 353 provides that the information must be made available on a website that is maintained by, or on behalf of, the company and identifies the company in question.

Access to the information on the website and the ability to obtain a hard copy of the information from the website must not be conditional on the payment of a fee or otherwise restricted, and the information must be made available as soon as is reasonably practicable and must be kept available throughout the period of two years, beginning with the date on which it is first made available on a website in accordance with this section.

Section 342 CA 2006 provides that members of a quoted company may require the directors to obtain an independent report on any poll taken or to be taken at a general meeting of a company.

The directors are required to obtain an independent report if they receive requests from:

(a) members representing not less than 5 per cent of the total voting rights of all the members who have a right to vote on the matter; or
(b) not fewer than 100 members who have a right to vote on the matter to which the poll relates and hold shares of the company on which there has been paid up on average not less than £100 per member.

A request may be made in hard copy or in electronic form, and must identify the poll or polls to which it relates and must be authenticated by the person or persons making it, and must be received by the company not later than one week after the date on which the poll is taken.

Section 343 provides that directors who are required under s 342 to obtain an independent report must appoint a person they consider to be appropriate (an independent assessor) to prepare a report for the company. The appointment must be made within a week after the company's being required to obtain the report. The directors must not appoint a person:

(a) who does not meet the independence requirement (s 344); or
(b) who has another role in relation to any poll on which he is to report (including in particular a role in connection with collecting or counting votes or with the appointment of proxies).

Section 344 CA 2006 provides that a person may not be appointed as an independent assessor if he is an officer or employee of the company, or a partner or employee of such a person, or a partnership of which such a person is a partner, or if he is an officer or employee of an associated undertaking of a company or a partner or employee of such a person or a partnership of which such a person is a partner. However, an auditor of a company is not regarded as an officer or an employee of the company for this purpose. Sections 345 and 346 deal further with the application of the independence requirement.

Section 347 provides for an independent assessor's report which must state whether:

(a) the procedures adopted in connection with the poll or polls are adequate;
(b) whether the votes cast including proxy votes were fairly and accurately recorded and counted;
(c) whether the issue of the validity of members' appointed proxies was fairly assessed;
(d) whether the notice of the meeting complied with the relevant requirements; and
(e) whether s 326 in relation to company's sponsored invitations to appoint proxies was complied with in relation to the meeting.

If he is unable to form an opinion on any of these matters, the report must record that fact and state the reasons for it. The report must state the name of the independent assessor (s 347 CA 2006).

An independent assessor who has been appointed to report on a poll is entitled to attend the meeting at which the poll is taken and any subsequent proceedings in connection with the poll (s 348 CA 2006). He is also entitled to be provided by the company with a copy of the notice and any other communication relating to it.

Section 349 provides that the independent assessor is entitled to access the company's records relating to any poll on which he is to report and the meeting at which the poll or polls may be or were taken.

He can require anyone who, at any time, was a director, secretary of the company, employee or accountable for the company's records, a member of the company or agent of the company, to provide him with relevant information of explanations for the purpose of preparing his report.

A person who fails to comply with a requirement under s 349, unless it was not reasonably practicable for him to provide the relevant information, commits an offence (s 350 CA 2006).

Where an independent assessor has been appointed to report on a poll, the company must ensure that the following information is made available on a website: the fact of his appointment, his identity, the text of the resolution that he is looking at and a copy of any report by him (s 351 CA 2006).

The provisions relating to results of a poll to be made available on a website by a quoted company (s 341) and the provision of an independent report on a poll (ss 342–351) apply in relation to class proceedings *mutatis mutandis* (ss 352–353 CA 2006).

16.12 Disability Discrimination Act 1995

The Act places a duty on those who provide goods, facilities and services not to discriminate against disabled people. The Act applies where these are provided to the public or a section of the public. It is likely that this would apply to meetings of quoted companies.

Summary

Meetings

Public companies must hold annual general meetings; private companies need not do so. Companies may hold general meetings between annual general meetings.

The Companies Act 2006 and the company's articles set out the rules which companies must follow.

Notice

The minimum period of notice is 21 days' notice for annual general meetings of public companies, and for other general meetings 14 days' notice if the company is limited. On occasion, short notice may be sufficient.

Notices must go to members and directors.

Chairman

The company's articles will generally specify who is to act as chairman. In the event that the articles make no provision, the members must act to fill the vacuum and elect one of their number.

The chairman's role is to take the meeting through the agenda, put matters to the vote and keep order.

Quorum

The rules on quorum are generally set out in the company's articles. They must be followed to the letter, although if members are deliberately boycotting meetings then the Secretary of State may seek the calling of an annual general meeting with a lower quorum or there may be an application to the court for the holding of a general meeting with a lower quorum.

Resolutions

If a special resolution is to be put to the vote at a meeting, then it should be set out verbatim in the notice, as should any amendment. In practice, ordinary resolutions are also set out verbatim in the notice. Any substantive amendment should also be set out in the notice.

There are provisions to permit private companies to resolve matters by written resolutions without the need for a meeting.

Votes

Initially, a vote is taken on a show of hands. This is not conclusive of the matter, however, except in two instances where the articles may state that a vote on a show of hands is decisive – namely, election of the chairman and adjournment of the meeting. In every other circumstance, a poll may be demanded by not fewer than five members or by members representing 10 per cent of the voting rights, or by members holding shares in the company conferring a right to vote at the meeting being shares on which an aggregate sum has been paid up equal to not less than 10 per cent of the total sum paid up on all the shares conferring that right.

Where a vote is taken on a poll, the outcome overrides the outcome on a show of hands.

Proxies

A member entitled to attend and vote at a meeting of a company with share capital may appoint somebody else to attend and vote in his place as a proxy. The notice sent to members must set out their right to appoint a proxy.

The proxy may speak.

Adjournment

The chairman of the meeting may adjourn the meeting if it is appropriate to do so – for example, to preserve order – and he must do so if so directed by the meeting.

Minutes

Companies must cause minutes and records of resolutions of general meetings to be kept.

Quoted companies

Additional requirements apply to quoted companies in relation to the publication of poll results on a website and the right of members to require an independent report on a poll taken at a general meeting.

Self-test questions

16.1 How long can a company go without holding an annual general meeting?

16.2 Set out the different ways in which company meetings may be called.

16.3 When may class meetings be necessary?

16.4 What matters have to be set out in the notice calling a company meeting?

16.5 What is the statutory provision in relation to a quorum at a company meeting?

16.6 How may a chairman of a meeting be elected?

16.7 How are polls conducted at company meetings?

16.8 Who may appoint a proxy?

16.9 How may electronic communications be used in relation to company meetings?

16.10 Set out the different types of resolutions that may be carried by a company.

16.11 What additional requirements exist in relation to company meetings of quoted companies?

Further reading

D Aherne and K Macher, 'The Continuing Evolution of Proxy Representation' [2011] JBL 125.

C Baker, 'Amending Special Resolutions' (1991) 12 Co Law 64.

JR Birds, 'The Deregulation Provisions of the Companies Act 1989' (1990) 11 Co Law 142.

R Grantham, 'The Unanimous Consent Rule in Company Law' [1993] CLJ 245.

HW Higginson, 'Written Resolutions of Private Companies' (1993) 109 LQR 16.

P Jaffey, 'Contractual Obligations of the Company in General Meeting' (1996) 16 LS 27.

Chapter 17

Accounts and returns

Chapter Contents

17.1 Accounts and reports

Part 15 of the 2006 Act deals with accounts and reports. Section 380 provides that this part of the Act applies to accounts and reports in relation to each financial year of a company.

17.1.1 Accounting records

Section 386 provides that every company must keep adequate accounting records. This means accounting records that are sufficient:

(a)   to show and explain the company's transactions;
(b)   to disclose with reasonable accuracy, at any time, the financial position of the company at that time; and
(c)   to enable the directors to ensure that any accounts required to be prepared comply with the requirements of the Act (and, where applicable, of Art 4 of Regulation (EC) No 1606/2002).

Quoted companies are required under European law to draw up accounts in compliance with Regulation (EC) No 1606/2002 (see section 1.4.3).

The accounting records must contain entries from day to day of sums received and expended, and a record of the assets and liabilities of the company.

If the company's business involves dealing in goods, the accounting records must contain statements of stock held by the company at the end of each financial year, statements of stock takings and, excepting goods sold by way of ordinary retail trade, statements of goods sold and purchased.

If a company fails to comply with the provisions of s 386 then every officer of the company in default is liable.

Section 388 provides that accounting records must be kept at the company's registered office or such other place as the directors may think fit, and must, at all times, be open to inspection by the company's officers. In the case of a private company, they must be kept for three years, and in the case of a public company, for six years from the date on which they were made.

Section 389 provides that failure to comply with maintenance of the records for these periods results in liability on every officer of the company in default.

17.1.2 Small companies

Section 381 relates to companies that are subject to the small companies regime. Companies that are subject to the small companies regime are sometimes treated differently, e.g. they are not subject to s 399 (duty to prepare group accounts), and are, subject to s 477, exempt from audit. The small companies regime for accounts and reports applies to companies for the financial year in relation to which the company:

(a)   qualifies as small (ss 382–383); and
(b)   is not excluded from the regime (s 384).

A small company qualifies as small in its first financial year if it fulfils the following qualifications.

It must fulfil two or more of the following requirements:

Turnover of not more than £5.6m.
Balance sheet total not more than £2.8m.
Number of employees not more than 50 (s 382).

Section 383 provides further that a parent company qualifies as a small company in relation to a financial year only if the group headed by it qualifies as a small group.

In subsequent years a company qualifies as small in relation to a subsequent financial year:

(a)   if the qualifying conditions are met in that year and the preceding year;
(b)   if the qualifying conditions are met in that year and the company qualified as small in relation to the preceding financial year; or
(c)   if the qualifying conditions were met in the preceding financial year and the company qualified as small in relation to that year.

A group qualifies as a small group in relation to the parent company's first financial year if the qualifying conditions are met in that year. These are that the group must satisfy two or more of the following requirements:

Aggregate turnover of not more than £5.6m net or £6.72m gross.
Aggregate balance sheet of not more than £2.8m net or £3.36m gross.
Aggregate number of employees not more than 50.

Net means after any set-offs and other adjustments made to eliminate group transactions; gross means without those set-offs and other adjustments.

A group qualifies as small in relation to a subsequent financial year of the parent company:

(a)   if the qualifying conditions are met in that year and the preceding financial year;
(b)   if the qualifying conditions are met in that year and the group qualified as small in relation to the preceding financial year; or
(c)   if the qualifying conditions were met in the preceding financial year and the group qualified as small in relation to that year.

Section 384 provides that certain companies are excluded from the small companies regime. The small companies regime does not apply to a company that is, or was, at any time within the financial year to which the accounts relate:

(a)   a public company;
(b)   a company that:

    (i)   is an authorised insurance company, a banking company, an e-money issuer, an ISD (Investment Services Directive) investment firm or a UCITS (Undertakings for Collective Investments in Transferable Securities) management company, or
    (ii) carries on insurance market activity, or

(c)   is a member of an ineligible group.

A group is ineligible if any of its members is:

(a)   a public company;
(b)   a body corporate (other than a company) whose shares are admitted to trading
       on a regulated market in an EEA (European Economic Area) state;
(c)   a person who has permission under Part IV of the Financial Services and
       Markets Act 2000 to carry on a regulated activity;
(d)   a small company that is an authorised insurance company, a banking company,
       an e-money issuer, an ISD (Investment Services Directive) investment firm or
       a UCITS management company; or
(e)   a person who carries on insurance market activity.

17.1.3 Medium-sized companies

Section 465 provides that a company qualifies as medium sized in relation to its first
financial year if the qualifying conditions set out in s 465(3) are met. Section 465(3)
provides that the qualifying conditions that must be satisfied by a company are two
or more of the following requirements:

Turnover not more than £22.8m.
Balance sheet total not more than £11.4m.
Number of employees not more than 250.

It qualifies as a medium-sized company in relation to a subsequent financial year:

(a)   if the qualifying conditions are met in that year and the preceding finan-
       cial year;
(b)   if the qualifying conditions are met in that year and the company qualified as
       medium sized in relation to the preceding financial year; or
(c)   if the qualifying conditions were met in the preceding financial year and the
       company qualified as medium sized in relation to that year.

Section 466 defines the companies that qualify as medium-sized companies where
they are parent companies.

Section 466(1) provides that a parent company qualifies as a medium-sized
company in relation to a financial year only if the group headed by it qualifies as a
medium-sized group.

A group qualifies as medium sized in relation to the parent company's first financial year if the qualifying conditions are met in that year. The group qualifies as
medium sized in relation to a subsequent financial year of the parent company:

(a)   if the qualifying conditions are met in that year and the preceding finan-
       cial year;
(b)   if the qualifying conditions are met in that year and the group qualified as
       medium sized in relation to the preceding financial year; or
(c)   if the qualifying conditions were met in the preceding financial year and the
       group qualified as medium sized in relation to that year.

The qualifying conditions, which must be satisfied as to at least two of the three, are as follows:

Aggregate turnover not more than £22.8m net (or £27.36m gross).
Aggregate balance sheet not more than £11.4m net (or £13.68m gross).
Aggregate number of employees not more than 250.

Section 467 deals with certain companies that are excluded from being treated as medium sized.

A company is not entitled to take advantage of the provisions of this part of the Act if it is:

(a)   a public company;
(b)   a company that:

    (i)   has permission under Part IV of the Financial Services and Markets Act 2000 to carry on a regulated activity, or
    (ii)   carries on insurance market activity; or

(c)   a member of an ineligible group.

A group is ineligible if any of its members is:

(a)   a public company;
(b)   a body corporate other than a company whose shares are admitted to trading on a regulated market;
(c)   a person other than a small company who has permission under Part IV of the Financial Services and Markets Act 2000 to carry on a regulated activity;
(d)   a small company that is an authorised insurance company, a banking company, an e-money issuer, an ISD investment firm or a UCITS management company (see section 17.1.2); or
(e)   a person who carries on insurance market activity.

Medium-sized companies enjoy certain exceptions in relation to filing obligations (s 445 CA 2006).

17.1.4 Quoted and unquoted companies

Quoted and unquoted companies are defined in s 385.

For the purposes of Part 15 of the Act, a company is a quoted company in relation to a financial year if it is a quoted company immediately before the end of the accounting reference period by reference to which that financial year was determined.

A quoted company means a company whose equity share capital:

(a)   has been included in the official list in accordance with the provisions of Part VI of the Financial Services and Markets Act 2000;
(b)   is officially listed in an EEA state; or
(c)   is admitted to dealing on either the New York Stock Exchange or the exchange known as NASDAQ.

An unquoted company is a company that is not quoted (s 385(3) CA 2006). Quoted companies are sometimes subject to additional rules, e.g. s 420 (duty to prepare directors' remuneration report) and s 428 (form and contents of summary financial statement: quoted companies).

17.1.5 A company's financial year

Section 390 deals with a company's financial year. A company's first financial year begins with the first day of its first accounting reference period and ends with the last day of that period, or a date not more than seven days before or after it, as the directors may determine.

Subsequent financial years begin with the day immediately following the end of the previous financial year, and end with the last day of the next accounting reference period or such other date not more than seven days before or after the end of that period, as the directors may determine.

The company's accounting reference period is determined according to its accounting reference date in each calendar year (s 391).

Section 392 provides for alteration of a company's accounting reference date. This may be done by giving notice to the Registrar specifying a new accounting reference date, having effect in relation to:

(a)   the company's current accounting reference period and subsequent periods; or
(b)   the company's previous accounting reference period and subsequent periods.

The notice must state whether the current or previous accounting reference period is to be shortened or extended, and a notice extending a company's current or previous accounting reference period is not effective if given less than five years after the end of an earlier accounting reference period of the company that was extended under this section.

A company's accounting reference period may not be extended so as to exceed 18 months, and a notice under this section is ineffective if the current or previous accounting reference period as extended in accordance with the notice would exceed that limit.

17.2 Annual accounts

Section 393 of the Companies Act 2006 provides that the directors of a company must not approve accounts for the purposes of the Act unless they are satisfied that they give a true and fair view of the assets, liabilities, financial position and profit or loss:

(a)   in the case of a company's individual accounts, of the company; or
(b)   in the case of a company's group accounts, of the undertakings included in the consolidation as a whole, so far as concerns members of the company.

It is further provided that the auditor of a company in carrying out his functions under the Act must have regard to the directors' duty under the section.

17.2.1 Individual accounts

Section 394 provides that the directors of every company must prepare accounts for the company for each financial year. These accounts are referred to as the company's individual accounts.

Section 395 sets out the appropriate accounting framework for the accounts, and s 396 provides that individual accounts must comprise:

(a) a balance sheet as at the last day of the financial year; and
(b) a profit and loss account.

The accounts must:

(a) in the case of the balance sheet, give a true and fair view of the state of affairs of the company as at the end of the financial year; and
(b) in the case of the profit and loss account, give a true and fair view of the profit or loss of the company for the financial year.

17.2.2 Group accounts

Section 399 provides that companies not subject to the small companies regime are liable to prepare group accounts if the company is part of a group.

Section 400 provides that a company is exempt from the requirement to prepare group accounts if it is itself a subsidiary undertaking and its immediate parent undertaking is established under the law of an EEA state in the following cases:

(a) where the company is a wholly owned subsidiary of that parent undertaking; or
(b) where that parent undertaking holds more than 50 per cent of the allotted shares in the company and notice requesting the preparation of group accounts has not been served on the company by shareholders holding in aggregate:

  (i)   more than half of the remaining allotted shares in the company, or
  (ii) 5 per cent of the total allotted shares in the company.

Additionally, in order to be able to claim exemption:

(a) the company must be included in consolidated accounts for a larger group drawn up to the same date or to an earlier date in the same financial year by a parent undertaking established under the law of an EEA state;
(b) those accounts must be drawn up and audited and that parent undertaking's annual report must be drawn up according to that law:

  (i)   in accordance with the provisions of the Seventh Directive as modified where relevant by the provisions of the Bank Accounts Directive (86/635/EEC) or the Insurance Accounts Directive (91/674/EEC), or
  (ii) in accordance with international accounting standards.

Section 401 provides that a company is exempt from the requirement to prepare group accounts if it is itself a subsidiary undertaking and its parent undertaking is not established under the law of an EEA state in the following cases:

(a) where the company is a wholly owned subsidiary of that parent undertaking; or
(b) where that parent undertaking holds more than 50 per cent of the allotted shares in the company and notice requesting the preparation of group accounts has not been served on the company by shareholders holding in aggregate:

  (i) more than half of the remaining allotted shares in the company, or
  (ii) 5 per cent of the total allotted shares in the company.

Section 402 provides that a parent company is exempt from the requirement to prepare group accounts if under s 405 all of its subsidiary undertakings could be excluded from consolidation in Companies Act group accounts.

Section 403 sets out the applicable accounting framework for group accounts, and s 404 provides that the group accounts must comprise a consolidated balance sheet and a consolidated profit and loss account.

Section 405 provides that subsidiary undertakings may be excluded from consolidation if the inclusion is not material for the purpose of giving a true and fair view (two or more undertakings may be excluded only if they are not material taken together), or if severe long-term restrictions substantially hinder the exercise of the parent company's rights over the assets or the management of that undertaking.

Furthermore, subsidiaries are exempted from inclusion if the information can only be acquired at disproportionate expense or undue delay. Subsidiaries are also excluded if the parent company's interest is only held with a view to subsequent resale.

Section 407 provides that the directors of a parent company must secure that the individual accounts of:

(a) the parent company; and
(b) each of its subsidiary undertakings

are all prepared using the same financial reporting framework, except to the extent that in their opinion there are good reasons for not doing so.

17.2.3 Notes to the accounts

Section 472 provides that information required to be given in notes to the company's accounts may be contained in the accounts or a separate document annexed to the accounts.

Sections 409 to 410 provide that the Secretary of State may make provision by regulations requiring information about related undertakings to be given in notes to a company's annual accounts.

Section 411 provides that information about employee numbers and costs must be included in notes to the company's accounts except in the case of companies that are subject to the small companies regime.

The information given should show the average number of persons employed by the company in the financial year and the average number of persons so employed within each category of persons employed by the company.

Section 412 provides that the Secretary of State may make provision by regulations requiring information to be given in notes to the company's annual accounts about directors' remuneration. Such a requirement extends to persons connected with a director or a body corporate controlled by a director.

Section 413 provides that in the case of a company that does not prepare group accounts, details of advances and credits granted by the company to its directors and guarantees of any kind entered into by the company on behalf of its directors must be shown in the notes to its individual accounts. In the case of a parent company that prepares group accounts, details of advances, credits and guarantees must be shown in the notes to the group accounts. The details required of an advance or credit include the amount, the interest rate, the conditions and any amounts repaid. In relation to guarantees, the details required include the main terms, the amount of the maximum liability that may be incurred, any amount paid and any liability incurred by the company for the purpose of fulfilling the guarantee.

Section 408 provides that where notes to the company's individual balance sheet show the company's profit or loss for the financial year, and the companies concerned prepare group accounts, then there is no need to supply the information specified in s 411 (employee numbers and costs).

17.2.4 Approval of the accounts

Section 414 provides that a company's annual accounts must be approved by the board of directors and signed on behalf of the board by a director of the company. The signature must be on the company's balance sheet.

17.3 Directors' report

The directors of a company must prepare a directors' report for each financial year (s 415).

If the company is a parent company, and the directors of the company prepare group accounts, the directors' report must be a consolidated report relating to the undertakings included in the consolidation.

The directors' report for the financial year must state the names of the persons who, during the financial year, were directors of the company, and the principal activities of the company in the course of the year (s 416).

Unless the company is subject to the small companies regime, the directors' report must contain a business review (s 417). The business review must contain a fair review of the company's business and a description of the principal risks and uncertainties facing the company.

The review requires a balanced and comprehensive analysis of:

(a) the development and performance of the company's business during the financial year; and
(b) the position of the company's business at the end of the year

consistent with the size and complexity of the business.

In the case of a quoted company, the business review must, to the extent necessary for an undertaking of the development, performance or position of the company's business, include:

(a) the main trends and factors likely to affect the future development, performance and position of the company's business; and
(b) information about:

    (i) environmental matters, including the impact of the company's business on the environment,
    (ii) the company's employees, and
    (iii) social and community issues

including information about any policies of the company in relation to those matters and the effectiveness of those policies.

Section 418 provides that the directors' report must contain a statement to the effect that in the case of each of the persons who are directors at the time a report is approved:

(a) so far as the director is aware there is no relevant audit information of which the company's auditor is unaware; and
(b) he has taken all the steps that he ought to have taken as a director to establish for himself that any relevant audit information has been made known to the auditor.

Section 419 provides for the approval and signing off of a directors' report by the board of directors on behalf of the board by a director or the secretary of the company.

If the report is prepared in accordance with the small companies regime, it must contain a statement to that effect in a prominent position above the signature.

If a directors' report is approved that does not comply with the requirements of the Act, every director of the company who:

(a) knew that it did not comply or was reckless as to whether it complied; and
(b) failed to take reasonable steps to secure compliance with those requirements or, as the case may be, to prevent the report from being approved commits an offence.

17.3.1 Quoted companies – directors' remuneration report

Section 420 provides that the directors of a quoted company must prepare a directors' remuneration report for each financial year. Failure to do so constitutes an offence.

Section 421 provides for the content of the report. The Secretary of State may make provision by regulations as to the information that should be in the report and how it is to be set out, and what is to be the auditable part of the report.

Section 422 provides that the directors' remuneration report must be approved by the board of directors and signed on behalf of the board by a director or the secretary of the company.

If a directors' report is approved and does not comply, then every director who knew of non-compliance or was reckless as to whether it complied, and who failed to take reasonable steps to secure compliance or, as the case may be, to prevent the report from being approved, commits an offence.

17.4 Publication of accounts and reports

Section 423 provides that every company must send a copy of its annual accounts and reports for each financial year to:

(a)   every member of the company;
(b)   every holder of the company's debentures; and
(c)   every person who is entitled to receive notice of general meetings.

The time allowed for sending out copies of the annual accounts and reports is as follows.

A private company must send them out not later than the end of the period for filing accounts and reports, or, if earlier, the date on which it actually delivers its accounts and reports to the Registrar.

In the case of a public company, the information must be given not later than 21 days before the relevant accounts meeting. If accounts are sent out later than that date, they shall, despite that, be deemed to have been duly sent if so agreed by all the members entitled to attend and vote at the relevant accounts meeting (s 424).

Section 425 provides for the situation in default. If there is a failure to comply with the sections above, the company and every officer of the company who is in default is guilty of an offence.

Section 426 provides the option of providing a summary financial statement. This is available to companies that may be specified in regulations by the Secretary of State.

Section 427 sets out the form and contents of summary financial statements for unquoted companies. The information must be derived from the company's annual accounts and be prepared in accordance with s 427 and regulations made under it.

Section 428 provides for the form and contents of summary financial statements for quoted companies.

If there is a failure in relation to any of these sections then the company and every officer in default is guilty of an offence.

A quoted company must ensure its annual accounts and reports are available on a website and remain so available until the annual accounts and reports for the company's next financial year are made available (s 430 CA 2006).

Section 431 provides for the rights of members or debenture holders to copies of accounts and reports for unquoted companies, and s 432 deals with the similar right for members and debenture holders of quoted companies.

In each case the member, debenture holder, etc. is entitled to the company's last annual accounts, the last directors' report and auditor's report on the accounts, and, in addition in the case of quoted companies, is also entitled to the last directors' remuneration report and the auditor's report on these reports.

Section 434 provides that where a company publishes any of its statutory accounts, they must be accompanied by the auditor's report unless the company is exempt from audit and the directors have taken advantage of that exemption.

If a company produces non-statutory accounts it must publish a statement stating they are non-statutory, and whether statutory accounts have been delivered to the Registrar, and whether an auditor's report has been made on the company's statutory accounts, and if so, whether the report is qualified or unqualified or includes a reference to any matters to which the auditor draws attention by way of emphasis without qualifying the report, or contains a statement under s 498(2) (records or returns inadequate, or accounts or directors' remuneration report not agreeing with records or returns) or s 498(3) (failure to obtain necessary information and explanations) (s 435 CA 2006).

17.4.1 Public companies: laying of accounts and reports

Section 437 of the Companies Act 2006 provides that the directors of a public company must lay before the company in general meeting copies of its annual accounts and reports.

Section 438 provides that it is an offence to fail to lay the accounts and the reports, although it is a defence for a person charged with such an offence to prove that he took all reasonable steps to secure that the requirements would be complied with before the end of the relevant period.

17.4.2 Quoted companies – members' approval of directors' remuneration report

Section 439 provides that a quoted company must, prior to the accounts meeting, give to the members of the company notice of the intention to move at the meeting an ordinary resolution approving the directors' remuneration report for the financial year.

Section 440 provides that it is an offence to fail to comply with this section, although it is a defence for a person charged with an offence to prove he took all reasonable steps to secure that the resolution was put to the vote at the meeting.

17.4.3 Filing of accounts and reports with the Registrar

Section 441 provides that the directors of a company must deliver to the Registrar for each financial year the accounts and reports required by:

(a) s 444 (filing obligations of companies subject to small companies regime);
(b) s 445 (filing obligations of medium-sized companies);
(c) s 446 (filing obligations of unquoted companies); or
(d) s 447 (filing obligations of quoted companies).

This is subject to s 448 (unlimited companies exemption from filing obligations).

Section 442 provides the period for filing accounts. The period is, for a private company, nine months from the end of the relevant accounting reference period, and, for a public company, six months from the end of that period.

Section 444 provides that the directors of a company subject to the small companies regime:

(a)   must deliver to the Registrar for each financial year a copy of the balance sheet drawn up as at the last day of that year; and
(b)   may also deliver to the company:

(i)   a copy of the company's profit and loss accounts for that year, and
(ii)   a copy of the directors' report for that year.

The directors must also deliver to the Registrar a copy of the auditor's report on the accounts (and on the directors' report).

There is provision for delivery of abbreviated accounts (s 444(3) CA 2006). Section 445 provides for the filing obligations of medium-sized companies. The directors of such a company must deliver to the Registrar a copy of:

(a)   the company's annual accounts; and
(b)   the directors' report.

They must also deliver a copy of the auditor's report on those accounts and on the directors' report.

There is again provision for delivery of abbreviated accounts (s 445(3) CA 2006).

In relation to both small and medium-sized companies, the obligations do not apply if the company is exempt from audit and the directors have taken advantage of that exemption.

Section 446 provides for the filing obligations of unquoted companies. The directors of an unquoted company must deliver to the Registrar for each financial year of the company a copy of:

(a)   the company's annual accounts; and
(b)   the directors' report.

They must also deliver to the Registrar a copy of the auditor's report on those accounts and the directors' report. Once again this does not apply to companies exempt from audit and where the directors have taken advantage of that exemption.

Section 447 provides for the filing obligations of quoted companies. The directors of a quoted company must deliver to the Registrar for each financial year of the company a copy of:

(a)   the company's annual accounts;
(b)   the directors' remuneration report; and
(c)   the directors' report.

They must also deliver a copy of the auditor's report on the accounts and on the directors' remuneration report, and the directors' report.

Section 448 provides for the exemption of unlimited companies from obligation to file accounts. The directors of an unlimited company are not required to deliver accounts and reports to the Registrar in respect of a financial year if the following conditions are met.

These conditions are that at no time during the relevant accounting reference period:

(a)   has the company been, to its knowledge, a subsidiary undertaking of an undertaking that was then limited;
(b)   have there been, to its knowledge, exercisable by or on behalf of two or more undertakings that were then limited, rights which, if exercisable by one of them, would have made the company a subsidiary undertaking of it; or
(c)   has the company been a parent company of an undertaking, that was then limited.

17.4.4 Abbreviated accounts

Section 449 provides that where the directors of a company deliver abbreviated accounts to the Registrar, and the company is not exempt from audit or the directors have not taken advantage of such an exemption, they must deliver to the Registrar a copy of the special report of the company's auditor, stating that in his opinion:

(a)   the company is entitled to deliver abbreviated accounts; and
(b)   the abbreviated accounts are properly prepared in accordance with regulations under that section.

The auditor's report on the company's annual accounts need not be delivered, but:

(a)   if the report was qualified, the special report must set out that report in full together with any further material necessary to understand the qualification; and
(b)   if that report contained a statement under:

(i)   s 498(2)(a) or (b) accounts, records or returns inadequate or accounts not agreeing with records and returns, or
(ii)   s 498(3) failure to obtain necessary information and explanations

the special report must set out that statement in full.

Section 450 provides for the approval and signing of abbreviated accounts: they must be approved by the board of directors and signed on behalf of the board by a director of the company. The signature must be on the balance sheet.

If abbreviated accounts are approved that do not comply with the requirements of regulations under the relevant section, every director of the company commits an offence if he knew that they did not comply or was reckless as to whether they complied and failed to take reasonable steps to prevent them from being approved.

17.5 Failure to file accounts and reports

Section 451 provides for the situation where there is default in filing accounts and reports.

It is an offence to fail to file accounts and reports, and every person who immediately before the end of the period was a director of the company commits an offence. It is a defence for a person charged with such an offence to prove that he took all reasonable steps to secure that the requirements would be complied with before the end of the period.

Section 452 provides for default in filing accounts and reports. If there is non-compliance with filing accounts and reports, and the directors of the company fail to make good the default within 14 days after the service of a notice on them requiring compliance, the court may, on the application of any member or creditor of the company, or of the Registrar, make an order directing the directors or any of them to make good the default within such time as may be specified in the order.

Section 453 provides for a civil penalty for failure to file accounts and reports. The liability falls on the company and the amount of the penalty is to be determined in accordance with regulations made by the Secretary of State by reference to the length of period between the end of the period for filing and the day on which the requirements are complied with, and whether the company is a private or public company.

The penalty may be recovered by the Registrar and is to be paid into the Consolidated Fund (s 453(3)).

17.5.1 Liability for false or misleading statements in reports

Section 463 deals with this situation. The reports to which the section applies are:

(a) the directors' report;
(b) the directors' remuneration report; and
(c) a summary financial statement so far as it is derived from either of those reports.

It is provided that a director of a company is liable to compensate the company for any loss suffered by it as a result of any untrue or misleading statement in a report, or the omission from a report, to which the section applies, of anything required to be included in it. He is liable only if he knew the statement to be untrue or misleading, or was reckless as to whether it was untrue or misleading, or knew the omission to be a dishonest concealment of a material fact.

17.5.2 Preparation and filing of accounts in euros

Section 469(1) provides that the amount set out in the annual accounts of a company may also be shown in the same accounts translated into euros.

Summary

Accounting records

Companies have to keep adequate accounting records.

Audit

Small companies are exempt from audit. Small companies are defined by reference to turnover, balance sheet total and the number of employees. Medium-sized companies, which are larger than small companies but defined by reference to the same three factors (though in their case of a higher amount), enjoy certain exemptions; otherwise companies' individual accounts are subject to audit.

Group accounts

Companies in a group must submit group accounts each year with a consolidated balance sheet and a consolidated profit and loss account.

Directors' report

The directors of a company must generally submit a directors' report each year setting out a business review of the company.

Directors' remuneration report

Every quoted company must prepare annually a directors' remuneration report.

Self-test questions

17.1   What accounting records must a company keep?

17.2   What constitutes the annual accounts of companies?

17.3   What information must be contained in the directors' report?

17.4   How must the accounts and reports be published?

17.5   What penalties apply in relation to the failure to file accounts and reports?

Further reading

K Lasok, 'The True and Fair View' (1989) 10 Co Law 13.

K Lasok and E Grace, 'Fair Accounting' [1988] JBL 235.

A Lev, 'Towards a Theory of Equitable and Efficient Accounting Policy' (1988) 63 Accounting Review 1.

A McGee, 'The True and Fair View Debate' (1991) 54 MLR 874.

D Prentice, 'A Director's Right of Access to Corporate Books of Account' (1978) 94 LQR 184.

Chapter 18

Auditors and annual return

18.1 Audit

Part 16 of the 2006 Act deals with audit. Chapter 1 deals with the requirement for audited accounts. Section 475 provides that a company's annual accounts for a financial year must be audited unless the company is exempt from audit under s 477 (small companies) or s 480 (dormant companies), or unless it is exempt under s 482 (non-profit-making companies subject to public sector audit).

If a company is so exempt, it must include a statement to that effect in its balance sheet (s 475(2)).

The statement must be to the effect that the members have not required the company to obtain an audit of its accounts for the year in question under s 476, and the directors acknowledge their responsibilities for complying with the requirements of the Act with respect to accounting records and the preparation of accounts.

Section 476 provides that the members of the company may require an audit. The members who wish for an audit must hold not less in total than 10 per cent in nominal value of the company's issued share capital or any class of it, or if the company does not have a share capital, must constitute not less than 10 per cent in number of the members of the company.

Section 477 provides for exemption from audit for small companies, provided that the company qualifies as a small company in relation to that year and that its turnover in the year is not more than £5.6m and its balance sheet total for the year is not more than £2.8m.

Section 478 provides for exclusion from the small companies exemption of a public company, a company that is an authorised insurance company, a banking company, an e-money issuer, a MiFID (Markets in Financial Instruments Directive) investment firm or a UCITS (Undertakings for Collective Investments in Transferable Securities) management company, or a company carrying on insurance market activity. A special register body within s 117(1) of the Trade Union and Labour Relations (Consolidation) Act 1992, or an employers' association under s 122 of the same Act, is similarly not exempt.

Section 479 provides that small companies are not entitled to exemption in the case of group companies unless the conditions in the section are complied with.

These are that the group must qualify as a small group and must not at any time in the year be an ineligible group, and that the group's aggregate turnover in the year is no more than £5.6m net or £6.72m gross, and the balance sheet total for that year is not more than £2.8m net or £3.36m gross.

Section 480 deals with dormant companies which are themselves exempt from audit.

18.1.1 Appointment of auditors

Section 485 provides that an auditor or auditors of a private company must be appointed for each financial year of the company unless the directors reasonably resolve otherwise on the ground that audited accounts are unlikely to be required. Part 42 CA 2006 provides for the qualification of such auditors.

Section 486 deals with the appointment of auditors of a private company and the default power of the Secretary of State. If a private company fails to appoint an auditor in accordance with s 485, the Secretary of State may do so in order to fill the vacancy.

An auditor or auditors of a private company hold office in accordance with the terms of their appointment (s 487).

Section 489 deals with the appointment of auditors of a public company. These must be appointed for each financial year of the company unless the directors reasonably resolve otherwise on the ground that audited accounts are unlikely to be required.

In default, once again, the Secretary of State may appoint somebody to fill the vacancy (s 490).

The 2014 edition repeats the 2012 edition of the UK Corporate Governance Code (para C.3.7) in providing that FTSE 350 companies should put the external audit contract out to tender at least every ten years. The Competition Commission, in its 2013 report, decided to make this a mandatory requirement as well as making clear that provisions in loan agreements which restrict a company's choice of auditor for example to categories or lists is prohibited.

Section 491 provides that the term of office of auditors of a public company is in accordance with the terms of their appointment.

Section 492 deals with the fixing of the auditor's remuneration. This must be fixed by the members by ordinary resolution or in such manner as the members may, by ordinary resolution, determine.

Section 493 provides that the Secretary of State may make provision by regulations for securing the disclosure of the terms of appointment of the companies' auditors, their remuneration and their duties.

Section 494 provides that the Secretary of State may make provision by regulation for securing the disclosure of the nature of any services provided for a company by the company's auditor whether as auditor or otherwise, or by his associates, and the amount of any remuneration received or receivable in this regard.

18.1.2 Functions of the auditor

Section 495 provides that a company's auditor must make a report to the company's members on all the annual accounts of the company which are sent out to the members in the case of a private company, and in the case of a public company, which are laid before the company in general meeting.

The report must state clearly whether in the auditor's opinion the annual accounts give a true and fair view, and have been properly prepared in accordance with the relevant financial reporting framework, and have been prepared in accordance with the requirements of the Act and, where applicable, Art 4 of Regulation 1606/2002/EC (on international accounting standards).

The auditor's report must be either unqualified or qualified, and must include a reference to any matters to which the auditor wishes to draw attention by way of emphasis without qualifying the report (s 495(4) CA 2006).

The auditor's report should include an introduction identifying the annual accounts that are the subject of the audit and the financial reporting framework that has been applied, and a description of the scope of the audit identifying the auditing standards in accordance with which the audit was conducted (s 495(2)).

Section 496 provides that the auditor is to report on the directors' report. The auditor must state in the report on the company's annual accounts whether, in the opinion of the auditor, the information given in the directors' report for the financial year for which the accounts are prepared is consistent with those accounts.

Section 497 provides for an auditor's report on the auditable part of the directors' remuneration report.

If the company is a quoted company the auditor must report to the company's members on the auditable part of the directors' remuneration report and state whether, in his opinion, that part of the directors' remuneration report has been properly prepared in accordance with the Act.

18.1.3 Auditor's statutory duties

Section 498 provides that a company's auditor in preparing his report must carry out such investigations as will enable him to form an opinion as to:

(a) whether adequate accounting records have been kept by the company and returns adequate for their audit have been received from branches not visited by him;

(b) whether the company's individual accounts are in agreement with the accounting records and returns; and

(c) in the case of a quoted company, whether the auditable part of the directors' remuneration report is in agreement with the accounting records and returns.

If the auditor is of the opinion that adequate records have not been kept or that the company's individual accounts are not in agreement with the records and returns, or in the case of a quoted company that the auditable part of the directors' remuneration report is not in agreement with the accounting records and returns, the auditor shall state that fact in his report (s 498(3) CA 2006).

Section 499 provides for the auditor's general right to information from the company in relation to the company's books, accounts and vouchers, and his right to require any officer or employee or person accountable for any of the company's books, accounts or vouchers, any subsidiary undertaking, any officer, employee or auditor of a subsidiary undertaking, or anybody who fell within the previous categories at a time to which the information or explanations required by the auditor relates or relate, to provide him with such information or explanations as he thinks necessary for the performance of his duties as auditor.

Section 500 deals with the auditor's right to information from overseas subsidiaries. Section 501 deals with offences. A person commits an offence who knowingly or recklessly makes to an auditor of a company a statement that conveys or purports to convey information that is misleading, false or deceptive in a material particular.

Section 502 provides for auditor's rights in relation to resolutions and meetings. In relation to a written resolution proposed to be agreed by a private company, the company's auditor is entitled to receive all such communications relating to the resolution, as are required to be supplied to a member of the company.

The company's auditor is entitled to receive all notices and other communications relating to general meetings which a member of a company is entitled to receive, and is entitled to attend any general meeting of the company and to be heard at any general meeting that he attends on any part of the business of the meeting that concerns him as auditor.

18.1.4 Disclosure in the auditor's report

The senior statutory auditor must sign the report in his own name on behalf of the audit firm (if it is an audit firm) (s 503 CA 2006).

The name of the individual who is the senior statutory auditor, as well as the name of the firm, must appear in all copies of the audit report (s 505 CA 2006).

There is an exemption from disclosing the name of the person who signed as senior statutory auditor if the company, on reasonable grounds, believes that a statement of the name would create, or be likely to create, a serious risk that the auditor or senior statutory auditor or any other person would be subject to violence or intimidation. If this is the case, the company must resolve that the name should not be stated and must give notice of the resolution to the Secretary of State, disclosing who the senior statutory auditor is.

18.1.5 Offences in connection with the auditor's report

Section 507 provides that in relation to any matter that is misleading, false or deceptive in a material particular, or where the company's report omits a statement that is required, then the auditor is guilty of an offence under this section.

This is a new criminal offence.

18.1.6 Auditors' liabilities – the case law

18.1.6.1 Conduct of the audit

The starting point of any survey of auditor's liability is the famous dictum of Lopes LJ in *Re Kingston Cotton Mill (No 2)* [1896] Ch 279, that 'an auditor is not bound to be a detective … he is a watchdog but not a bloodhound'. The auditors in this case had taken on trust a management assessment of the amount of yarn in stock, failing to make a physical check themselves. The assessments were frauds, which had been perpetrated by a manager to make the company appear to flourish by exaggerating the quantity and value of cotton and yarn in the company's mills.

The auditors took the entry of the stock in trade at the beginning of the year from the last preceding balance sheet, and they took the values of the stock in trade at the end of the year from the stock journal.

The book contained a series of accounts under various heads purporting to show the quantities and values of the company's stock in trade at the end of each year and a summary of the accounts which was adopted by the auditors.

The auditors always ensured that the summary corresponded with the accounts but they did not enquire into the accuracy of the accounts. The auditors were held not liable; the court concluded they were entitled to accept the certificate of a responsible official. This is a decision that would almost certainly be reversed today. The dictum of Lopes LJ, however, still finds approval and has fossilised into an immovable principle of law, though it is now generally accepted that an auditor is a watchdog which must bark loudly and relentlessly at any suspicious circumstance. Professional standards have advanced and duties have become stricter since the 1890s.

At the outset of the audit, an auditor must familiarise himself with the company's articles of association, so that he can ensure that payments shown in the accounts have been properly incurred. It will be no defence to assert that he has not read the company's constitution.

In *Leeds Estate Building and Investment Co v Shepherd* (1887) 36 ChD 787, the terms of the articles had not been carried out, and it was held that it was no excuse that the auditor had not seen them. As a result of this neglect, dividends, directors' fees and bonuses were improperly paid and the auditor was therefore held liable for damages.

An auditor is required to investigate suspicious circumstances. In *Re Thomas Gerrard* [1968] Ch 455, Pennycuick J noted at p. 475 that 'the standards of reasonable care and skill are, upon the expert evidence more exacting than those which prevailed in 1896' (i.e. in *Re Kingston Cotton Mill*). Here, in addition to an overstatement of stock, there had been fraudulent practice in changing invoice dates to make it appear that clients owed money within the accounting period, when in fact it was due outside of it, and to make it appear that suppliers were not yet owed money for goods when such liability did exist.

In holding Kevans, the auditors, to be liable, Pennycuick J considered (p. 476) that the changed invoice dates should have aroused suspicion:

> I find the conclusion inescapable, alike on the expert evidence and as a matter of business common sense that at this stage (of discovering the altered invoice dates) he ought to have examined the suppliers' statements and where necessary have communicated with the suppliers.

18.1.6.2 The USA experience

In the absence of much British authority, transatlantic experience is instructive as the accounting standards adopted in Britain and the USA are similar.

In the USA, in 1939, there occurred a case of far-reaching significance, *McKesson and Robins* (1939) 18 Cal App 2d 648, which involved the most ingenious of frauds. The fraud was engineered by four brothers who were operating under different names and who accomplished a massive deception in the operation of a wholly fictitious crude drug business.

Purchases were claimed to have been made by the McKesson company from Canadian vendors who, it was alleged, sold the goods on to customers. The firms to whom it was alleged that the goods had been sold were real but had done no business of the type claimed. The Canadian vendors were either fictitious or blinds used to support the fictitious transactions. The fraud was supported by fictitious invoicing, advice notes and records of communication. The auditors, Price Waterhouse, failed to discover the fraud. The stocks and debtors of the company were consequently overstated by $23 million.

The US Securities and Exchange Commission was extremely critical of the practice of the auditors, emphasising the need for physical contact with the inventory, and the case led to a general change in auditing practice.

The report stated:

> It is unusually clear to us that, prior to this case, many independent public account-
> ants depended entirely too much upon the verification of cash as the basis for the
> whole auditing programme and, hence, as underlying proof of the authenticity of
> all transactions. Where, as here, during the final three years of the audit, physical
> contact with the operations of a major portion of the business was limited to exam-
> inations of supposed documentary evidence of transactions carried on completely
> off-stage through agents unknown to the auditors ... it appears to us that the reli-
> ability of these agents must be established by completely independent methods.

Another notorious US case is also instructive. This is the Salad Oil Swindle case of
1963. De Angelis, an Italian American, had built up a massive vegetable oil empire.
He was able to negotiate warehouse receipts from American Express to commodity
brokers on the basis of his stock.

The stocktaking exercise affords an illustration of the ludicrous acceptance of
fiction as fact. De Angelis's employees would climb to the top of each tank to make
a depth sounding of the oil, which would be shouted down to the American Express
man below, who would slavishly take down the figures. While the team moved from
one vat to the next, the oil would be pumped from one tank to the adjacent one and
this process would continue throughout the warehouse.

The case has had a salutary effect on auditing practice in the USA and in the
UK. The importance of a physical stock check is now established. An auditor is
unwise to take anything on trust from his client, and it is advisable to treat any management statement or assertion with healthy suspicion. Thus a check should be made
of petty cash held (random checks for large firms are probably sufficient). Thus, in
London Oil Storage Co Ltd v Seear Hasluck & Co (1904) (unreported), where the
auditors failed to check the petty cash which, according to the books, amounted to
£760 but which, in fact, amounted to £30, they were held liable in damages.

The balance of moneys in the bank should be verified by a bank statement (*Fox
v Morrish* (1918) 35 TLR 126) and similarly certificates of investments held should
be examined (*Re City Equitable Fire Insurance Co Ltd* [1925] Ch 407).

It may thus be seen that auditing practice has blown the sails of legal practice on
a fresh tack, so that now the standard expected of an auditor is much higher than at
the time of *Re Kingston Cotton Mill*. An auditor might still not be a bloodhound but
he must be a watchdog at the very peak of his performance and must never go to
sleep on the audit – even with one eye open!

18.1.6.3 The auditor's contractual liability

Liability may arise in contract. The auditor will be liable for failing to perform properly what he has undertaken to do. The other party to the contract – the company – is
the only person who can sue the auditor under this head of liability.

The extent of the auditor's liability will be to pay damages resulting from the
breach of contract if the damages are in the contemplation of the parties; for instance,
if the breach is for failure to detect fraud, damages will be awarded to compensate
for further fraud that has been perpetrated after the date when the fraud should have
been detected.

18.1.6.4 The auditor's tortious liability

An auditor may be liable in negligence to his client or in the tort of negligent misstatement to third parties. Formerly, it was the law that there was no duty owed to third parties to exercise care in drawing up accounts. In *Candler v Crane Christmas & Co* [1951] 2 KB 164, the auditors prepared inaccurate accounts which were relied upon by the claimant as the basis of investing money in the company. A majority of the Court of Appeal refused to allow an action in such circumstances.

However, in a historic decision in *Hedley Byrne & Co Ltd v Heller & Partners Ltd* [1964] AC 465, the House of Lords overruled the *Candler* decision. Liability could henceforth arise where an auditor knew or ought to have known that his report would be relied upon and he was negligent in preparing it. Initially, the precise scope of an auditor's liability was not clear. The Institute of Chartered Accountants among others took an optimistic view that it was limited to those persons whom the auditor specifically knew would rely upon the audited accounts.

This view was blown sky high by *JEB Fasteners Ltd v Marks Bloom & Co (a firm)* [1983] 1 All ER 583, affirmed on other grounds. In 1975, the defendants had audited the accounts of BG Fasteners. The audited accounts massively overvalued the company's stock. JEB Fasteners had read the negligently audited accounts. Woolf J held that the defendants owed a duty to the claimants. In the event, there was no liability as the judge held that the negligently audited accounts did not induce the JEB Fasteners' purchase of BG Fasteners. Woolf J relied in his judgment on an earlier unreported English case, *Grover Industrial Holdings Ltd v Newman Harris & Co* (1976) and the judgment of Stocker J in that case, as well as two Commonwealth authorities, the Canadian case of *Haig v Bamford, Hagan, Wicken and Gibson* [1976] WWR 331 (Canada) and the case of *Scott Group Ltd v McFarlane* [1978] NZLR 553 (New Zealand). Both resulted in liability being placed on auditors in similar circumstances to JEB Fasteners.

In the later Scottish case of *Twomax Ltd v Dickson, McFarlane and Robinson* (1982) SC 113, Twomax had acquired a majority stake in a private company, Kintyre Knitwear Ltd. Twomax claimed that in purchasing shares in the company it had relied upon the accounts negligently prepared by the defendants. The court held that the audit was perfunctory and negligent, and the auditors were held liable in damages to the claimants.

In *Caparo Industries plc v Dickman* [1990] 2 AC 605, the House of Lords considered the position of the liability of an audit firm. The third defendants were the auditors Touche Ross. The first and second defendants were the chairman and chief executive of a company called Fidelity. The contention of the claimant, Caparo, was that it was misled by the fraudulent misrepresentations of the first and second defendants which the third defendants, the auditors, had been negligent in failing to detect and report. The House of Lords considered the possible liability of the auditors. It was held in the circumstances that the auditors did not have liability. The auditors owed a duty to the company and not to individual shareholders.

It is clear post-*Caparo* that liability is restricted to cases where the auditor knows of the user and the use to which he will put the information – see *Morgan Crucible Co plc v Hill Samuel Bank Ltd* [1991] 1 All ER 148. Even here, an auditor will not be liable in tort if he reasonably believes that the user will also seek independent advice: see *James McNaughten Paper Group Ltd v Hicks Anderson and Co* [1991] 2 QB 113.

However, a duty may extend beyond the client itself. Thus in *Barings plc v Coopers & Lybrand* [1997] 1 BCLC 427, the Court of Appeal accepted the argument that in principle the auditor of a subsidiary company can owe a duty of care to the parent company. In this case, Barings sought to lay responsibility for the collapse of Barings on the auditors for failure to report on Nick Leeson's fraud in unauthorised futures trading. These activities were carried out through a subsidiary, Barings Securities Ltd. Coopers & Lybrand prepared the consolidated group accounts for Barings, and Coopers & Lybrand, Singapore, audited Barings Securities' consolidation schedules.

The auditors argued that they owed no duty of care to Barings and that the damages being claimed by Barings as a shareholder in its subsidiaries ought to be claimed by the subsidiary.

The Court of Appeal held that Barings had a right of action independent of the company. The court stressed that Coopers & Lybrand, Singapore, knew that their report on Barings Securities' consolidation schedules was required by Barings to enable Barings to demonstrate that the group accounts should give a true and fair view of the group's business.

In the Scottish decision of *The Royal Bank of Scotland plc v Bannerman Johnstone Maclay* (2005) SLT 579, Lord MacFadyen in the Scottish Court of Session (Outer House) had to consider the extent of tortious liability of auditors.

The defendants had audited the accounts of APC Ltd. The bank that advanced money to the company brought an action alleging that a duty was owed to them as the defendant's chartered accountants knew that the company required a substantial overdraft facility from the bank and that the bank required to see monthly management accounts and relied on the annual audited accounts. The defendant argued that for a duty of care to arise, there had to be an intention on their part that the bank should rely on the audited accounts. Lord MacFadyen held that intention was not essential and that knowledge of reliance was sufficient. His Lordship stated that it was open to the defendants to attach a disclaimer of responsibility to the bank, which they had not done. The decision did not deal with the question of whether any loss suffered by the bank fell within the duty. This was not dealt with in this action. The bank had to produce evidence to show negligence.

18.1.6.5 Limiting liability

The Institute of Chartered Accountants of England and Wales recommends that auditors clearly limit their duty to the company's members as a body. Thus, the class of persons to whom an auditor may be liable is somewhat larger than originally envisaged.

If liability is proved, damages are awarded to compensate the claimant for the loss he has sustained by reason of the negligence of the auditor insofar as the losses that they compensate are foreseeable consequences of the auditor's breach of duty.

Section 532 provides for the voidness of provisions protecting auditors from liability which would otherwise attach to them in connection with any negligence, default, breach of duty or breach of trust in relation to the company, occurring in the course of the audit of accounts, or by which a company directly or indirectly provides an indemnity for an auditor of the company or an associated company against any such liability.

Any such provision is void except as permitted by s 533 (indemnity for costs of successfully defending proceedings) or ss 534–536 (liability limitation agreements).

Sections 534 to 536 provide for liability limitation agreements. These are agreements that purport to limit the amount of a liability owed to a company by its auditor in respect of any negligence, default, breach of duty or breach of trust, occurring in the course of the audit of accounts. The liability limitation agreement must not apply in relation to more than one financial year and must specify the financial year in relation to which it applies.

The Secretary of State may by regulations require liability limitation agreements to contain specified provisions or provisions of a specified description, and may prohibit liability limitation agreements from containing specified provisions or provisions of a specified description.

Section 536 provides for the authorisation of liability limitation agreements. It provides for a liability limitation agreement between a private company passing a resolution before it enters into the agreement, waiving the need for approval, or by the company passing a resolution before entering into the agreement approving the agreement's principal terms, or by the company passing a resolution after entering into the agreement approving the agreement itself.

In relation to a public company's auditor, the agreement may be authorised by the company passing a resolution before it enters into the agreement approving the principal terms, or after the agreement is entered into approving the agreement itself.

Section 537 provides that a liability limitation agreement is not effective to limit the auditor's liability to less than such amounts as is fair and reasonable having regard to the auditor's responsibilities, the nature and purpose of the auditor's contractual obligations, and the professional standards expected of him.

Section 538 provides that a company that has entered into a liability limitation agreement must make such disclosure in connection with the agreement as the Secretary of State may require by regulations.

Section 1157 empowers the court to relieve auditors of liability for negligence, default and breach of trust. In addition, it is open to accountants to insure against potential liability, but some of the sums of compensation are potentially so great that this is not always feasible.

18.1.6.6 The auditor's statutory liability

An auditor may be liable in a winding up for misfeasance or breach of duty to the company (s 212 of the Insolvency Act 1986). If this were to be so, the court would order whatever compensation it thinks fit.

18.1.7 Removal, resignation etc. of auditors

Section 510 provides for the removing of an auditor from office. The members of a company may remove an auditor from office at any time. Section 511 provides that this power is only exercisable after special notice has been served (see section 16.4.1). The company must then send a copy of the notice to the person proposed to be removed.

The auditor proposed to be removed may make, with respect to the intended resolution, representations in writing to the company and request their notification to members of the company and the company must circulate those representations.

If the representations are not circulated, then the auditor may require them to be read out at the meeting and this is without prejudice to the auditor's right to be heard at the meeting in any event.

Section 514 deals with the failure to reappoint an auditor and the special procedure that is required if this is to be done by written resolution (private companies only, of course).

If such a resolution is proposed as a written resolution, and its effect would be to appoint a person as auditor other than a person whose term of office has expired or is to expire, then the company must send a copy of the proposed resolution to the person proposed to be appointed and to the outgoing auditor, and the outgoing auditor may, within 14 days of the notice, require that written representations should be circulated to members of the company, and the company must then circulate those representations. If any requirement of the section is not complied with, the resolution is ineffective.

Section 515 deals with the failure to reappoint an auditor at a meeting. The section applies to a resolution at a general meeting whose effect would be to appoint somebody other than the retiring auditor whose term of office has ended.

In such a situation, special notice is required in the case of a private company if the period for appointing auditors has not yet ended since the outgoing auditor ceased to hold office, or such a period has ended and an auditor or auditors should have been appointed but were not.

In the case of a public company, where there has been no accounts meeting of the company since the outgoing auditor ceased to hold office, or there has been an accounts meeting at which an auditor or auditors should have been appointed but were not, in such situations special notice is required.

The outgoing auditor may require his written representations to be circulated and the company must then circulate those written representations.

Section 516 deals with the resignation of an auditor. An auditor may resign by depositing a notice to that effect at the company's registered office. Section 517 provides for the notice to the Registrar of the resignation of an auditor.

Section 518 deals with the rights of a resigning auditor. He may deposit with the notice a signed requisition calling on the directors to convene a general meeting for the purpose of receiving and considering such explanation of the circumstances connected with his resignation as he may wish to place before the meeting, and he may request the company to circulate to its members before the meeting a statement in writing of the circumstances connected with his resignation.

Section 519 provides that where an auditor of an unquoted company ceases for any reason to hold office, he must deposit at the company's registered office a statement of the circumstances connected with his ceasing to hold office unless he considers there are no circumstances in connection with the ceasing to hold office that need to be brought to the attention of members or creditors of the company, and if that is the case he must deposit at the company's registered office a statement to that effect.

Section 520 provides that within 14 days of the deposit of such a statement, the company must send a copy of it to every person entitled to be sent copies of the accounts or apply to the court, and if it applies to the court it must notify the auditor of the application.

Section 521 provides that a copy of the statement must also be sent to the Registrar. Section 522 provides that it is the duty of the auditor to notify the appropriate audit authority where, in the case of a major audit, an auditor ceases for any reason to hold office, or in the case of an audit that is not a major audit, ceases to hold office before the end of his term of office.

Section 523 similarly provides that it is the duty of a company to notify the appropriate audit authority where an auditor ceases to hold office before the end of his term of office and that this statement must be accompanied by a statement by the company of the reason for his ceasing to hold office, or, if a copy of the statement deposited by the auditor at the company's registered office in accordance with s 519 contains a statement of the circumstances in connection with the ceasing to hold office, must annex that statement.

Section 524 provides that the information given to the audit authority must then be passed to the accounting authorities and they may, if the appropriate audit authority considers it appropriate, forward to those authorities a copy of the statement or statements accompanying the notice.

The accounting authorities are the Secretary of State and any other person authorised by him under s 456.

18.1.8 Quoted companies and the rights of members to raise audit concerns at accounts meetings

Section 527 provides that members of a quoted company may require the company to publish on a website a statement setting out any matter relating to the audit of the company's accounts or any circumstances connected with the auditor of the company ceasing to hold office since the previous accounts meeting, that the members propose to raise at the next accounts meeting.

To exercise rights under the section, members must represent at least 5 per cent of the total voting rights of all members who have a relevant right to vote, or at least 100 members who have a relevant right to vote and hold shares in the company on which there has been paid up an average sum per member of at least £100.

Section 528 deals with website availability. The information must be made available on a website that is maintained by or on behalf of the company, and identifies the company in question, and access to the information on the website and the ability to obtain a hard copy of the information from the website must not be conditional on the payment of a fee or otherwise restricted. The statement must be made available within three working days of the company being required to publish it on a website, and must be kept available until after the meeting to which it relates.

Section 529 provides that a quoted company must, in the notice it gives of the accounts meeting, draw attention to the possibility of placing a statement on the website and the effect of the provisions of the Act.

Section 530 provides that it is an offence for any company officer to fail to comply with these website requirements.

18.2 Annual return

Section 853 provides that every company must deliver to the Registrar successive annual returns, each of which is made up to a date not later than the date that is, from time to time, the company's return date.

The company's return date is the anniversary of the company's incorporation, or if the company's last return delivered in accordance with the Act was made up to a different date, the anniversary of that date.

Section 855 provides for the contents of the annual return. The following information must be detailed:

(a) the address of the company's registered office;
(b) the type of company it is and its principal business activities;
(c) the prescribed particulars of:

   (i) the directors of the company, and
   (ii) in the case of a private company with a secretary or a public company, the secretary or joint secretaries;

(d) if the register of members is not kept available for inspection at the registered office, the address of the place where it is kept available for inspection, and if there is a register of debenture holders which is not kept available for inspection at the company's registered office, the address of where it is kept available for inspection;
(e) a statement of the company's capital and the total number of shares, the aggregate nominal value of the shares, and the rights attaching to different classes of shares, together with the aggregate nominal value of shares of that class. It should also set out the amount paid and the amount, if any, unpaid on each share. Clearly these provisions only apply if the company has a share capital; and
(f) prescribed particulars of every person who is a member of the company or who ceased to be a member of the company during the period since the last return. It must also state the number of shares held by each member of the company at the date the return is made up and the number of shares that have been transferred since the date of the last return by each member or person who has ceased to be a member.

Section 858 provides that if a company fails to deliver an annual return before the end of the period of 28 days after the return date, this constitutes an offence by the company, and every director of the company and every secretary of the company and every officer of the company who is in default.

A procedure now exists for updating existing information: the so-called shuttle return.

Summary

Auditors

All companies except dormant companies and certain exempt private companies must appoint auditors. The auditors have statutory protection if they are to be removed from office. They also have rights to bring matters to the attention of members where they resign.

Auditors must be qualified with a recognised body.

The auditor must adopt a strict approach in conducting the audit. There is a statutory obligation to report to the company on the accounts. There will also be contractual duties owed to the company flowing from the contract concluded between the company and the auditors.

Auditors also owe a duty of care to third parties whom they know are going to rely on the audited accounts for specific purposes without the benefit of other independent advice.

Auditors may, subject to restrictions, limit their liability.

Members of a quoted company may require the company to publish their audit concerns on a website.

Annual return

Every company must file an annual return concerning information about the company's activities, officers, shares and debentures. There is now a simplified 'shuttle return' procedure for updating existing information.

Self-test questions

18.1   What type of company must make provision for the audit of their accounts?

18.2   What is the annual return?

Further reading

S Chua, 'The Auditor's Liability in Negligence in Respect of the Audit Report' [1995] JBL 1.

H Cohen, 'Auditors' Liability for Negligence: A Time for Reform?' (1993) 8 JIBL 133.

W Doralt and others, 'Auditors' Liability and Its Impact on the European Financial Markets' [2008] CLJ 62.

M Hemraj, 'Audit Failure Due to Negligent Audit: Lessons From DTI Investigations' (2003) Co Law 45.

PE Morris, 'Contractual Limitations on the Auditor's Liability' [2009] 72 MLR 607.

PE Morris and J Stevenson, 'Accountancy: Auditors Negligence and Incorporation' (1996) 176 Bus LR 54.

A Underwood, 'Can Auditors Be Held Liable for Third Party Losses Resulting From Company Fraud?' (2009) 158 NLJ 1175.

Chapter 19

Secretary

Chapter Contents

19.1 Introduction

One hundred years ago, a company secretary would have found his powers were few. The question of the authority of the company secretary was considered many years ago in *Barnett Hoares & Co v South London Tramways Co* (1887) 18 QBD 815.

In this case, the South London Tramways Co had made an agreement with Messrs Green and Burleigh, who were contractors, to construct part of the tramline. The company, as is common in building and construction contracts, retained a certain percentage of the amounts for which their engineer had certified completion, since Green and Burleigh were to maintain the line for a period of time. The retention money was payable to the contractors at the end of this period. The contractors had applied to the bankers, Barnett Hoares & Co, for a loan and had given them as security a letter that purported to assign to them the retention money of £2,000 under the contract.

The bankers had then written to the Tramways company's secretary for the confirmation that £2,000 was held and the required confirmation had been given. When Barnett Hoares were not paid back by the contractors, they had claimed the retention money. They then discovered that only £675 was held as retention money, despite the written assurances of the secretary. The issue in the case they brought against the company concerned the authority of the company secretary. Had he had the authority to bind the company?

The outcome in the case was clear and unequivocal: the company secretary had not had the authority to bind the company.

As Lord Esher MR said (p. 817):

> A secretary is a mere servant; his position is that he is to do what he is told and no person can assume that he has any authority to represent anything at all, nor can anyone assume that statements made by him are necessarily to be accepted as trustworthy without further enquiry.

Things have changed. In 1971, the Court of Appeal again considered the role and significance of the company secretary in *Panorama Developments (Guildford) Ltd v Fidelis Furnishing Fabrics Ltd* [1971] 2 QB 711.

Panorama Developments (Guildford) Ltd ran a car hire business which was called Belgravia Executive Car Rental. The company fleet comprised limousines which included Rolls-Royces and Jaguars. Fidelis Furnishing Fabrics Ltd was a company of good repute, and its managing director was a man of integrity. However, its company secretary, RL Bayne, was not of the same cloth. He told Panorama that Fidelis wished to hire cars so that he could meet important customers at Heathrow Airport. He claimed that he took these customers to the company's office and the company's factory in Leeds.

This was not true. No customers were met at Heathrow and the company did not have a factory in Leeds. The cars had been used by Bayne personally. Panorama sued Fidelis Fabrics for their hire charges.

As in the earlier Barnett case, the defendants argued that they were not bound by the acts of their company secretary, who fulfilled a very humble role and had no authority to make any contracts or representations on behalf of the company.

However, the Court of Appeal decided that, on the contrary, the company secretary had bound the company. In considering the Barnett case, Lord Denning MR said (p. 20):

> But times have changed. A company secretary is a much more important person nowadays than he was in 1887. He is an officer of the company with extensive duties and responsibilities. This appears not only in the modern Companies Acts, but also by the role which he plays in the day-to-day business of companies. He is no longer a mere clerk. He regularly makes representations on behalf of the company and enters into contracts on its behalf which come within the day-to-day running of the company's business. So much so that he may be regarded as held out as having authority to do such things on behalf of the company. He is certainly entitled to sign contracts connected with the administrative side of a company's affairs, such as employing staff, and ordering cars, and so forth. All such matters now come within the ostensible authority of a company secretary.

Today, then, the secretary is one of the principal officers of the company and he is the agent through whom much of the company's administrative work is done. Indeed, when making contracts on behalf of the company, it is advisable for the secretary to ensure that he does so as agent of the company to avoid any personal liability.

As an officer, the secretary will be liable to a default fine for contravention along with directors under many provisions of the Companies Acts. The Department of Business, Innovation and Skills brings many prosecutions for offences under the Companies Acts, especially concerning failures to lodge documents with the Registrar of Companies.

The secretary will in all probability be an employee, entitled as a 'clerk or servant' to rank as a preferential creditor, and as such will be paid off first in a liquidation. However, secretaries who do not give their whole time to the company and perform their duties through a deputy are not within the scope of the provision. This was decided in the case of *Cairney v Back* [1906] 2 KB 746.

In this case, the company secretary of Consolidated Mines Ltd had to attend directors' meetings, deal with the correspondence and callers, and keep the minute book. Walton J considered that, if the evidence had stopped there, then the defendant would have been a clerk or servant. However, although the defendant was generally at the office from 12 pm to 2 pm, he had no particular hours of attendance. He also paid a clerk who worked regularly from 10 am to 5 pm. In other words, the general work of the company falling within his purview was really done by the clerk. The defendant did not, therefore, exactly serve the company. Rather he provided services, attending himself occasionally when required. He was not an employee.

With the Companies Act 2006 it is no longer necessary for a private company to have a secretary (s 270 CA 2006). If it chooses to have one it will still have to enter particulars in its register of secretaries and send details of any changes to Companies House as with the secretary of a public company (s 276 CA 2006).

A company secretary will henceforth be able to register a service address which, just as in the case of directors, may be stated as the company's registered office so that a secretary, just as a director, does not have to disclose his home address (s 277 CA 2006).

19.2 Duties of the secretary

As an officer, the secretary owes fiduciary duties to the company and is liable for any secret gain made from the company. An illustration of this principle is *Re Morvah Consols Tin Mining Co* (1875) 2 ChD 1. One James Hammon sold a tin mine in Cornwall to a certain McKay, who set up a company to purchase the mine. McKay became company secretary. Hammon was to be paid partly in cash and partly in shares, and McKay was to receive some shares for setting up the deal. The company knew nothing of this.

Later, the company was wound up by the Stannary Court. (The tin mines of Devon and Cornwall, or Stannaries, were formerly subject to a special legal regime. The jurisdiction is now exercised by the Cornish County Court.) McKay was ordered to pay over the value of the shares to the liquidator because he was in breach of his fiduciary duty.

19.3 Responsibilities of the secretary

Formerly, when companies tended to be smaller, their affairs less complex and the legal requirements less onerous, the company secretary was typically a clerk who was employed to perform routine work under orders. Today, the responsibilities of the company secretary would usually include:

(a) preparing and keeping minutes of board and general meetings (s 248 and s 355 CA 2006);
(b) dealing with share transfers and issuing share and debenture certificates;
(c) keeping and maintaining the register of members and debenture holders (s 113 and s 743 CA 2006) (in large public companies, a professional share registrar often maintains these registers as well as dealing with share transfers);
(d) keeping and maintaining the register of directors and secretary (s 162 and s 275 CA 2006);
(e) the registration of charges and the maintaining of the company's register of charges (s 860 and ss 875–876 CA 2006);
(f) keeping copies of directors' contracts (s 228 CA 2006);
(g) keeping and maintaining the register of share interests (s 808 CA 2006);
(h) sending notices of meetings, copies of accounts, etc.;
(i) keeping the company's articles up to date;
(j) preparing and submitting the annual return (s 854 CA 2006);
(k) filing with the Registrar of numerous returns and documents;
(l) preparation of the numerous returns required by government departments and official bodies;
(m) witnessing documents – that is, signing as witness (together with a director) against the company seal or otherwise; and
(n) payment of dividends and the preparation of dividend warrants.

Depending on the size of the headquarters staff, the company secretary may also be the chief accounting officer, have charge of staff employment and pension matters, obtain legal advice from solicitors and confer with the auditors. If the company is quoted, he may also deal with the Stock Exchange. It is entirely possible that still other responsibilities may be placed upon the secretary and staff by the company's articles.

19.4 Qualifications

Because of the great welter of statutory duties and the increasing responsibilities placed on company secretaries, it was inevitable that a company secretary should have to possess a relevant qualification. Although there are no mandatory qualifications for a company secretary of a private company, there are for a public company. According to s 273 CA 2006, it is the duty of directors of a public company to take all reasonable steps to ensure that the secretary or each joint secretary of the company is a person with the requisite knowledge and experience and who:

(a) was the secretary of a public company for at least three of the five years immediately preceding the appointment as secretary; or

(b) is a member of one of the following professional bodies:

> The Institute of Chartered Accountants in England and Wales;
> The Institute of Chartered Accountants of Scotland;
> The Association of Certified Accountants;
> The Institute of Chartered Accountants in Ireland;
> The Institute of Chartered Secretaries and Administrators;
> The Institute of Chartered Management Accountants;
> The Chartered Institute of Public Finance and Accountancy; or

(c) is qualified in the United Kingdom as a barrister, or an advocate or a solicitor; or

(d) is a person who, by virtue of holding or having held any other position or being a member of any other body, appears to the directors to be capable of discharging the functions of a secretary.

It should be noted that the obligation is a continuing one so that, for example, if a person ceases to hold an appropriate qualification, the directors should reconsider his appointment.

It is somewhat ironic that there should be minimum qualifications for the company secretary of a public company but not for directors. Nothing could better illustrate the change in the role of the company secretary and the law's perception of this.

Summary

Responsibilities

Responsibilities include: the preparation and keeping of minutes of board and general meetings; dealing with share transfers and issuing share and debenture certificates;

keeping and maintaining the register of members and debenture holders; keeping and maintaining the register of directors and secretary; the registration of charges and the maintaining of the company's register of charges; keeping and maintaining the register of directors' share interests; sending notices of meetings and copies of accounts; keeping the company's articles up to date; preparation and submission of the annual return; payment of dividends and the preparation of dividend warrants.

Duties

The secretary owes fiduciary duties to the company and is liable for any secret gain made from the company: *Re Morvah Consols Tin Mining Co* (1875).

Qualifications

Private companies are not required to have a secretary, but may do so. In a public company, a company secretary must possess a recognised qualification. A company secretary may be a director but need not be one.

Self-test questions

19.1   What is the function of a company secretary?

19.2   What are the duties of a company secretary?

19.3   Set out the major statutory responsibilities of a company secretary.

19.4   What qualifications are needed in relation to the company secretary of a public company?

Further reading

D Armour, *The ICSA Company Secretary's Checklists*, 6th edn 2009, published by the Institute of Chartered Secretaries and Administrators.

D Armour, *ICSA Company Secretary's Handbook*, 9th edn 2012, published by the Institute of Chartered Secretaries and Administrators.

K Eddy, *Chartered Secretary Magazine*, published by DSA. This magazine provides useful updates and insights into company secretarial practice.

R Severn, 'Protection and Respect Are Due to the Company Secretary' (1996) 43 IHL 21.

Chapter 20

Debentures and the law of mortgages

20.1 Introduction

Debentures are, in general, subject to the same principles as ordinary mortgages. Equitable principles protect mortgagors against 'clogging the equity of redemption', that is, making it difficult to redeem or placing some restriction on redemption. These clogs may include making the mortgage irredeemable or redeemable only after a long time or providing some commercial advantage to the lender of money as against the borrower of the money. In relation to debentures, there is no rule prohibiting debentures from being irredeemable or redeemable only after a long period of time. Section 739 of the Companies Act 2006 provides that:

> A condition contained in debentures, or in a deed for securing debentures, is not invalid by reason only that the debentures are made irredeemable or redeemable only on the happening of a contingency (however remote), or on the expiration of a period (however long), any rule of equity to the contrary notwithstanding.

In *Knightsbridge Estates Trust Ltd v Byrne* [1940] AC 613, a company that had secured a loan by mortgaging its property to the lender of the money argued that the provision that the mortgage would last for 40 years was void as an unreasonable restriction on the mortgagor. The court held that the mortgage constituted a debenture within the Companies Act and, therefore, was not void. Other restrictions placed upon the mortgagor may well be invalid. Thus, in *Kreglinger v New Patagonia Meat & Cold Storage Co Ltd* [1914] AC 25, the court recognised that requiring the borrower to sell sheepskins to the lender of finance for a period of time could constitute an unfair clog on the equity of redemption. In the event, on the facts of the particular case, it was held not to be unreasonable. The agreement provided that for five years the borrower should sell the skins to the lender so long as the lender was willing to buy at the best price offered by any other person.

20.2 Types of debentures

Every trading or commercial company has an implied power to borrow for the purposes of its business. Thus, for example, an auctioneer was held to have the implied power to borrow money in *General Auction, Estate and Monetary Co v Smith* [1891] 3 Ch 432. Clearly, any company incorporated under the Companies Act 2006 without any restriction on its objects may do so. Companies with objects clauses will be able to borrow money to achieve their objects unless there is some express prohibition in the objects clause.

A company's articles may restrict the company's powers to borrow money. There was such a provision in Table A of the Companies Act 1948, but there was no similar provision in the 1985 Table A. Nor do the model articles of private or public companies under the Companies Act 2006 contain any restriction.

The term debenture is used in many senses. Usually, debentures are secured, but they need not be. A debenture is generally under the company seal, but once again need not be.

There may be a single debenture, typically a secured loan from a bank. By contrast there may be an issue of debenture stock where a loan is raised, usually by means of an offer to the public via the Stock Exchange. Where there is debenture stock, there will be a debenture trust deed. The trust deed will set out the terms of the loan. There may also be a debenture trust deed where there is a series of debentures – that is to say, several separate loans made to people that rank for payment *pari passu* (equally one with the other). By virtue of s 738 CA 2006, a debenture covers any form of borrowing by a company whether secured or unsecured. The definition reads as follows:

'Debenture' includes debenture stock, bonds and any other securities of a company, whether constituting a charge on the assets of the company or not.

In practice, the term debenture is used to describe a secured borrowing. A mortgage that is created by a company is also a debenture: see *Knightsbridge Estates Trust Ltd v Byrne* (1940). The claimants owned freehold property in Knightsbridge. The property was mortgaged to a friendly society and the mortgage was to be repaid over a period of 40 years. The company wanted to redeem the mortgage early.

The House of Lords held that the company had no right to redeem the mortgage early as the equitable doctrine that provided for early redemption did not apply to mortgages granted by companies.

20.3 Debentures compared with shares

Debentures and shares have certain similarities. They are both collectively termed securities. Dealings in debentures on the Stock Exchange are carried out in much the same way as dealings in shares. Prospectus rules are applicable to both shares and debentures in much the same way. There are certain distinctions between shares and debentures, however.

The main distinctions are as follows:

(a) the essential distinction between the two is that a debenture holder is a creditor of the company whereas a shareholder is a member of the company;
(b) the company is free to purchase its own debentures;
(c) debentures may be issued at a discount whereas shares cannot be issued at less than par value (see s 580 CA 2006); and
(d) interest on a debenture when due is a debt which can be paid out of capital. There is no automatic right to a dividend and dividends are payable out of profits.

(See also section 4.1.)

20.4 Debenture trust deeds

Where there is a debenture trust deed, which there will be if debenture stock has been issued, the trustee acts as the company's creditor. He acts on behalf of all debenture holders. It is his duty to ensure that the terms of the debentures are enforced.

The trustee of debentures may, for example, act to appoint an administrative receiver on behalf of all the debenture holders where there has been a breach of the terms of the debenture. The receiver (see Chapter 21) will be responsible for taking possession of the property that is the subject of the charge with a view to realising the property and paying off the debenture holders. This process is explained in Chapter 21 (see sections 21.3 and 21.4).

Certain conditions are uniform:

(a) a covenant to repay the amount of the loan at the appropriate time and to pay interest upon the due dates. In default of either of these requirements, the whole loan becomes immediately repayable;

(b) the creation of a floating charge over some or all of the company's assets;

(c) the creation of a fixed charge over the company's fixed assets;

(d) on the happening of certain events, the whole amount of the loan to become immediately repayable – for example, the company ceasing business;

(e) a covenant to keep the company's property insured;

(f) a covenant to keep the company's property in good repair; and

(g) the powers and the duties of the debenture trustee will also be set out in the debenture trust deed.

The advantages of a debenture trust deed are clear. It enables the company to deal with the trustee for debenture holders on behalf of all of the debenture holders and thus to act expeditiously. The trustee of debentures will be supplied with information by the company on the state of the company's business. The trustee of debentures would generally be somebody expert in business and he will thus be able to act with alacrity and with expert knowledge where the debenture holders may lack the appropriate knowledge and would in any event find it difficult to act as promptly as the trustee for debenture holders.

Once it was common to exonerate trustees of debentures in advance for any breach of trust by a provision in the trust deed. Now such provisions are generally void (s 750 CA 2006). Debenture holders may give a release to a trustee for past defaults at a meeting of debenture holders by special resolution (s 750(2) CA 2006).

Section 751 CA 2006 also provides for the continuation of certain earlier provisions relieving trustees of debentures from liability.

20.5 A fixed charge

Although technically, under s 738 CA 2006, any form of borrowing by a company is a debenture, in practice the term is used to describe a secured borrowing. The borrowing may be secured in one or both of two different ways. The debenture may be secured by a fixed charge. This is similar to an ordinary mortgage. The charge attaches to the property subject to the charge at the time of its creation. A fixed charge over land is the most common form of fixed charge. A fixed charge may be created over other assets, however. Thus a fixed charge may be created over investments held by the company. It seems in addition that a fixed charge may be created over a company's book debts provided that these book debts are paid into a separate bank account: see *Re Keenan Bros Ltd* [1986] BCLC 242 (Irish Supreme Court) and *Siebe Gorman & Co Ltd v Barclays Bank Ltd* [1979] 2 Lloyds Rep 142.

This latter case concerned RH McDonald Ltd, who executed a debenture in favour of Barclays Bank. This debenture charged, by way of a fixed charge, all book debts and other debts owing to McDonald Limited. McDonald were required to pay the proceeds of book debts into a separate account with Barclays. They were further prohibited from charging or assigning the proceeds to any other person. Later Siebe Gorman, a supplier of safety equipment to McDonald, who were chasing payment for unpaid debts, agreed to accept an assignment of certain book debts from McDonald.

McDonald went into liquidation and this case concerned a dispute between Barclays, claiming under the debenture, and Siebe Gorman, claiming under the later assignment.

Slade J held that the debenture conferred a fixed charge in favour of Barclays Bank. This fixed charge over book debts was effective.

However, in *Re New Bullas Trading Ltd* [1994] 1 BCLC 485, Knox J held that a charge over the company's book debts constituted a floating charge. In this case, the charge was over book debts which also provided that money paid was to be paid into an account at a named bank. It was then for the chargee to direct how the money was to be used but, in default, the money was removed from the fixed charge and became subject to a floating charge. The Court of Appeal held that uncollected debts were subject to a fixed charge.

In the Privy Council appeal from the Court of Appeal from New Zealand, *Agnew v Commissioner of Inland Revenue, Re Brumark* [2001] 2 AC 710, the case concerned a debenture that was closely modelled on the *New Bullas* debenture.

Lord Millett, delivering the judgment of the board in *Agnew*, held that the critical feature distinguishing a floating charge from a fixed charge lay in the chargor's ability, freely and without the chargee's consent, to control and manage the charge assets and withdraw them from the security. The Privy Council considered that *New Bullas* had been wrongly decided and the decision in *Siebe Gorman* was treated in guarded terms as a case in which Slade J had found sufficient restrictions on the use to which the chargor could put the collected debt payments to warrant that the charge was a fixed charge.

The issue arose once again in the House of Lords decision in *Re Spectrum Plus Ltd (in liquidation)* [2005] 2 AC 680. Here a charge over present and future book debts, where the chargor was required to collect and place the debts in a designated account with the chargee bank, but where the chargor was free to draw on the account for its business purposes provided the overdraft limit was not exceeded, was held in law to be a floating charge, even if it was expressed as being a fixed charge.

The House of Lords held that the unrestricted use by the chargor of the proceeds in the account was inconsistent with the creation of a fixed charge, since it allowed the debt and its proceeds to be withdrawn from the security.

The House of Lords held, following the Privy Council decision of *Re Brumark* in which *New Bullas* had been held to be wrongly decided, that *Siebe Gorman* was wrong and should be overruled. Although the decision in *Re Spectrum* overruled long-standing authority which had been relied upon for many years by banks and other commercial lenders, the House of Lords felt that it was inappropriate to depart from the normal circumstances in which a decision has retrospective effect and did not feel that this was an appropriate case for a decision that only had prospective effect.

20.6 A floating charge

The second type of security is called a floating charge. The ability to create a floating charge is one of the advantages of incorporation; however, since the impact of the Enterprise Act 2002, holders of floating charges created on or after 15 September 2003, with few exceptions, will not be able to appoint an administrative receiver (a narrow category of specialist financing transactions are exempted from this general prohibition – see ss 72B–72G of the Insolvency Act 1986). The floating charge enables a company to raise finance by mortgaging its entire assets and undertaking back to the provider of the finance and yet continue to trade. A floating charge does not attach to the property that is the subject of the charge until the charge crystallises. Until this time, the company is free to carry on trading with the property that is the subject of the charge. The characteristics of the floating charge are set out in *Re Yorkshire Woolcombers Association Ltd (Illingworth v Houldsworth)* [1904] AC 355. These are: that the floating charge is over a class of assets present and future; that the company can continue to do business and to dispose of the assets in the course of that business; and that the assets within the class of assets subject to the floating charge will fluctuate and change as the company trades.

In the House of Lords, the Lord Chancellor, the Earl of Halsbury, described a floating charge thus (p. 357):

> In the first place, you have that which in a sense I suppose must be an element in the definition of a floating security, that it is something which is to float, not to be put into immediate operation, but such that the company is to be allowed to carry on its business. It contemplates not only that it should carry with it the book debts which were then existing, but it contemplates also the possibility of those book debts being extinguished by payment to the company, and that other book debts should come in and take the place of those that had disappeared. That, my Lords, seems to me to be an essential characteristic of what is properly called a floating security.

In *Re GE Tunbridge Ltd* [1995] 1 BCLC 34, the charge was expressed to be a fixed charge over all the company's assets other than land or trading stock. This would have included office equipment and book debts. Since the characteristics of a floating charge, as set out in *Re Yorkshire Woolcombers Association*, were present, these were held to be subject to a floating charge.

Generally, if the company is able to deal with the charged property in the normal course of business, the charge is a floating charge but, in *Re Cimex Tissues* [1995] 1 BCLC 409, although the company had a limited power to deal with the charged machines, the charge was still held to be a fixed one.

A floating charge will crystallise in certain circumstances:

(a) if the company goes into liquidation;

(b) if a receiver is appointed either by the court or under the terms of the debenture;

(c) if there is cessation of the company's trade or business: *Re Woodroffes (Musical Instruments) Ltd* [1986] Ch 366; or

(d) if an event occurs which by the terms of the debenture causes the floating charge to crystallise.

There is doubt as to whether the happening of an event specified in the debenture would cause automatic crystallisation of the charge or whether the happening of the event merely permits the debenture holders to act to bring about crystallisation. In *Re Manurewa Transport Ltd* [1971] NZLR 909, the New Zealand court held that crystallisation could occur automatically on the happening of the specified event. This view was approved *obiter* by Hoffmann J in *Re Brightlife Ltd* [1986] 3 All ER 673, and confirmed by him in *Re Permanent Houses (Holdings) Ltd* [1988] BCLC 563. In this case Hoffmann J held that a clause providing for default events involving crystallisation and becoming immediately enforceable was effective to trigger automatic crystallisation.

20.7 Registration of charges

The charges that require registration are set out in s 860 CA 2006. They are:

(a) a charge on land or an interest in land other than a charge for rent;
(b) a charge on goods or any interest in goods;
(c) a charge on intangible movable property which includes:

> goodwill,
> intellectual property,
> book debts,
> uncalled share capital of the company or calls made but not paid, and
> a charge for securing an issue of debentures;

(d) a floating charge on the company's property or undertaking; and
(e) a charge on a ship or aircraft, or any share in a ship.

The Secretary of State may amend the categories of registrable charges by regulation (s 894 CA 2006).

Sections 860 to 862 CA 2006 require registration of prescribed particulars of these charges within 21 days of their creation. Failure to register the prescribed particulars of a charge renders the charge void under s 874. It does not affect the validity of the debt, of course. The obligation to register the prescribed particulars of the charge is an obligation placed upon the company and therefore failure to register a charge constitutes an offence by the company and any officer who is in default. Since the creditor has an interest in registering the prescribed particulars of the charge, it may well be that he will undertake to effect the registration (s 860(2) CA 2006).

The Act requires that the prescribed particulars are delivered to the Registrar of Companies for registration.

The obligation to register prescribed particulars also extends to the situation where the company acquires a piece of property that is already mortgaged (s 862 CA 2006). Failure to register particulars of such a charge, however, does not render the charge invalid but merely results in the liability of the company and any officer in default (s 862(4); and see s 874). Provision is made in s 873 for late delivery of particulars to the Registrar after the 21 days' time limit has passed. Rectification of the register of charges may be made on application of the company or a person interested and on such terms and conditions as seem to the court just and expedient. If the court is satisfied that the failure to register the charge before the end of the permitted period or the omission of any particular:

(i)   was accidental or due to inadvertence or to some other sufficient cause; or
(ii)   is not of a nature to prejudice the position of creditors or shareholders of the company, or alternatively that on other grounds it is just and equitable

then late registration may be permitted.

If at the time of delivery of the particulars the company is unable to pay its debts as they fall due, or subsequently becomes unable to do so as a result of the transaction involving the charge, and insolvency proceedings begin before the end of the relevant period, then the charge is void against the administrator, liquidator or other person. The relevant time period is two years in the case of a floating charge in favour of a connected person, one year in the case of a floating charge in favour of an unconnected person and six months in any other case (see section 25.2).

20.8 Discharge of charges

Section 872 CA 2006 provides for entries of satisfaction and release.

This statement is delivered to the Registrar verifying with respect to a registered charge that the debt for which the charge was given has been paid or satisfied in whole or in part. When part or all of the property or undertaking charged has been released from the charge, then the Registrar may enter on the register a memorandum of satisfaction in whole or of the fact that part of the property or undertaking has been released from the charge or ceased to form part of the company's property, as the case may be.

Where the Registrar enters a memorandum of satisfaction in whole, the Registrar will send the company a copy of it.

20.9 Priorities amongst charges

As has been noted, a fixed charge applies to the property it covers from the point of creation. A fixed charge will usually take priority over a subsequent fixed charge and over any floating charge no matter when created. This is, however, subject to the proviso that, if a floating charge is created prior to a fixed charge, and the floating charge prohibits the creation of any subsequent charge with priority over that floating charge, and this condition is actually registered with the prescribed particulars at the company's registry, then that floating charge will take ahead of a subsequent fixed charge.

A floating charge attaches to the property that it covers when it crystallises. Generally, a floating charge will take priority over a subsequent floating charge: see *Re Benjamin Cope & Sons Ltd* [1914] 1 Ch 800. An exception to this general principle is if a company retains the power to create a later floating charge that covers only a particular class of assets enjoying priority over an earlier floating charge: see

Re Automatic Bottle Makers [1926] Ch 412. The company here manufactured glass bottles and other glassware. The company issued a series of debentures and by a debenture trust deed created a general floating charge over all its undertaking and assets present and future. The company retained the power to create in priority to that charge such mortgages or charges as the company should think proper

> by the deposit of any dock warrants, bills of lading, or other similar commercial documents, or upon any raw materials, or finished or partly finished products and stock for the purpose of raising moneys in the ordinary course of the business of the company.

In pursuance of this, Automatic Bottle Makers charged documents, material and stock to raise money by way of floating charge to rank ahead of the floating charge created by the trust deed.

The Court of Appeal held that the company had the power to create a second specific floating charge with priority over the first general floating charge.

20.10 Special circumstances affecting priorities

In relation to floating charges, three particular situations need to be noted:

(a) a judgment creditor in all probability takes priority over a floating charge if he has been paid at the time the charge crystallises or if the company's goods have been seized and sold, even though the proceeds are still retained by the bailiff;

(b) a landlord may retain goods belonging to the company and any subsequent proceeds from the sale of those goods where he is distraining for rent before the floating charge has crystallised; and

(c) any preferential debts of the company are to be paid out of assets that are subject to a floating charge if there are no other assets free of the charge sufficient to pay off the preferential debts. Preferential debts are examined in detail below in section 25.4.

Furthermore, a floating charge may be invalid in certain circumstances. Under s 245 of the Insolvency Act 1986, a floating charge that is created in favour of a connected person within the period two years before the onset of insolvency is invalid, except to the extent that it is made for good consideration or within 12 months of the onset of insolvency if it is made in favour of an unconnected person. If it is made in favour of an unconnected person, it also needs to be demonstrated that at the time that the charge was created, the company was unable to pay its debts. This condition does not apply where the charge was created in favour of a connected person.

The following are connected with a company:

(a) a director or shadow director of the company;

(b) an associate of a director or shadow director of the company; and

(c) an associate of the company.

An associate includes a person's spouse, relatives, partners and their spouses and relatives, employers, employees and companies that the person and his associates control.

The charged property cannot be used for securing certain debts but the debts are still payable.

In *Re Fairway Magazines Limited* [1993] BCLC 643, also considered below, a floating charge was created in favour of a director. The company subsequently went into insolvent liquidation, and the liquidator argued that the charge constituted a preference under s 239. He also argued that £15,000 had been paid in advance of the creation of the charge and was not protected by s 245(2)(a) insofar as it was argued by the liquidator that it was not for money paid or goods or services supplied at the same time or after the creation of the charge. Mummery J considered that the advance of cash could pre-date the creation of the charge, saying that as a matter of common sense it was impossible for the two to be made simultaneously and that there would inevitably be a gap between payment and the creation of the charge. What was necessary was to look at the substance of the transaction.

In *Re Shoe Lace Ltd, Power v Sharp Investments Ltd* [1992] BCLC 636, however, Hoffmann J, at first instance, thought the wording of the section required one to ask whether a reasonable businessman would consider that the money was paid at the same time as the charge was created.

In *Re Shoe Lace Ltd, Power v Sharp Investments Ltd* [1994] 1 BCLC 111, in the Court of Appeal, it was decided that, where there was a gap between the advance of cash and the creation of the charge, s 245 would come into play unless it was the briefest of delays. Any delay in the execution of the debenture will result in invalidity unless it really is de minimis.

In *Rehman v Chamberlain* [2011] All ER (D) 127 (Sep), the timing of the creation of a floating charge was at issue.

Rehman had advanced money to the company on 12 February 2009. The advance was later secured by a floating charge dated 27 February 2009. During the course of the year the company went into liquidation. The liquidator sought to avoid the charge on the basis that it was created within the relevant time.

Rehman claimed that the charge was agreed on 12 February 2009 and that that was the date that the debenture should be dated. The court held that the advance of money in anticipation of the charge did not amount to a contract for immediate security. Rehman's appeal was accordingly dismissed, and the charge was held to be void.

The company went into administration on 15 October 2009 and into creditors' involuntary liquidation on 18 February 2010.

The debenture was dated 27 February 2009 and would therefore be caught within the 12 months prior to the administration; see s 245 of the Insolvency Act 1986. However, the credit was advanced on 12 February 2009, i.e. outside of the period, and if the register were to be rectified to demonstrate this as the date of the charge then it would not be caught by s 245.

It was held that the debenture was created within the 12-month period.

It is also possible that a fixed or floating charge may be found to be invalid under s 239 of the Insolvency Act 1986 as a preference. If it is made in favour of a connected person, once again, the period of time is two years preceding the onset of insolvency. If it is made in favour of an unconnected person, the period is six months, ending with the onset of insolvency.

One of the guiding principles behind the insolvency legislation is to achieve equal treatment for like creditors. Therefore, preferring some creditors to others has to be tackled. In *Re Beacon Leisure Limited* [1991] BCC 213, rent was paid to a director before the due date by the company. The date of payment had not arrived and the assets of the company were diminished by the payments. However, the judge accepted that there was no preference. On the face of it, the decision seems somewhat surprising.

In *Re Fairway Magazines Limited* (1993), Mummery J held that there was no preference where a director of a company that was in financial difficulties and who had guaranteed the company's overdraft agreed to extend the borrowing facility to the company in return for a floating charge over the company's assets. It was held that the creation of the charge was part of a scheme that would enable the company to continue to do business. This was not a case of asset depletion but rather of survival of the company. It was held that the transaction was not motivated by a desire to prefer (see also section 25.2).

20.10.1 Reservation of title

There are certain additional features that need to be borne in mind in relation to priority of charges (the same features will need to be borne in mind in relation to liquidations). If a company has goods that are let out under a hire purchase agreement, or are leased and, therefore, do not belong to the company, the owner of the goods clearly retains title to them. A similar principle applies where there is a valid reservation of title clause. In *Aluminium Industrie Vaassen BV v Romalpa Aluminium Ltd* [1976] 1 WLR 676, we have a classic exposition of the law in relation to reservation of title. The supplier of aluminium foil in the Netherlands supplied aluminium foil to the company in the United Kingdom. The aluminium foil was supplied on credit terms. The supplier expressly reserved title in the goods until they were paid for. The supplier required the purchaser to store the aluminium foil separately and imposed fiduciary obligations upon the purchaser in relation to the property. Mocatta J held that there was an effective reservation of title. He was upheld unanimously by the Court of Appeal. The relevant clause of the contract of sale provided:

> The ownership of the material to be delivered by [AIV] will only be transferred to [Romalpa] when [it has] met all that is owing to [AIV]. Until the date of payment [Romalpa could be required] to store the material in such a way that it is clearly the property of [AIV].

Three particular features were stressed in the case:

(a) there must be a clear and unambiguous reservation of the title in the property;
(b) the goods must not be inextricably linked with other goods and must be capable of being separated from other people's property; and
(c) a fiduciary obligation must be placed on the purchaser by the supplier. In *Romalpa*, agency and bailment relationships had been created.

The principles in the *Romalpa* case (interestingly, Romalpa was the company suffering from the so-called *Romalpa* clause, which was actually a clause in the supplier's terms and conditions) were applied in subsequent cases. In *Borden (UK) Ltd v Scottish Timber Products Ltd* [1981] Ch 25, the supplier of resin reserved title in the resin. This was problematic because, although the resin had not been paid for, it was inextricably linked with chipboard. It was held that the supplier of the resin could not effectively reserve title where the resin was mixed with other products and could not be separated out. As Templeman LJ said (p. 44):

> When the resin was incorporated in the chipboard, the resin ceased to exist, the seller's title to the resin became meaningless and the seller's security vanished. There was no provision in the contract for the buyers to provide substituted or additional security. The chipboard belongs to the buyers.

In *Re Bond Worth Ltd* [1980] Ch 228, there is an object lesson in how not to create a valid retention of title (or *Romalpa* clause). Acrilan Fibre had been supplied by Monsanto Ltd to Bond Worth. It was to be used in the manufacture of carpets. The sale agreement reserved 'equitable and beneficial ownership' of the fibre. Slade J held that the effect of such a reservation was to create the necessary implication that legal title had not been reserved by the supplier. The effect of this was that the supplier was creating a charge over the property rather than reserving effective title. As such, the charge required registration. It was not registered and was, therefore, void. Similarly, in *Stroud Architectural Systems Ltd v John Laing Construction Ltd* [1994] 2 BCLC 276, the claimants supplied glazing units on terms where they reserved the equitable and beneficial ownership in the goods. This was held to create a floating charge as they had not reserved the legal title or full title.

In *Re Peachdart Ltd* [1984] Ch 131, the supplier of leather reserved title in the leather. This leather was used in the manufacture of handbags. Once again, there was an inextricable mixing of the different properties and therefore there could be no valid reservation of title in such circumstances. The provision concerned created a charge and this charge was void for lack of registration. In *Re Clough Mill Ltd* [1985] 1 WLR 111, there was a valid reservation of title in relation to yarn. The Court of Appeal restated the requirements of a valid reservation of title which had been earlier expressed in the *Romalpa* case. In *Chisholm Textiles v Griffiths* [1994] 2 BCLC 291, the supplier of cloth to a dress manufacturer sought to reserve title in dresses into which the fabric had been incorporated. The judge held that this created a charge over the manufactured articles which was void for non-registration.

An interesting case on reservation of title is *Hendy Lennox (Industrial Engines) Ltd v Graeme Puttick Ltd* [1984] 1 WLR 485. In this case, the supplier of diesel engines had sought to reserve title in them. The engines were installed into generators. It was contended that there could be no valid reservation where such mixing had taken place. The court held, however, that there was no inextricable linking in such a situation as the engine could be removed from the generator.

A rather curious situation arose in *Chaigley Farms Ltd v Crawford, Kaye and Grayshire (t/a Leylands)* [1996] BCC 957. In this case, the retention of title clause was over livestock. The judge considered that the exchange of correspondence made it clear that the reservation of title was over live animals. It was held that animals that had been slaughtered were not within the clause.

20.10.2 Liens

Another feature that should be watched for in insolvency situations, whether involving the enforcement of charges or a liquidation, is the situation involving liens. A lien is the situation that exists where a person who has done work for another retains property belonging to that other, for example, a car repairer or a watch repairer.

In circumstances where a person holds property belonging to the company where that property is subject to a charge (or would otherwise come under the direct control of a liquidator if the company is in liquidation), the holder of the property must be paid off first so that the lien is discharged before the property becomes subject to the control of the administrative receiver or liquidator. Thus, in *George Barker (Transport) Ltd v Eynon* [1974] 1 WLR 462, a transport contractor was held entitled to retain possession of a consignment of meat belonging to the company until it had been paid in respect of money owed to it. Once paid, the lien is released and the property then becomes subject to the control of the administrative receiver (or liquidator). In fact, in *George Barker*, the transport contractors had a specific provision in their contract giving them a lien – a contractual lien. Some liens such as repairers' liens arise by operation of law. The transporting company in fact released the meat to the company's receiver without prejudice to any lien that it had.

20.10.3 Overseas companies

The principal change in the provisions relating to company charges is that charges created by overseas companies have now been replaced by a regulation making power to require registered overseas companies to register charges over property in the United Kingdom (s 1052 CA 2006).

Summary

Debentures

Technically, a debenture is any form of borrowing by a company but, in practice, a debenture is a secured borrowing. A debenture may be a single loan, for example, from a bank or one of an issue of debentures made to the public. An issue of debentures to the public is very similar in many respects to an issue of shares to the public. However, a debenture holder is a lender to the company, not a member of the company. Debentures and shares issued to the public are collectively called securities.

Where debentures are issued to the public, there must be a debenture trust deed and, in other cases of lending, there may be. The debenture trustee who is given the task of guarding the debenture holders' interests will act to enforce the security in appropriate situations and will ensure that the terms of the lending are honoured.

Charges

The security given to a company's borrowings may take one of two forms. It may be in the shape of a fixed charge, which is basically similar to an ordinary mortgage, and may be granted over the fixed assets such as land, investments, etc. It seems it may also be granted over a company's present and future book debts where these are paid into a separate bank account.

The other type of charge is a floating charge, which is unique to company law and which a company may grant over its entire assets and undertaking. Unlike a fixed charge, a floating charge is not effective from the date of its creation but rather when it crystallises upon the happening of certain events. Crystallisation may occur automatically if the company goes into liquidation, if a receiver is appointed, if the company ceases business and possibly on the happening of an event specified in the debenture agreement.

Registration of charges

Particulars of most, but not all, charges have to be registered within 21 days of their creation at the companies' registry. Failure to register the prescribed particulars of the charge renders it void against an administrator, liquidator or a person who acquires an interest or right over the charged property.

Late registration is permitted but subject to any rights acquired in the meantime. In respect of matters required to be placed on the register of charges with the companies' registry, deemed notice still operates.

When a charge is discharged, an entry of satisfaction and release to that effect should be registered with the Registrar of Companies.

Priorities

Fixed charges are generally paid off ahead of all floating charges and later fixed ones.

A first floating charge will generally take ahead of a subsequent floating charge unless the first preserves the possibility of a subsequent limited floating charge taking ahead of the earlier one.

Points to note on priorities

In determining priorities in relation to floating charges, certain creditors will take ahead of floating chargees. These are judgment creditors, landlords distraining for rent and preferential creditors.

On occasion, floating charges may be held to be invalid where a company goes into liquidation or an administration order is made and fixed or floating charges, if created as preferences (over other creditors), may also be found to be invalid where a company goes into liquidation or an administration order is made.

It is important to watch out for valid reservation of title clauses. If there are such clauses the property concerned does not belong to the company.

Where a person has a valid lien over company property – for example, a repairer's lien over lorries belonging to a company which are with the repairer following work being done on them – then the lien must be released by payment before the receiver or liquidator can take control of the property in question.

Self-test questions

20.1 Define a debenture.

20.2 Describe different types of debenture.

20.3   How do debentures differ from shares?

20.4   What is the nature of a debenture trust deed?

20.5   What is a fixed charge?

20.6   Define a floating charge.

20.7   Describe the system of registration of charges.

20.8   What happens when charges are discharged?

20.9   Set out the priorities amongst competing charges.

20.10 How is a judgment creditor protected where a company's assets are subject to a floating charge?

Further reading

A Berg, 'Charges Over Book Debts: A Reply' [1997] JBL 433.

A Berg, 'Brumark Investments Ltd and the Innominate Charge' [2001] JBL 531.

D Capper, 'Fixed Charges Over Book Debts – Back to Basics But How Far Back?' [2002] LMCLQ 246.

E Ferran, 'Floating Charges – The Nature of the Security' [1988] CLJ 213.

R Goode, 'Charges Over Book Debts: A Missed Opportunity' (1994) 110 LQR 592.

R Gregory and P Walton, 'Book Debt Charges – The Saga Goes On' (1999) 115 LQR 14.

M Lawson, 'The Reform of the Law Relating to Security Interests in Property' [1989] JBL 287.

G Mitchell and A Start, 'Fixed and Floating Charges After Spectrum' (2005) 155 NLJ 1309.

KJ Naser, 'The Juridical Basis of the Floating Charge' (1994) 15 Co Law 11.

RR Pennington, 'The Genesis of the Floating Charge' (1960) 23 MLR 630.

D Turing, 'Retention of Title: How to Get Value From a Bad Penny' (1995) 16 Co Law 119.

S Worthington, 'Floating Charges – An Alternative Theory' [1994] 53 CLJ 81.

S Worthington, 'Fixed Charges Over Book Debts and Other Receivables' (1997) 113 LQR 562.

Chapter 21

Receivership

Chapter Contents

21.1 Introduction

Since the advent of the Enterprise Act 2002, for all new floating charges (save exceptional floating charges involving financial market operations), administration and not receivership has been the appropriate vehicle of enforcement. Banks and other trade creditors that have floating charges created before 15 September 2003 may, however, continue to enforce them in the traditional way. Because of this fundamental change in the law, the matter is covered here only for the sake of completeness without going into undue detail.

Where it is sought to enforce the terms of a debenture where there has been a default, the appropriate remedy used generally to be to secure the appointment of a receiver. If it is sought to appoint a person under the terms of a floating charge, the person appointed was generally an administrative receiver who had to be a qualified insolvency practitioner: see s 388 of the Insolvency Act 1986. Since the coming into force of the Enterprise Act 2002, generally holders of floating charges created on or after 15 September 2003 have not been able to appoint administrative receivers. Exceptionally, in special circumstances in relation to specialist financing transactions, administrative receivers may still be appointed (see ss 72B–72G of the Insolvency Act 1986).

Where an administrative receiver is appointed over the entire assets and undertaking of the company, he will need to act as manager as well as receiver. It is likely where there are substantial contracts that the receiver will also be appointed as manager, as the company will wish to continue its business during the receivership.

21.2 Appointment

An administrative receiver may, if the debenture is issued under the common seal of the company, be appointed where the company is in default under s 101(1) of the Law of Property Act 1925. In such a circumstance, the debenture holder or a trustee for debenture holders has the opportunity to appoint a receiver of the company's income.

An alternative course of action is to enforce any express power given by the debenture to appoint a receiver.

In the last resort, the debenture holder can apply to the court for an order of sale of the property, foreclosure, delivery of possession or the appointment of a receiver of the property that is subject to the charge. The court will generally only appoint a receiver if the principal sum or interest is in arrears, if the company has gone into liquidation or if the security is in some way jeopardised. A receiver will not be appointed merely because it can be demonstrated that the company's assets will on realisation be insufficient to meet the amount of the secured debt: see *Re New York Taxicab Company* [1913] 1 Ch 1.

21.3 Procedure on appointment

The appointment of an administrative receiver will be in writing unless it is by court order. The person who it purports to appoint as administrative receiver must agree to the appointment.

The person appointed as administrative receiver must notify the company of his appointment and all of the company's creditors so far as their addresses are known to him. This must be done within 28 days of the appointment (s 46(1) of the Insolvency Act 1986).

In every receivership, there must be publicity given to the fact that there is a receivership. This must be stated on every invoice, order for goods or business letter issued by or on behalf of the company or the receiver or manager where the company's name appears (s 39 of the Insolvency Act 1986).

21.4 The course of the administrative receivership

On the appointment of an administrative receiver, the administrative receiver will require the directors of the company to produce a statement of affairs of the company giving details of the company's assets, debts, liabilities (the names and addresses of creditors), any securities held by the creditors and the dates those securities were given (s 47 of the Insolvency Act 1986). The administrative receiver should send a report to the Registrar of Companies, to any trustees for secured creditors and to all secured creditors for whom he has an address. The report should detail:

(a)   the events leading up to his appointment;
(b)   the disposal and proposed disposal of property by him;
(c)   the carrying on or proposed carrying on of any business by him;
(d)   sums owed to debenture holders and preferential creditors; and
(e)   the amount, if any, likely to be available to pay other creditors (s 48 of the Insolvency Act 1986).

In the course of this report, the administrative receiver is likely to comment on the content of the statement of affairs.

It should be the aim of the administrative receiver to get in the property that is subject to the charge and generally convert it to cash for payment of the sums owed to chargeholders and, where appropriate, to pay off any preferential creditors.

It may well be that, in seeking to achieve this aim, the administrative receiver elects to carry on running the business. In relation to existing contracts, the appointment of an administrative receiver would generally have no effect on the liability under such contracts. An administrative receiver is not the agent of the person appointing him, rather he is the company's agent (s 44(1)(a) of the Insolvency Act 1986). The administrative receiver may conclude new contracts and will be personally liable on them (s 44(1)(b) of the Insolvency Act 1986), but is entitled to an indemnity out of the assets of the company in respect of that liability (s 44(1)(c) of the Insolvency Act 1986).

When an administrative receiver is appointed by the court, he will need the approval of the court for most of his actions. Since such an administrative receiver has been appointed by the court, he is an officer of the court and interference with his functions will therefore constitute a contempt of court. Such an administrative receiver is, therefore, not an agent of the debenture holders or of the company, rather he is an officer of the court. He still has a right of indemnity out of the company's assets in the same way as an administrative receiver appointed out of court.

The powers of administrative receivers are set out in s 42 and Sch 1 of the Insolvency Act 1986 and these powers include taking possession of the property, selling it, borrowing money, bringing or defending legal proceedings, appointing agents, carrying on the company's business, etc. The powers are extensive. A person dealing with an administrative receiver in good faith and for value is not concerned to enquire whether the receiver is acting within his powers (s 42(3) of the Insolvency Act 1986).

In general, therefore, it may be seen that administrative receivers owe duties to the persons appointing them where they are appointed out of court; and when they are appointed in court, the administrative receivers are officers of the court. It is clear that administrative receivers also owe duties to other people. In *Downsview Nominees Ltd v First City Corporation* [1993] AC 295, a Privy Council case on appeal from New Zealand, it was held that a duty was owed by a receiver and manager to a second debenture holder to act in good faith for proper purposes in conducting the receivership, although the primary duty was to realise the assets for the benefit of the debenture holders. Liability was based on a breach of duty in equity rather than in negligence. The case centred on two debentures issued by the mortgagor company, Glen Eden Motors Ltd, who traded as new and used motor dealers.

21.5 Priority of payments in an administrative receivership

The priority of payments in an administrative receivership is as follows:

(a)   it is first necessary to pay the expenses of the administrative receivership including the administrative receiver's remuneration;
(b)   where the charge is a floating charge and there are preferential creditors, these preferential creditors should be paid off out of the proceeds of the sale of property subject to the floating charge before the secured creditors are paid off (preferential creditors are considered in section 25.4); and
(c)   paying off the debenture debt and interest that is due.

21.6 Termination of administrative receivership

Where an administrative receiver has completed his task, he may vacate office. He must give notice forthwith to the Registrar of Companies that he is ceasing to act (s 45(4) of the Insolvency Act 1986).

An administrative receiver may also be removed by an order of the court (s 45(1) of the Insolvency Act 1986). Once again, here, the administrative receiver would need to serve notice under s 45(4) of the Insolvency Act 1986. Similarly, an administrative receiver may resign from office. He must give notice to his appointer and the company of his intention to resign. The notice must be of at least seven days' duration. There must be notice given to the Registrar.

An administrative receiver must also vacate office if he ceases to be qualified to act as an insolvency practitioner (s 45(2) of the Insolvency Act 1986) and also if an administration order is made in respect of the company (s 11(1) of the Insolvency Act 1986).

Summary

Administrative receivership for floating charges created before 15 September 2003

Where there is a default in honouring the terms of a debenture, a receiver may be appointed. If a receiver is appointed under a floating charge over all of the company's assets and undertaking, he will generally act as receiver and manager (managing the company's business) and he is termed an administrative receiver. He must be a qualified insolvency practitioner. Where a person is appointed under a fixed charge, he is a receiver and need not be a qualified insolvency practitioner.

It is the role of the administrative receiver to realise the assets subject to the floating charge and to pay off in priority the charges of the receivership, preferential creditors and money owing to chargees.

Section 72A of the Insolvency Act 1986 (inserted by s 250 of the Enterprise Act 2002) provides that 'The holder of a qualifying floating charge in respect of a company's property may not appoint an administrative receiver of the company'.

From 15 September 2003 onwards only certain specialist financing transactions may be enforced by the creations of new floating charges. These include where a debt of £50 million or more is financed, where the company is an air traffic control, railway or water company, or where the company is a registered social landlord.

Self-test questions

21.1 Describe the impact of the Enterprise Act 2002 on receivership.

21.2 How may administrative receivers be appointed?

21.3 What is the procedure on the appointment of an administrative receiver?

21.4 Set out the course of an administrative receivership in brief.

21.5 What is the priority of payments in an administrative receivership?

21.6 What happens when an administrative receivership is terminated?

Further reading

H Anderson, 'Receivership Preferential Creditors' (1994) 15 Co Law 195.
A Berg, 'Duties of a Mortgagee and a Receiver' [1993] JBL 213.
G Doyle, 'A Residual Status of Directors in Receivership' (1996) 17 Co Law 131.
R Grantham, 'The Purpose of a Company Receiver's Powers' [1993] Conv 401.
A Hogan, 'Receivers Revisited' (1996) 17 Co Law 226.
Mr Justice Lightman, 'The Challenges Ahead: Address to the Insolvency Lawyers' Association' [1996] JBL 113.

Chapter 22

Voluntary arrangements and administration

Chapter Contents

22.1 Voluntary arrangements

Part I of the Insolvency Act 1986 (ss 1–7B) provides a simple procedure whereby a company that is in financial difficulties may enter into a voluntary arrangement with its creditors. This arrangement may involve either a composition in satisfaction of its debts – that is, provision for creditors to receive a percentage of what is due to them – or a scheme of arrangement of its affairs.

The voluntary arrangement must be supervised by a person, 'the nominee', who must be a qualified insolvency practitioner. The proposal for a voluntary arrangement may be made by the directors of a company or where an administration order is in force by the administrator or where the company is being wound up by the liquidator (s 1 of the Insolvency Act 1986).

If the nominee is not the company's administrator or liquidator, then the proposal should be submitted to him, together with a statement of the company's affairs containing particulars of the company's assets, creditors, liabilities and debts. The nominee must then submit a report to the court stating whether, in his opinion, meetings of the company and of its creditors should be summoned to consider the proposal, and if, in his opinion, such meetings should be summoned, the date on which and place at which they should be held (s 2 of the Insolvency Act 1986).

If the nominee is the company's liquidator or administrator, he should summon meetings of the company and of its creditors to consider the proposal (s 3(2) of the Insolvency Act 1986).

The meetings summoned must then determine whether to approve the proposed voluntary arrangement with or without modifications. A meeting may not approve:

(a) any proposal that affects the right of a secured creditor of the company to enforce his security except with his consent;

(b) the withdrawal of the priority of a preferential debt over other debts, except with the consent of the creditor; or

(c) the payment of a proportion of preferential debts to a preferential creditor that is a smaller proportion than is to be received by other preferential creditors except with the consent of the creditor.

The proposal must be approved by three-quarters in value of the creditors present and voting and by a simple majority of the members, according to the Insolvency Rules.

If the voluntary arrangement is approved, then, if the company is being wound up or if an administration order is in force, the court may stay the winding-up proceedings or discharge the administration order, or it may give such directions as it thinks appropriate to facilitate the implementation of the voluntary arrangement (s 5 of the Insolvency Act 1986). There is a period of 28 days from the date when the nominee reports the results of the meetings' consideration to the court for members, creditors and others to object to the court (s 4(6) of the Insolvency Act 1986).

On the application of a member, contributory creditor, nominee or, if appropriate, liquidator or administrator, the proposal may be challenged on the ground that it unfairly prejudices the interests of a creditor, member or contributory of the company, or that there has been some material irregularity at or in relation to either of the meetings.

Once the proposal for the voluntary arrangement has taken effect, the nominee becomes the supervisor of the composition of the voluntary arrangement. The supervisor may apply for a winding up to be ordered or for an administration order to be made.

If any creditor or some other interested party is dissatisfied with any act, omission or decision of a supervisor, he may apply to the court to give the supervisor directions or to alter the decision etc. in question (s 7 of the Insolvency Act 1986).

The voluntary arrangement procedure is a valuable one. It was added to British company law at the behest of the Cork Committee 1982 (Cmnd 8558, 1982: paras 400–403), which considered that companies, like individuals, should be able to enter into binding arrangements with their creditors.

On 6 April 1995 the government announced proposals for a new form of procedure for dealing with companies in financial trouble (Revised Proposals for a New Company Voluntary Arrangement Procedure). The directors of a company would be given 28 days to put together a rescue plan. During this moratorium the company would be supervised by a licensed insolvency practitioner.

There are safeguards for lenders and creditors. There has to be a reasonable prospect of success in the opinion of the insolvency practitioner before the plan can be put into force. There must be a creditors' meeting within 28 days of the commencement of the moratorium. If more than 75 per cent of the creditors in value support the proposals, it is binding on all creditors. The creditors can reject the entire project. They can also extend it.

22.2 Administration

Following the report of the Review Committee on Insolvency Law and Practice – the Cork Report 1982 (Cmnd 8558, 1982) – a government white paper (*A Revised Framework for Insolvency Law* (Cmnd 9175, February 1984)) echoing some of its recommendations set out a procedure to facilitate the rehabilitation or reorganisation of a company. This process was the administration process and it was incorporated into the Insolvency Act of 1985, which was in turn consolidated in the Insolvency Act 1986. In essence, the scheme of administration is to make possible the rescue of a company by placing its management in the hands of an administrator. For as long as the administration is in force, it is not possible to commence winding-up proceedings or any other process against the company or to enforce any charge, hire purchase or retention of title provision against the company without the leave of the court.

The corporate insolvency provisions of the Enterprise Act 2002, which came into force on 15 September 2003, made fundamental changes to the law of insolvency.

Henceforth the holder of a floating charge created on or after 15 September 2003 cannot generally appoint an administrative receiver but must instead appoint an administrator. The court-based administrative procedure of Part II of the Insolvency Act 1986 is replaced by a new system. There are now three ways of appointing an administrator:

(a)   by the court;
(b)   out of court by the company or its directors; or
(c)   out of court by the holder of a floating charge.

The powers and role of an administrator are now set out in the Insolvency Act 1986 Sch B1 para 3 (inserted by the Enterprise Act 2002).

The administrator must now seek to rescue the company and maintain it as a going concern. If this is not reasonably practicable then the administrator should seek to achieve a better result for the company's creditors than would be likely if the company were to be put into liquidation. If neither of these is reasonably achievable, then the administrator, without unnecessarily harming the interests of creditors, should seek to realise the company's property to make a distribution to one or more secured or preferential creditors.

22.3 Appointment by the court

Appointment by the court may be made at the behest of the company by ordinary resolution or unanimous written resolution, by a majority of the company's directors, or by one or more creditors. Additionally, a holder of a floating charge may seek appointment of an administrator by the court. For this to be successful, the floating charge must be a 'qualifying floating charge'.

A floating charge is a 'qualifying floating charge' if it satisfies the requirements set out in the Enterprise Act 2002 Sch 16, inserting Sch B1 to the Insolvency Act 1986. It must either state that the relevant paragraph of the Act applies to the floating charge making it a 'qualifying floating charge' or purport to give the holder of the floating charge the power to appoint an administrator or an administrative receiver. It should be noted that this last provision means that even those pre-Enterprise Act 2002 floating charges, where there was the power given to appoint an administrative receiver, will fall within the scope of this part of the Act allowing the floating charge holder to apply for an administration order.

Additionally, the floating chargeholder must hold security that relates to the whole or substantially the whole of the company's property.

It is worth noting that a 'qualifying floating chargeholder' can intervene where others apply to the court for an order to seek the appointment of an administrative receiver (if it is an appropriate case where he is entitled to do so) or of an administrator.

A 'qualifying floating chargeholder' seeking to enforce the floating charge in obtaining an administration order need only show that the charge is enforceable. Others who seek a court administration order must demonstrate that the company is or is likely to become unable to pay its debts, and that the court order is likely to achieve the purpose of administration.

On appointment the administrator must advertise the court order in the *London Gazette* and in a newspaper that circulates in the area of the company's principal place of business, and additionally send a copy of the court order to the Registrar of Companies.

22.4 Appointment by the company or the company's directors

If the appointment is to be made by the company or its directors, five written business days' notice must be given of the intention to appoint to those persons with the right to appoint an administrative receiver (in the exceptional case where this applies) or to persons having a right to appoint an administrator under the Act.

Additionally, a notice of the appointment must be filed in court, together with a statutory declaration by the appointer that he is entitled to make the appointment and that it is made under the Act. The administrator must additionally file a statement that he consents to the appointment and that the purpose of the administration is reasonably likely to be achieved in his opinion.

22.5 Appointment by a qualifying floating chargeholder

An appointment may be made out of court by a qualifying floating chargeholder. The qualifying floating chargeholder must give two written business days' notice to any prior qualifying chargeholder unless such earlier qualifying chargeholder has consented to the appointment.

The notice of intention may be filed in court. The qualifying chargeholder must file in court a notice of the appointment and a statutory declaration that he is a qualifying floating chargeholder and that the floating charge is enforceable. Additionally, the administrator must file a statement that he has consented to the appointment and that in his opinion the purpose of the administration is reasonably likely to be achieved.

22.6 The administrator's proposals

However the administrator is appointed, the following steps apply.

Within eight weeks of the company entering administration, and as soon as is reasonably practicable, the administrator must file proposals as to how the purpose of the administration is to be achieved. This is sent to the Registrar of Companies as well as to creditors and members of the company.

An initial creditors' meeting must be called within ten weeks, and as soon as is reasonably practicable, to consider the administrator's proposals. This meeting need not be convened if the administrator considers there is insufficient property to make a distribution to unsecured creditors above the ring-fenced amount that they are guaranteed under the Act (see section 25.4). In any event, creditors whose debts amount to at least 10 per cent of the company's debts may require a meeting of the creditors.

At the creditors' meeting the creditors must vote on the administrator's proposals. A simple majority in value of debts is decisive of the issue.

In relation to secured creditors, the relevant amount relating to their vote is in terms of any shortfall between their debt and the value of their security. However, the administrator's proposals cannot include action that is detrimental to their rights unless this has been agreed.

'Inability to pay debts' is determined by s 123 of the Insolvency Act 1986. This provides that inability to pay debts may be demonstrated by one of the following:

(a)   if a creditor is owed a debt exceeding £750 for three weeks after making a written request for payment of that debt;

(b) execution or process issued on a judgment is returned unsatisfied in whole or in part (in practice, the minimum sum owed must exceed £750);

(c) if it is proved to the satisfaction of the court that the company is unable to pay its debts as they fall due (in practice, the same minimum sum applies);

(d) if the company's assets are worth less than the amount of its liabilities, taking account of contingent and prospective liability (in practice, the same minimum sum applies);

(e) in Scotland, a charge for payment on an extract decree or extract registered bond or extract registered protest has expired without payment being made (in practice, the same minimum sum applies); or

(f) in Northern Ireland, a certificate of unenforceability has been granted in respect of a judgment against the company (in practice, the same minimum sum applies).

22.7 Effects of administration

The effect of an application for an administration order is set out in Sch B1 of the Act. Once a petition has been presented for an administration order and during the currency of an administration, there must be:

(a) no resolution passed or order made to wind up the company;

(b) no steps taken to enforce any security of the company's property or to repossess goods in the company's possession under any hire purchase or leasing agreement except with the leave of the administrator and the court, and subject to such terms as the administrator or the court may impose (note that hire purchase agreements are defined to include retention of title agreements in this part of the Insolvency Act 1986); or

(c) no other proceedings and no execution or other legal process commenced or continued, and no distress may be levied against the company or its property except with the leave of the court, and once again subject to such terms as it may impose.

Once a petition for an administration order has been made, and during the currency of an administration order, a landlord's right to re-enter for forfeiture of the lease is not possible except with the permission of the court or the administrator.

22.8 Powers of the administrator

The person appointed to administer the company must be a qualified insolvency practitioner (see s 388 of the Insolvency Act 1986). He is given wide powers of management to do what is necessary for the management of the affairs, business and property of the company. These powers include taking possession of the property, selling and otherwise disposing of it, raising or borrowing money, appointing a solicitor or accountant, bringing or defending legal proceedings, effecting and maintaining insurances, appointing agents, carrying on the business of the company, establishing subsidiaries, granting or accepting surrender of a lease or tenancy and power to do all such things that are incidental to these powers.

22.9 Contracts of employment and the Enterprise Act 2002

The appointment of an administrator does not effect the dismissal of the company's employees. The administrator acts as agent of the company.

Section 19 of the Insolvency Act 1986 provided that nothing done or omitted to be done within 14 days of the appointment of an administrator, shall be construed as adoption of employment contracts by the administrator. This provision created some doubt as to whether failing to act within those 14 days could be construed as adoption of employment contracts.

Schedule B1 of the Insolvency Act 1986, as inserted by the Enterprise Act 2002, provides that in relation to administrations on or after 15 September 2003, action taken within the period of 14 days after an administrator's appointment shall not be taken to amount or contribute to the adoption of a contract of employment. The clear effect of this is to indicate that an omission to act cannot amount to adoption. The decision in *Powdrill v Watson* [1995] 1 AC 394 is thus unambiguously endorsed by this provision.

22.10 Fair dealing

The Insolvency Act makes provision for certain transactions at an undervalue (s 238), preferences (s 239), extortionate credit transactions (s 244) and floating charges to be invalidated where an administration order has been made. These are considered in more detail below (see section 25.2).

22.11 Termination of administration

Administration is terminated automatically 12 months after the effective date of appointment. This period may be extended on a single occasion for a period of an additional six months with the consent of the creditors, or any number of times by the court on the application of the administrator for such period as the court deems appropriate. In relation to creditor consent there must be the consent of at least half in value of the unsecured creditors and all of the secured creditors.

If the company is rescued in accordance with the provisions of the Act, then the administration will terminate.

Additionally, if there are funds available after secured and preferential creditors have been paid, the company may go into a creditors' voluntary winding up. The administrator would, in these circumstances, become the liquidator, unless the creditors make a different choice.

If there are no funds available for distribution to creditors, the administrator must give notice to that effect to Companies House unless the court orders otherwise. The company will then be deemed dissolved after three months of the giving of the notice unless the court orders otherwise.

Summary
Voluntary arrangements
In response to recommendations made by the Cork Committee 1982, Pt I of the Insolvency Act 1986 makes provision for companies in financial difficulties to come to voluntary arrangements with their creditors agreeing to pay a percentage of debts that are due. A proposal for a voluntary arrangement may be made by a company's directors, liquidator or administrator. The supervisor charged with implementing the proposal must be a qualified insolvency practitioner.

Administration
First introduced in 1985 at the behest of the Cork Committee, administration enables a company's survival – often though not always where it has been unable to pay its debts or is likely to become unable to do so.

Since the Enterprise Act 2002, the administration procedure has taken over from administrative receivership as the main method of enforcement of rights for holders of floating charges. The Enterprise Act 2002 has introduced a massive shift in the nature of insolvency law, putting, as it does, the emphasis on the survival and rescue of the company rather than on its dissolution.

Self-test questions

22.1 How may the system of voluntary arrangements assist a company in financial difficulties?

22.2 What is the nature of administration?

22.3 When may an administrator be appointed by the court?

22.4 When may an administrator be appointed by the company or the company's directors?

22.5 When may an appointment be made out of court by a qualifying floating charge holder?

22.6 Describe the course of an administration.

22.7 What are the effects of a company going into administration?

22.8 Set out the powers of an administrator in brief.

22.9 What is the effect of administration on a company's employees?

22.10 Describe the fair dealing provisions in the Insolvency Act 1986 in brief.

22.11 How may an administration be terminated?

Further reading

V Finch, 'Pre-packed Administrations: Bargains in the Shadow of Insolvency or Shadowy Bargains' [2006] JBL 568.

T Green, 'The Process of Administration – A Potted Summary' (1994) 10 IL & P 77.

G McCormack, 'Rescuing Small Businesses: Designing an "Efficient" Legal Regime' [2009] JBL 299.

D Milman, 'Rescuing Corporate Rescue' (1993) 14 Co Law 82.

M Phillips, 'The Administration Procedure and Creditors' Voluntary Arrangements: The Case for Radical Reform' [1996] 17 Insolv L 14.

O Radley-Gardner and M Sefton, 'Closing the Doors: The Complexities Involved in Administrations' (2009) 159 NLJ 18.

J Tribe, 'Company Voluntary Arrangements and Rescue: A New Hope and a Tudor Orthodoxy' [2009] JBL 454.

A Walters, 'Corporate Insolvency After the Enterprise Act 2002' (2004) 25 Co Law 1.

Chapter 23

Investigations

Chapter Contents

23.1 Introduction

Minority remedies have already been considered (Chapter 15). On occasion, powers are given to the Companies Investigation Branch of the Department for Business, Innovation and Skills, which buttress the minority remedies which are available. In particular, investigations, or inspections (as they are sometimes called), may be held into companies.

23.2 Production of documents

If it believes that there is good reason to do so, the Department for Business, Innovation and Skills may require a company to produce documents at such time and place as is specified or it may authorise an officer of the Department or any other competent person to require a company to produce to him any documents that may be specified (s 447 of the Companies Act 1985 as amended by s 21 of the Companies (Audit, Investigation and Community Enterprise) Act 2004). The power extends to requiring production of documents from any person who appears to be in possession of documents but without prejudice to any lien that may be held over the documents. The section also provides for the Secretary of State to require questions to be answered and not just those relating to any papers handed over. The power is reinforced by a power of entry and search of premises set out in s 448 and ss 453A and 453B CA1985. Section 450 of the Act provides a punishment for destroying, mutilating or falsifying a document, and the offence is punishable by imprisonment and/ or a fine. Section 453C of the Act makes it an offence treatable as contempt of court to fail to comply with the requirements of s 447. It is usual for an officer of the Department to arrive at an early stage to inspect documents to prevent destruction of the documents.

23.3 Investigation of affairs of a company

In addition to the power to require the production of documents, the Department for Business, Innovation and Skills can in certain situations appoint inspectors to investigate the affairs of a company. Very often, the investigation is preceded by requiring the production of documents that may then demonstrate that a full-blooded investigation is appropriate. Section 431 of the Act provides that the Secretary of State may appoint one or more inspectors to investigate the affairs of a company and to report on them in such manner as he may direct. The appointment may be made in the case of a limited company with share capital on the application of not lower than 200 members or members holding one-tenth of the issued shares and in the case of a company without share capital on the application of one-fifth of the members of the company, and in any case an investigation may be held on the application of the company. In general two joint inspectors are appointed – one is usually a senior solicitor or barrister and the other is usually a senior accountant. For the sake of convenience here, the appointment will be referred to as the appointment of an inspector. The appointment of an inspector to investigate into the affairs of the company is not a judicial proceeding but an administrative one and the decision of the Department for Business, Innovation and Skills is final and cannot be challenged provided that the power is exercised bona fide: see *Norwest Holst Ltd v Secretary of State for Trade and Industry* [1978] Ch 201. It was stated in this case that an investigation is an administrative act and that the full rules of natural justice did not therefore apply. In the case of such an application, it should be supported by such evidence as the Secretary of State may require to demonstrate that there is good reason for requiring the investigation. The Secretary of State may before appointing an inspector require the applicant or applicants to give security for the costs of the investigation.

Section 432 provides that an investigation must be held into the affairs of a company where it is ordered by the court (s 432(1) of the Companies Act 1985). Furthermore, the Secretary of State may order that an investigation should be held if there are circumstances suggesting that:

(a) the company's affairs are being or have been conducted with intent to defraud creditors or otherwise for a fraudulent or unlawful purpose, or in a manner that is unfairly prejudicial to some part of the members;

(b) an actual or proposed act or omission is or would be so prejudicial or that the company was formed for any fraudulent or unlawful purpose (note that the wording of the section was not amended by the Companies Act 1989 when s 459 was amended to permit petitions where all of the members have been prejudiced. The odd result is that it would seem that an investigation cannot be ordered if all of the members are prejudiced);

(c) persons connected with the company's formation or management have been guilty of fraud, misfeasance or other misconduct towards the company or its members; or

(d) the company's members have not been given all the information with respect to the company's affairs that they might reasonably expect (s 432(2) of the Companies Act 1985).

Section 432(2A) provides that inspectors may be appointed under s 432(2) on terms that their report is not for publication. In every other case, the Secretary of State may if he thinks appropriate provide that the report is to be published.

23.4 Investigation of ownership or control

Section 442 of the Companies Act 1985 provides that the Secretary of State may order an investigation into the ownership or control of a company to find out who the true owners of the company are if he thinks there is good reason to do so. He must order an investigation if an application is made by 200 or more members or by members holding 10 per cent or more of the company's issued shares unless he thinks that the investigation is vexatious or that it would be sufficient to carry out an investigation under s 444 (this provides for information being given direct to the Secretary of State without the need for the appointment of inspectors).

If the difficulty in obtaining information about any shares appears due to the non-cooperation of persons, then the Secretary of State may make an order that:

(a) any transfer of the shares will be void;
(b) voting rights in respect of the shares may not be exercised;
(c) additional shares may not be issued in respect of those shares; and
(d) sums due on the shares will not be paid except in a liquidation (s 454 of the Companies Act 1985).

An aggrieved person may appeal against such an order (s 456 of the Companies Act 1985).

In every case where an inspector is appointed under ss 431, 432 or 442, the inspector may investigate any other company in the group.

23.5 Investigation into insider dealing

Section 97 and ss 167–169 of the Financial Services and Markets Act 2000 confer on the Financial Conduct Authority (as successor to the Financial Services Authority) and the Secretary of State power to set up investigations.

23.6 Consequences of inspections

As well as a final report made by the inspector, there may be interim reports. This will particularly be the case if there is a long and complex investigation. Generally speaking, the reports will be published without delay, but occasionally there will be a time lag. A delay was challenged unsuccessfully in *R v Secretary of State for Trade ex p Lonrho plc* [1989] 1 WLR 525.

Some of the more important consequences of the report or the inspection of documents under the Companies Act 1985 may include the following:

(a) The Secretary of State may petition under s 124(4) of the Insolvency Act 1986 if he considers it is expedient in the public interest to wind the company up on the just and equitable ground. The matter does not have to be considered personally by the Secretary of State but may be considered by an official: see *Re Golden Chemical Products Ltd* [1976] Ch 300. The report will be evidence in the proceedings; see *Re Tower and Holiday Clubs Ltd* [1967] 1 WLR 711. The report itself, however, is open to challenge and other evidence may need to be adduced; see *Re Koscot (Interplanetary) (UK) Ltd* [1972] 3 All ER 829.

(b) If it appears to the Secretary of State that in the case of a company that has received a report under s 437 CA 1985 (Inspectors Report), or where the Secretary of State has exercised his powers under s 447 or s 448 of that Act (powers to require documentation and information or to enter and search premises) or the Secretary of State or the Financial Conduct Authority has exercised powers under Part 11 of the Financial Services and Markets Act 2000 (information gathering and investigations), or the Secretary of State has received the report from an investigator appointed by him or the Financial Conduct Authority, then the Secretary of State may, if it appears to him that the company's affairs are being or have been conducted in a manner that is unfairly prejudicial to the interests of members generally or some part of the members, or that an actual or proposed act or omission of the company, including an act or omission on its behalf would be so prejudicial, apply to the court for a petition under s 995 CA 2006 in relation to unfairly prejudicial conduct. He may do this in addition to or instead of presenting a petition for the winding up of the company (s 995 CA 2006).

(c) An application may be made for a disqualification order against any person who is or has been a director or shadow director of any company if it appears to the Secretary of State from the report or from information gleaned from documents that have been disclosed that a disqualification order should be made in the public interest. The maximum period for such a disqualification is 15 years.

If matters come to light during the course of an investigation that suggest that a criminal offence has been committed and those matters are referred to the appropriate prosecuting authority, the Secretary of State can halt the inspection or confine it to specific matters (s 437(1A) CA 1985).

23.7 Expenses of investigation

The expenses of investigation are borne by the Department for Business, Innovation and Skills. It may, in appropriate cases, recover them from persons, particularly those convicted as a result of prosecutions consequent upon a report.

23.8 Impact of the Companies Act 2006

The 2006 Act makes some minor amendments to the law on company investigations.

The Inspector may now be given general directions by the Secretary of State with regard to exercising his functions. He may also be asked to take no further steps in the investigation (s 1035 CA 2006).

The 2006 Act also makes provision in relation to the resignation, removal and replacement of Inspectors (s 1036 CA 2006), and the power to obtain information from former inspectors (s 1037 CA 2006).

Summary

Investigations

The Department for Business, Innovation and Skills is given various powers to investigate the affairs, ownership or directors' share dealings within a company. There are also powers to investigate insider dealing.

As a prelude to an investigation, the Department may order a company to disclose specified documents to it. This may conclude the matter by revealing what action should be taken or that nothing is amiss, or it may be the prelude to a full-blooded investigation. Where inspectors are appointed, one is generally a senior lawyer and one a senior accountant. Their report may be published. The inspection is an administrative proceeding, not a judicial one.

As a consequence of the inspection, the Secretary of State may do one or more of the following:

(a) initiate winding-up proceedings on the just and equitable ground;

(b) petition on the grounds of unfair prejudice; or

(c) apply for a disqualification order against a director or shadow director.

Self-test questions

23.1 What powers does the Department for Business, Innovation and Skills have in relation to requiring a company to produce documents, and requiring questions to be answered?

23.2 How may an investigation into the affairs of a company be instituted?

23.3 Set out how an investigation of ownership or control of a company may be instigated.

23.4 Under what provision may an investigation into insider dealing be set up?

23.5 What are the various consequences of inspections?

23.6 Who bears the expenses of an investigation?

23.7 What is the impact of the Companies Act 2006 in relation to the holding of investigations?

Further reading

M Griffiths, 'The DTI Is Watching You' (2005) 155 NLJ 198.

M Griffiths, 'DTI: Power to Enter and Remain' (2005) 155 NLJ 738.

P Mitchard, 'Judicial Review of DTI Inspectors Appointed Under s 432(2) of the Companies Act 1985' [1985] 1 CJRB 6.

Chapter 24

Takeovers, reconstructions and amalgamations

Chapter Contents

Certain terms are used repeatedly in this area of 'takeovers'.

24.1 Takeovers

The term 'takeover' is generally used to describe the situation where one company acquires the shares of another company (target company). The acquiring or bidding company becomes the holding company of the acquired or target company, which therefore becomes a subsidiary. Takeovers may be accomplished by agreement or a takeover bid, which may be a 'hostile' bid.

24.2 Reconstructions

A reconstruction is generally accomplished where the shareholders of the transferring company and the shareholders of the company to which the business has been transferred are the same. The people who are carrying on the reconstructed business are thus generally the same as those who carried it on before. Reconstructions may involve an external element such as where a particular company sells its business and assets to another company in exchange for shares in that company; alternatively reconstructions may be internal within a particular group where the capital structure within the group is altered.

24.3 Amalgamations

The term 'amalgamation' is usually used where two companies are brought together. The two companies may become one new company, for example, X plc and Y plc becoming Z plc, or alternatively X plc may be subsumed by Y plc or vice versa. Here, clearly, there is an overlap with the term 'takeover'.

24.4 Takeovers Directive

The United Kingdom was obliged to take action in relation to takeovers by virtue of the EU Takeovers Directive (2004/25/EC). This had to be implemented in the UK by 20 May 2006. In consequence the government made the Takeovers Directive (Interim Implementation) Regulations 2006 (SI 2006/1183). These regulations came into force on 20 May 2006. The provisions in the regulations have been replaced by the relevant provisions of the Companies Act 2006.

24.5 Key changes

The key changes relate to new statutory rules that have been introduced and also to revisions in the City Code on Takeovers and Mergers (the Code may be found on the Panel on Takeovers and Mergers website at: www.thetakeoverpanel.org.uk).

The new statutory rules generally apply to companies whose shares are admitted ⸴ing on an EEA (European Economic Area) regulated market, while the Code has been amended to bring its provisions into line with the Takeovers Directive for all companies and for all transactions that come within the jurisdiction of the Panel on Takeovers and Mergers (see section 24.10).

The new statutory rules include: a requirement for directors' reports every year containing detailed information on the share and management structures of the company (s 992 CA 2006); a new offence for failure to comply with the Code's rules on documentation in relation to takeover bids (s 953 CA 2006); changes relating to compulsory purchase of outstanding shares where there is a takeover offer ('squeeze-out' and 'sell-out') (Part 28 Chapter 3 of the 2006 Act), as well as provisions enabling companies to 'opt in' to the 'breakthrough' provisions which have the effect of removing pre-bid defences for opting-in companies (s 966 CA 2006).

Most of the new statutory rules only apply where there is a takeover bid within the Directive. It is important therefore to understand what takeover bids are captured by the Directive. The jurisdiction only relates to a public offer for the transferable securities of an EEA company where the securities carry voting rights and are admitted to trading on an EEA-regulated market provided that the bid's object is control of the company or where control has already been acquired.

Voting rights are defined as votes in a general meeting, including rights that may only arise in certain circumstances.

24.6 Directors' reports

The statutory rules require additional disclosure in directors' reports if the company had securities carrying voting rights admitted to trading on a regulated market at the end of the financial year, whether or not the company is presently subject to a takeover bid. The aim is to ensure transparency in relation to the share and management structures of companies that may become subject to a bid within the terms of the Directive (s 992 CA 2006).

24.7 The new offence relating to bid documentation

The Act introduces a new criminal offence for failure to comply with rules relating to the documentation on a takeover bid. This applies if there is a bid within the terms of the Directive to which the Code's rules apply. If the document does not comply with the document rules then an offence is committed.

In relation to an offer document, the offence could be committed by a company or by a company's directors, officers or shareholders. In relation to a response document responding to a bid, the offence could be committed by any of the target company's directors or other officers, but not the target company itself.

Liability would only lie where the person knew of or was reckless as to the non-compliance of the relevant documents and where that person failed to take all reasonable steps to ensure that the documents did comply (s 953 CA 2006).

24.8 Takeovers – 'squeeze-out' and 'sell-out' rules

The offeror has to reach the relevant 90 per cent threshold before and cannot give a 'squeeze-out' notice after the end of the period of three months after the closure of the last date on which the offer can be accepted. It should be remembered that the purpose of the provisions is to ensure that where an offer is made to acquire all the shares or shares of a class that the offeror does not already hold, then if the offer is accepted by 90 per cent in value of shareholders, the offeror can give notice to acquire the other 10 per cent. Similarly there is reciprocity in that the remaining percentage of 10 per cent or less can serve notice to be acquired. These are the 'squeeze-out' and 'sell-out' principles in the Act and existed in the 1985 Act although they have now been amended (Part 28 Chapter 3 of the 2006 Act).

24.9 'Opting in' and 'opting out' in relation to pre-bid defences

The Takeover Directive provides for the cancellation of companies' pre-bid defences. The pre-bid defences are where minority shareholders can issue disproportionate voting rights and where they have restrictions on the transfer of shares in the company's articles or in separate contractual agreements. The Act permits UK companies to 'opt in' to a regime, which has the effect of cancelling these pre-bid defences. A company may 'opt in' by passing a special resolution. It can 'opt out' again by passing similarly a further special resolution (s 966 CA 2006).

If a person suffers loss by reason of the rendering invalid of a pre-bid defence, that person is entitled to such just and equitable compensation as may be ordered by the court (s 968(6) CA 2006).

24.10 Changes to the Code

Section 942 CA 2006 provides the definition of the Panel (i.e. the Panel on Takeovers and Mergers), which has functions in relation to the supervision of takeovers and mergers within the Takeovers Directive and beyond.

The Panel is responsible for issuing Principles, Rules, Rulings and Directions. The everyday business of the Panel is conducted by the Panel Executive. The Panel Executive can institute legal proceedings before the Hearings Committee in relation to any alleged breach of the City Code on Takeovers and Mergers (i.e. the Code). This could result in a notice of censure, a report to a regulatory or professional body or payment of a sum of money to the holders of the offeree securities. There is a possible appeal from the Hearings Committee to the Takeover Appeal Board.

Furthermore, of course, decisions of the Panel are subject to judicial review in ˄ normal way.

˅e Act makes provision for this in ss 943–946 CA 2006. Section 952 provides ˄s in relation to breach of rules issues by the Panel.

Furthermore, s 953 provides that it is an offence for failure to comply with rules about bid documentation within this section, and s 954 provides that rules may confer power on the Panel to order a person to pay such compensation as it thinks just and reasonable if he is in breach of a rule, the effect of which is to require the payment of money.

Section 955 provides for enforcement by the court on the application of the Panel, if the court is satisfied there is a reasonable likelihood that a person will contravene a rule of the Panel or contravene an order requiring disclosure of information or documents under s 947.

It is further provided, however, by s 956 that contravention of a rule or disclosure requirement does not give rise to any right of action for breach of statutory duty.

Provision is made in ss 957–959 for funding the Panel's activities.

A prime change in the law relates to the scope of the Code's jurisdiction. Previously the Code's jurisdiction limited the Panel's ability to act in relation to takeover bids, but now the jurisdiction has been extended to cover all takeover bids within the Takeover Directive where there is a United Kingdom element in terms of registered office or where the securities of the company are traded on a UK-regulated market.

Sometimes there will be shared jurisdiction as to where the registered office is in the United Kingdom but the regulated market is in a different EEA member state.

If the target company has its registered office in the United Kingdom, the Isle of Man or the Channel Islands, and its securities are regulated on a UK-regulated market or on any stock exchange in the Isle of Man or the Channel Islands, then the Code applies to that company, whether or not the main place of management is within the United Kingdom, the Isle of Man or the Channel Islands. The law in applying the provisions to the Isle of Man and the Channel Islands goes beyond the scope of the Directive, which does not require this (s 965 CA 2006).

Other companies are also within the jurisdiction if the registered office and the main place of management is within the United Kingdom but the securities are admitted to trading on a regulated market elsewhere within the EEA, then the companies are subject to the jurisdiction of the Panel within the Code.

In certain cases there is shared jurisdiction as where the target company has its registered office in an EEA state and securities are admitted to trading on a regulated market in another EEA Member State and the UK is one of those states in one or the other situation. If there is shared jurisdiction then only part of the Code applies, dependent on whether it is a matter of the company's registered office being within the UK or the company's securities being traded in the UK. If there is shared jurisdiction then, in those cases, the Code would only cover takeover bids within the meaning of the Directive. If, however, the jurisdiction is not shared then the Code will continue to regulate transactions that were previously covered. These are takeover bids and mergers, together with other transactions where the objective is obtaining or consolidating control as well as partial (and tender) offers. However, it would only regulate these additional transactions if the company is a UK, Isle of Man or Channel Islands company, or it is the type of public or private company that it regulated previously.

24.11 General principles, definitions and rules

New general principles contained in the Directive have now been enacted.

A major change to the definitions is the extension of the definition of acting 'in concert'. This has been extended to include a person who cooperates with the target company to frustrate the bid.

There are certain rule changes as well to bring the Code into line with the requirements of the Directive. Some of these rule changes involve detailed provisions relating to the contents of offer documents. There are also more detailed rules regarding the disclosure of the offeree board's views.

24.12 Substantial Acquisition Rules abolished

The Substantial Acquisition Rules, which were introduced in response to the dawn raid syndrome of parties acting in concert, and which required those establishing significant shareholdings in companies above 15 per cent to declare this, have now been abolished.

It is worth noting that stakeholders must still disclose within two days of acquiring an interest of 3 per cent or above, and within an offer period those 'interested' in 1 per cent or more of a company's securities are required to disclose their dealings under the Code.

24.13 Arrangements and reconstructions

Part 26 of the Companies Act 2006 deals with arrangements and reconstructions.

Sections 895 to 901 deal with compromise or arrangements between a company and its creditors or any class of them or its members or any class of them (s 895 CA 2006).

However, these provisions essentially apply to arrangements and reconstructions of private companies. Part 27 of the Companies Act 2006 deals with mergers and divisions of public companies, and there are more onerous rules to be followed in relation to these companies.

With respect to private companies, however, application should be made to the court under s 896 to order a meeting of the creditors or class of creditors or members or class of members to be summoned as the court may direct to consider the proposed arrangement.

Where a meeting is summoned under s 896, the notice summoning the meeting must explain the effect of the compromise or arrangement and in particular state any material interests of the directors, whether as members or as creditors of the company,
' the effect on those interests of the compromise or arrangement that is proposed.

⊣ion 899 provides that if a majority in number representing 75 per cent in
  ⁀ creditors or class of creditors or members or class of members (as the

case may be) present and voting, either in person or by proxy, agree a compromise or arrangement, the court may, on an application under this section, sanction the compromise or arrangement.

The application to the court may be made by the company or any creditor or member of the company, or if the company is being wound up, or an administration order is in force in relation to it, the liquidator or administrator.

As noted, Part 27 of the Act deals with mergers and divisions of public companies. Section 903 provides that the requirements applicable to a merger for public companies are specified in ss 905–914, and that certain of these requirements modify or exclude the provisions of Part 26.

Furthermore, the requirements applicable to a division are specified in ss 920–930 and similarly these requirements modify or exclude in some respects the provisions of Part 26 by ss 931–934.

Section 904 defines the mergers that are affected by Part 27 of the Act.

Section 905 provides that a draft of the proposed terms of the scheme must be drawn up and adopted by the directors of the merging companies. These draft terms must be published and forwarded to the Registrar (s 906).

The scheme must be approved by a majority in number representing 75 per cent in value of each class of members present and voting (s 907).

The directors of each of the merging companies must draw up or adopt reports explaining the effect of the compromise or arrangement and must adopt this report. Furthermore, s 909 provides that an expert's report must be drawn up on behalf of each of the merging companies. The report that is required is the written report on the draft terms to the members of the company. The expert's report must indicate the methods to be used in arriving at the share exchange ratio, describing the valuation difficulties that may have arisen, giving an opinion of the method or methods used, and stating whether they consider the share exchange ratio to be reasonable.

Section 910 provides that the last annual accounts of any of the merging companies are to be supplemented by an accounting statement if there are more than seven months before the first meeting of the company summoned to consider and possibly approve the scheme.

Section 911 provides for inspection of the documents relating to merger, setting out the draft terms, the directors' explanatory report, the expert's report and the company's annual accounts and reports, supplemented, if appropriate.

Section 912 provides for articles of the new company to be approved by ordinary resolution of the transferor company or each of the transferor companies, and s 913 provides for protections of holders of special rights attaching to securities.

Sections 915 to 918 provide for some circumstances where particulars in reports are not required. Section 916 provides that meetings of members of a transferee company are not required where the merger is one by absorption when 90 per cent or more of the relevant securities of the transferor or company are held by or on behalf of the transferee company, and s 917 provides that no meetings are required if conditions are met regarding disclosure of documents where minority members of not less than 5 per cent of the paid-up capital of the company would have been able, during the period, to require a meeting of each class of members and did not require such.

In a similar way, Chapter 3 of Part 27 deals with division of companies where the scheme involves a division where under the scheme the undertaking properties and liabilities of the company, in respect of which the compromise or arrangement is proposed, are to be divided among and transferred to two or more companies, each of which is either an existing public company or a new company, whether or not a public company.

In such a situation, draft terms of the scheme must be drawn up and adopted by the directors (s 920 CA 2006) and the draft terms must be published by the directors, delivering a copy of the draft terms to the Registrar (s 921 CA 2006).

The members must approve the division by 75 per cent in value of each class of members of the company present in voting in person or by proxy (s 922 CA 2006).

The directors of the transferor company and each existing transferee company must draw up and adopt an explanatory report which sets out the legal and economic grounds for the draft terms, and details of the criteria for the allocation to members of shares in the transferee company (s 923 CA 2006).

Section 924 CA 2006 provides for an expert's report to be drawn up on behalf of each company involved in the division, setting out the methods used to arrive at the share exchange ratio, describing any special valuation difficulties that have arisen, describing the method or methods used for valuation, and stating whether in the expert's opinion the share exchange ratio is reasonable.

Section 925 provides for a supplementary accounting statement if the last annual accounts ended more than seven months before the first meeting of the company summoned for the purposes of approving the scheme.

Section 926 provides that members of the company must be able, during the period before the scheme is adopted, to be able to inspect the following documents: the draft terms, the directors' explanatory report, the expert's report, the company's annual accounts and reports, and, if appropriate, any supplementary accounting statement that has been required by s 925.

Once again, there are circumstances in which meetings of members of a transferee company may not be required. One such is if documents are appropriately disclosed and there is the right for members representing 5 per cent or more of paid-up capital to require a meeting and no such meeting has been required (s 932 CA 2006).

Furthermore, s 933 provides that all of the members may agree to dispense with the requirements of certain reports such as the directors' explanatory report, the expert's report and the supplementary accounting statement.

Section 934 provides for the power of the court to exclude certain requirements where conditions regarding disclosure of documents and publication of draft terms have been complied with.

24.14 Sale of assets in return for shares

Another way of accomplishing a reconstruction is under ss 110 and 111 of the Insolvency Act 1986. This involves the following procedure. The company that is to be transferred is in the course of a voluntary winding up or being proposed for voluntary winding up. The company in voluntary liquidation sells its assets in exchange for shares in the transferee company. The transferee company's shares are then distributed to the former members of the transferor company. Section 111 of the Insolvency Act provides that dissentient members of the transferor company who did not vote in favour of the special resolution placing the company in voluntary liquidation may, within seven days, by writing to the liquidator, require that their interests be purchased for cash.

There is no need to apply to the court here. The main disadvantage for the transferee company is the provision that dissentients may require that their interests be purchased for cash. Indeed, the right of a dissentient member to dispose of his shares for cash is sacrosanct and cannot be excluded by the company's constitution: see *Bisgood v Henderson's Transvaal Estates Ltd* [1908] 1 Ch 743.

Summary

Takeovers, reconstructions and amalgamations

The Companies Act 2006 makes provision for the compulsory acquisition of up to 10 per cent of a target company's shares where the bidding company has acquired 90 per cent. The acquisition of the minority holding would be ordered on the same terms as the majority was acquired. Not only does the majority have a right to acquire the minority, but the minority has a corresponding right to be acquired.

The Act also provides for schemes of arrangement to be made between a company and its creditors or members. These provisions are usually utilised where there is an internal reconstruction. The procedure involves application to the court on two occasions, so it can be costly. There are additional requirements if the reconstruction involves the merger of at least one public company or a division where at least one of the companies is a public company or a new company.

A straightforward procedure for merger is presented by the Insolvency Act where a company goes into voluntary liquidation. The liquidator accepts shares from a transferee company in exchange for the assets of the company. The shares are then distributed to the former members of the transferor company. A dissentient in the transferor company can insist on his interest being purchased for cash.

Where there is a takeover involving a quoted company, the City Code on Takeovers and Mergers is of crucial importance. It is extra-statutory but policed by the Panel on Takeovers and Mergers. The City Code is made up of general principles and detailed rules governing the conduct of takeovers.

Self-test questions

24.1 What is a takeover?

24.2 What is a reconstruction?

24.3 What is an amalgamation?

24.4 Describe the importance of the EU Takeovers Directive (2004/25/EC).

24.5 Set out the rules and regulations that govern takeovers and mergers in the UK.

24.6 Describe the impact of s 992 CA 2006 in relation to disclosure in annual directors' reports.

24.7 Set out in brief the offence relating to bid documentation in the Companies Act 2006.

24.8 Describe the 'squeeze-out' and 'sell-out' rules.

24.9 What is the nature of 'opting in' and 'opting out' in relation to pre-bid defences?

24.10 Describe the interrelationship between the Companies Act 2006 and the Panel on Takeovers and Mergers.

24.11 What is the structure of the City Code?

24.12 What is the status of the Substantial Acquisition Rules?

24.13 What are the legislative arrangements in the Companies Act 2006 in relation to arrangements and reconstructions?

24.14 Set out how a reconstruction may be accomplished under ss 110 and 111 of the Insolvency Act 1986.

Further reading

M Adenas, 'European Takeover Directive and the City' (1997) 18 Co Law 101.

D Calcutt, 'Company Law Lecture – The Work of the Takeover Panel' (1990) 11 Co Law 203.

B Clarke, 'Articles 9 and 11 of the Takeover Directive (2004/25) and the Market for Corporate Control' [2006] JBL 355.

A Johnston, 'Takeover Regulation: Historical and Theoretical Perspectives on the City Code' (2007) CLJ 422.

G Morse, 'Takeover Regulation' [2008] JBL 96, 460.

F Oditah, 'Takeovers, Share Exchanges and the Meaning of Loss' (1996) 112 LQR 424.

Chapter 25

Liquidation

Chapter Contents

It is beyond the scope of this work to give a detailed survey of the law on liquidation. This area of law is a complex one. Not only is the Insolvency Act 1986 devoted in part to the law on liquidation (or winding up), but this is supplemented by detailed insolvency rules governing the practice of insolvency (Insolvency Rules 1986, SI 1986/1925).

The law on winding up as well as personal bankruptcy was updated by the Insolvency Act 1985 following the Report of the Review Committee on Insolvency Law and Practice (the Cork Report – Cmnd 8558, 1982). The Committee had been appointed as long ago as 1977 with the allotted task of making proposals to reform the law on personal bankruptcy and corporate insolvency. This was then consolidated in the Insolvency Act 1986. The Enterprise Act 2002, as has been noted, makes some fundamental changes to insolvency law (Chapter 21).

25.1 Types of winding up

There are essentially two types of winding up. There is compulsory winding up – a winding up by court order – and voluntary winding up – winding up initiated by the members of the company. Voluntary winding up then splits into two types:

(a) members' voluntary winding up, which is largely under the control of the members where the directors swear a statutory declaration of solvency; and
(b) creditors' voluntary winding up, which is largely under the control of the creditors as the directors have seen fit not to swear a statutory declaration of solvency.

25.1.1 Compulsory winding up

Section 122(1) of the Insolvency Act 1986 sets out the grounds of compulsory winding up. They are as follows.

A company may be wound up if:

(a) the company has by special resolution resolved that the company be wound up by the court;
(b) the company is a public company that has registered as such on initial incorporation but has not been issued with a certificate to do business under s 761 of the Companies Act 2006 and more than a year has expired since it was so registered;
(c) it is an old public company, within the meaning of the Companies Consolidation (Consequential Provisions) Act 1985;
(d) the company has not commenced business within a year of incorporation or suspends business for a year;
(e) the number of members is reduced below two, unless it is a private company to which the exemption relating to a membership of one now applies;
(f) the company is unable to pay its debts; or
(g) the court is of the opinion that it is just and equitable that the company should be wound up.

The court clearly has a discretion as to whether or not to grant a petition. This point receives support from s 125 of the Insolvency Act 1986, which provides that the court may dismiss a petition or adjourn the hearing conditionally or unconditionally, or make an interim order or any other order that it thinks fit. In exercising its discretion, the court may take into account factors such as the ability of the company to secure additional finance or if the majority of creditors support the liquidation; see *Re Hewitt Brannan (Tools) Co Ltd* [1990] BCC 354.

Only the last two grounds in s 122(1) are of great importance. The inability to pay debts is 'fleshed out' in s 123 of the Act. This has been covered above (section 23.6). In considering the various grounds that demonstrate inability to pay debts, the court will take account of any disputed debts and if it feels that there is a bona fide dispute concerning a debt, no winding-up order will be granted unless it is clear that more than £5,000 is owed by the company.

In *Re Welsh Brick Industries Ltd* [1946] 2 All ER 197, the Court of Appeal held that a judge was competent to grant a petition on the basis of the evidence before him even though unconditional leave to defend the debt had been given to the company. The fact that the debt is the subject of an application for appeal to the Court of Appeal is not in itself sufficient grounds for dismissing a winding-up petition; see in the matter of *Re BLV Realty II Ltd* [2010] EWHC 1791 (Ch) applying *Re A & BC Chewing Gum Ltd* [1975] 1 WLR 579. In *Re Ringinfo Ltd* [2002] 1 BCLC 210, however, the judge, Pumfrey J, considered that a debt disputed on genuine and substantial grounds cannot support a petition. As a general rule, there is a low threshold whether there is a genuine dispute. See *Tallington Lakes Ltd v South Kestevan District Council* [2012] EWCA Civ 443.

Even if it is demonstrated that there is a dispute concerning the debt, a winding-up petition may be granted if it is established that at least £750 is owing. Thus it was established in *Re Tweeds Garages Ltd* [1962] Ch 406 that the garage owed at least the minimum amount then required by the Act and the petition was granted.

Yet the existence of a debt of the requisite amount is not sufficient of itself to force a winding-up petition. The court has a discretion and will consider the views of contributories and especially of other creditors. In *Re ABC Coupler and Engineering Co Ltd* [1961] 1 All ER 354, a judgment creditor with a debt of in excess of £17,500 petitioned for an order that the company be compulsorily wound up. The petition was not supported by any other creditor and was opposed by a number of them. The company had extensive goodwill and a considerable excess of assets over liabilities. The petition was not granted.

The various grounds on which a petition to wind up the company on the just and equitable ground may be granted have also been considered above (see section 15.6). The petition here is presented by a member or contributory, as he is termed in a liquidation situation (see s 124(2) of the Insolvency Act 1986). The presence of the remedy of just and equitable winding up is a clear demonstration of the fact that winding up is available in situations other than where the company is in financial difficulties. The appellation insolvency as applied to the Insolvency Act is in some ways misleading. Indeed, it seems that the contributory whose shares are fully paid must show that he has an interest in the winding up, which means that he must demonstrate that assets will be available for distribution, i.e. that the company is solvent. The question was left open in *Re Rica Gold Washing Co* (1879) 11 ChD 36. In the more recent case of *Re Leyland Printing Company & Anor* [2010] EWHC 3788 (Ch), a solvent company was wound up on the 'just and equitable ground', where the company was a shell company having sold its entire business and assets, and liquidation was the most efficient mechanism for distributing assets to its creditors.

In addition, s 124(2) of the Insolvency Act 1986 provides that a contributory may only present a petition if the number of members is reduced below the statutory minimum or he holds shares that were originally allotted to him, or have been transmitted to him on the death of a former holder, or he has held the shares for at least six months from the previous 18 months before the commencement of the winding up.

The progress of a compulsory liquidation is that the petition is presented, for example, by a creditor if it is on the ground of inability to pay debts or by a contributory if it is on the ground that it is just and equitable that the company should be wound up.

The Secretary of State may also, on occasion, present a petition and also if, following a report made or information received in relation to company investigations or information obtained under s 2 of the Criminal Justice Act 1987 in relation to fraud investigations or under s 83 of the Companies Act 1989 in relation to assisting overseas regulatory authorities, he thinks that it is expedient in the public interest that a company should be wound up.

Once the petition has been presented, it is then for the court to decide whether the case has been made out. If it has been made out, the petition may be granted at the court's discretion and an order to wind the company up may be made. The commencement date of the liquidation is the date the petition is presented; that is, retrospectively the date of the commencement of liquidation is the date of the petition. This is material in many situations as certain acts or transactions may be rendered invalid within certain time limits.

As has been noted, s 125 of the Insolvency Act 1986 provides that on hearing a winding-up petition, the court can grant the petition or adjourn the hearing conditionally or unconditionally, or make an interim order. It should not refuse to grant a winding-up petition solely on the ground that the company's assets have been mortgaged equal to or in excess of the company's assets, or on the basis that the company has no assets.

Once a winding-up petition has been presented, the company or any creditor or contributory can apply to the court for a stay of proceedings where proceedings are pending in the High Court or Court of Appeal and in any other case may apply to restrain further proceedings (s 126 of the Insolvency Act 1986). The actual making of the order operates to stay all proceedings but this provision enables action to be taken to stay proceedings upon presentation of the petition.

Once a winding-up petition has been presented, any disposition of the company's property and any transfer of shares or alteration of its status is void unless the court orders otherwise where it has been committed after the commencement of the winding up (s 127 of the Insolvency Act 1986). Since the commencement date of a winding up is the presentation of the petition, this renders void dispositions after the presentation of the petition.

Section 127 includes payments that are made into and out of a company's bank account; see *Re Gray's Inn Construction Co Ltd* [1980] 1 All ER 814. The principles on which dispositions may be validated were discussed by the Court of Appeal in *Re Gray's Inn Construction Co Ltd*. Buckley LJ said that in general the interests of the unsecured creditors will not be prejudiced in making any validation decision. He went on to say that a disposition carried out in good faith in the course of business at a time when the parties are unaware that a petition has been presented would normally be validated by the court.

Where a winding-up order is granted, the court will appoint a provisional liquidator and that liquidator will be the official receiver (s 136(2)). The official receiver may require some or all of the company's officers, those involved in its formation within the previous year, those in its employment or previous employment within the last year, or those who are officers or in the employment of a company which was within the previous year an officer of the company, to provide a statement of affairs to the official receiver setting out the company's assets, debts, liabilities, names and addresses of its creditors, securities held by them and the dates on which the securities were given.

Section 139 provides that separate meetings of creditors and contributories may be called for the purpose of choosing a permanent liquidator. The creditors and the contributories at their respective meetings may nominate a person to be liquidator. The liquidator will be the person nominated by the creditors in the event of any conflict. Yet the contributories may go to court to overturn the decision, seeking the appointment of the person nominated by them. The same meetings of creditors and contributories may nominate people to a liquidation committee. The purpose of the liquidation committee will be to liaise with the liquidator during the course of the winding up. The liquidation committee is not able or required to function whilst the official receiver is liquidator.

Certain powers of the liquidator in a compulsory winding up can only be exercised with the sanction of the liquidation committee (see s 167(1)(a) of the Insolvency Act 1986).

It is the function of the liquidator to realise the company's property for cash during the liquidation. The proceeds should then be distributed to the company's creditors, and, if there is a surplus to the persons entitled to it, generally the contributories (class rights are again relevant here – see section 7.6): s 143 of the Insolvency Act 1986.

The liquidator takes into his custody and places under his control all the company's property and things in action (s 144 of the Insolvency Act 1986).

25.1.2 Voluntary liquidation

Voluntary liquidation may commence in the following ways:

1   If a fixed period has been settled for the duration of the company and the fixed period has now passed or if the company is to come to an end after a certain event, then the company may be wound up by ordinary resolution.
2   If the company resolves to be wound up voluntarily by special resolution.
3   If the company resolves by special resolution to be wound up on the basis that it cannot by reason of its liabilities continue its business (s 84 of the Insolvency Act 1986).

Notice of any resolution to wind up should be published in the *London Gazette* within 14 days (s 85(1) of the Insolvency Act 1986).

In a voluntary winding up, the winding up commences on the date that the resolution is passed (s 86 of the Insolvency Act 1986).

If the directors of the company or a majority of them swear a statutory declaration of solvency to the effect that the company will be able to pay its debts in full together with interest within the next 12 months, then this represents a statutory declaration of solvency. If such a declaration is made, then the declaration should be delivered to the Registrar of Companies. Where there is such a declaration, the liquidation proceeds as a members' voluntary winding up as the interests of creditors are supposedly protected by the statutory declaration of solvency that has been sworn. The statutory declaration of solvency should be passed within the five-week period immediately before the resolution to wind up (ss 89–90 of the Insolvency Act 1986).

If the winding up proceeds as a members' voluntary winding up, then there will be a general meeting of members or contributories to pass a resolution to wind up and to appoint somebody as liquidator.

If no statutory declaration of solvency is sworn then the liquidation proceeds as a creditors' voluntary winding up. In such a situation, a general meeting of members is needed to resolve to wind up, to nominate a liquidator and to appoint members (up to five) for the liquidation committee.

(Note that a liquidation committee implies a compulsory winding up or a creditors' voluntary winding up. No liquidation committee is appointed in a members' voluntary winding up as it is believed that the interests of creditors are protected by the statutory declaration of solvency. In a compulsory winding up and a creditors' voluntary winding up, there may be a liquidation committee.)

In the creditors' voluntary winding up, a meeting of creditors will be called to appoint a liquidator and if the creditors so wish to appoint up to five creditors' representatives on to a liquidation committee. In the event of a dispute on the choice of liquidator, the creditors' choice will prevail unless the court orders otherwise (ss 100–101 of the Insolvency Act 1986).

25.2 Fair dealing

Certain matters that should be watched for in relation to a liquidation have already been noted: invalidity of floating charges (s 245 of the Insolvency Act 1986) and invalidity of preferences (s 239 of the Insolvency Act 1986) (see section 20.9).

There are other provisions in the Insolvency Act concerned with the adjustment of prior transactions (administration and liquidation). These are the so-called fair dealing provisions.

Section 238 of the Insolvency Act 1986 provides that an administrator or liquidator may apply to the court for an order of restitution where the company has entered into a transaction at an undervalue as where it makes a gift of property or receives significantly less consideration for property than its true value. The court will not make an order if it is satisfied that the company entered into the transaction in good faith and for the purpose of carrying on its business, and that at the time it did so there were reasonable grounds for believing that the transaction would benefit the company.

An order may be made, just as in the case of preferences, if the transaction is in favour of a connected person, within two years of the onset of insolvency or, if in favour of an unconnected person, within six months of the onset of insolvency. (The onset of insolvency means the date of presentation of a petition to appoint an administrator or the date of commencement of the winding up. Any transaction between the presentation of a petition for administration and the granting of the order is also caught.)

A transaction would amount to a preference if the benefit given to a recipient places the recipient in a better position than the position the recipient would otherwise have been in a subsequent insolvency of the company and at the time of the transaction the company is influenced by a desire to better the recipient's position.

A transaction would be at an undervalue if the company either received no consideration or a consideration that was considerably less than the value of the transaction.

Either of the above transactions may amount to a breach of directors' duties if the directors were not acting in good faith or had not properly and reasonably considered whether there was corporate benefit for the company in entering into the transactions.

In *Re Bacon MC Ltd* [1991] Ch 127, the court had to consider whether the granting of a floating charge in favour of a bank amounted to a preference or a transaction at an undervalue, or neither.

The company imported bacon. Its main customer withdrew and two of the company's directors retired; one of them was obese and could not perform the manual work required of him. The bank was worried at the decline in the company's fortunes. It sought and obtained a floating charge to secure the company's overdraft. The directors knew they needed the continued support of the bank. Subsequently, the company went into insolvent liquidation and the liquidator sought to set aside the charge and the appointment of an administrative receiver. The judge considered that the decision to grant the floating charge to the bank had been made to prevent the bank calling in its overdraft. Furthermore, he considered that the transaction was not at an undervalue.

Payments made to three directors (husband, wife and son) from accounts that each held with the company less than three months before the company went into administration were held to be preferences in *Re Exchange Travel (Holdings) Ltd (In Liq)* [1996] BCC 933.

In *Progress Property Company Ltd v Moorgarth Group Ltd* [2010] UKSC 55, the Supreme Court held on 8 December 2010 that in assessing whether a transaction was a transaction at an undervalue, the court had to look at the purpose and substance of the transaction. The mere fact that the price was lower than the market value with hindsight was not enough to show that it was a transaction at an undervalue, as the issue of bad faith was a material issue.

Extortionate credit transactions where credit is supplied to the company on terms where the payments are grossly exorbitant or where the terms otherwise grossly contravene ordinary principles of fair dealing are also caught (s 244 of the Insolvency Act 1986). The time limit here is a transaction within the three-year period terminating with the date of the administration order or the date when the liquidation commenced (s 244(2) of the Insolvency Act 1986).

368 BOURNE ON COMPANY LAW

The court may order the transaction to be set aside or some part of it. It may vary the terms or order the surrender of money or property or order accounts to be taken. It may order any combination of these.

25.3 Malpractice

Another area of law of importance in a liquidation concerns the penalisation of directors and officers for malpractice. Section 212 of the Insolvency Act 1986 provides a summary remedy in winding up where a person who has been an officer, liquidator, administrator or administrative receiver, or concerned in the promotion, formation or management of the company has misapplied or retained or become accountable for the company's money or property or been guilty of any misfeasance or breach of any fiduciary or other duty in relation to the company. The court may order repayment of money or restoration of property or such contribution for breach of duty as the court thinks just. It would appear that s 1157 CA 2006 enabling the court to give relief to any officer does not cover liquidators, administrators or administrative receivers (see section 12.11.4).

A provision of some importance enables the court on the application of the liquidator to declare that any persons knowingly party to the carrying on of the business of a company with intent to defraud creditors or for a fraudulent purpose be ordered to contribute to the company's assets. This is the so-called 'fraudulent trading' section (s 213 of the Insolvency Act 1986). The Cork Committee had recommended that, while retaining the high standard of proof for criminal proceedings for fraudulent trading (now s 993 CA 2006), a lower standard of proof founded on unreasonable behaviour should become the basis for civil liability. In the event, a new provision – s 214 of the Insolvency Act – based on unreasonable behaviour – wrongful trading – supplements rather than replaces s 213 of the Act. Under s 213, actual deceit on the part of the person carrying on the business must be shown. In *Re Gerald Cooper Chemicals Ltd* [1978] Ch 262, it was said that where the company received forward payment for the supply of indigo knowing that it could not continue to trade because of insolvency and used this to pay off part of a loan, the company was carrying on business fraudulently. The person receiving the money was stated to be liable if he accepted money which he knew full well to have been obtained by the carrying on of a business with intent to defraud creditors.

When an order is made on the application of the liquidator, the sum that the person is ordered to pay will generally contain a punitive element as well as a compensatory one: see *Re William C Leitch Bros Ltd* [1932] 2 Ch 71 and *Re a Company (No 001418 of 1988)* [1991] BCLC 197.

Section 213 was considered in *Morphitis v Bernasconi* [2003] Ch 552. The case concerned Transmetal Chimica Ltd, who were hauliers operating from a trading estate in Sandwich. Bernasconi was a director of the company. The company misleadingly claimed that a certain payment of £10,000 would be made when it was known that it could not be made and the company carried on incurring debts that the company knew would never be paid (these included rents owed to Ramac Holdings Ltd). The liquidator brought a claim under s 213 of the Insolvency Act 1986, which provides for payments where a company is indulging in fraudulent trading. At first instance Antony

Ellery QC held that there was liability. The Court of Appeal reversed this, holding that it does not follow that because a person has defrauded in the course of a company's business the business was carried on with intent to defraud.

Savirimuthu criticises the Court of Appeal for failure to provide a coherent explanation of the basis of liability in s 213 (A. Savirimuthu, 'Casenote on Morphitis' (2005) 26 Co Law 245).

Section 214 of the Insolvency Act 1986 extends liability to directors or shadow directors who should have known or ought to have concluded that there was no reasonable prospect that the company would avoid going into insolvent liquidation. The section is therefore more limited in catchment than s 213 as s 213 applies to any person knowingly party to the carrying on of the business. Furthermore, s 214 has no corresponding criminal sanction.

It seems that only the liquidator can bring proceedings under s 214.

In *Re Oasis Merchandising Services Ltd* [1998] Ch 170, the liquidator had entered into an agreement with a specialist litigation support service. The service was to fund the litigation as the company had no funds. In exchange for this, the liquidator was to sell and assign the fruits of the action. The litigation service was given a significant degree of control over the proceedings.

The Court of Appeal held that the liquidator had no power to enter into such an agreement and that, although the liquidator had power to sell any of the company's property, this did not extend to the fruits of any litigation bought by the liquidator under s 214.

The section was considered in *Re Produce Marketing Consortium Ltd (No 2)* [1989] BCLC 520. The liquidator of the company sought an order under s 214 of the Insolvency Act 1986 against two directors. The auditors of the company, which was in the business of importing fruit, had warned the directors of the company's serious financial position. The judge found the directors liable to contribute £75,000. In determining how to decide whether directors ought to have known of the company's position, Knox J had this to say (p. 550):

> The knowledge to be imputed in testing whether or not directors knew or ought to have concluded that there was no reasonable prospect of the company avoiding insolvent liquidation is not limited to the documentary material actually available at the given time. This appears from s 214(4) which includes a reference to facts which a director of a company not only should know but those which he ought to ascertain, a word which does not appear in s 214(2)(b). In my judgement this indicates that there is to be included by way of factual information not only what was actually there, but what given reasonable diligence and an appropriate level of general knowledge, skill and experience, was ascertainable.

In *Re Purpoint Ltd* [1991] BCLC 491, Vinelott J held a director of the company liable under s 214 where it should have been plain to him that the company could not avoid going into insolvent liquidation. The purpose of an order under s 214 is to ensure that any depletion of the company's assets that occurs after a time when there is no reasonable prospect of the company's avoiding an insolvent winding up is made good. The company's business is being conducted at such a time at the risk of creditors.

In *Re Hydrodam (Corby) Ltd* [1994] 2 BCLC 180, the extent to which wrongful trading may extend to others was at issue. Liability is imposed under s 214 on shadow directors (s 741(2) CA 1985 defines a shadow director as 'a person in accordance with whose directions or instructions the directors of the company are accustomed to act'. The subsection continues: 'However, a person is not deemed a shadow director by reason only that the directors act on advice given by him in a professional capacity.' The provision is preserved in s 251 CA 2006).

Hydrodam was a wholly owned subsidiary of Eagle Trust plc. The liquidator made a claim for wrongful trading against Eagle Trust plc, one of Eagle Trust's subsidiaries, and all of Eagle Trust's directors. Two of Eagle Trust plc's directors applied to have the claim struck out. The company had duly appointed directors, two Channel Island companies. Millett J was prepared to assume that Eagle Trust could be a shadow director. He did not accept, however, that it followed that Eagle Trust's directors were also shadow directors. Although they attended the ultimate holding company's board meetings, they were still not thereby without other factors shadow directors. Millett J held that no case had been made out against either of the defendants.

Previously, it had been thought that banks and substantial creditors ran risks when they gave instructions to companies in financial difficulties. *Re Hydrodam* makes it very clear that cogent evidence will be needed of giving instructions to those people running the company before the shadow directorship is made out.

In *Re Onslow Ditching Ltd* [2011] EWHC 257 (Ch), the Chancery division of the High Court considered the issue of breach of directors' duties under the Companies Act 2006. This issue was intermingled with consideration of wrongful trading under s 214 of the Insolvency Act 1986.

The directors in question had not stopped the company's actions when it should have been clear to them that the company was insolvent. They were found liable, both for misfeasance and breach of duty, as well as for wrongful trading. Their breach of duties to the company originated from the time when they should have known that the company could no longer meet its obligations as they fell due.

A person is only liable for wrongful trading if the court is not satisfied that he took every step with a view to minimising the potential loss to the company's creditors as (assuming him to have known that there was no reasonable prospect that the company would avoid going into insolvent liquidation) he ought to have taken. Directors should therefore raise concerns with other board members and urge action, such as discontinuing trading, as is appropriate. This appears to be the only defence available under s 214. Section 727 of the Companies Act 1985 (now s 1157 CA 2006) was considered and rejected as a defence in *Re Produce Marketing Consortium Ltd (No 2)* (1989).

As well as the potential liability of directors for matters occurring before the liquidation commences, there are various offences of fraud and deception that may be committed during a liquidation.

These include:

(a) fraud etc. in anticipation of a winding up (s 206 of the Insolvency Act 1986);

(b) past or present officers making gifts or transfers of or charges on company property (s 207 of the Insolvency Act 1986);

(c) misconduct by past or present officers during the course of the winding up (s 208 of the Insolvency Act 1986);

(d) falsification, destruction, mutilation, etc. of the company's books, papers, etc. (s 209 of the Insolvency Act 1986); and

(e) material omission from the statement relating to company's affairs (s 210 of the Insolvency Act 1986).

25.4 The conduct of the liquidation

While it is not intended to go into the minutiae of the conduct of the liquidation, it is proposed here to mention one or two miscellaneous facets of the process of liquidation and to consider the priority of payments in a liquidation.

Section 233 of the Insolvency Act, implementing a recommendation of the Cork Committee, provides that suppliers of gas, water, electricity and telephone services cannot make it a condition of continued supply, where there is an administration, administrative receivership, voluntary arrangement or liquidation, that all moneys owing be paid. The section is a recognition of the dominant bargaining position of such utility suppliers and it prevents them using their 'economic muscle'. The supplier can, however, insist on a personal guarantee in relation to continued supplies.

Another matter to consider in a liquidation is the right of the liquidator to disclaim onerous property under s 178 of the Insolvency Act 1986. Onerous property means any unprofitable contract and any other property of the company that is unsaleable or not readily saleable, such as a wasting lease. This power must be exercised within 12 months of the commencement of the liquidation. Where it is exercised, any person sustaining loss or damage is deemed a creditor and can prove for the extent of the loss or damage in the winding up.

Another matter that may arise in a liquidation situation concerns the reuse of company names. Section 216 of the Insolvency Act 1986 deals with the so-called 'phoenix syndrome' and places certain limitations on the reuse of company names. The section provides that the old name or a similar one cannot be used by the directors or shadow directors for a period of five years from the commencement of the liquidation. In *Thorne v Silverleaf* [1994] 1 BCLC 637, the defendant was a director of two companies that had gone into liquidation, Mike Spence (Reading) Ltd and Mike Spence (Motor Sport) Ltd. He had personally guaranteed their overdrafts. The defendant established and became a director of a third company, Mike Spence Classic Cars Ltd. The company dealt in vintage cars. The claimant provided the company with finance. The company's financial position deteriorated and the claimant complained that the defendant was personally liable for its debts since the company had a name so similar to the two previous companies as to suggest an association with them. The court held that this was so and the defendant was held personally liable under s 216 of the Insolvency Act 1986. However, the old name may well have a value and the court can give leave to a director of a failed company to buy over the old name (see *Re Bonus Breaks Ltd* [1991] BCC 546).

In *Re Lightning Electrical Contractors Ltd* [1996] 2 BCLC 302, leave was granted respecting a company that was already trading. This was not a 'phoenix syndrome' situation. The liquidating company's administrative receivers supported the application and it was not opposed by the Secretary of State.

When the liquidator has realised the company's assets, he is faced with paying off the company's debts. Many features of priority that applied in relation to receivership also apply here (see section 21.4). The order of priority is as follows:

(a)   the costs of the liquidation, including the liquidator's remuneration;

(b)   preferential creditors are paid next. The categories of preferential debts are set out in Sch 6 of the Insolvency Act 1986 as amended by the Enterprise Act 2002. The categories rank equally and are as follows:

   (i)   any sums owing to occupational and state pension schemes;

   (ii)   wages due to employees for the four-month period before liquidation up to £800 per employee; and

   (iii)   any accrued holiday pay owed to employees.

Note that any sum advanced by a bank etc. for paying salaries and accrued holiday pay which would otherwise have been preferential becomes preferential by subrogation;

(c)   debts secured by fixed charges;

(d)   debts secured by floating charges are paid off next (subject to the ring-fencing provisions of the Enterprise Act 2002). The Enterprise Act provides for ring-fencing of assets where there is a floating charge to provide funds for unsecured creditors. Currently the following provisions determine the amount that is ring-fenced:

   (i)   if the amount available for distribution is less than £10,000 and it is considered that the cost of making provision for the unsecured creditors would be disproportionate, then no assets are available,

   (ii)   50 per cent of the first £10,000 realised, and thereafter 20 per cent of further realisations,

   (iii)   a maximum ring-fenced fund of £600,000 (Insolvency Act 1986 (Prescribed Part) Order 2003 (SI 2003/2097));

(e)   ordinary trade creditors who have no security (subject to the Enterprise Act 2002 provisions);

(f)   any deferred debts such as dividends which have been declared but not paid.

If there is a surplus of assets (many liquidations are solvent ones), the surplus will be distributed amongst the company's members according to their class rights (see section 7.6).

Summary

Liquidations (or winding ups) fall into two basic categories: compulsory by court order and voluntarily initiated by the members of the company. Voluntary liquidations are of two types: members' voluntary winding up under the control of the members, where the directors have sworn a statutory declaration of solvency, and creditors' voluntary winding up. In the latter case, there has been no statutory declaration of solvency and the predominant interest of the creditors is recognised.

In a liquidation, certain prior transactions may be reopened if they are made at an undervalue, or if they are extortionate credit agreements or if they constitute preferences. Floating charges made in the run-up to a liquidation may also be held to be invalid.

If the company has been trading when it was known that it could not pay its debts, those trading will be civilly and possibly criminally liable. Directors and shadow directors may even be civilly liable where they ought to have known that the company could not survive. There are also various areas of liability for officers during a liquidation such as falsification of a company's books, transferring company property during a liquidation, etc.

The suppliers of utility services – gas, water, electricity and telephone – cannot insist on payment of moneys due as a condition for continued service. During the liquidation, the liquidator may disclaim onerous property such as a lease or an unprofitable contract, but the other party may then prove as a creditor in the liquidation.

There is a set order for payment of debts – liquidation expenses, preferential debts, floating charges, ordinary debts and deferred debts. If there is a surplus this should be distributed to members, taking account of their class rights.

Self-test questions

25.1 Set out the different types of winding up or liquidation.

25.2 Set out in brief the nature of the fair dealing provisions under the Insolvency Act 1986.

25.3 What is the importance of s 212 of the Insolvency Act 1986?

25.4 Set out the conduct of a typical liquidation in brief.

Further reading

LG Doyle, 'Anomalies in the Wrongful Trading Provisions' (1992) 13 Co Law 96.

E Ferran, 'Timing Requirements of the Companies and Insolvency Legislation' [1994] 3 CLJ 37.

V Finch, 'Doctoring in the Shadows of Insolvency' [2005] JBL 690.

M Griffiths, 'The Phoenix Syndrome' (2006) 156 NLJ 530.

T Hooke and A Hicks, 'Wrongful Trading – Predicting Insolvency' [1993] JBL 338.

A Judge, 'Look Before You Leap – Negotiating the Minefield of Insolvency Purchasing' (2008) 158 NLJ 432.

A Keay, 'What Future for Liquidation in the Light of the Enterprise Act Reforms?' [2005] JBL 143.

R Nolan, 'Less Equal Than Others – Maxwell and Subordinated Unsecured Obligations' [1995] JBL 485.

F Oditah, 'Wrongful Trading' [1990] LM CLQ 205.

F Oditah, 'Aspects of the Treatment of Claims in Insolvency' (1992) 108 LQR 459.

DD Prentice, 'Preferences and Defective Floating Charges' (1993) 109 LQR 371.

A Savirimuthu, 'Morphitis in the Court of Appeal: Some Reflections' (2005) 26 Co Law 245.

J Townsend, 'Schemes of Arrangements and Asbestos Litigation in *Re: Cape plc*' (2007) 70 MLR 837.

S Turnbull and S Crofts, 'Directors in Danger' (1992) 110 Accountancy 115.

J Ulph and T Allen, 'Transactions at an Undervalue, Purchasers and the Impact of the Human Rights Act 1998' [2004] JBL 1.

S Wheeler, 'Swelling the Assets for Distribution in Corporate Insolvency' [1993] JBL 256.

Index